The

Political Economy
of the **Asian**

Financial

Crisis

The

Political Economy

of the Asian

Financial

Crisis

Stephan Haggard

INSTITUTE FOR INTERNATIONAL ECONOMICS
Washington, DC
August 2000

Stephan Haggard, visiting fellow, is a professor at the University of California, San Diego Graduate School of International Relations and Pacific Studies and is an adjunct in the Department of Political Science. In July 1997 he became Director of the University of California's systemwide Institute on Global Conflict and Cooperation, where he chairs the Northeast Asian Cooperation Dialogue. He has been a consultant to AID, the World Bank, the United Nations Conference on Trade and Development, and the OECD and is a member of the Council on Foreign Relations. He is a member of the Advisory Committee of the Institute.

INSTITUTE FOR INTERNATIONAL ECONOMICS
11 Dupont Circle, NW
Washington, DC 20036-1207
(202) 328-9000 FAX: (202) 328-5432
http://www.iie.com

C. Fred Bergsten, *Director*
Brigitte Coulton, *Director of Publications and Web Development*
Brett Kitchen, *Marketing Director*

Printing and typesetting by
 Automated Graphic Systems
Cover design by
 Naylor Design Inc.

Printed in the United States of America
02 01 00   5 4 3 2 1

Library of Congress Cataloging-in-Publication Data

Haggard, Stephan.
  The political economy of the Asian financial crisis / Stephan Haggard.
    p. cm.
  Includes bibliographical references and index.
  1. Finance—Asia—Case studies.
  2. Financial crises—Asia—Case studies.
  I. Title.
  HG187.A2 H34 2000
  332′.095—dc21   00-038312

  ISBN 0-88132-283-0

For Nancy

Contents

Tables

Figures

Preface

The study of financial crises in emerging market economies has, unfortunately, been a staple of the Institute's research from its inception. William Cline's *International Debt and the Stability of the World Economy* (1983) and *International Debt: Systemic Risk and Policy Response* (1984) were the first systematic analyses of the debt problems of the developing countries. C. Fred Bergsten, Cline, and John Williamson authored *Bank Lending to Developing Countries: The Policy Alternatives* (1985). Williamson helped make the case for a new strategy in *Voluntary Approaches to Debt Relief* (1988). Cline reviewed the entire debt crisis of the 1980s in *International Debt Re-examined* (1995).

The Institute has been equally active in analyzing the financial crises in emerging market economies in the 1990s. Guillermo Calvo, Morris Goldstein and Eduard Hochreiter examined *Private Capital Flows to Emerging Markets after the Mexican Crisis* (1996). Goldstein made one of the first presentations on *The Asian Financial Crisis: Causes, Cures, and Systemic Implications* (1998) and Marcus Noland, et al. laid out the *Global Economic Effects of the Asian Currency Devaluations* (1998). In an effort to help head off future crises, we recently published Goldstein's analysis, with Graciela Kaminsky and Carmen Reinhart, of *Assessing Financial Vulnerability: An Early Warning System for Emerging Markets* (2000).

By mid-2000, the Asian economies outside of Indonesia were showing strong signs of recovery. But troubling questions remained about whether the reforms undertaken in the wake of the crisis had eliminated future sources of risk. The answer to that question was not simply economic but rested ultimately on politics. Had the crisis generated reforms that were politically sustainable over the long run? To address these questions, the Institute turned to political scientist Stephan Haggard to write *The Political Economy of the Asian Financial Crisis.*

Haggard's first objective was to consider how politics might have affected the onset of crises in the most-seriously affected countries: Thailand, Indonesia, Malaysia, and South Korea. He notes that the nature of business-government relations in East Asia had troubling as well as beneficial aspects. The problem was not so much industrial policy, as traditionally conceived in earlier literature on the region, but rather the role of the government in the financial system. Direct state intervention in the allocation of financial resources generated various well-known risks, including that of moral hazard.

But efforts to liberalize the financial system also produced risk. Regulatory agencies lacked the capacity to monitor new activities. Banks and other intermediaries lobbied for lax regulation and exceptions. They sought to shift the cost of their activities onto the government and ultimately onto taxpayers.

Politics also affected how governments managed financial distress once it occurred. Across the region, business resistance slowed the reform process. Electoral politics played a role in the democracies but an important finding is that the democracies did no worse than the authoritarian governments in responding to the crisis. In South Korea, Kim Dae Jung in fact drew on broad public and legislative support early in his term to launch wide-ranging reforms. Thailand's fragmented party system proved slower in responding but also chalked up some important accomplishments.

By contrast, Indonesia's increasingly vulnerable president proved utterly incapable of breaking through long-standing patterns of cronyism and corruption. Economic mismanagement sparked popular protest and led to the defection of the military. While this had the positive effect of bringing democracy to Indonesia, the resulting political uncertainty contributed to the longest and deepest recession in the region.

Haggard also dissects the unorthodox approach undertaken by Malaysia's Prime Minister Mahathir. The imposition of capital controls was designed to regain some macroeconomic policy autonomy. But the move also had political roots in Prime Minister Mahathir's campaign against the "speculators" in the fall of 1997, a campaign which compounded Malaysia's difficulties. The continuity in Malaysia's political system also had the effect of slowing the pace of economic reform.

In addition to painful short-run adjustments, the crisis posed two longer-term tasks for governments in the region—financial and corporate restructuring, and recrafting the social contract. Financial and corporate restructuring proved difficult as banks and firms sought to shift losses onto the government. Some governments, notably South Korea, moved swiftly to address these issues while Indonesia still faces daunting adjustment problems.

However, Haggard argues that a variety of legal and policy reforms undertaken in the wake of the crisis are reshaping the terms of competition in the region. These include liberalization of foreign direct investment and new rules governing bankruptcy and corporate governance. East Asian capitalism may not be converging on a Western model but the crisis has had a profound influence on the nature of business organization in the region.

Finally, Haggard addresses the social fallout of the crisis. He finds that the extent of backlash was limited by the presence of reformers who saw both political and social gains from more market-oriented reform. However, he also notes that governments in the region were poorly positioned to manage the social consequences of the crisis, having relied for too long on informal social insurance mechanisms.

Haggard's findings thus mirror those of Dani Rodrik's Institute study *Has Globalization Gone Too Far?* (1997). Open economies reap the gains of international trade and investment but require strong social safety nets to make that openness sustainable. Haggard sketches out a social agenda for the future that will permit Asia to continue to combine growth with a relatively equitable distribution of income.

The Institute for International Economics is a private nonprofit institution for the study and discussion of international economic policy. Its purpose is to analyze important issues in that area and develop and communicate practical new approaches for dealing with them. The Institute is completely nonpartisan.

The Institute is funded largely by philanthropic foundations. Major institutional grants are now being received from the William M. Keck, Jr. Foundation and the Starr Foundation. A number of other foundations and private corporations contribute to the highly diversified financial resources of the Institute. About 26 percent of the Institute's resources in our latest fiscal year was provided by contributors outside the United States, including about 11 percent from Japan. The Korea Foundation, the Starr Foundation, the GE Fund, and the Freeman Foundation provided generous support for this project.

The Board of Directors bears overall responsibility for the Institute and gives general guidance and approval to its research program—including the identification of topics that are likely to become important over the medium run (one to three years), and which should be addressed by the Institute. The director, working closely with the staff and outside Advisory Committee, is responsible for the development of particular projects and makes the final decision to publish an individual study.

The Institute hopes that its studies and other activities will contribute to building a stronger foundation for international economic policy around the world. We invite readers of these publications to let us know how they think we can best accomplish this objective.

C. Fred Bergsten
Director
August 2000

Acknowledgments

This book was less the result of competence and expertise than of curiosity and a dare. For some time, I had worked on the political economy of reform and on the East Asian newly industrializing countries, but I had never ventured deeply into Southeast Asia. Fred Bergsten's challenge—to write a book on the political economy of the Asian financial crisis—presented an opportunity to educate myself. Thankfully, I found help from a number of colleagues: on Korea, Chung-in Moon and Jongryn Mo; on Indonesia and all of Southeast Asia, Andrew MacIntyre, who co-authored chapter 2; on Malaysia and Singapore, Linda Low, who co-authored Appendix 2.1; and on social issues, Nancy Birdsall, who helped me think through the social dimensions of the crisis and co-authored chapter 5.

I also learned much from a seminar at the Graduate School of International Relations and Pacific Studies at the University of California San Diego on the Asian financial crisis. The group, which included among its stalwarts Miles Kahler, Peter Gourevitch, Andrew MacIntyre, and Takeo Hoshi, provided me a number of chances to present work. Lawrence Krause was also a member of that seminar, and his wisdom and insight deserves special mention.

Several people read the entire manuscript and deserve special thanks for their perseverance and particularly detailed comments: Robert Ayres, Catherin Dalpino, Sandra Eccles, Jorg Faust, Bernard K. Gordon, Peter Gourevitch, Kevin Hewison, Charles Morrison, Stephen Parker and T. J. Pempel. A number of other people had the generosity to comment on portions of the manuscript or offered assistance that proved particularly useful, including Gabriel Aguilera, Sri-Ram Aiyer, Peter Brimble, Ha-joon Chang, Michele Chang, Jason Cheah, Yun-han Chu, David Cole, Deunden Nikomborirak, Larry Diamond, Rick Doner, Kimberly Elliott, Don Emmerson, Carol Graham, Natasha Hamilton-Hart, Kevin Hewison, Jomo K.S., Ethan Kapstein, Juho Lee, David Lipton, Ashok Mody, Vali Nasr,

Joan Nelson, Greg Noble, Lant Pritchett, John Ravenhill, Nita Rudra, Shanker Satyanath, Adam Schwarz, Amar Siamwalla, Dennis Tachiki, Peter Timmer, John Williamson, Chris Woodruff, and Ngaire Woods. A number of policymakers in Washington, Seoul, Jakarta, Kuala Lumpur, and Bangkok—some wishing to remain anonymous—entertained my questions.

In addition to these individuals, several institutions provided me opportunities to present pieces of this book: the Departments of Political Science at the University of Minnesota, Carleton College, and National Taiwan University; the School of International and Public Affairs, Columbia University; the Center for Social Theory and Comparative History at the University of California, Los Angeles; the Monash Asia Institute and the Research School of Pacific and Asian Studies, Australian National University; and the Gaston Sigur Center of George Washington University.

A number of graduate students served as research assistants or were kind enough to let me draw on their work. I am particularly indebted to Allen Hicken, Kit Panupong, Dan Pinkston, and James Schopf, all excellent young scholars on the region. Shu Fan provided outstanding research assistance, as did Jessie Zhou. I also owe a great debt to members of the class I taught on the Asian financial crisis in the spring of 1999, who forced me to organize my thoughts on these issues and produced first-class research papers on a number of issues related to the crisis.

This study could not have been completed without financial support, and in addition to the Institute, I would like to thank Peter Cowhey and the Institute on Global Conflict and Cooperation, which provided me with travel, research assistance, and the time to complete the study. The Carnegie Foundation, the Korea Foundation, and the Asia Research Fund (Korea) also provided funding. The World Bank supported my research on the politics of financial and corporate restructuring, but takes no responsibility for the views expressed here.

Introduction:
The Political Economy of the Asian
Financial Crisis

The Asian economic crisis of 1997-98 was a singular event in the region's postwar economic history. Adverse external shocks had struck the developing countries of East and Southeast Asia in the past, most notably the oil price increases of the 1970s and early 1980s. Individual countries had also experienced episodic difficulties. South Korea had a sharp, short recession in 1980, and the Philippines experienced a debt crisis in the early 1980s. Falling oil prices forced substantial adjustments on Indonesia in the mid-1980s, and a number of Southeast Asian countries experienced recession in 1985-86. But since the period of high growth began—a period that dates to the 1960s for Hong Kong, Singapore, South Korea, and Taiwan—East Asia had not experienced a collective shock of this magnitude.

The question of why these rapidly growing countries got into so much trouble and how they managed to return to growth has now been picked apart from a number of different angles, primarily by economists. Somewhat less attention has been paid to the political economy of the crisis (see, however, Jomo 1998c; Pempel 1999b). This book redresses this imbalance by posing three basic questions. First, did political factors contribute to Asia's vulnerability to crisis, and if so how? Second, how did incumbent governments and their successors manage the contentious politics of adjustment, including both short-term crisis measures and longer-term structural change? Third, what if any were the political and institutional *consequences* of the crisis of 1997-98, including for the consolidation of democratic rule?

The central arguments of the book can be stated briefly:

- Close business-government relations that had proven an asset during the period of high growth generated moral hazard, distorted the liberalization process, increased vulnerability to shocks, and complicated the adjustment process once the crisis hit. Reducing the risks of crisis in the future requires not only discrete policy and regulatory changes, but political and institutional changes that check particularistic business influence and increase transparency in business-government relations (chapters 1 and 6).

- Once countries enter a "zone of vulnerability," political uncertainty plays an important, but neglected, role in both the onset and depth of financial crises. Early *economic* warning indicators need to be supplemented with a greater understanding and appreciation of the *political* sources of market uncertainty (chapter 2).

- Contrary to defenders of "Asian values," nondemocratic governments had no apparent advantages over democratic ones in adjusting to the crisis, and a number of disadvantages. These included arbitrary actions on the part of chief executives, political instability, and profound uncertainties about the succession process. Democracies such as South Korea that moved swiftly to build legislative and interest group support were capable of instituting wide-ranging institutional and policy reforms that contributed to rapid recovery (chapters 2 and 3).

- In the four most seriously affected countries—South Korea, Thailand, Indonesia, and Malaysia—"backlash" against the market was partly offset by "market-oriented populists." These reformist leaders, parties, and movements saw the introduction of more market forces, coupled with appropriate and independent regulation, as an antidote to corruption and the undue influence of favored business interests (chapter 3).

- The crisis generated pressures for financial and corporate restructuring, but the process faced substantial political resistance and the reform movement appears to have slowed. However, longer-run institutional, legal, and policy changes put in place in the wake of the crisis are gradually transforming financial systems, corporate governance, and business-government relations in important ways, making them more accountable and transparent, if not fully "Western" (chapter 4).

- Governments were poorly positioned, both politically and administratively, to respond to the social dimensions of the crisis. Their interventions did not always reach the most seriously affected groups, which tended to be in the urban middle, working, and marginal classes. A new social contract is required to mitigate the costs of such crises in the future (chapter 5).

- The crisis showed the democracies to be resilient and has advanced the cause of economic reform in the region. But a deepening of financial, corporate, and social reforms will also require a parallel process of deepening democracy by enhancing the accountability and transparency of government and by reducing the influence of particularistic interests (chapter 6).

The Debate over Causes: A Brief Intellectual History

The Asian financial crisis unfolded in several overlapping phases, beginning in Thailand and spreading first to other Southeast Asian countries. A convenient date for its onset is 2 July 1997, when the Thai baht was allowed to float. On 11 July, the Philippines followed suit, and for the remainder of the year, all the Southeast Asian currencies were allowed to float and depreciated sharply. The Philippines extended an existing International Monetary Fund standby arrangement in July, Thailand reached agreement with the Fund after some delay in August, and Indonesia signed a large standby arrangement in November. The Thai and Indonesian programs were both backed by supplementary resources from other multilateral institutions and donors and were among the largest multilateral rescue programs ever assembled. Nonetheless, neither succeeded in restoring confidence quickly and both required revision during 1998 and 1999.

Malaysia was also forced to give up its currency peg in July 1997. In contrast to the other Southeast Asian countries, however, it avoided recourse to the Fund. On 1 September 1998, the government took the unorthodox choice of fixing its exchange rate and imposing capital controls.

The second phase of the crisis began with Taiwan's decision to float its currency on 17 October 1997. Speculation immediately shifted to the Hong Kong dollar, which had been pegged to the US dollar since an earlier foreign exchange crisis in 1983. Massive reserves and a well-institutionalized currency board allowed Hong Kong's financial authorities to defend the peg. But the sharp increase in interest rates required to do the job produced a dramatic sell-off in the Hong Kong stock market, which has a heavy weighting of interest-rate-sensitive property development firms. For the first time, markets in the United States and Europe felt the events in Asia, and all emerging markets faced a dramatic widening of spreads.

South Korea marked the next stage of the crisis. A number of large South Korean groups failed in early 1997, but in the wake of Hong Kong's difficulties, the country suffered a severe liquidity crisis and on 21 November was also forced to abandon support for the South Korean won. On

3 December, South Korea agreed to a massive Fund program backed by additional resources from the World Bank, Asian Development Bank, and other countries in the region. Within weeks, this package proved inadequate, and on Christmas Eve a new program was unfurled, including additional resources and conditions and negotiations with foreign banks over the terms of a short-term debt restructuring. The events in South Korea did not mark the end of the currency crises of 1997-99; the effective Russian default of August 1998 provided another shock to emerging markets and Brazil faced difficulties in early 1999. But this book focuses on the four Asian countries hit hardest by the crisis: Indonesia, Malaysia, South Korea, and Thailand—with a brief comparative look at two broadly comparable countries that escaped the worst of the crisis, the Philippines and Taiwan.

This sequence of events was not only a shock to the region but a shock for the economics profession and the international policy community as well. Few outside the region had foreseen the nature or depth of the economic problems that followed.[1] Three distinct schools dominated the ensuing post mortem: "fundamentalists," who emphasized macroeconomic and particularly exchange rate mismanagement; "internationalists," who focused on the inherent volatility of international financial markets, self-fulfilling speculative attacks, and contagion; and "new fundamentalists," who underlined regulatory and structural problems, particularly in the financial sector. A fourth controversy surrounded the IMF's prescriptions, and whether the adoption of overly restrictive monetary and fiscal policies and ambitious structural adjustment mitigated or compounded the crisis.

Before turning to these central causal arguments, all would agree on a number of factors that played a background role in the crisis or constituted permissive conditions. The Chinese devaluation of 1994, that country's increasing entry into export markets, and the continued sluggishness in the Japanese economy all had implications for the middle-income countries of the region. The unexpected depreciation of the yen posed difficulties for a number of Asian countries (Noland et al. 1998), particularly for South Korea, which competed head to head with Japan in a number of sectors. Different countries also faced particular terms of trade shocks. For example, South Korea and Malaysia were adversely affected by a collapse of semiconductor prices. But it is highly implausible that these developments were enough, in themselves, to generate crises of the magnitude that ensued.

The process of deeper financial integration constituted a necessary condition for the crisis to occur. Asia witnessed a dramatic increase in international capital flows in the early 1990s, including not only the mobile

---

1. One prescient warning was Park (1996).

portfolio capital of hedge funds and "speculators," but extensive bank lending as well (Kahler 1998; Institute for International Finance 2000). This increase in capital flows was partly the result of an important policy development. All the high-growth countries in the region (with the notable exception of China and arguably Taiwan) had either opened their capital accounts some time earlier or made moves to do so in recent years.

A major source of vulnerability in South Korea was the fact that the maturity profile of external debt was increasingly skewed toward the short run, partly as a result of policy. In Southeast Asia, much private borrowing, for example by ethnic Chinese banks and enterprises, had always been relatively short-term. But the maturity profile of foreign debt did not appear to be a central determinant of Indonesia's crisis—or Malaysia's.

The massive reversal of capital flows clearly did not fit the profile of the "traditional" balance of payments crisis first modeled by Krugman (1979) in which monetary and particularly fiscal policy generated unsustainable current account deficits.[2] In none of the most seriously affected countries were budget deficits problematic, and a number of the countries in the region were even in surplus.

However, a common feature of policy in the region was a commitment to fixed or heavily managed exchange rates, and the related problems of overvaluation that can ensue (Corsetti, Pesenti, and Roubini 1998). Moreover, there is evidence in several countries of a basic failure to understand the policy constraints associated with an open capital account. When governments recognized overheating and sought to slow economic activity, the use of monetary policy instruments only had the effect of inducing more capital inflows, thus further contributing to real appreciation.

But there is both ongoing debate and important differences across countries with respect to their external position. Export growth slowed in all countries in the region in 1996, and Thailand's current account deficit was quite large at the time its crisis broke. But South Korea and Indonesia had deficits that did not deviate substantially from levels that had been financed by private capital inflows in the past. Moreover, the extent of overvaluation was certainly not profound.[3] However, the fixed rate regime nonetheless encouraged excessive risk-taking because it was perceived

---

2. However, there arguably were massive budget deficits associated with the implicit or explicit guarantees to faltering banking systems.

3. Using consumer price index-deflated trend real rates, Chinn (1998) finds overvaluation as of May 1997 of 30 percent in Indonesia—almost certainly too much—and 13 percent in Thailand. But South Korea shows a slight *undervaluation* using the same measure, and if deviations from a purchasing power parity rate are considered, the extent of overvaluation in Thailand is nearly halved, and Indonesia shows up as slightly undervalued (see Furman and Stiglitz 1998).

as constituting a guarantee to investors; the fact that so much offshore borrowing was unhedged suggests just such a perception.

Critics of this "fundamentalist" view place greater emphasis on self-fulfilling speculative attacks and contagion (Obstfeld 1996; Radelet and Sachs 1998a, 1998b; Baig and Goldfajn 1999; Masson 1999). In this class of models, creditors are not responding to fundamentals but to the actions of other creditors and what Radelet and Sachs (1998b) have neatly labeled "rational panic." Prima facie evidence of the panic-driven nature of the crisis include the fact that it was largely unanticipated and the substantial overshooting of exchange rate adjustments that followed its onset (Radelet and Sachs 1998a, 1998b).

When such crises start in one country, there are a variety of channels through which they can be propagated to other countries, including fears of competitive devaluation or financial linkages of various sorts (Calvo 1999, Masson 1999). As we have seen from the brief sketch above, Thailand begat Indonesia and Malaysia; Taiwan's devaluation begat the market meltdown in Hong Kong in late October; and that meltdown begat South Korea, which in turn resonated back through the Southeast Asian markets at the end of 1997.[4]

As the depth of domestic financial and corporate distress became more apparent, attention shifted to a third set of domestic vulnerabilities. "New fundamentalists" focused particular attention on the weakness of Asian financial sectors, included rapid lending growth, high corporate leveraging, and excessive risk-taking (Krugman 1998d; Caprio 1998; Pomerleano 1998; Harwood, Litan, and Pomerleano 1999; Goldstein, Kaminsky, and Reinhart 2000).[5] Malaysia, South Korea, and Thailand all underwent bank-financed investment booms before the crisis, during which lending grew rapidly (despite low and declining returns on capital) and bank balance sheets deteriorated.

Krugman (1998d) pushed this line of analysis back toward more fundamental issues of business-government relations. As he put it succinctly, "the problem began with financial intermediaries—institutions whose

---

4. Malaysian Prime Minister Mahathir's imposition of capital controls fed directly into this debate about the weight of external influences (Krugman 1998d, 1999; Montes 1998; Wade and Veneroso 1998). If short-term capital movements were the proximate cause of the crisis, couldn't such vulnerability be reduced by maintaining capital controls, or at least exercising extreme caution in their removal? Interestingly, none of Malaysia's neighbors followed Mahathir's departure from orthodoxy, although the international policy community became somewhat less hostile to controls in the wake of the crisis.

5. Among the oft-cited regulatory failures were low capital adequacy ratios; weak, and weakly enforced, lending limits to related managers and enterprises; permissive asset classification systems and provisioning rules; and, in general, poor disclosure and transparency of bank operations. These problems compounded the effects of weak institutional development by the banks themselves, which tended to lend on the basis of collateral and personal relationships rather than cash flow; see chapter 1.

liabilities were perceived as having an implicit government guarantee, but were essentially unregulated and therefore subject to severe moral hazard problems." When the bubble burst and asset prices started to fall, collateral values also fell, and the illiquidity and insolvency of financial institutions became apparent. This development in turn forced banks either to curtail lending or cease operations altogether, leading to yet further asset deflation. Kaminsky and Reinhart (1998) and Goldstein, Kaminsky, and Reinhart (2000) provide support for the conclusion that the causal relationship between foreign exchange crises and financial crises ran in both directions, and that domestic financial weakness increases vulnerability to foreign exchange crises.

The final, most heated controversy surrounded the policy content of IMF-supported programs. Critics argued that fiscal and monetary policy tightening had perverse effects (Radelet and Sachs 1998a, 1998b; Furman and Stiglitz 1998, Krugman 1999). Rather than stabilizing the exchange rate, they sent markets the signal that further decline was in store, contributed to the overshooting of exchange rate adjustments, and severely compounded problems in the financial and corporate sectors. Feldstein (1998) argued that the IMF's efforts at financial market reform were also overly ambitious and intrusive and had similar adverse consequences.

The IMF cannot be held blameless in the crisis, but any assessment hinges on some counterfactual and a weighing of unpleasant tradeoffs (Corden 1998; World Bank 2000b, 29). For example, critics of the IMF tended to discount the risks of even further currency depreciation and its effects on the servicing costs of foreign debt (Fischer 1998). The evidence for perverse exchange rate effects is mixed at best (Goldfajn and Baig 1998; Dekle, Hsiao, and Wang 1998), and the IMF did in fact move—albeit perhaps too slowly—to reverse its initial monetary and fiscal policy prescriptions. Given the extent of the collapse, it was also impossible to avoid reform of the financial and corporate sectors. Moreover, any assessment requires attention to how the actions—and inaction—of governments affected markets, and that brings us back to the central role of politics.

Bringing Politics Back In

With the exception of the implicit political economy of those emphasizing moral hazard, the striking feature of the debates among economists just outlined is the absence of systematic political analysis.[6] The arguments

6. A number of political scientists and political economists did enter the intellectual fray, but their analyses had little apparent influence on the debates among economists on the causes of the crisis. Political economy accounts include Jomo (1998b), Arndt and Hill (1999), and particularly Pempel (1999b). *The Journal of Democracy* also published a number of essays on the politics of the crisis; see Suchit (1999), Harymurtri (1999), Mo and Moon (1999), and Emmerson (1999). Also see Noble and Ravenhill (2000a).

of both the "fundamentalists" and "internationalists" are seriously limited by this lacuna. In both interpretations, investors are clearly responding to what governments do. A given exchange rate can be sustained if the government is willing to take the necessary actions (Frieden 1997), but these actions carry substantial political cost in the form of an adequate increase in interest rates, a decline in real wages, or—if necessary—an adjustment of the peg. It is thus not economic developments alone that trigger the exit of investors, but the expectation that the government is unwilling or unable to adjust.

Similarly, in the model of self-fulfilling speculative attacks adopted by Radelet and Sachs (1998a, 1998b), it is not evident why the first investor decides to panic; the trigger of the panic is exogenous to the model. But because the model is based on the subsequent reaction of investors to the first in the queue to exit, this is a serious analytic flaw. In fact, the earlier speculative attack models made much more explicit room for politics along the lines already noted: The government would choose to defend a pegged exchange rate, but crises would arise when the markets believed that the government would not have the political capability to sustain it (Obstfeld 1996). Moreover, such models require a trigger or coordinating mechanism, and while that trigger might be provided by an exogenous shock, it can also be provided by political developments that produce uncertainty about government policy (Krause 1998, Leblang 1999, Mei 1999).[7]

Considerations of political economy are also clearly germane to the debate between critics and defenders of IMF programs. As shown in chapter 2, the onset of the crisis was preceded by a period of substantial uncertainty about the course of government policy in South Korea and Thailand; similar periods of uncertainty followed the collapse of the currency in all four of the countries examined here. Yet the debate has proceeded on the assumption that the consequences of a given monetary policy stance (or any other policy measure, for that matter) are independent of market assessments of government credibility and political capacity.

The "new fundamentalists" who focus on deeper vulnerabilities associated with regulatory weaknesses and problems of moral hazard veered the farthest into political territory, but their analysis also begged a number of important questions. Why was the financial sector weakly regulated? Was it the result of sins of omission, simply the lack of administrative capacity and know-how? Or was it in fact due to sins of commission, in the form of forbearance to favored parties? If the latter, the source of vulnerability and moral hazard is not simply bad policies but the politics and institutions that generate them.

---

7. Radelet and Sachs (1998a) revert to these factors at a number of points (e.g., p. 28 on Thailand).

If most accounts by economists paid only passing attention to the way politics contributed to the crises, then they demonstrated even less interest in its political *consequences*. But for citizens of the affected countries, the crisis was major political as well as economic news: Governments, and even regimes, fell as a result of it; politically significant groups saw a destruction of their wealth and sharp declines in income; and citizens vented their frustrations at the ballot box, in the streets, and sometimes in disturbing social violence. Contending parties and coalitions, incumbents and oppositions struggled to balance strong external pressures from international financial institutions and markets and equally strong pressures from domestic constituents.

Our experience of other severe economic crises suggest that they not only have political roots, but are followed by important, sometimes fundamental, political changes (Gourevitch 1991). The advanced industrial democracies came out of the Great Depression, and the world war to which it contributed, with altogether new economic theories, policy commitments, and political alignments and institutions. The debt crises of the 1980s transformed the economic models developing countries had pursued since the 1940s, particularly in Latin America. In a number of countries in that region and elsewhere, crises played a direct role in the transition to democratic rule as well (Haggard and Kaufman 1995). And whereas the transition from socialism ultimately had international political roots in the transformation of the Soviet Union, the economic crisis of the 1990s in the former socialist countries of Europe has had wide-ranging consequences for political alignments in that region as well.

The Asian financial crisis does not rank with these other three economic cataclysms in either its depth or duration; therefore, its longer-term political significance may well be less profound. However, the crisis contributed to the collapse of the Suharto regime, the installation of new governments in both South Korea and Thailand, and the birth of a new political reform movement in Malaysia. The crisis has also forced reforms that have profound longer-term implications for the role of government in the economy and society.

The Arguments in More Detail

Chapter 1 sets the stage by looking at the nature of business-government relations in the most seriously affected countries. Close interaction between the public and private sectors is a hallmark of the region, and a feature of governance that contributed to its high levels of investment and rapid growth in the past. But such relationships and the interventions they spawned are not without risks, particularly in an era of greater capital mobility. In all four countries, government intervention in and through the financial sector created perverse incentives with respect to the ability of banks to monitor their clients and politicized both lending decisions and subsequent losses.

However, it is important to underline that equal if not greater risks were associated with poorly conceived and regulated liberalization and privatization. These reforms are often seen as antidotes for rent seeking and corruption. But they can also be "captured" by business and distorted in ways that shift risk back to the government and increase vulnerability to shocks, typically by weakening the regulatory process.

Underneath these discrete policy problems lie deeper political and institutional features of business-government relations in the region. In Western commentary, these are frequently reduced to corruption, cronyism, and nepotism. In some instances, particularly in Indonesia, these problems were indeed acute. But the sources of vulnerability were not limited to the illegal and illicit. They sprang, rather, from the political commitments of governments to favored portions of the private sector, the absence of countervailing political checks on business influence, and the lack of transparency in business-government relations.

Whatever the long-run sources of vulnerability, we still need some explanation for the onset of the crisis. Chapter 2 outlines the responses of the governments that were incumbent when the crisis struck—Kim Young Sam in South Korea, Chavalit in Thailand, Mahathir in Malaysia, and Suharto in Indonesia. Political uncertainty was implicated in the onset of the crisis, but political factors were even more important in shaping the subsequent adjustment process.

One source of difficulty was precisely in the way business-government relations hindered the government from reacting to emerging difficulties in a timely, coherent fashion. However, broader political uncertainties were also relevant. Given the heated controversy during the past decade over "Asian values," and the purported advantages of authoritarian and democratic rule, it is worth asking to what extent these uncertainties were correlated with the type of political regime.

One purported advantage of authoritarian rule is the capacity for decisive action. In the past, Suharto had responded aggressively, even preemptively, to economic challenges. But the events of late 1997 exposed a number of weaknesses of authoritarian rule in both Indonesia and Malaysia. These weaknesses included the risk of arbitrary action, the lack of transparency surrounding business-government relations, and the uncertainties that surround succession in such systems. These problems were particularly acute in Indonesia, which differed from Malaysia in lacking any meaningful channels for political participation. Once Suharto's grip on power became uncertain, challenges to the regime mounted, and the credibility of the government underwent a swift deflation. It is not coincidental that the country undergoing the most profound political change also experienced the deepest economic crisis.

In the two democracies, South Korea and Thailand, electoral and non-electoral challenges and the nature of government decision-making processes delayed initial reform efforts and diluted their coherence; Malaysia's semi-democracy faced these problems to some extent as well. But the democracies had an important self-correcting mechanism that the authoritarian regimes lacked: The system of government enjoyed support even if incumbents did not, and elections could bring new reformist governments to office. In Indonesia, this could occur only through a change of regime, which—however desirable in the long run—was of necessity traumatic and destabilizing in the short run.

Chapter 3 turns to the political consequences of the crisis and the reform efforts of "successor" governments. In the two democracies—South Korea and Thailand—new reform-oriented governments came into office. Kim Dae Jung was able to advance a wide-ranging reform program early in his term, while in Thailand, the Chuan government was somewhat more hamstrung by features of Thai institutions, including a fragmented party system. Nonetheless, the democracies not only survived this first major economic test to their stability but were able to initiate important policy reforms.

Malaysia's semi-democratic government is the one of the four in which there was continuity in both the political system and its leadership. That continuity did not go unchallenged; the crisis gave birth to a *reformasi* movement, spawned by the arrest and prosecution of Anwar Ibrahim, and breathed new life into the Islamic opposition. The opposition put a dent in the ruling UMNO party's dominance, but Prime Minister Mahathir was able to use the advantages of office and a hierarchical political party to gain reelection. The result, however, was that the crisis did not generate the extent of reform visible in the democracies.

In Indonesia, the crisis played a direct role in the fall of the Suharto regime. Suharto's successor, B.J. Habibie, confronted a variety of non-electoral challenges, any number of which threatened his tenure, including splits within the military, serious ethnic and communal violence, continuing democracy and student protests, and a resurgence of Islam. The transitional Habibie government also faced strong electoral challenges from a variety of new parties that sprang up following Suharto's fall. These political challenges were not inimical to reform; to the contrary, political competition pushed Habibie to remake himself as a reformer. But the transitional nature of his government, the near-revolutionary nature of political change in 1998 and 1999, and severe administrative constraints on government limited the government's capacity to undertake meaningful reform.

Despite the very important differences across these four countries, certain commonalties are also visible in the political fallout from the crisis, including in the nature of the political opposition. All governments had to contend with pressures from business and social reactions to the crisis, but the focus of the opposition was not necessarily directed against the reforms sought by the international financial institutions. Some reformist leaders and parties arose or gained strength by targeting the weaknesses of the old growth model: demanding more accountable and transparent government; greater attention to social welfare; and a revision of the explicit and implicit rules governing business-government relations. Reforming business-government relations implied greater transparency and more independent regulation, but also the introduction of more competition and an end to various forms of protection, subsidy, and privilege. In sum, it is misguided to see the course of policy solely as a response to external political pressures from the international financial institutions and the United States (Wade and Veneroso 1998). At least in some important policy areas, domestic groups were reaching surprisingly similar conclusions on the need for reform.

Initiating policy change is one thing; implementing it is another. To explore the political economy of reform in more detail, chapters 4 and 5 examine the two issues that will define the nature of the region's development model in the future: the restructuring of the financial and corporate sectors and the redefinition of the social contract.

A central feature of the Asian financial crisis is systemic distress: the simultaneous illiquidity if not insolvency of large numbers of banks and firms. Systemic distress posed two political questions in the short run. First, how quickly would governments recognize losses and seek to allocate them among parties? Second, would governments engage in forbearance and bailouts of banks and firms? Or would they exploit the crisis to close nonviable entities, devise new regulatory regimes, and—most basically—reform the patterns of business-government relations that had generated vulnerability to crisis in the first place?

Under conditions of systemic distress, the line between a viable and nonviable bank or firm is blurred; all the countries of necessity engaged in forbearance and public losses in all cases were large. South Korea's political system produced a more ambitious restructuring program than those of the other countries, but the government continued to confront entrenched *chaebol* resistance to a number of its efforts to reform corporate governance, particularly among the largest companies. Even greater continuity is visible in Thailand's relatively arms-length approach to restructuring, Malaysia's continuing defense of favored enterprises, and Indonesia's cronyism.

However, these discouraging judgments on the extent of financial and corporate reform are misleading in one crucial regard: They underestimate the longer-term consequences of the legal and regulatory changes and liberalization measures governments adopted in response to the crisis. These changes include strengthened financial regulation and rules on corporate governance, improved bankruptcy procedures, and the liberalization of foreign direct investment. Such measures necessarily take time to make themselves manifest in the capital markets, in corporate practice, and in the terms of competition in particular markets, but they are gradually reforming the nature of business-government relations in the region.

The problems of financial and corporate restructuring are closely related to the social dimensions of the crisis: How will governments manage the social dislocation arising from the crisis and the policy reforms and firm-level restructuring efforts that ensued (chapter 5)?

In the past, Asian governments generally relied heavily on growth to resolve social welfare questions. They invested in human capital (with Thailand a partial exception), but limited formal social insurance. This approach had already come under pressure from a combination of political as well as economic changes—democratization, urbanization, aging, and increased openness to trade and investment. The crisis only underlined that governments in the region did not have good information on those vulnerable to crises, and the coverage in place was limited in both scope and depth. Although many were adversely affected by the crisis, those hardest hit included urban workers in lower-paid construction and manufacturing jobs, particularly in small and medium-sized enterprises, and in those rural areas linked to or dependent on these workers. These social groups were not effectively represented in the political system; what representation they did have stemmed from political forces without clear or compelling programmatic alternatives.

The governments in the region quickly developed short-term programs to defend social spending and provide relief to the most vulnerable through public employment programs. Outside South Korea, however, neither the nature of the dominant political parties nor of organized interest groups appeared propitious for a redefinition of the social contract. Governments advanced models that continued to rely heavily on informal mechanisms.

It is still too soon to determine the implications of the crisis for the "Asian model," of which there is in any case clearly more than one. But this preliminary review of the crisis suggests cautious optimism that goes beyond the swift economic recovery the region witnessed beginning in 1999. On the social front, the crisis has not spawned the backlash that many feared, but has at least generated debate over the need to revise the implicit social contract to cushion more social groups from the risks of greater openness.

The financial and corporate picture remains the least settled, and it is naturally in this area where interests are most strongly entrenched. But reforms in train include not only increased openness to foreign investment, but efforts to strengthen the regulatory environment and to place business-government relations and corporate governance on a more transparent footing. It is doubtful that these policy changes will lead soon to convergence with Western practice, but there is no reason they should. The diversity of national systems of regulation and corporate governance has served both Asia and the world economy in the past, and will no doubt continue to do so.

Finally, the crisis has shown the resilience of democratic forms, contributed to a remarkable political transition in Indonesia, and generated reformist pressures in Malaysia as well. The crisis has mobilized new social forces for greater participation, accountability, and transparency in government. This deepening of democracy remains the most crucial task, both in its own right and as a key to sustaining other economic, institutional, and social reforms.

1

Business-Government Relations and Economic Vulnerability

Rapid lending growth, an increase in corporate leveraging, declining returns on capital, and weaknesses in the financial sector contributed to the vulnerability of the most seriously affected countries well before the Asian financial crisis actually broke. Even if we acknowledge the central role of capital movements in triggering the crisis, any full account of its onset and depth must encompass these domestic conditions as well. To what extent can they be traced back to political factors and of what sort?

This chapter focuses on business-government relations and their effect on the policy environment in the period before the crisis. In the past, it was believed that the nature of business-government relations in Asia contributed to *good* policy, at least by developing-country standards; even the World Bank came around to this view in its *East Asian Miracle* report (World Bank 1993). But quite strict political requirements are required for such a "good equilibrium" to occur, including political counterweights to private economic power, meritocratic bureaucracies, independent regulatory agencies, and transparency in business-government relations.

These conditions were frequently missing, and as a result the patterns of business-government relations that had evolved in the region carried with them certain risks (see table 1.1). A first problematic fact is the highly concentrated nature of private economic power. A second cluster of potential risks has to do with the moral hazard that arises from various forms of government intervention (Krugman 1998d; Corsetti, Pesenti, and Roubini 1998), particularly government involvement in the financial sector and the conduct of industrial policy. Although the role of industrial policy in the crisis has almost certainly been exaggerated, political involvement

15

Table 1.1 Risk in business-government relations

Policy and political conditions	Risks
Industrial and financial concentration	Undue political influence; capacity for firms to blackmail government; moral hazard and "too big to fail" problem
Government intervention	
Financial sector	Management of past financial crises and government intervention in financial markets create moral hazard
Industrial policy	Government support for particular sectors or projects generates moral hazard
Liberalization, privatization, and deregulation	Capture of liberalization produces poorly designed reforms and weak regulation and provides opportunities for corruption and private fraud and malfeasance
Politics of business-government relations	Dependence of politicians on particular firms generates corruption, policy biases, and economic mismanagement

in the financial sector has unquestionably been a source of moral hazard, even in the absence of explicit guarantees.

However, a third source of policy and political risk arises as a result of liberalization, particularly of financial markets. In the absence of independent and capable regulatory institutions, financial market liberalization provides ample opportunities for private actors to engage not only in risky behavior, but also in fraud and outright expropriation. Political factors can have profound consequences for the opening of the capital account as well, leading to premature liberalization, inauspicious sequencing (such as opening short-term transactions before long-term ones), and weak regulation. Liberalization measures are as vulnerable to capture and distortion as other forms of government intervention.

These particular policy risks—whether from intervention or liberalization—result from certain political institutions and processes. I argue that overly close and nontransparent political relationships between politicians and particular firms contributed to the economic vulnerabilities outlined. Chapter 2 shows that these same conditions also affected how governments responded to early signs of difficulty and played an even more important role in how the crisis was initially managed.

The Microeconomics of the Crisis

Microeconomic explanations for the crisis do not ignore larger risks associated with the conduct of macroeconomic and exchange rate policy, nor the vulnerabilities associated with increasing exposure to international capital flows (Caprio and Klingebiel 1997; Caprio 1998; Kahler 1998; Ito

Table 1.2 Growth of investment and bank credit (percent)

	1991	1992	1993	1994	1995	1996	1997
Indonesia							
GDP growth	8.9	7.2	7.2	7.5	8.2	8.0	2.2
Gross domestic investment as share of GDP	27.0	25.8	26.3	27.6	28.4	29.6	28.4
Bank credit to private sector as share of GDP	46.2	45.5	48.9	51.9	53.5	55.4	61.0
South Korea							
GDP growth	9.2	5.0	5.8	8.6	9.0	7.1	5.5
Gross domestic investment as share of GDP	38.4	36.6	36.0	35.7	36.6	36.9	35.0
Bank credit to private sector as share of GDP	56.8	56.8	57.9	60.4	60.7	65.7	73.4
Malaysia							
GDP growth	8.8	7.8	8.4	9.4	9.4	8.6	7.7
Gross domestic investment as share of GDP	35.7	36.0	38.3	40.1	43.0	42.2	42.4
Bank credit to private sector as share of GDP	75.3	74.6	74.8	74.9	85.1	93.1	103.9
Thailand							
GDP growth	8.0	8.1	8.3	8.8	9.3	6.4	-0.5
Gross domestic investment as share of GDP	41.6	39.3	39.5	40.0	41.1	41.1	35.6
Bank credit to private sector as share of GDP	67.7	72.2	79.8	90.9	97.5	100.0	118.7

Sources: Mody (1999); World Bank (1999d).

1999; Edwards 1999). However, features of the financial and corporate sectors—rapid lending growth, high corporate leveraging, excessive risk taking, and declining returns on capital—increased vulnerability to external shocks and magnified their effects (Kaminsky and Reinhart 1998; Krugman 1998d; Caprio 1998; Pomerleano 1998; Goldstein, Kaminsky, and Reinhart 2000; and on earlier crises, Caprio and Klingebiel 1997).

Prior to the crisis, lending growth in all four countries outpaced GDP growth by substantial margins (table 1.2). Rapid lending growth was accompanied by an increase in corporate leveraging. Korean companies have long sustained high debt-equity ratios, and saw them increase still further in the 1990s. Thailand also saw increases in leveraging, as did Malaysia, although from a lower base. Lending growth and high leveraging were matched at the national level by continuing high levels of aggregate investment. In Thailand, gross domestic investment averaged over 40 percent from 1991 to 1996. Malaysia saw a sharp increase in

Table 1.3 Corporate leverage, short-term debt, and return on assets (percent)

	1990	1991	1992	1993	1994	1995	1996
Corporate leverage							
Indonesia	n.a.	1.94	2.10	2.05	1.66	2.11	1.88
South Korea	3.11	3.22	3.37	3.63	3.53	3.77	3.55
Malaysia	1.01	0.61	0.62	0.70	0.99	1.10	1.18
Thailand	2.18	2.01	1.84	1.91	2.13	2.22	2.36
Short-term debt/total debt							
Indonesia	n.a.	47.6	59.2	60.4	58.4	58.2	56.7
South Korea	50.2	50.2	55.8	56.3	58.6	59.6	58.5
Malaysia	67.5	72.9	73.1	73.4	72.8	72.2	70.1
Thailand	61.2	65.7	74.8	73.6	72.4	67.1	67.2
Return on assets							
Indonesia	9.4	9.1	8.6	7.9	7.4	6.2	6.5
South Korea	4.1	4.0	3.9	3.6	3.4	3.6	3.1
Malaysia	5.4	6.2	6.0	6.5	6.3	6.1	5.6
Thailand	11.7	11.2	10.2	9.8	9.3	7.8	7.4

n.a. = not available

Source: Claessens, Djankov, and Lang (1998).

investment to over 40 percent as well. Investment in South Korea was somewhat lower but still extraordinarily high by world standards. Indonesia also registered a modest increase in aggregate investment albeit from a lower base than the other three crisis countries.

A striking feature of the financial profile of the Asian corporates was the bias in the maturity structure of their debt toward the short term.[1] Not only did short-term debt increase during the decade, but it also began from a very high level. The numbers in table 1.3 capture both domestic and foreign short-term obligations. The fact that foreign debt accounted for a growing share of total debt, and that it was increasingly short-term and often unhedged, made firms and the economy as a whole particularly vulnerable to adverse shocks (e.g., on Mexico, see Sachs, Tornell, and Velasco 1996; on Asia, see Radelet and Sachs 1998a, 1998b, and Ito 1999).

The dramatic increase in lending was accompanied by decreasing rates of return as a result of the declining availability of good projects, poor project evaluation, and a decline in the credit standards of banks. Thai and Indonesian companies had among the highest rates of return in the world during the early 1990s, but both saw declines over the course of

---

1. When banks lend on a line-of-credit basis, these loans are recorded as short-term lending even if they are rolled over, including coverage of interest payments. This process is called "evergreening." Outstanding loans can thus grow without new cash flow to the borrower.

the decade of nearly 30 percent. South Korea saw a decline in returns on assets from performance that was already strikingly poor.

How developments in the corporate sector affected the banks *before* the onset of the crisis is not straightforward (World Bank 1998a, chapter 3). Except for South Korea, where bank profitability has historically been very low, the boom meant rising profits for banks. But accounting standards in the region do not differentiate between "income" derived from "ever-greening"—the practice of lending to cover interest payments—and actual interest payments. As a result, some (unknown) share of bank income and additions to net worth in each country was fictitious.

Moreover, each country saw important segments of the financial sector fare poorly during the 1990s, including the state-owned banks in Indonesia, finance companies in Thailand, and merchant banks in South Korea. Portfolio growth in these segments was typically tied to the property sector and equity markets.[2] Property prices were volatile in Malaysia, and vacancy rates in both Indonesia and Thailand by mid-decade were high, around 14 percent and increasing. As early as the end of 1996, property indexes on the Indonesian and Thai stock markets were off by one-third and three-fourths, respectively, from their 1993 peaks, suggesting that the asset bubble had begun to burst—and with it the value of collateral—well before the external crisis hit.

A final source of vulnerability is the weakness of regulation and poor disclosure and transparency (Corsetti, Pesenti, and Roubini 1998; Radelet and Sachs 1998a, 1998b; Ito 1999). A comparative overview by Caprio (1998) ranked 12 middle-income countries in East Asia and Latin America on a number of indicators of the regulatory environment. The four most seriously affected countries consistently ranked toward the bottom of this group.[3] Caprio constructed a measure of transparency that includes, among other things, whether banks require ratings and whether the top banks have international ratings; South Korea tied for 5th among the 12, Thailand came in 7th, and Indonesia and Malaysia tied for 8th. A ranking done in 1993 by Capital Information Services (CIS) included judgments

---

2. Corsetti, Pesenti, and Roubini (1998) estimate bank exposure to real estate at the end of 1997 from 15-25 percent of loans in South Korea, to 25-30 percent in Indonesia, to 30-40 percent in Malaysia and Thailand.

3. On capital adequacy requirements, Malaysia tied with one other country for 5th, and Indonesia, South Korea, Thailand tied with one other country for 7th (last place). On loan classification requirements, Indonesia ranked 8th, Malaysia and South Korea tied for 9th, and Thailand ranked 11th (again, last place). On liquidity requirements, Malaysia and Thailand tied for 8th, South Korea 9th, and Indonesia 10th (last place). Finally, Caprio ranked the countries on foreign ownership of banking assets, on the assumption that foreign banks are likely to introduce best practice and higher levels of transparency. Malaysia ranked 8th, Indonesia 9th, South Korea 10th, and Thailand 12th. On the summary rankings of these four indicators, plus an additional one on the overall operating environment, Malaysia ranked 7th, South Korea 9th, Thailand 11th, and Indonesia 12th.

about the quality of information provided by banks on a range of indicators, from profits and losses to assets and liabilities, including substantial contingent ones (Delhaise 1998). All the Asian countries fared poorly.[4] Despite such a weak informational base, both international and domestic lenders continued to extend credit; we return to this issue below. The relevant point here is that when investors, creditors, and outside analysts do not have a clear picture of the health of financial institutions, adverse shocks are more likely to feed assumptions that things are even worse than they look.

Business-Government Relations: The Benefits

Before turning to how business-government relations might have contributed to these problems, we first have to address how—and whether—countries in Asia had previously combined the advantages of close business-government relations while avoiding the risks. Chalmers Johnson's (1983) pioneering analysis of Japan outlined an answer to this question that influenced all subsequent writing on the subject. Johnson argued that a "developmental" state guaranteed a policy commitment to economic growth and cooperation with the private sector that "avoided an emphasis either on private profit or the state's socialization of wealth" (Chalmers Johnson 1999, 57-8). Others placed even greater emphasis on how "strong" governments (in some cases authoritarian ones) enjoyed political independence from private actors (Haggard 1990, 1994). This autonomy allowed governments to control the policy agenda and granted them the capacity to "discipline" firms (Amsden 1989): to condition various government supports on performance, and thus to assure that industrial policy did not result in the gross misallocation of resources so common elsewhere in the developing world.

Competent, meritocratic bureaucracies and the concentration of decision-making power in relatively insulated economic agencies played a crucial role in the model of the developmental state. By socializing government officials toward common goals, meritocratic bureaucracies limited the opportunities for rent-seeking (Evans 1995, 1997). Governments in a number of developing Asian countries also granted substantial independence to reformist technocrats and shielded them from political pressures. Such independence remains critical with respect to the conduct of monetary and fiscal policy and the regulation of financial markets.

Finally, governments of the region were able to limit rent-seeking by controlling the way business was politically organized and interacted

---

4. Out of a maximum possible score of 1000, Thailand ranked the best in the Asia-Pacific region, but it received a score of only 442; Malaysia, Indonesia, and South Korea had scores of 423, 401, and 329, respectively.

with government. "Deliberation councils" made up of government, business, and other representatives signaled government commitment, increased the credibility of policy, and established trust while guaranteeing a certain degree of transparency that limited the opportunities for private dealing (Fukuyama 1995; World Bank 1993; Campos and Root 1996, chap. 5; and Chang 1994, but see MacIntyre 1994a). Policy networks linking business and government also increased the flow of information, thus improving the quality of policymaking on the one hand and communicating the government's policy objectives to private actors on the other. As Maxfield and Schneider (1997, 13) summarize, "Trust between business and government elites can reduce transaction and monitoring costs, diminish uncertainty, lengthen time horizons and . . . increase investment."

But where effective, these relations rested on the political preconditions noted above—relatively independent governments and bureaucracies that were not beholden to particular business interests. Moreover, where direct business-government consultation was successful, it occurred through mechanisms that were relatively open, if not to the public at large at least to diverse private-sector groups. These arrangements guaranteed that opportunities for private dealing and rent-seeking by individual firms could be checked.

The Concentration of Private Economic Power

Against these potential benefits of close business-government relations must be set a number of important risks. The first lies in the increasingly concentrated industrial structure that accompanied developing Asia's rapid growth, and the potential this brought for business influence on policy and even blackmail of government.

Bird (1999) has collated average four-firm concentration ratios; that is, the average share of total sales in each sector accounted for by the top four firms (see table 1.4). These ratios are surprisingly similar for Indonesia, Malaysia, and South Korea. Although high in comparison with the United States and United Kingdom, they are less than for several other developing countries (Pakistan, Turkey, and Sri Lanka).[5]

As Bird acknowledges, however, these numbers miss a crucial feature of industrial organization in Asia: the existence of highly diversified family-owned or -controlled conglomerates that operate in many markets at once. The best known example of this phenomenon are the Korean *chaebol*. In

---

5. Bird also argues (against received wisdom) that concentration has been trending down in Indonesia as a result of greater openness to trade, although concentration is more constant over time in Malaysia and South Korea.

Table 1.4 The concentration of private economic power (percent)

	Indonesia	South Korea	Malaysia	Thailand
Average concentration ratios (4-firm level)	54.0 (1993)	57.0 (1987)	53.0 (1990)	n.a.
Ownership concentration in 10 largest firms (3 largest shareholders)	53.0	23.0	46.0	44.0
Share of total outstanding shares owned by 5 largest shareholders (unweighted)	67.5	38.1	58.8	56.6
Share of total market capitalization controlled by top 15 families	61.7	38.4	28.3	53.3
Market share of five largest banking institutions, end-1997 (share of bank loans)	41.0	75.0[a]	41.0	70.0
Share of firms unable to cover interest expenses from operational cash flow (peak number and year)	63.8 (1st half 1999)	33.8 (1998)	34.3 (1998)	32.6 (1997)

n.a. = not available

a. Market share for South Korea is for 8 dominant nationwide banks.

Sources: Concentration ratios, Bird (1999); ownership concentration in 10 largest firms, La Porta, Lopez-de-Silanes, and Schleifer (1999); family control, Claessens, Djankov, and Lang (1998); concentration of outstanding shares, Asian Development Bank (1998, all listed companies in Indonesia, Malaysia, and Thailand, sample of 81 listed firms for South Korea); market share of banks, Casserly and Gibb (1999); debt-servicing problems, Claessens, Djankov, and Klingebiel (1999).

1995, the top five *chaebol* accounted for 25.9 percent of all shipments in the manufacturing sector, and 27.2 percent of value added (Yoo 1999).

In Southeast Asia, diversified Chinese business groups have been among the largest firms in both Indonesia and Malaysia, but the last decade has also witnessed a particularly rapid expansion of new "local" (*pribumi* in Indonesia, *bumiputra* in Malaysia) business groups as well (Gomez and Jomo 1997, Searle 1999 on Malaysia; Pangestu and Harianto 1999 on Indonesia). In Indonesia in 1992, the top 10 groups accounted for half of the total turnover of the top 100 companies in the country, and 80 percent of the assets of the country's top 300 groups were controlled

Table 1.5 Ownership of South Korean business groups by insiders
(percentage of common shares held)

Business group	Founder	Relatives	Member companies	Total
Hyundai	3.7	12.1	44.6	60.4
Samsung	1.5	1.3	46.3	49.3
LG Group	0.1	5.6	33.0	39.7
Daewoo	3.9	2.8	34.6	41.4
Sunkyong	10.9	6.5	33.5	51.2
Sangyong	2.9	1.3	28.9	33.1
Hanjin	7.5	12.6	18.2	40.3
Kia	17.1	0.4	4.2	21.9

Source: World Bank (1998a), 60.

by Indonesian-Chinese conglomerates (Pangestu and Harianto 1999). By the early 1980s, 50 of Thailand's 100 largest manufacturing firms belonged to 1 of 16 conglomerates, which jointly accounted for fully 90 percent of the assets of all Thai enterprises (Rock 1995, 14).

A starker indication of the concentration of private economic power can be seen in the data on the extent of ownership concentration in table 1.4. Indonesia appears particularly concentrated on these measures, whereas South Korea, and by at least one measure Malaysia, would appear to be somewhat less so.[6] But in Korea, lax rules on corporate governance have allowed families to control firms and whole groups through mechanisms such as cross-ownership within the group and deviation from one-share-one-vote rules (Yoo 1999). For example, the founder of Hyundai and his relatives own a little over 15 percent of the group, but through intra-group cross-holdings effectively control 60 percent (see table 1.5). Similar mechanisms have been documented for Malaysia as well (see Gomez and Jomo 1997).

The role of finance in the concentration of private economic power varies in important ways across the countries. In South Korea, the financial system is relatively concentrated, but the government has limited the ability of business groups to control financial institutions (Woo 1991; Choi 1993). In Thailand, by contrast, the banking sector is highly concentrated and has long been privately owned. Family-owned private banks such as Bangkok Bank and the Farmer's Bank have been at the center of diversified business groups. In Indonesia before the crisis, the majority of the 144 private commercial banks were also controlled by four or five family groups (Kahn 1999).

The relationship between the concentration of private economic power and political influence is not necessarily straightforward. In Indonesia,

---

6. Malaysia's difference in this regard reflects the government's self-conscious efforts to offset the dominance of Chinese business by promoting *bumiputra* firms.

the fact that ethnic Chinese account for a small share of the population and a large share of wealth makes them more, not less, politically vulnerable.

In general, however, economic concentration implies that private actors can bring relatively large resources to bear on the political process. When banks and firms are very large relative to the economy as a whole, their distress necessarily has systemic implications. Some sense of the magnitude of this problem can be gained from the last row in table 1.4, which shows the number of firms facing liquidity problems at the height of the crisis. Large banks and firms facing distress used their size in a "too big to fail" blackmail game: support us or else!

The Politics of Moral Hazard I: The Government and the Financial Sector

A second source of economic vulnerability is the pursuit of policies that generated moral hazard. With the exception of insurance for small depositors—and even that policy is controversial in some circles—no government has an incentive to extend guarantees in an explicit way; such a policy would be akin to the childhood prank of pinning a sign on someone's back that says "kick me." Nonetheless, firms might form expectations about the government's future behavior from its handling of past financial crises. Could banks and borrowers count on the government to come to their rescue, or had the government limited the risks of moral hazard by forcing shareholders, creditors, and borrowers to absorb losses and aggressively prosecuting fraud and malfeasance?

In Malaysia and Thailand, banking authorities responded to financial crises in the 1980s in ways that strengthened the legal framework and sought to limit moral hazard. Yet despite these efforts, the continued involvement of the government in the financial sector in Indonesia, Malaysia, and South Korea created the ongoing risk of politicization of both lending decisions and any subsequent losses that arose, even in equity markets.

Thailand had a financial crisis in 1983-84 that resulted in the collapse of Asia Trust Bank (the 12th largest bank in terms of assets) and a number of finance companies.[7] In return for orchestrating liquidity support, the government pushed mergers, took over partial ownership of some institutions, placed public officials into executive positions, and expanded the Bank of Thailand's regulatory powers. By the time the crisis eased, 13 finance companies had had their licenses revoked.

In a pattern that was again visible in the 1997-99 crisis, however, the treatment of the banking sector was more lenient. One bank was effectively

---

7. My thanks to Kit Panupong for his assistance on this section.

nationalized, but a number of other major banks received extensive liquidity support through a newly created Financial Institutions Development Fund (FIDF). The FIDF, which was under the control of the central bank, had a wide range of powers at its disposal to assist and rehabilitate financial institutions, including the power to write down capital and replace management. However, the fund also enjoyed substantial discretion and could support institutions through low-interest loans, deposits, or purchase of convertible debentures and shares.

The crisis of the mid-1980s occurred under a liberalizing but semi-authoritarian regime and involved an expansion of the government's regulatory authority, the closing of a number of institutions, and the imposition of conditions on others; even under those political conditions, forbearance was shown toward the largest banking institutions. The crisis of the 1990s by contrast occurred under a democratic opening that provided multiple new channels for business lobbying of government.

The problems facing the country's financial institutions became apparent as early as 1991 when the Bank of Thailand detected irregularities in a struggling mid-sized bank, the Bangkok Bank of Commerce (BBC). A bank examination in 1991 revealed that 27 percent of BBC's total assets were nonperforming (Nukul Commission Report 1998, para. 283). Subsequent examinations in 1993 and 1994 showed that the problem had only worsened. The government agreed to purchase a substantial stake in the bank through the FIDF, but without any writedown of shareholder capital or replacement of management. The central bank governor defended this action on the grounds that similar forbearance had been shown toward banks in the past (Nukul Commission Report 1998, para. 300 and 306)!

As the extent of mismanagement at BBC became public in mid-1996 following disclosure by the opposition, there was a run on the bank. After having indulged BBC for an extraordinary period, the central bank finally took formal control of BBC. Ultimately, a total of $7 billion was spent to keep BBC afloat. Although the FIDF recovered some of that money, the bailout set a dangerous regulatory precedent and severely damaged the reputation of the Bank of Thailand. The Nukul Commission, established in 1998 to investigate the causes of the crisis, sidestepped the issue of outright corruption, stating somewhat obliquely that "in a [sic] recent past, top BOT officials were inclined toward political interests" (para. 317). But several politicians within Prime Minister Banharn's Chart Thai party were known beneficiaries of large loans from BBC (*The Nation*, 13 March, 18 April 1997; Pasuk and Baker 1998, 105-10, 259).

Indonesia is frequently invoked as the quintessential case of crony capitalism. As longtime observers of the Indonesian financial sector Cole and Slade (1998, 65) put it, "in the 1990s the 'Suharto connection' became the 'guarantee' or collateral underlying the viability of many enterprises and financial institutions, most obviously in banking and securities markets. Any financial regulator who attempted to apply prudential rules to such connected financial institutions or transactions ... was removed from his position. Politics and connections dominated."

The power and value of a genuine Suharto connection were widely understood. This was starkly illustrated in 1990 when Bank Duta, a private bank housing the substantial deposits of several political foundations controlled by Suharto, lost nearly half a billion US dollars in foreign exchange speculation. Bank Duta was promptly rescued by two other large corporate groups with very close financial ties to Suharto, which in turn were quickly rewarded with other forms of state largesse (Schwarz 1994, 112).

The failure of Bank Summa, only 2 years after the Bank Duta case, demonstrates that what Suharto gave he could easily take away. Bank Summa was owned by the Astra group, the second largest industrial conglomerate in Indonesia. Despite its early association with Suharto, the group had consciously distanced itself from the Suharto circle and refused to participate in the Bank Duta restructuring. The regulators were subsequently turned loose on Bank Summa, and the bank was forced into liquidation at enormous cost to the parent company. Moreover, other cronies were allowed to buy up a number of Astra assets (Cole 1999).

The problems in the Indonesian banking sector were not limited to crony banks; the direct involvement of the government in the banking sector created additional moral hazard problems. Of the top 15 banks in Indonesia before the crisis, 6 had the government as the largest shareholder (Nasution 1999, 83).[8] Nonperforming loans at state-owned banks in 1996 totaled 16.6 percent of their total credits, in comparison with 13.8 percent for private nonforeign exchange banks and 3.7 percent for private foreign exchange banks—although, as we will see in chapter 4, these numbers must be treated with appropriate suspicion.

Following a recapitalization of a number of state-owned banks in 1992, Bank Indonesia announced plans to prosecute bad debtors in 1994, and the next year publicized a list and prevented them from leaving the country. Nonperforming loans temporarily fell. But the high-profile case of Eddie Tansil suggests the government's unwillingness to monitor private borrowers (Backman 1999, 32; Delhaise 1998, 132). Following parliamentary queries and revelations, Tansil was convicted of bribing officials at the state-owned development bank Bapindo to obtain $430 million of unsecured loans, on which he later defaulted. Tansil was jailed, but he is thought to have subsequently bribed his way out; his whereabouts remain unknown.

---

8. These 6 banks controlled fully 30 percent of assets in the banking system, and that underestimates the government's role because of a number of banks controlled indirectly by the central bank, line ministries, and the military.

Malaysia had a financial crisis in 1985-87 involving three banks, a number of deposit-taking cooperatives (DTCs), and illegal deposit-taking institutions (Sheng 1992; Thillainathan 1998). The government forced the banks to recognize all losses, despite substantial management and shareholder resistance, changed management, and required existing shareholders to inject as much capital as possible through a new share issue; the central bank recapitalization was conditional. When the economy began to rebound, however, the central bank changed its approach by establishing a fund to support select *bumiputra* enterprises; this more interventionist approach was again visible during the current crisis.

The political economy of the DTCs was contentious. After the government suspended 24 of them, depositors argued that their deposits should be guaranteed in full. However, the government committee charged with overseeing the rescue rejected this argument and imposed partial losses on depositors. Those responsible for mismanagement were charged in court; some were sentenced to jail. Few of the DTCs survived the crisis.

But if Malaysia did somewhat better than Thailand in managing its financial crisis in the 1980s, it shared with Indonesia the problems associated with growing government involvement in the financial sector.

As in Indonesia, the problems were not simply ones of how the financial crisis was managed, but of the deepening general involvement of the government in the banking sector. Between 1970 and 1990, 8 of the top 10 banking institutions that had been controlled by Chinese and foreign interests were brought under the control of either *bumiputra* or government companies (Gomez and Jomo 1997, 60-66; Searle 1999, 75).[9] The second largest bank, Bank Bumiputra, was established by the government in 1965 to help ethnic Malays; problems of moral hazard were particularly acute there. In 1984, Bank Bumiputra reported massive losses stemming from loans to Hong Kong-based speculators in Malaysia's largest banking scandal and was taken over by the state-owned oil company Petronas. Petronas came to the rescue a second time in 1989, and the bank was bailed out again in 1998 (see chapter 4). The sixth largest bank, United Asian Bank, was controlled by a company that was itself controlled by the ruling UMNO party.

9. The first, third, and fifth largest banks in the country before the crisis began their lives as Chinese-owned institutions but came under government control (Maybank and United Malayan Banking Corporation, or UMBC) or had substantial government ownership (D and C Bank). In some cases, government control of banks, particularly smaller ones, came following runs or other problems of mismanagement that forced government intervention. In other cases, however, such as the government's acquisition of shares in UMBC, the motives were explicitly political and involved efforts to counter concerns about Chinese ownership of banks. UMBC was later acquired by a prominent UMNO party leader and then sold back to the state when the government required ministers to divest their holdings of listed companies (Lee 1987, 328; Searle 1999, 142)!

Thus the appearance of a private banking sector in Malaysia is somewhat misleading. Government involvement in the banking sector has in fact been pervasive and motivated by a particular political strategy of developing *bumiputra* interests, with the strong implicit commitments such a program implies.

The government's involvement in the financial sector in Malaysia extends to the stock market (Gomez and Jomo 1997, 34-39; Perkins and Woo forthcoming). One component of the New Economic Policy was the requirement that firms over a certain size—with some exceptions such as export-oriented enterprises—sell 30 percent of their shares to *bumiputras*. One way of doing this was simply to allow certain individuals to acquire shares at a discount, making share allocation a vehicle for patronage. But this was unwieldy and did not achieve the social objective of increasing the wealth in *bumiputra* hands because the shares could simply be sold. Beginning in the 1980s, discounted shares were acquired by unit trusts set up by the government-owned Permodalan Nasional Berhad (National Equity Corporation, or PNB). The shares were acquired by government grants and interest-free loans and the trusts offered guaranteed rates of return. As a result, the government came to have a particularly strong interest in the performance of the stock market, opening another window for moral hazard.

South Korea's financial history, finally, has been anything but smooth (Cole and Park 1983; Woo 1991; Choi 1993). The events of 1997-98 were the third in a cycle of lending and investment booms dating to the 1960s, each of which was followed by financial crisis. The most recent of these occurred in the wake of the heavy and chemical industry drive of the 1970s, when a rapid expansion of credit from state-owned banks resulted in significant surplus capacity in a number of sectors. Under authoritarian auspices, the government undertook a forced restructuring of a number of major heavy industries in 1981-82 and a second round of corporate restructuring and debt rescheduling for 78 troubled enterprises in 1986-88. The government steered a middle course between bailouts and allowing firms to fail by forcing takeovers and mergers. But this required giving generous financial incentives to the acquiring firms, including long grace periods on interest payments, tax breaks, and outright grants (Moon 1994, 149).

Following the transition to democracy in 1987-88, the political opposition protested the substantial costs of the 1980s bailouts and the close nature of business-government relations more generally. The governments of both Roh Tae Woo and Kim Young Sam reverted to a variety of direct means to limit *chaebol* borrowing.[10] However, as the data in

---

10. These included limitations on borrowing for "noncore" business, requirements to sell idle buildings and land, and limits on intra-group investments.

table 1.2 show clearly, these efforts had very little influence on the extent of corporate leveraging in the 1990s. Moreover, the combination of high spreads between lending and deposit rates and the notoriously low profitability of Korean banks was a clear sign of extensive nonperforming loans (Dalhaise 1998, chap. 5). Rather than being called, bad loans were compensated by overdraft privileges at the central bank (Park 1999).

Although the government's ownership of banks was not as extensive as in Indonesia, neither was it trivial (Haggard and Mo 2000). During the 1994-96 period, the Korean Development Bank increased credit for facility investment at a rapid pace. This lending signaled government commitment to larger projects, again raising moral hazard questions. The Roh and Kim governments also prolonged the government's involvement in the banking sector in other ways. The government did not even abandon its practice of reviewing the appointment of top bank managers until 1993, and even after that point, policy continued to play a role in bank lending decisions (Park 1999). For example, the Kim Young Sam government made concerted efforts to press banks to channel credit to small and medium-sized enterprises.

But in some cases, government involvement was altogether lacking in a policy rationale, as the Hanbo scandal of 1997 showed.[11] With a total of 24 subsidiaries, the Hanbo group was the country's 14th largest *chaebol* (by assets) in 1995. With government blessing, the group had developed a proposal for a massive steel complex. During the final stages of construction in 1996, the firm ran into serious delays and construction costs more than doubled. After a number of secondary financial institutions cut the supply of new credit to the firm in late 1996, Hanbo's main banks stepped in temporarily to prop up the group, but by January it was clear that Hanbo was insolvent and creditors took control.

Once under bank control, the full extent of Hanbo's difficulties became apparent. The firm was able to borrow more than $3.5 billion for the steel project because top bank managers circumvented normal loan review processes. The subsequent legislative investigation revealed that the chairman of Hanbo directed bribes toward the presidents of his main creditor banks, but also to members of the National Assembly Finance Committee (including members of the opposition) and to one of Kim Young Sam's aides, who directed the president's economic advisors to pressure Hanbo's banks to continue to lend.[12]

The Hanbo case was unique in the extent of malfeasance but probably not altogether exceptional. The scandal severely weakened the govern-

---

11. The following two paragraphs draw on Schopf (2000).

12. Additional money was also spent to secure the license for the plant in the first place, to secure support from local politicians around the site who faced opposition on environmental grounds, and to subsequently quiet legislators who might blow the whistle.

ment's ability to manage emerging problems in the banking and corporate sector before the crisis broke (see chapter 2). As in the other crisis countries, continued government involvement in the banking sector weakened bank incentives to aggressively monitor their corporate clients.

The Politics of Moral Hazard II: Industrial Policy

A second, related explanation for the crisis in Asia is that moral hazard arose from the conduct of industrial policy (Wolf 1998; *The Economist*, 15 November 1997). Was industrial policy—in the specific sense of government targeting of particular industries—present in the crisis countries, and if so, was it pervasive enough to contribute significantly to the financial weaknesses noted above?

In Thailand and South Korea, the answer is almost certainly "no." In Thailand, the government was involved in extending protection to capital goods industries in the 1970s and early 1980s (Rock 1995). However, a brief infatuation with mimicking Northeast Asian industrial policy by creating a "Thailand Inc." passed with the export-led growth of the mid-1980s. Large-scale, state-led efforts such as the Eastern Seaboard project were scaled back and transferred to private hands (Pasuk and Baker 1998, 81-89). The government has played no role in the allocation of credit to industry (although it has required banks to extend credit to agriculture) or the granting of subsidies for particular activities, and the Board of Investments has taken a permissive approach to the designation of "priority" sectors for investment incentive purposes.

South Korea, of course, does have a very long history of industrial policy. But the heavy industry drive of the 1970s—the heyday of industrial targeting—was held responsible for a variety of economic ills. After seizing power in a coup in 1980, Chun Doo Hwan began to gradually dismantle the industrial policy regime (Haggard et al. 1994; Chang, Park, and Yoo 1998). These efforts accelerated with the inauguration of the Kim Young Sam administration in 1993. By the time of the crisis, Korea's industrial policy was limited to a handful of R&D supports in some high-technology industries. The long legacy of industrial policy may have contributed indirectly to the bank-*chaebol* relations described in the foregoing section, but there is little ground for arguing that the investment boom of the 1990s resulted from government targeting of particular industries.

Assessing the significance of industrial policy in Malaysia presents some complications because of the centrality of ethnic considerations in economic policymaking (Bowie 1988; Jesudason 1989; Gomez and Jomo 1997; Mahathir 1999; Jomo 1986, 1994, 1995; Gomez 1990, 1991, 1994, 1999; and Searle 1999). Following ethnic riots in May 1969, the government adopted a New Economic Policy (NEP), which explicitly sought to redistribute wealth from non-Malays, particularly foreigners and Chinese, to Malays.[13] Dissatisfied with the meager results of these policies, then-Minister of Trade and Industry Mohamed Mahathir shifted course in 1980 by initiating a "Look East" policy, modeled explicitly on Japan and South Korea. The state-owned Heavy Industries Corporation of Malaysia (HICOM) was the central agent of this big push, and undertook joint ventures with foreign companies in a variety of sectors, including steel, cement, natural gas, and most controversially, a national car project, the Proton.

Virtually all the HICOM ventures ended up losing money. When the country experienced a recession in the mid-1980s, Mahathir moved to professionalize the management of state-owned enterprises (SOEs), corporatize and privatize selectively, revamp incentives for foreign investors, and pay greater attention to exports. Nonetheless, protection for some state-supported projects continued, and the government remained committed to certain other projects, such as the national car effort, despite the fact that it was nominally privatized.

Indonesia, finally, is the case in which government involvement in the economy was most extensive, indeed even bewildering. In contrast to South Korea, where industrial policy was conducted primarily by channeling financial subsidies to private firms, SOEs played a more central role in Indonesia, particularly during the oil boom of the 1970s. By the mid-1980s, there were more than 200 public enterprises, sales of which accounted for approximately a quarter of GDP.

With the decline in oil prices in the early 1980s, technocratic reformers gained greater control over the policy agenda and gradually shifted the emphasis toward a private-sector led import-substitution approach, supplemented after 1985-86 with greater emphasis on export promotion. Among the instruments for achieving the development of domestic industries were "officially sanctioned cartels (cement, glass, plywood and paper), price controls (cement, sugar, automobiles); entry and exit controls (plywood and automobiles); [and] exclusive licensing (clove marketing, wheat flour milling)," not to mention the continued role of public-sector monopolies in a range of sectors, including energy and mining, public utilities, fertilizer, plantations, and some "strategic"—although not rapidly growing—sectors such as steel (Jomo et al. 1997, 144). The Investment Coordinating Board maintained complicated lists of activities eligible for various incentives, but "the list served more as an instrument of discretionary control over both foreign and domestic private investors than as a tool for guiding investment incentives into potential high-growth areas" (Felker and Jomo 1999, 47; see also MacIntyre 1993).

---

13. To implement these objectives, the government established a number of public corporations as well as a licensing system to ensure that new investments complied with the NEP's objectives.

After 1988, the government embarked on a modest reform program for SOEs, including some selective privatization after 1994, but more imporant a further liberalization of both trade and foreign direct investment (Bresnan 1993, chap. 10; Winters 1996, chap. 4; Felker and Jomo 1999). At the same time, the government grouped 10 "strategic industries" under the Coordinating Agency for Strategic Industries controlled by the state minister for research and technology, B.J. Habibie. Although deemed "strategic," these industries were in fact dominated by SOEs in sectors such as aircraft, shipbuilding, and steel, all of which benefited from direct and indirect state subsidies, government procurement, and other restrictive arrangements. Although the operations and finances of the firms are far from transparent, the assessments that exist find substantial losses and failure to meet policy objectives (McKendrick 1992). In 1991, the World Bank found that Habibie's projects accounted for fully half of all losses by SOEs (cited in Schwarz 1999, 87).

In sum, industrial policy played some role in generating moral hazard in Indonesia and Malaysia, but it seems difficult to argue that it was a central factor in the financial weaknesses outlined in the previous section. Except for the Habibie projects, the general trend in the four countries was in the direction of less rather than more industrial targeting. Indeed, it was the process of liberalization, rather than industrial policy, that was subject to some of the most damaging forms of political manipulation.

The "Capture" of Liberalization

If government interventions of various sorts can generate moral hazard, a different but no less significant set of risks is posed by weakly regulated liberalization, particularly of the financial sector. These problems may reflect either "sins of omission" or "sins of commission." In the first case, well-intentioned reforms, typically championed by technocrats and supported by international financial institutions, are undertaken without adequate legal, administrative, or informational capacity to check private ineptitude, malfeasance, or fraud. In the second case, political interference in either the design or implementation of the reform undermines its stated objectives. It is important to distinguish between the two problems. The first can be solved by increasing bureaucratic capacity, but the latter requires more fundamental institutional and even political reform, such as increasing the independence of central banks and regulators.

The problems of financial liberalization were clearly most acute in Indonesia, and centered not on the capital account, which had been relatively open since the late 1970s, but on domestic liberalization. Ironically, the financial reforms of the 1980s and 1990s were seen by technocrats as a way of minimizing abuses in the banking system (Cole and Slade 1996, chapter 10; Hamilton-Hart 1999). These efforts began with the removal of credit controls and interest rate ceilings in June 1983 and accelerated through a wide-ranging set of reforms in 1988 that included reduced restrictions on establishment and branching of banks and finance companies and issuing of equities and the adoption of extraordinarily low (2 percent) reserve requirements. The number of private banks mushroomed from 74 before the reform to 239 in 1996. Nonbank financial institutions proliferated even more rapidly, and the capitalization of the stock market increased dramatically (Cole and Slade 1996, chapter 6; Hamilton-Hart 1999).

The private sector supported decontrol and promotion of the private financial markets. Chinese businessmen and bankers were particularly well-positioned to take advantage of the new regime, including the opportunities to finance their banking and corporate expansion through share issues with minimal disclosure (Cole and Slade 1996, 334). However, the "opportunities" created by the reforms included the ability to form "swindle" banks:

> The typical swindle bank makes loans to non-bank companies owned by its principal owner(s) to finance questionable investment projects, usually at inflated prices. Liabilities of such banks are mainly deposits owned by the general public, liquidity credit from Bank Indonesia, unsecured commercial paper sold to the general public (including foreigners), and equity shares owned by Bank Indonesia and other state-related institutions. . . . Such banks typically really have negative net worth. (Nasution 1999, 85-86)

The technocrats were not unaware of these problems and after a series of delays, Bank Indonesia tightened the framework for banking regulation in 1991 and strengthened the regulation of the stock exchange over the first half of the 1990s. But the complicated nature of banking regulations, competition between the Ministry of Finance and central bank, and the lack of information and personnel all limited the capacity of the government to implement the new regulatory regime (Cole and Slade 1996; Hamilton-Hart 1999; Hill 1999, 61-67).

However, there can be little doubt that politics also limited the ability of the regulators to confront bankers and problem debtors. The president showed a continuing propensity to intervene in the loan decisions of both state-owned and private banks. Any financial regulator who attempted to enforce prudential rules on connected financial institutions was removed from his position, including the managing director of the central bank in 1992 and the minister of finance in 1996 (Cole and Slade 1998, 65).[14]

Political considerations also influenced the liberalization process in Thailand. Following the cleanup of the crisis of 1983-84, technocrats turned their attention to initiatives designed to mobilize financial savings and

---

14. Prudential regulation of the stock market was similarly complicated by a variety of interest group pressures (Cole and Slade 1998, 229-34).

force greater competition on a protected and oligopolistic financial sector dominated by a handful of powerful, family-controlled banks (Pakorn 1994, Alba, Hernandez, and Klingebiel 1999; Yos and Pakorn 1999; LoGerfo and Montinola 1999).[15]

Early efforts in 1989-90 to remove or increase ceilings on both deposit and loan rates met resistance from the larger commercial banks, which feared competition from smaller banks, foreign entrants, and finance companies (Doner and Unger 1993, 119-120). However, the major banks quickly realized that they could benefit quite substantially from deregulation. The first liberalization program (1990-92) relaxed controls on banks' portfolios and branching and allowed commercial banks to underwrite debt instruments and sell mutual funds. Expanded opportunities for non-bank financial institutions did not necessarily hurt the banks; of the 93 finance and securities companies in the country, no fewer than 26 were affiliated with private Thai commercial banks. A number of these companies, which played a central role in making the multibillion-dollar commercial paper market, began to experience distress as early as mid-1996 (Overholt 1999).

The further opening of the capital account began with the acceptance of the obligations of the IMF's Article VIII in May 1990 and culminated with the launching of the Bangkok International Banking Facility (BIBF) in 1993. The 49 Thai and foreign banks with BIBF licenses were allowed to borrow offshore and relend to domestic borrowers at substantial spreads, with the additional benefit of a fixed exchange rate and a number of tax advantages.

The external imbalances and macro and microeconomic problems created by financial liberalization have been a leitmotif of virtually all writing on Thailand's crisis, as has been the inadequacy of prudential regulation, particularly with respect to the finance companies (Pakorn 1994; Nukul Commission Report 1998, para. 434; Alba, Hernandez, and Klingebiel 1999; Yos and Pakorn 1999; LoGerfo and Montinola 1999; Overholt 1999). To what extent did politics affect the design and implementation of liberalizing initiatives?

The creation of the BIBF had a complex of competing motives, including geostrategic and regional ones (Thorn 1994; LoGerfo and Montinola 1999). Economic reform and opening in Indochina appeared to offer tremendous opportunities for Bangkok to serve as a financial center for the region while expanding trade through the poorer East and Northeast of the country, from which—not coincidentally—a number of politicians drew support. Thai commercial banks saw opportunities in entering the Indo-

---

15. Technocrats also sought to promote the capital market as an alternative to dependence on bank financing, while asserting greater control over a stock exchange (the Stock Exchange of Thailand, or SET), which had become the locus of a variety of fraudulent practices (Handley 1997, 100).

china market, and the initial expectation was that the BIBF would focus primarily on offshore or so-called "out-out" transactions. However, it became clear that the scope for "out-in" transactions exploiting large interest rate differentials and tax breaks dwarfed the offshore potential of the BIBF, and those transactions quickly came to dominate.

The consequences of both international and domestic liberalization hinged crucially on the regulatory capacity of the Bank of Thailand, and that in turn rested on the larger political milieu (LoGerfo and Montinola 1999). In 1988, the semi-democratic regime of Prem was replaced by a democratically elected coalition government under Chatichai. Although the transition to democratic rule was interrupted by a year and a half of military rule (February 1991 to September 1992), the introduction of democratic politics meant fundamental changes in the relationship among business, politicians, and regulators. Chatichai naturally expanded the role of the party politicians in the cabinet, including at the Ministry of Finance, while technocrats who had exercised influence over the budget process through the National Economic and Social Development Board (NESDB) saw their influence radically devalued.

The Bank of Thailand retained greater independence than the NESDB, but the governor holds his position at the pleasure of the minister of finance. In the early 1980s, the power of dismissal was used twice, resulting in what Amar Siamwalla has called "implicit intervention:" "Instead of submitting to explicit orders from the Minister [of Finance], the Governor would anticipate the Minister's desires and follow the current political line" (Ammar 1997, 71). The Nukul Commission, established to look into the causes of the crisis, found increasing politicization of the bank and a declining willingness as well as capability[16] to make supervisory decisions (1998, para. 429, 434). The Securities and Exchange Commission, only formed in 1992, was also subject to intense lobbying throughout the 1990s to limit its oversight of insider dealing and other fraudulent practices on the stock exchange (Handley 1997, 108). Thailand's problems were clearly not limited to lack of bureaucratic capacity.

As in Thailand, the banking crisis of the mid-1980s led to a strengthening of the legal framework of financial regulation in Malaysia; unlike Thailand, the process of financial market liberalization was more incremental and modest (Lin and Chung 1995; Thillainathan 1998, 14). Lending rates were freed up in 1991, and the government's requirements that banks channel some share of total credit to "priority" sectors eased. The government also established an offshore financial center on the island of Labuan, but this center remained small and some administrative measures were used after 1994 to limit short-term capital movements (see appendix 2-1).

---

16. One serious problem the Bank of Thailand faced was the departure of a number of skilled personnel to the rapidly expanding private financial sector; see *Manager* (Bangkok), February 1995, 27-31.

Given that the capital account was already relatively open, Labuan cannot be held responsible for the growth of Malaysia's foreign debt. Foreign banks did have a strong presence in the country—accounting for roughly 30 percent of loans and deposits when the crisis hit—but the government restricted both foreign and domestic entrants.

Nonetheless, there were a number of ways in which the government's interest in both ethnic redistribution and supporting favored enterprises complicated other liberalizing reforms and created incentives for lax financial regulation. The privatization program was envisioned as a new tool for achieving the objective of ethnic redistribution, but the line between this objective, political goals, and outright corruption sometimes blurred (Jomo 1995). The privatization of both infrastructure and state-owned companies typically occurred through negotiated tenders and involved a small number of firms.[17] Favored individuals benefited handsomely from the transfer of large blocks of shares in government companies without open tender (Gomez and Jomo 1997, chaps. 4, 5). But privatization did not serve to eliminate the problem of moral hazard because of the government's political as well as economic interest in seeing the projects successfully completed; in effect, the government took on large contingent liabilities as a result of a privatization process that should have shifted risk onto the private sector.

The government's political objectives also had a number of consequences for the regulation of the financial system. The government had a strong interest in lending to *bumiputra* entrepreneurs (to support the privatization program), in supporting the buoyancy of the stock market (due to the growing number of *bumiputra* investing in discounted shares and government-run unit trusts), and in supporting non-*bumiputra* Chinese firms that were linked to the government. As a result, limits on lending to speculative activities such as property development and share purchases were weak and weakly enforced. In 1997, the proportion of total loans to these activities reached 43 percent. In March 1997, just before the crisis, the central bank did finally move to curb these speculative excesses (Bank Negara Malaysia, *Annual Report 1997*, 78). But by that time, property and shares had already been used as collateral to secure additional bank credit, creating a financial system that was highly vulnerable to shocks (Perkins and Woo forthcoming).

South Korea's crisis was also preceded by a complex set of liberalization measures with respect to both the real and financial sectors; as in Malaysia, the two must be understood in tandem. In 1993, the Kim Young Sam government sought to curb increasing concentration by requiring *chaebols* to designate core industries and phase out their noncore businesses. In

---

17. Of 13 large national projects that the government awarded between 1992 and the onset of the crisis, 8 were awarded to Renong Bhd, which had previously been the investment arm of the ruling party (UMNO) (Perkins and Woo forthcoming).

return, the government offered exemptions from a complex system of credit controls and regulations on entry, investments, acquisition of assets, and real estate holdings (Yoo 1999). Because the government had limited entry into a number of sectors in the past, and because of the opportunities posed by the strong yen, deregulation was followed by a rush of facility investments in a number of key industries, including steel, petrochemicals, semiconductors, and most controversially autos.[18]

As in the past, the rapid growth of facility investment during the boom of 1994-96 relied heavily on borrowing; domestic and international liberalization further encouraged this tendency (Chang 1998). In 1991, the government initiated major institutional changes in the financial markets. The most important of these was the licensing of merchant banks and the lifting of administrative controls on the yields and supply of commercial paper (CP), in which the merchant banks were the major market makers.

The creation of new merchant banks and the liberalization of the CP market was a major factor in the expansion of short-term financing (Cho 1998); it is also a case study in how financial reforms can be captured not only in their implementation but in their basic design.[19] In the early 1980s, the government expanded the number of investment and finance companies (IFCs) in an effort to bring informal financial market players under government regulation. In the 1990s, the IFCs expressed a strong interest in transforming themselves into merchant banks because of a number of privileges those institutions enjoyed. The government licensed 24 IFCs as merchant banks in two separate rounds, 9 in 1994, and 15 in 1996, supposedly to contribute to a more market-based financial system.

In fact, the licensing process was the result of intense lobbying efforts which, like the Hanbo scandal, involved kickbacks from the new merchant banks to bureaucrats and politicians (*Korea Herald*, 11 April 1998). According to an investigation by the Board of Audit and Inspection (BAI), three of the IFCs licensed in 1996 were insolvent *at the time they were licensed* (*Chosun Ilbo*, 18 March 1998)! Of the 16 merchant banks whose licenses were revoked by the government in 1998, 15 were new entrants in 1994-96.

These domestic developments took place against the backdrop of a gradual opening of the capital account (Park 1998; Cho 1998). The United States exerted pressure for greater financial openness beginning in the late 1980s. These pressures then accelerated in anticipation of OECD membership in 1996. The Korean government's strategy for liberalization of

---

18. After a long controversy, the president granted Samsung a permit to build a passenger car factory in December 1994 over strong opposition by incumbent firms and bureaucrats at the Ministry of Trade and Industry. What appeared to break the stalemate in favor of Samsung was the decision to locate the plant in Pusan, the economically struggling hometown of President Kim Young Sam.

19. I am indebted to Jungkun Seo for this analysis of the merchant banks.

the capital account was a gradual one. Fearful of destabilizing portfolio movements and facing resistance from domestic underwriters, the government liberalized transaction-based flows such as short-term trade credits first while only gradually opening portfolio investments and restricting investments in domestic fixed-income assets. The government also sought to control direct borrowing by the *chaebol*. However, the government was unduly lax with respect to bank borrowing, particularly with the merchant banks.[20] Behind a number of the merchant banks were the *chaebol*; denied ownership of banks, they had acquired stakes in nonbank financial institutions as a conduit for financing their own operations.

As in the other cases, regulators lacked both the independence and capacity to monitor the international operations of banks adequately. The Kim Young Sam government recognized this problem and in early 1997 created a financial reform committee to devise a more independent regulatory structure. Instituting these changes not only came too late but, as will be shown in the next chapter, the government faced substantial political and bureaucratic resistance to its efforts. Reform had to await the coming of the Kim Dae Jung government.

The Politics of Business-Government Relations

The foregoing review suggests strongly that the sources of economic vulnerability were not limited to particular policies but were rooted in basic features of the business-government relationship. In Western accounts, these political and institutional weaknesses are typically reduced to the problem of cronyism and corruption. As we have seen, problems of corruption and cronyism were certainly in evidence. But the political problem extended beyond the illicit to the influence that business interests exercised over legislation, regulation, and the legal process more generally.

Of course, the quality of the quantitative data on corruption is of somewhat questionable quality, usually taking the form of subjective valuations of businesspeople (Elliott 1997b).[21] But even if we take the data with a grain of salt and focus primarily on orders of magnitude and the general

---

20. Over objections by the Ministry of Finance and Economy, merchant banks lobbied successfully to engage in international business, resulting in extraordinary risk-taking, such as investments in Thailand and in Russian bonds (*Business Korea*, September 1997, 24).

21. The problem with subjective assessments of experts or market participants is that corruption is likely to be confounded with a number of other things in respondents' evaluations, from policy to economic performance; e.g., all the crisis countries show an increase in corruption, according to Transparency International, between 1996 and 1997 when the crisis hits. Even the teams that generate the data issue cautions (see table 1-6). These caveats aside, some research has found statistically significant effects of corruption on growth and foreign investment (Mauro 1995; Wei 1997; Elliott 1997a).

direction of change, it is not particularly supportive of a simple corruption story (see table 1.6).

The two data sets examined here do confirm some suspicions. Hong Kong, the Philippines, Singapore, and Taiwan are, on average, less corrupt than the four most seriously affected countries discussed here. Among those, Indonesia is the most corrupt, and South Korea or Malaysia least, with Thailand in between. All are more corrupt than the OECD countries and three central European countries (Czech Republic, Hungary, and Poland).

But the data also present a number of anomalies. The "Asian eight" have, as a group, become less, rather than more corrupt since the first half of the 1980s. Moreover, corruption in these countries is less virulent than in Latin America, Africa, or the Soviet successor states. By the Transparency International data, the reduction in corruption in the region is greater than in other developing regions. If we turn from these averages to the performance of individual crisis countries, South Korea and Indonesia show improvements over time, including before the crisis, and Thailand improves by one measure while worsening by the other. There is little difference in scores between Indonesia—the hardest hit of the crisis countries—and the Philippines, which was affected but did not experience the profound shocks of the four countries analyzed here (see appendix 3-1).

What such indices do not capture is the broader political relationships between politicians and the private sector. These include the extent to which politicians rely on particular firms and groups for political support, the transparency of business-government relations, and whether institutions encourage healthy or perverse private-sector influence on policy.

The changing nature of business-government relations is most apparent if we focus first on the democracies. As in the other Southeast Asian countries, Sino-Thai business developed clientelistic ties with military leaders and bureaucrats not simply to pursue rents but for political protection (Doner and Ramsay 1998). Over time—and in contrast to Malaysia and Indonesia—the Chinese community became assimilated. Business associations formed in key sectors, including rice and banking, and established more institutionalized consultative processes with the government. In the early 1980s General Prem's liberalizing military regime developed a Joint Public-Private Consultative Committee that provided a forum for the discussion of major policy issues (Anek 1992). However, this occurred during a period when the military-led government still dominated politics and granted the technocrats substantial control over key areas of policy, particularly macroeconomic policy. Such delegation limited to some extent the adverse consequences of continuing clientelism.

Table 1.6 Indicators of corruption

	ICRG Data				TI Data					
	1982-85	1992-95	Change[a]	1982-95	1980-85	1988-92	1996	Change[b]	1997	1998
Most affected countries in Asia										
South Korea	4.58	8.33	3.75	5.30	3.93	3.50	5.02	1.09	4.29	4.2
Thailand	5.63	5.00	−0.63	5.18	2.42	1.85	3.33	0.91	3.06	3.0
Malaysia	8.96	6.67	−2.29	7.38	6.29	5.10	5.32	−0.97	5.01	5.3
Indonesia	1.67	4.79	3.12	2.15	0.20	0.57	2.65	2.45	2.72	2.0
Other Asia										
Hong Kong	8.96	8.33	−0.63	8.52	7.35	6.87	7.01	−0.34	7.28	7.8
Taiwan	7.29	6.67	−0.63	6.85	5.95	5.14	4.98	−0.97	5.02	5.3
Singapore	10.00	6.67	−3.33	8.22	8.41	9.16	8.80	0.39	8.66	9.1
The Philippines	0.42	4.79	4.37	2.92	1.04	1.96	2.69	1.65	3.05	3.3
Average Asian	5.94	6.41	0.47	5.82	4.45	4.27	4.98	0.53	4.89	5.0
China	6.25	7.29	1.04	6.53	5.13	4.73	2.43	−2.7	2.88	3.5
A.I.S.[c]	9.01	8.88	−0.13	8.90	7.60	7.65	7.68	−0.08	7.82	7.77
Latin America[d]	4.79	5.03	0.23	5.01	3.71	3.37	3.54	0.17	3.16[e]	3.34
Africa[f]	4.10	5.49	1.39	4.78	3.00	2.95	2.77	0.23	3.36[g]	2.75
Eastern Europe[h]	6.39	8.06	1.67	7.36	3.47	5.21	5.27	−1.80	5.15	4.8
Soviet Union/Russia	6.67	5.21	−1.46	6.18	5.13	3.27	2.58	−2.55	2.27	2.4

A.I.S. = Advanced Industrial States

Note: The Center for Institutional Reform and the Informal Sector (IRIS) at the University of Maryland compiles a data set from data originally collected by Political Risk Services and published in the International Country Risk Guide (ICRG). This data set includes a number of political risk variables, including an assessment of the degree to which payments are required at high political levels for large transactions and at the lower levels for routine government functions such as customs clearance. The scale ranges from 0, indicating payments are "generally accepted" to 6, indicating little corruption. Data in table 1.6 are converted to a 10-point scale. Transparency International (TI), a Berlin-based NGO established in 1993, began its ranking of perceived corruption in 1995. The ranking, which starts at zero for the most corrupt and goes to 10 for the least, is based on a number of surveys. In 1996, for example, these included the ICRG/IRIS index, World Competitiveness Report of Institute for Management and Development, Hong Kong-based Political and Economic Research Consulting (PERC), DRI/McGraw-Hill Global Risk Service, Economist Intelligence Unit, and a survey of embassies and chambers of commerce from Göettingen University. Researchers from Göettingen University in collaboration with Transparency International subsequently created historical data, also based on other surveys (usually one or two for 1980-85 and three or four for 1988-92, depending on the country). For more details on the sources of these data by country, see the Web site maintained by Johann Graf Lambsdorff of Göettingen University, http://www.gwdg.de/~uwvwicr.htm. See also Elliott (1997 a), appendix B, for caveats about the use of these and other data.

a. Period of change measured: 1982-85 to 1992-95.

b. Period of change measured: 1980-85 to 1996.

c. Based on data for Australia, Canada, Europe, Japan, New Zealand, and United States.

d. Based on data for Argentina, Bolivia, Brazil, Chile, Colombia, Ecuador, Mexico, and Venezuela.

e. 1997 score for Ecuador not available.

f. Based on data for Cameroon, Egypt, Kenya, Nigeria, South Africa, and Uganda.

g. 1997 score for Cameroon, Egypt, Kenya, and Uganda not available.

h. Based on data for Czech Republic, Hungary, and Poland.

The direct involvement of business in politics not only showed a secular increase (Anek 1992, 33), but also leapt upward whenever politics were liberalized or became more democratic (1973-76; gradual liberalization in the 1980s; 1988-91; 1992-present). Thailand's constitutions have produced a fragmented and weak party system, and the electoral system encourages personal rather than partisan campaign strategies (Hicken 1998, 1999). Campaigns are expensive and politicians of all major parties have turned to both Bangkok financial and industrial interests, and increasingly to the emergent provincial business elite, for support.[22] A number of business-people entered politics directly (Ockey 1992; Pasuk and Sungsidh 1996; Handley 1997).

To accommodate these political investments, coalition governments would form by allocating cabinet and subministerial positions to their members and channeling fiscal resources through the ministries to relevant supporters (Pasuk and Sungsidh 1996). These institutional arrangements naturally meant a diminished role for the technocrats, particularly after the transition to fully elected democratic governments in 1988-91 under Chatichai, and after 1992.

In sum, the new Thai democracy faced a number of problems in maintaining the political and institutional conditions required to hold private influences over public policy in check. Some parties, particularly the Democrats, expressed concern about these issues and sought to project an image of clean government. But as we will see in chapter 3, they also had to secure electoral support and ruled in coalition with other parties.

In South Korea, political liberalization and democratization have made business-government relations increasingly contentious (Haggard and Moon 1990; Moon 1994; Kim 1997). In the early 1960s, the military government of Park Chung Hee initially acted quite decisively to break up rent-seeking relationships between the government and the private sector. However, the new government quickly made peace with the private sector and established a variety of consultative mechanisms, including meetings between the president and chairmen or representatives of the major *chaebol*.

As the *chaebol* grew in size and the government undertook its heavy industry drive in the 1970s, the nature of business-government relations again became increasingly controversial. When Chun Doo Hwan seized power in 1980, the government instituted tighter controls on credit, passed an anti-monopoly law, and forced the major restructuring of business outlined above (Haggard and Moon 1990; Moon 1994).

However, at the same time, both Chun and particularly his protégé Roh Tae Woo required resources to compete as the political system was

---

22. The provincial nouveaux riche not only provided funding but also organized the regional and local machines that were critical for Bangkok-based parties to mobilize (and buy) votes in the provinces and rural areas.

slowly liberalized. Roh Tae Woo won the first democratic election for president by a plurality when Kim Dae Jung and Kim Young Sam split the opposition vote in 1987. But in 1995, under the Kim Young Sam administration (1993-98), an opposition lawmaker accused Roh of having amassed an enormous political slush fund (West 1997). Prosecutors were able to trace the funds because the new government had implemented a "real name" account system precisely to end the practice of hiding funds for tax and political purposes. The size of the fund Chun bequeathed to Roh—$285 million—and the comparable amounts Roh added to it were stunning. The revelations immediately raised questions about the favors that firms had received in return, from licensing and finance to lax tax and regulatory treatment.

Beginning in the 1980s, and accelerating with democratization, the relationship between government and business became more contentious, and the consultative mechanisms that had existed in the past atrophied. The private sector became more assertive in lobbying against unwanted controls and openly supporting sympathetic candidates. As the Hanbo incident showed, democratization provided new channels for business influence through the legislature (Schopf 2000). But at the same time, Roh Tae Woo, Kim Young Sam, and Kim Dae Jung were all under continual political pressure—from labor, students, nongovernmental organizations, and the broader public—to "do something" about the increasing concentration of business and ongoing allegations of corruption and corporate malfeasance. These larger political battles over the nature of business-government relations were very much part of Korea's adjustment efforts under both Kim Young Sam and Kim Dae Jung.

In Malaysia and Indonesia, the issue of business-government relations has much wider political implications because of the question of how to manage inter-ethnic inequalities. In Malaysia, where the Chinese community is much larger (approximately 27 percent vs. 3-4 percent, depending on definitions), those efforts have always been more institutionalized. In the West, Mahathir is associated with public sector initiatives, such as the Proton car project. But the core of his approach was to create a more competitive Malay private sector through privatization (Jomo 1995).

This shift in policy mirrored a fundamental transformation in the political base of the UMNO. At the time of its foundation, the UMNO was dominated at the grass roots by rural teachers; in 1981, a full decade after the NEP, school teachers still accounted for 41 percent of delegates to the UMNO's General Assembly. However, this dropped to 19 percent in 1987, while businessmen constituted 25 percent in that year. By one estimate, almost 20 percent of the UMNO's 165 division chairmen in 1995 were millionaire businessmen (Gomez and Jomo 1997, 26). Drawing on East Asian examples, the Mahathir administration devised a set of business consultative mechanisms to engage this important new constituency (Biddle and Melor 1999).

Yet at the same time, the dominant position of the UMNO and the increasing discretion in the hands of the prime minister (Milne and Mauzy 1999, chap. 2) sometimes resulted in a blurring of the boundary between government, party, and private interests. The UMNO deepened its involvement in business during the 1970s, in part to reduce its dependence on Chinese financing through its coalition partner, the Malaysian Chinese Association. In the 1980s, several party-controlled companies became among the largest conglomerates in the country. When the UMNO was forced to divest its holdings as a result of a challenge from a rival faction within the party, it did so to sympathetic business supporters. Ironically, this business base of support increasingly came to encompass Chinese as well as Malay entrepreneurs (Gomez 1999).

The discretion in the hands of the prime minister with respect to key policies such as privatization and the intertwining of party and business interests made conflicts of interest—at least as they would be understood in the United States—unavoidable. Moreover, they ran the risk of generating expectations that public and party enterprises or private firms with close political ties to the government would get bailed out (even if they in fact were not). It is again not surprising that, as in South Korea, the opposition focused substantial attention on cronyism and how to restructure business-government relations (see chapter 3).

Indonesia is the country to which the trio of sins—"corruption, collusion (or cronyism), and nepotism" (KKN in Indonesian)—was most frequently applied during the crisis, and with good reason (see Robison 1986; MacIntyre 1991, 1994b). The scale of corruption was clearly related to the highly concentrated nature of authoritarian rule in Indonesia. President Suharto could and did use presidential decree powers and other forms of discretion to benefit cronies and family (Indonesia Corruption Watch 1998) and gained from the general lack of transparency in government. The number of cronies—those with a continuing, close personal relationship with the president—appeared fairly small, and the number of extended family members involved in business numbered fewer than 20 (Schwarz 1999, chap. 6; Backman 1999, 263). But the diversified nature of their businesses cut across a large swath of the Indonesian economy (*Time*, 24 May 1999; Backman 1999, chapters 13, 14; Schwarz 1999, chapters 5, 6). Crony and family business empires of this scope would almost certainly have been impossible under more democratic, open, transparent political circumstances.

Business-government relations in Indonesia are further complicated by the fact that Chinese-Indonesians dominated the emerging private sector and were big beneficiaries of the liberalization of the 1980s and 1990s. Given Indonesia's volatile political history and periodic violence against the Indonesian-Chinese, they naturally had incentives to form political alliances that could offer protection, including with the military. At the same time, their minority status and wealth made them highly reluctant to engage in any overt political activity (MacIntyre 1991, 1994b). Rather, political relationships were more likely to be personal, clientelistic, and nontransparent, exactly the circumstances under which corruption and private dealing flourish.

Suharto (and lower-level political and military leaders) had to balance lucrative relationships with private Chinese-Indonesian businesses against demands for greater inter-ethnic redistribution. Suharto resisted a Malaysian-style program, but he periodically had reasons to respond to the *pribumi* private sector. The availability of oil money first provided the opportunity for a variety of programs that advanced *pribumi* businesses, from preferential awarding of contracts to bank lending (Winters 1996, chap. 3). Habibie's strategic industry initiative was partly a way to counter the weight of Chinese business and appeal to *pribumi* nationalism. Particularly after Suharto's reelection in 1993, the relative influence of Habibie supporters, cronies, and family rose at the expense of the technocrats.

Conclusion

A number of features of the business-government relationship in the crisis countries increased their vulnerability to external shocks. These risk factors include the concentration of the private sector, government involvement in banking, industrial policy, and weakly regulated and "captured" liberalization. Of these risks, industrial policy appears to weigh least heavily, although its role cannot be dismissed altogether in Indonesia and Malaysia.

Yet a skeptic might still point out that these are all problems of long standing and that developing Asia managed to grow rapidly with them in the past. Again, why should these factors become a source of vulnerability now?

A first point this review should make clear is that the crisis of 1997-98 was not developing Asia's first. Thailand, South Korea, and Malaysia have had financial crises in recent memory, and although they were not on the scale of the crisis of 1997-98, neither were they costless. Some of the sources of financial vulnerability highlighted here are of long standing, but so is the propensity to financial crisis.

Second, it is misleading to say that the nature of the risks has been constant. Critics of liberalization like to underscore that it is the new element in the policy mix, and thus the factor likely to be of most obvious causal weight (Wade and Veneroso 1998; Chang 1998, 1999). But the risk of government intervention and poorly regulated liberalization are not mutually exclusive, and a demonstration of the significance of the latter does not constitute proof for the unimportance of the former. Unfortunately, it is quite possible to have the worst of both worlds: government intervention that generates moral hazard and political uncertainty and precipitous liberalization that creates risks of a different sort.

Moreover, other things *were* changing. The trend toward increasing concentration of private economic power has been a secular one, and some patterns of government intervention (such as the new strategies for advancing favored entrepreneurs in Malaysia or the increasing presence of the Suharto family in Indonesian business) are of relatively recent vintage. More important, we have seen that the politics of business-government relations has not been constant either, with the government becoming more porous to private influence in Indonesia, Malaysia, and Thailand, and in some ways in South Korea well.

Perhaps more important, the overall context of policy had changed. In the early phases of growth, both the social and private returns on capital are very high. Close business-government relations served the function of assuring investors, often in highly uncertain political environments, and thus inducing the high levels of capital accumulation that was central to the Asian model. But as the returns to capital fall over time, the political order becomes more stable, and efficiency in the allocation of resources becomes more important for sustained growth, the logic of costly assurances to private actors becomes less clear. The inability of investors to monitor both business-government relations and the firm also becomes more costly. In short, relationships that might have had some use at one point in time may prove dysfunctional at a later stage of growth.

A final response accepts that the catalog of vulnerabilities outlined here does not, in itself, constitute a theory of financial crises but only a set of factors that can increase the propensity to crisis and compound their costs when they strike. However, the problems in business-government relations we have noted also affect how governments manage problems in the financial sector and foreign exchange markets and how they are perceived by those markets; chapter 2 takes up these questions.

2

Incumbent Governments and the Politics of Crisis Management

with ANDREW MacINTYRE

Almost by definition, crisis settings are ones in which all options are unattractive and the optimal policy response is either unknown or sharply contested.[1] Yet even if we must have sympathy with policymakers struggling under adverse circumstances, it is also clear that their actions—or inaction—are highly consequential. When countries enter a zone of vulnerability or when crises break, markets are highly sensitive to indications that the government is unwilling or unable to act in a decisive, coherent fashion. Political developments can serve as a trigger or focal point that shifts expectations in adverse ways. Politics can also affect the course of adjustment once a crisis hits, and thus mitigate or compound its severity. This chapter explores the effects of three factors that might be considered political early warning indicators for countries vulnerable to crisis (table 2.1): electoral and non-electoral challenges to incumbent governments; inefficiencies in the government's decision-making processes; and features of business-government relations that might impede a government's ability to act. To what extent were these political risk factors present in each case and what influence did they have on both the onset and initial course of the crisis? In taking this inventory, this chapter also stands back to address a particular controversy about the link between politics and economic performance in East Asia. Are democracies

Andrew MacIntyre is associate professor in the Graduate School of International Relations and Pacific Studies, University of California, San Diego.

1. This chapter draws in part on Haggard and MacIntyre (2000).

Table 2.1 Political constraints on crisis management: The incumbents

	Thailand	South Korea	Malaysia	Indonesia
Government in office, dates in office (onset of crisis[a])	Prime Minster Chavalit Yongchaiyudh, 11/1996-11/1997 (7/1997)	President Kim Young Sam, 2/1993-2/1998(11/1997)	Prime Minster Mohammed Mahathir; first assumed office 7/1981[b], most recently elected 4/1995 and 11/1999 (7/1997)	President Suharto. First assumed office 3/1966; most recently elected (indirectly) 3/1993 and 3/1998, resigned 5/1998 (widened exchange rate band 7/1997, floated 8/1997)
Political challenges				
Electoral	Six-party coalition government with recurrent threats of defections	National presidential elections in 12/1997	Substantial electoral victory for ruling coalition in 1995; general elections not required until 4/2000, but UMNO Party elections in 6/1998	Indirect presidential election in 3/1998
Non-electoral	Antigovernment demonstrations in early 11/1997	Some limited strikes and demonstrations in sensitive sectors (Kia workers, central bank employees)	Minimal	Student demonstrations from 2/1998; protests against price increases and large-scale riots in Jakarta 5/1998; mounting social violence 1-5/1998
Decision-making process	Parliamentary, six-party coalition	Presidential, unified government but executive-legislative and intraparty splits	Parliamentary, coalition government, but UMNO dominant	Authoritarian, highly concentrated
Government links to business	Close links between legislators of all parties and business	Some evidence of corruption involving executive and legislators (Hanbo), intense lobbying by distressed firms	Close to politically favored groups	Close links between executive and cronies and family businesses

a. Onset of crisis is the date exchange rates were allowed to float.

b. Mahathir succeeded Hussein Onn after the latter's heart operation in July 1981, and was elected in the April 1982 general elections.

more prone to the risks just outlined, as defenders of "Asian values" have implied, or do authoritarian regimes suffer from similar or even greater disabilities?

Political Sources of Uncertainty

The question of how electoral cycles affect government policy and the real economy has been a central theme of political economy for some time (for a recent synthesis, see Alesina, Roubini, and Cohen 1997). In the next chapter, we address the policy consequences of actual changes in government, and what sorts of oppositions gained from the crisis. But impending elections and non-electoral challenges, in the form of demonstrations, strikes, or riots, can also weaken the ability of incumbent governments to make difficult decisions.[2] Moreover, the prospect that a political challenge—again, either electoral or non-electoral—will result in a change of government can itself generate political uncertainties; this is particularly likely when there are substantial differences in the policy positions of incumbents and their challengers or simply uncertainty about what a change of government might bring.[3]

A second source of uncertainty about the course of policy lies in the decision-making process itself, in which a trade-off can arise between decisiveness and credibility (Tsebelis 1995; Haggard and McCubbins 2000; MacIntyre 1999a, 1999b). This trade-off is related to the nature of institutional checks and balances in the decision-making process, or more specifically the number and preferences of different veto gates.[4] A decision-

---

2. Critics of early political business cycle approaches argued that if voters were fully rational, they would see through politicians' efforts to manipulate the economy for short-term electoral ends and react accordingly, both in the market and at the ballot-box (see Alesina 1994 for a review). Yet despite this objection, incumbent governments facing electoral or non-electoral challenges may nonetheless be prone to delay policy actions that impose short-run costs, for the simple reason that their time horizons are too short to capture the benefits. Such hesitation is particularly plausible if we consider not only electoral challenges, but extra-parliamentary actions that can also threaten the survival of the government.

3. Such uncertainty will be especially great when the change of government is irregular (e.g., through a coup) or when there is a change of regime (e.g., from authoritarian to democratic rule). Recent cross-national statistical work by Leblang (1999) and Mei (1999) has shown that changes of government (Leblang) and elections (Mei) increase the propensity to financial crisis, even when controlling for a variety of other determinants.

4. A veto gate is an institution that has the power to veto a policy proposal, thus forcing a reversion to the status quo. Veto gates can include the president, legislature, a second chamber of the legislature, a committee within a legislature, or the courts; in authoritarian governments, they may include the military. The preferences of these veto gates may be more or less closely aligned; thus, the president and legislature may represent distinct veto gates, but may either be of the same party (unified government) or of different parties (divided government).

making system with few checks on executive decisions—a single or very few veto gates—has the advantage of being decisive. Policy can be changed easily, but precisely for that reason may not be credible, and can even become erratic (MacIntyre 1999a, 1999b). By contrast, a system with multiple veto gates has the advantage of checks and balances that force deliberation and bargaining. It will be slow-moving and less decisive. At the extreme, such systems can generate outright stalemate. Such an outcome may be desirable if the policy status quo is favorable, but can be highly costly during crises when there is strong pressure for policy change.

A final source of uncertainty about the course of government policy arises out of the nature of business-government relations. We have seen the ways in which these relationships generated vulnerability over the longer run. But business lobbying complicates economic policymaking in the short run as well, particularly where governments have a history of responding to business pressures or the interests of particular firms.

How did different types of governments—democracies, dictatorships, and varieties of each—fare in managing the crisis?

There can be little question that the two democracies—South Korea and Thailand—both experienced difficulties responding to the crisis and that some of these difficulties can be traced directly to features of democratic rule, including electoral pressures and divided decision-making processes. In Thailand, a weak coalition government proved slow in reacting to early warning signals before the crisis struck and had difficulty formulating a coherent response once it did. In Korea, impending presidential elections split the ruling party, created tensions between the executive and National Assembly, and made the government particularly sensitive to lobbying. However, as will become evident in chapter 3, the democracies also had an advantage over their authoritarian counterparts, including the ability of oppositions to mobilize support and new governments to take office and initiate reform with electoral and legislative support.

As one would expect, semi-democratic Malaysia and authoritarian Indonesia initially faced fewer political constraints. The absence of meaningful electoral or non-electoral challenges and concentrated decision-making structures seemed to position them to respond decisively to the crisis. In fact, these purported advantages of authoritarian rule proved illusory, particularly in Indonesia, and for at least three different reasons. First, the advantages of decisive decision-making were more than offset by the erratic behavior of chief executives. In Malaysia, Prime Minister Mahathir exacerbated his country's problems by mounting a campaign against international "speculators," thus encouraging the very behavior he was decrying. In Indonesia, Suharto's commitment to reform in the initial IMF program was followed almost immediately by derogations that called that commitment into question.

A second closely related source of uncertainty centers on the role of the private sector and particular firms. All four governments faced challenges to policymaking as a result of business lobbying; the findings of this chapter thus extend the conclusions of chapter 1 that the nature of business-government relations was implicated in the onset and depth of the crisis. But authoritarian governments were no more immune to appeals from privileged segments of business than their democratic counterparts, and arguably were less so. Political challenges to authoritarian leaders made it even more imperative that they maintain links with privileged private sector supporters, while the absence of democratic accountability and the lack of transparency made it difficult for oppositions and interest groups to monitor these relationships. In both Indonesia and Malaysia, commitments to reform ran into particularly strong business resistance.

However, the greatest source of uncertainty in any authoritarian regime centers on the question of succession. In Malaysia, divisions within the policymaking apparatus reflected deeper political divisions within the government and a succession battle between Mahathir and his deputy prime minister, Anwar Ibrahim. In contrast to Indonesia, Mahathir's control over a strong party apparatus allowed him to organize political support, reassert his authority, and pursue an unorthodox response to the crisis.

In Indonesia, the very concentration of authority in Suharto made the system vulnerable both to his discretion and any signs that his rule might be in jeopardy. The absence of institutionalized mechanisms to generate mass support and manage opposition—as existed in Malaysia—ultimately generated profound political uncertainty. When serious opposition emerged, the very fate of the regime, and the property rights associated with it, were at stake. It is no accident that the authoritarian regime facing the most extensive political challenges, and ultimately undergoing the most wide-ranging political change, was also the country that experienced the deepest policy uncertainty and the most profound crisis.

Thailand

By late 1996, Thailand was coming off a remarkable economic boom, prolonged by the inflow of foreign capital. As real GDP growth slowed in 1996, two issues were of particular policy concern—the widening current account deficit (growing from an already-large 8.1 percent of GDP in 1995 to 8.4 percent in 1996), and unease about the health of the recently liberalized financial sector. Although the baht had been tested at the time of the Mexican crisis, these factors fueled growing speculation against the currency in the second half of 1996 (Bhanupong 1998; Warr 1998). But Thai authorities failed to address either of these problems in a credible way, clung to a strategy of defending the pegged exchange rate, and ultimately fell victim to a massive speculative attack on 2 July 1997.

We have already seen how political links between members of the government and financial institutions generated severe moral hazard problems earlier in the decade. These problems did not go away, but broader constitutional weaknesses compounded them. All of the democratically elected governments before the crisis—Chatichai, Chuan, Banharn, and Chavalit—rested upon shaky multiparty coalitions, made up of internally weak and fragmented parties that not only provided access for private interests but made policymaking extraordinarily contentious (Hicken 1998, 1999). Governments were constructed from a pool of approximately a dozen parties, and cabinet instability was a chronic problem. As leader of the governing coalition, the prime minister was vulnerable to policy blackmail by coalition partners threatening to defect in pursuit of better deals in another alliance configuration.

In September 1996, Banharn's government collapsed after key coalition partners deserted him. After what was widely regarded as the country's dirtiest election, Chavalit's New Aspiration Party (NAP) narrowly emerged as the largest party in Parliament (*Far Eastern Economic Review*, 26 November 1996, 16-22). Chavalit proceeded to construct a six-party coalition made up of most of the parties from the previous government. Nonetheless, he also signaled that he would appoint a cabinet built around an "economic dream team" of highly respected technocrats, most notably Amnuay Viruwan as minister of finance, to address the country's mounting economic difficulties.

The biggest area of concern in the financial sector was not the banks themselves, but the finance companies (Pakorn 1994; Yos and Pakorn 1999; Alba, Hernandez, and Klingebiel 1999; Overholt 2000).[5] On 5 February 1997, the first Thai company (Somprasong Land) defaulted on a foreign loan repayment. Late in the month, it was announced that the largest of the finance companies, Finance One, was seeking a merger with a bank to stave off collapse. By the end of February, Financial Institutions Development Fund (FIDF) assistance extended to 14 companies and totaled Bt50 billion (Nukul Commission 1998, para. 343).

In the face of widespread fears of an impending financial implosion, Finance Minister Amnuay and Central Bank Governor Rerngchai Marakanond suspended trading of financial sector shares on the stock exchange on 3 March and went on national television to announce a series of emergency measures designed to reassure nervous markets.[6] These mea-

---

5. By the end of 1996, Thailand's 91 finance companies (25 were pure finance companies, and 66 performed both finance and securities functions) accounted for nearly 25 percent of total credit and were suffering from the end of a prolonged property boom and mounting nervousness about unhedged foreign liabilities.

6. The two key elements of the policy intervention were a requirement that all banks and finance companies make much stronger provision for bad loans and an announcement that

sures did little to reassure financial markets. Underlying the market's nervousness were doubts about the health of other finance companies and banks as well as about the government's ability to follow through with its restructuring plans.

Such fears proved well founded. The original Ministry of Finance report showed that 18 finance companies and 3 banks faced difficulties, but the list was trimmed following direct intervention from the prime minister (Nukul Commission 1998, para. 368). Several senior members of Chart Pattana, the second largest party in the coalition, had controlling interests in some of the 10 targeted institutions. They succeeded in vetoing the plan and ensuring that no action was taken against the 10 companies. Moreover, the very fact that they were permitted to remain open meant that—as with the Bangkok Bank of Commerce—the central bank had to provide liquidity to keep them afloat in the face of runs by creditors and depositors.

The management of the financial market problems in March constituted a critical juncture in the development of the larger crisis in Thailand. Both Thai and foreign analysts expressed concern about the scale of the bad loan problem (e.g., *Far Eastern Economic Review*, 13 March 1997, 61-62; Overholt 2000); it was not unknown. Even the modest path they opted for—lifting capital adequacy provisions and singling out the weakest institutions for immediate attention—were effectively vetoed by other members of the ruling coalition, some with direct stakes in the institutions. Rather than risking the collapse of his new government by alienating Chart Pattana, Chavalit preferred to gamble on compromise and delaying measures.

The finance minister's inability to follow through on the modest plans he had outlined had a corrosive effect on investor confidence. Moreover, there were debilitating costs to delay. At the same time as the government was pumping money into insolvent finance companies to keep them afloat, the central bank was also spending down reserves to prop up the exchange rate and avoid any substantial increase in interest rates. This was clearly not a sustainable strategy, and in mid-May the baht suffered its heaviest assault to date.

Amnuay had encountered resistance with respect to macroeconomic policy as well. The question of if and when to adjust the exchange rate involved judgments about timing; as pressures on the rate mounted, the central bank argued that it was risky to float, and Amnuay ultimately deferred on the issue. The need to make fiscal adjustments, by contrast, engaged the cabinet. As in the past (Pasuk and Sungsidh 1994), coalition partners successfully reversed Amnuay's efforts to trim more pork from

ten of the weakest financial companies would have to raise their capital base within 60 days (*The Nation*, 4 March 1997).

the budget, and he resigned from the government on 19 June. Within two weeks—on 2 July—the baht was cut loose.

The onset of the crisis did not, of itself, guarantee effective action. Upon taking office, Amnuay's successor, Thanong Bidaya, announced the suspension of 16 finance companies (including 7 of the original 10), giving them 30 days to implement merger plans (*Bangkok Post*, 6 August 1997). At the same time, however, the prime minister announced that no further finance companies would be closed, and that the government would guarantee the closed finance companies loans and deposits. Both measures had profound implications for the FIDF, to which the remaining finance companies increasingly turned for support. Not only did Chart Pattana succeed in preventing the closure or merger of the 16 finance companies, it also managed to persuade the central bank to continue injecting liquidity into the institutions.[7]

A week later, on 5 August,[8] Thanong announced that a further 42 finance companies would be suspended. However, charges of corruption and conflict of interest surfaced with respect to the committee given the responsibility of reviewing the finance companies' rehabilitation efforts. This resulted in further delays until a new chairman, Amaret Sila-on, the respected head of the Thai Stock Exchange, was appointed to oversee the process in August (*Bangkok Post*, 26 August 1997).

With the deadline for deciding the fate of the suspended finance companies looming, lobbying intensified. By mid-October, Amaret had resigned, claiming that he was being undercut by forces within the government (*Bangkok Post*, 12 October 1997).[9]

Developments were equally unpromising in other policy areas. Within a week of announcing the IMF program on 14 October, the government reversed a decision to raise gasoline taxes. Minister of Finance Thanong resigned, stating succinctly that the country needed a "genuinely independent, credible economic team which is accepted by the public, monetary institutions both domestic and foreign and the International Monetary Fund and World Bank" (*Far Eastern Economic Review*, 30 October 1997, 60). In downgrading Thailand's credit rating on 24 October, Standard & Poor's argued explicitly that "patronage-based politics increasingly has impaired the ability of technocrats to manage ongoing financial stress, while Thailand's fragmented political landscape offers little prospect of

---

7. In late July, it was revealed that loans to the 16 finance companies equaled about 10 percent of GDP (*Bangkok Post*, 14 August 1997).

8. The IMF's $17.2 billion package was unveiled in Tokyo on 11 August.

9. Further concessions were soon made to Chart Pattana and the finance companies, including an indefinite extension of the deadline for their restructuring and the conversion of previous government loans into equity. Chart Pattana also succeeded in guaranteeing that two new restructuring agencies would not be independent of the government.

cohesive government in the near term" (*Far Eastern Economic Review*, 6 November 1997, 21). The international financial institutions had come to quite similar conclusions.

By this stage, as we will see in the next chapter in more detail, the crisis was forcing broader political realignments. On 3 November, on the eve of a special session of Parliament called to approve six executive decrees that were central to the economic reform effort, Chavalit resigned, paving the way for a new government under the Democrat Party.

Politics in Thailand exerted a powerful influence over both the onset and initial management of the crisis. Intracoalitional politics delayed action on the budget, and politicians with direct and indirect interests in regulated financial institutions prevented an effective resolution of their mounting problems. These political failings contributed to the onset of the crisis directly by weakening confidence in the Thai financial sector, and deepened it once the devaluation occurred by further delaying adjustment and generating uncertainty about the capacity of the government to act.

South Korea

South Korea[10] did not face Thailand's current account difficulties, but like Thailand it did face a number of problems associated with the end of a domestic investment boom. This boom was concentrated not in real estate but in manufacturing, and within manufacturing in heavy and chemical industries dominated by the largest *chaebol* (Haggard and Mo 2000). Rather than attention focusing initially on the insolvency of banks and finance companies, it was the weakness of several large *chaebol* that triggered concerns about bank solvency.

As in Thailand, a number of vulnerable companies lobbied aggressively for government support. As in Thailand, pressures from business were compounded by broader political factors, including in South Korea the impending presidential election scheduled for December and the fragmentation of the ruling party; in combination, these factors blocked the passage of an important set of financial reforms and contributed to a more general uncertainty about the capacity of the government to respond to the crisis.

Any account of the onset of Korea's financial crisis must begin with the political effects of the Hanbo scandal. The government made no effort to save Hanbo's management; the firm was effectively nationalized through the injection of new money (*Far Eastern Economic Review*, 20 February 1997, 16-17; 13 March 1997, 16-17; 24 April 1997, 19; *Business Korea*, February 1997, 13). But when two more of the top-30 *chaebol* folded—Sammi in March and Jinro in April—the government adopted a

---

10. A more detailed account of the events of 1997 is contained in Haggard and Mo (2000). For the World Bank's input into the structural adjustment process, see World Bank 1998c.

more concerted response to the problem. On 18 April, 35 commercial and state banks announced an "anti-bankruptcy" pact that allowed them to continue to lend to troubled borrowers.[11] The government supplemented the program by injecting liquidity into the banking system through the purchase of nonperforming assets by the Korean Asset Management Corporation.

Market response to the plan was positive, and the stock market rallied sharply. However, beginning in July, Korean financial and foreign exchange markets entered a period of marked uncertainty, and the government's management of the Kia bankruptcy was clearly a major cause.

The Kia crisis broke on 23 June, when Kim Sun-Hong, chairman of the group, appealed to the government for assistance in persuading creditors not to call maturing loans. On 15 July, the group's creditor banks placed it under the anti-bankruptcy pact (Ministry of Finance and Economy, *Economic Bulletin*, August 1997, 22-23). A highly politicized battle ensued over the future of Kia. Refusing to resign, the group's chairman quickly denounced the initial support package as inadequate and mobilized support for the company from suppliers, employees (who were substantial shareholders), and the public at large through a "Save Kia" campaign (*Korea Newsreview*, 26 July 1997, 16).

Because of the high concentration of both the financial and corporate sectors, and the extraordinary leveraging of the latter, the difficulties of three or four major groups affected the entire banking sector. In August, the government announced an additional $8 billion of support for the banking system (*Korea Newsreview*, 30 August 1997, 24-25). But it also signaled impatience with the campaign Kia was waging. The entire anti-bankruptcy pact was becoming a source of uncertainty, and the government began to send stronger signals that it wanted Kia's creditors to let the firm go bankrupt (*Korea Newsreview*, 2 August 1997, 27).

The Kia management was unwilling to submit to court receivership (*pasan*), however, under which existing management would be replaced, and exploited an important loophole in Korean bankruptcy law—court "protection" or "mediation" (*hwa ui pob*)—to avoid it.[12] One powerful weapon the government maintained in pushing the creditors toward the receivership option was the threat that the government would not guarantee the foreign obligations—$687 million—of the firm if it sought court protection (*Korea Newsreview*, 27 September 1997, 25-26). On 29 September,

---

11. Banks would continue to extend credit to any top-50 *chaebol* at risk and defer debt payments for 90 days if the company was "basically sound" and came up with a "self-rescue" package of measures including layoffs, sale of assets, and organizational consolidation.

12. Under Korean law, firms may file for court "protection" or "mediation." Under this procedure, management maintains its rights and, if three-fourths of creditors agree, debt payments can be postponed and new credits extended. Banks may have an incentive to go along with this option, because court receivership implies liquidation and certain losses.

the creditors delivered an ultimatum that no further credit would be extended. Nonetheless, it took a full month, until 22 October, before the government intervened to definitively settle the Kia issue by ousting management and effectively nationalizing it (Ministry of Economic Affairs, *Economic Bulletin*, November 1997, 25-28; *Far Eastern Economic Review*, 6 November 1997, 65).

The Korean banking system had thus been through a string of corporate bankruptcies and was already in deep distress when the shock from Hong Kong hit in the third week of October. Foreign banks refused to roll over short-term foreign credits to Korean financial institutions and pressure on the exchange rate mounted, culminating in the floating of the exchange rate on 21 November.

While the Hanbo scandal, the anti-bankruptcy pact, and conflict over Kia were taking place, the government faced an additional set of problems in strengthening financial regulation. In the wake of the Hanbo scandal, the president initiated a Financial Reform Commission. The fate of this reform effort also influenced foreign perceptions of the government's capacity to act; to understand its fate requires further explication of the government's political weaknesses in 1997.

Following the Hanbo scandal, Kim Young Sam distanced himself from the party and the nomination process.[13] Lee Hoi Chang captured the nomination on 21 July, and appeared on his way to an easy victory in December. However, his popularity plummeted when it was revealed that his two sons had avoided military service. The party began to fragment.[14] In the meantime, Kim Dae Jung's electoral chances were improving not only as a result of the crisis, but through an unlikely alliance with conservative candidate Kim Jong Pil.

In sum, the political background to policymaking before the crisis includes a severely weakened president and a divided ruling party headed by a candidate desperately trying to differentiate himself from the incumbent. Although National Assembly elections are not concurrent with the presidential elections in Korea, ruling party legislators were disinclined to take any actions that would damage the party in the run-up to the presidential elections.

In the meantime, the Financial Reform Commission had moved ahead with its institutional reform proposals. These included increasing the independence of the Bank of Korea (BOK) from the Ministry of Finance and Economy (MOFE) and stripping regulatory powers out of both the BOK and MOFE and forming an independent regulatory agency. With strong bureaucratic opposition to the reform and few politicians seeing

---

13. The Korean Constitution prohibits re-election of the president.

14. Another presidential hopeful, Rhee In Je, left the ruling party and launched his own campaign on 13 September, taking many of Kim Young Sam's supporters with him.

any gain from it, the ruling party and opposition agreed to postpone the legislation until after the elections.

The question of financial reform resurfaced in late October, in part at the insistence of the IMF. At the end of the second week of November, the package of financial reform bills was headed for passage. However, one of the contentious and unresolved issues was whether the Financial Supervisory Board (FSB), which would consolidate a number of existing regulatory agencies, would fall under the control of the prime minister or of the minister of finance and economy, where the National Assembly believed it would have more oversight powers (*Korea Herald,* 14 November 1997). In addition, the labor unions representing the Bank of Korea and the four agencies targeted for elimination were opposed to the consolidation, undertook a number of protest actions, and threatened to strike (*Korea Herald,* 15 November 1997).

In principle, the ruling party could have passed the bills over these objections. But Lee Hoi Chang's supporters were rightly concerned about the political cost of doing so. They wanted to secure opposition support for the legislation in order to defuse it as a campaign issue (*Korea Herald,* 17 November 1997). The opposition had few incentives to cooperate. If they signed on, they would be associated with potentially costly reforms that affected Kim Dae Jung's labor constituents. If they postponed their assent, any negative economic effects would be laid at the feet of the president and the ruling party. For markets already increasingly unsettled by a number of other developments, failure to pass the reform legislation was but one additional piece of bad news.

With the financial reform legislation blocked in the National Assembly, Finance Minister Kang Kyung Shik turned his attention to drafting short-term policy measures that would address the weakness of the financial sector and the turmoil on the foreign exchange markets without recourse to the IMF. The centerpiece of Kang's plan was $10 billion of support from foreign central banks, but the United States argued that Korea should work through the IMF (Cho and Pu 1998, 114-15). With economic policy in a shambles, the president decided to replace his economic team.

The effects of this sequence of events on the markets are unmistakable. The won plunged to the maximum limit of 2.25 percent for three consecutive days beginning on the 17th, the day after the National Assembly postponed the financial reform legislation. On the 19th, it only took 10 minutes for the won to reach its limit, triggering the closure of the foreign exchange market (*Korean Herald,* 20 November 1997). On the 21st, the won was cut free.

Much analysis of the Korean crisis has focused on the response of the markets to the first IMF program in early December, and whether its failure was due to the design of the program (as critics of the Fund argue), to the revelation that reserves were completely exhausted (as Fund officials hold), or to politically generated uncertainty (see Graham 1998 for a review). Particular attention has been given to remarks by Kim Dae Jung that were interpreted to suggest that he would renegotiate the terms of the IMF program. In the two days following these remarks, the won fell nearly 10 percent against the dollar. The decline was only stopped—and then only briefly—when the three main candidates signed a joint pledge to honor the IMF agreement. Despite this political commitment, the program had to be supplemented by a new agreement and new resources on Christmas Eve (*Far Eastern Economic Review*, 25 December 1997 and 1 January 1998).

However, these events were only the last in a long series that had affected investor confidence in the second half of the year. Contrary to the often-repeated assertion that no one foresaw the crisis, prominent market analysts were expressing serious doubts about Korea and its banking system before the Thai crisis broke in July. First, there was substantial uncertainty about how the government would respond to the failure of major firms, which invited the test posed by Kia. These uncertainties were compounded by a larger political milieu, which made it difficult for the government to act. By November, it is doubtful that passage of the reform legislation would have been able to reverse Korea's fortunes. However, the failure reflected a more fundamental stalemate in Korean politics of which investors and analysts were perfectly aware. Only with the election of Kim Dae Jung did expectations stabilize and the government gain the ability to initiate much-needed reforms.

Malaysia

From the end of the mid-1980s recession in 1986 through the first half of 1997, the Malaysian economy accumulated an enviable record of economic growth with budget surpluses and consistently low inflation. In retrospect, there were several signs of vulnerability, but it is important to stress that none of them appeared particularly severe (Jomo 1998a; Athukorala 1998). On the external front, the ringgit did show signs of real appreciation that were reflected in a large current account deficit. Between 1994 and 1997, external debt tripled—with a particularly rapid increase in short-term foreign borrowings. However, overall debt remained modest when compared with GNP (45.6 percent), its maturity structure did not appear particularly troubling (76.1 percent in medium- and long-term debt), and debt service ratios were extremely modest (5.7 percent of exports) (*Bank Negara Annual Report 1997*, 51).

A second concern was that Malaysia was experiencing symptoms of a bubble. As we have seen, the rapid expansion of credit in late 1996 and early 1997 was increasingly channeled into the financing of purchases of property and shares, and in March 1997 the central bank moved to curb speculative excesses by placing ceilings on bank lending to property and shares. But the banking system seemed to many observers less vulnerable to crisis than in South Korea and Thailand because of the strengthening of prudential regulation in the mid-1980s (Chua 1998, but see also Jomo 1998a, 183). Before the Thai crisis, analysts were speaking approvingly of a "soft-landing," as the economy began to gradually slow in comparison with the torrid pace of 1995 and 1996.

Following the attacks on the Thai baht in May, the central bank briefly defended the ringgit but quickly gave up the effort. For the remainder of the year, the ringgit continued a steady, and largely uninterrupted, fall. Given the relatively favorable starting point, why did Malaysia fare so poorly?

Although regional contagion clearly bears substantial responsibility for Malaysia's troubles, the country's problems were compounded by a series of political factors that created substantial uncertainty about government intentions. These events began with Mahathir's "war on the speculators" in the second half of 1997, a series of self-fulfilling prophecies that soured foreign investors on the country. Mahathir's speech of 20 September 1997 to the joint annual meetings of the IMF and World Bank in Hong Kong, in which he attacked "speculators" and called for a ban on "unnecessary, unproductive, and immoral" currency trading, received wide publicity (Mahathir 1998). However, this speech was not an isolated event: from July until December, the prime minister engaged in a running battle with the markets.[15] After each speech, the foreign exchange and stock markets responded negatively.

Fiscal policy also became a source of uncertainty. Following a meeting of the UMNO's supreme council on 4 September, Mahathir deferred several large infrastructure projects, and the budget unveiled on 17 October by then-Deputy Prime Minister Anwar Ibrahim combined slowed spending growth with a small corporate tax cut. But in November, Anwar announced that the government would assume responsibility of the Bakun dam from the project's main developer, the Ekran group, the first major sign that the government would step in to assist politically connected groups. In early December, the prime minister declared that a

---

15. His first attack on the foreign exchange markets came on 28 July, and already hinted at the possibility that the government might impose controls. On 3 August the central bank limited ringgit sales for noncommercial purposes, and on 27 August the Kuala Lumpur Stock Exchange (KLSE) moved to stop short-selling of 100 blue chip stocks (*Far Eastern Economic Review*, 18 September 1997, 65). Mahathir's comments continued even after the hostile response of the markets to the Hong Kong speech. In Chile on 30 September, Mahathir argued for a new non-US dollar peg because the dollar was "unstable" and later spoke against raising interest rates to defend the ringgit (*Financial Times*, 2 October 1997; *Far Eastern Economic Review*, 9 October 1997; *Straits Times*, 28 October 1997).

RM$10 billion road, rail, and oil-pipeline project linking northeastern Malaysia and Thailand would, in fact, go forward (Economist Intelligence Unit, *Quarterly Economic Report*, 1st quarter 1998, 15-19).

In early December, Malaysian economic policy took a completely new turn. Closely identified with Anwar, this new direction amounted to "an IMF package without the IMF." The government cut spending dramatically, delayed "non-strategic" construction projects, deferred capital imports of several major state-owned enterprises, and canceled controversial overseas investments (*Bank Negara Annual Report 1997*, 111-12). Anwar also signaled to the banking community that firms facing fundamental difficulties should not be kept afloat artificially and that prudential regulation would be tightened. Most dramatic among these measures was a plan to consolidate the country's vulnerable finance companies as a prelude to restructuring the entire banking sector (*Bank Negara Annual Report 1997*, 113).

Two further elements of the Anwar package are noteworthy because they underscore emerging policy differences within the government that would widen over time. First, Anwar stated that Malaysia remained committed to a flexible exchange rate and that further controls on capital flows would not be forthcoming. Second, the program coincided with the end of the effort by the central bank to restrain interest rates. Anwar did not control monetary policy, but he defended the central bank and warned that interest rates would rise, as they did beginning in December 1997.

The 5 December program seemed to mark the ascent of a relatively orthodox policy stance. However, just before its announcement—on 20 November—Mahathir created a contending center of economic policymaking authority in the National Economic Action Council (NEAC). The NEAC was chaired by Daim Zainuddin, a former finance minister who was an architect of the high-growth strategy of the late-1980s and early 1990s and highly influential within the party. Daim's position as treasurer of the UMNO meant that he was closely connected both to the UMNO's business interests and to the new class of entrepreneurs who had benefited from privatization and other government policies in the 1990s.

The NEAC generated substantial uncertainty over economic policymaking authority. Anwar was made deputy chairman of the council, but this undermined his authority as finance minister, given that the NEAC was vested with the authority to develop plans to overcome the crisis. On most controversial issues, the final NEAC report was at odds with the Anwar approach (National Economic Action Council 1998). The council argued that a fiscal stimulus (to which Anwar would be converted) and lower interest rates (to which he was not) were necessary for recovery, thus calling into question the already tenuous independence of the central bank. Throughout April and May, a more or less open conflict raged on interest rate policy between Mahathir and Daim, on the one hand, and Anwar and Central Bank Governor Ahmad Don, on the other. The NEAC also deemed assistance for firms hurt by the crisis as wholly appropriate, undercutting Anwar's focus on the risks of moral hazard and corruption.

With the elevation of Daim to cabinet status on 24 June, the debate between the two sides was effectively resolved in Daim's favor. Monetary policy eased from July to deal with the ballooning crisis in the financial sector, and Anwar launched a number of important new institutions for recapitalizing the banks (Danamodal), acquiring, rehabilitating, and disposing of assets (Danaharta) and restructuring corporate debt (chapter 4). Beginning in June, the government accelerated its efforts to raise foreign funds to finance these efforts, seeking support from Japan, Taiwan, Singapore, and the World Bank. However, the plan to float US$2 billion of bonds for Danaharta was shelved when international agencies cut Malaysia's credit ratings. Standard & Poor's claimed nonperforming loans had reached 30 percent of total loans—roughly double government estimates—and was concerned with the lack of transparency in the restructuring process. Moody's also expressed concern over the growing conflict between Mahathir and Anwar (*Far Eastern Economic Review*, 13 August 1998, 10-13).

On 27 August, the central bank issued its second quarter report on the performance of the economy, and the news was uniformly bad: During the second quarter, GDP shrank by 6.8 percent. On 1 September, Mahathir imposed capital controls and fixed the exchange rate (see appendix 2.1). On 2 September, Mahathir removed Anwar from office (*Far Eastern Economic Review*, 17 September 1998, 10-14).

Why did the Malaysian government pursue such a zig-zagging policy course that appeared to undermine confidence and ended with the imposition of capital controls? The answer certainly does not appear to lie in the electoral cycle or a strong opposition. The ruling Barisan Nasional (National Front) government took over 65 percent of the popular vote and 84.3 percent of seats in the 1995 general elections, and new ones were not scheduled until 2000. Moreover, a number of well-known restrictive features of the Malaysian political system, including an erosion of judicial autonomy and tight government control over the formation of independent political and interest groups, allowed it to manage any dissent that might arise in the wake of the crisis (for overviews, see Case 1996, Crouch 1996, and Milne and Mauzy 1999).

Rather, the pattern of policy emanates from two closely related political factors. The first was the government's particularly strong commitment to the Malay private sector. Mahathir had staked his political status on a new approach to inter-ethnic redistribution that centered on the development of *bumiputra* firms through privatization. Unfortunately, these firms, as well as non-*bumiputra* firms with close political connections with the government, were heavily concentrated in trading and services, finance, property, and construction—in sum, in the nontraded sectors most vulnerable to the shocks that occurred in 1997-98. The recommendations of the NEAC and the imposition of capital controls were designed not simply to provide an overall stimulus but to protect these favored companies.

But issues of economic policy also became linked to conflicts within the party over leadership and succession. To understand how requires a closer look at UMNO politics. The UMNO had long exercised dominance within the party system. Internally, the party leadership exerted its power over the party machinery through its control of nominations, appointments, and campaign financing, as well as economic rents. However, the UMNO also had democratic features that required the leadership to court support at the party's base, particularly when leadership challenges and succession struggles emerged.[16]

The immediate background to the political crisis of September 1998 can be traced to the triennial party elections in March for local policy leadership positions.[17] Despite some discontent, Mahathir prevailed; 105 division chiefs were returned without challenge, and only 12 incumbents were voted out.

This vote should have signaled the power that Mahathir continued to hold over the party, but the fall of Suharto in May and the continuing problems in the economy emboldened Anwar and his supporters to issue a more direct challenge to the prime minister in anticipation of the UMNO General Assembly. In a series of speeches, Anwar raised the issue of "corruption, cronyism, and nepotism" in an increasingly pointed fashion, including before foreign audiences (Economist Intelligence Unit, *Country Economic Report: Malaysia and Brunei*, 3rd quarter 1998, 13). While agreeing with Mahathir that the sources of the crisis were primarily external, Anwar also underscored the importance of domestic policy change—increasing transparency, improving corporate governance, and battling corruption.

---

16. Intra-party political conflicts under Mahathir were not new, and had from the beginning of his administration focused on dissent over executive powers and corruption. A·split between Mahathir and Deputy Prime Minister Musa Hitam was resolved by the latter's resignation in 1986 (Gill 1998a, 1998b; Crouch 1996, chap. 7 and p. 116), but was followed immediately by a challenge from Hamzah Razaleigh for the presidency of the party in 1987. In a preview of Anwar's challenge, Razaleigh charged that Mahathir had centralized decision-making power and used those powers to distribute government contracts and business opportunities to a narrow range of favored cronies.

17. The party is organized into roughly 4,500 branches that elect leaders to represent them at the divisional level; divisions correspond with parliamentary districts. These divisions select the delegates to the UMNO General Assembly, which in turn chooses the president and deputy president of the party (who, given the Barisan Nasional's electoral dominance, have historically been the prime minister and deputy prime minister, respectively). Positions as division chief are also coveted as a stepping stone to electoral office. The races naturally engage local rivalries, but also provide an opportunity for expression of discontent within the party. In 1998, this discontent centered in part on the role of Islam in society but also on the deteriorating state of the economy and corruption (*Far Eastern Economic Review*, 9 October 1997).

Anwar emphasized issues of poverty alleviation and social justice, citing the Koran (LIX 7), "in order that (they) may not (merely) make a circuit between the wealthy" (*New Straits Times,* 19 June 1998).

The General Assembly belonged to Mahathir. He undertook an extensive defense of his pro-*bumiputra* policies. Appealing to his expanded business constituency, Mahathir argued that allegations of cronyism and nepotism were being used by foreigners to ensure the failure of the New Economic Policy (*New Straits Times,* 18 June 1998). He also seized the corruption issue from his opponents by publishing lists of the companies and individuals who had been beneficiaries of a number of important government policies.[18] The lists encompassed large swaths of the Malay and Chinese private sectors, and included a number of Anwar supporters and even his father.[19]

The outcome of these political battles had immediate policy consequences. Anwar's authority on economic policy was formally undercut by the elevation of Daim Zainuddin to the cabinet immediately following the UMNO General Assembly. The release of the new stimulus package was timed to coincide with the UMNO General Assembly, and the government pressed the central bank to ease monetary policy in early July. In late August, the central bank governor, Ahmad Mohamed Don, resigned under pressure, setting the stage for the concentration of all economic policymaking authority around Mahathir. Following Anwar's exit, Mahathir announced that he would take over the Finance Ministry himself, and he appointed close associates to the central bank.

In the first year after the crisis broke, Prime Minister Mahathir succeeded in drawing attention to weaknesses in the international financial architecture and the benefits of capital controls. However, his interpretation of events conveniently ignores the ways in which he himself contributed to Malaysia's difficulties. The "war against the speculators," uncertainty about both the general direction of policy and the locus of decision-making authority, and close government links to favored firms all compounded the country's economic difficulties.

---

18. These included a list of public works and infrastructure projects that had been let to private companies; individuals who had been allocated company shares under the Special Bumiputra Share Allocation between 1993 and 1997; and recipients of public transport licenses, haulage permits, and government contracts (*New Straits Times,* 21 and 22 June 1998).

19. The assembly also marked the onset of the personal attack on Anwar. A short book by a journalist, Khalid Jafri, entitled *Fifty Reasons Why Anwar Cannot Be Prime Minister,* was distributed widely to assembly delegates, and included a range of charges from sexual impropriety to corruption. Although Khalid was later charged at the insistence of Anwar's supporters, his detractors called for investigation of the charges raised in the book. Given the harshness of Malaysian libel laws and subsequent testimony at Anwar's trial, it is difficult to avoid the conclusion that the UMNO leadership acquiesced to the personal attack on Anwar.

Indonesia

Of all the countries swept up in the Asian financial crisis, Indonesia's case is the most dramatic, particularly given the fact that key macroeconomic indicators provided few early warnings of impending collapse (Soesastro and Basri 1998; Hill 1998; Radelet and Sachs 1998a, 1998b). The current account deficit was substantial, with evidence of overvaluation, but the deficit was less than half of Thailand's and with no telltale signs of capital flight or speculation against the currency before the fall of the baht. Nonetheless, the Indonesian rupiah suffered by far the steepest depreciation of all the crisis currencies, and in the real economy the largest fall in output.

Indonesia did not show the signs of an asset bubble or overinvestment visible in South Korea or Thailand. Nor is there a case to be made that the external crisis originated in the financial sector, as was at least in part the case in Thailand and Korea. Indonesia's banking sector had a number of serious weaknesses, but through the third quarter of 1997 these issues were not seen as pivotal for overall investor confidence. And yet by the fourth quarter of 1997 the situation had changed dramatically, and the Indonesian banking system was on the verge of complete collapse.

Indonesia's distress is made even more puzzling if we consider that Suharto's initial approach to the crisis appeared both more decisive and coherent than the Chavalit or Kim governments' and more cooperative than the bellicose policy pronouncements of Prime Minister Mahathir (MacIntyre 1999a). In contrast to Thailand's costly and futile effort to defend the baht, Indonesia's response to regional contagion was to quickly widen the band within which the rupiah traded, and when this proved inadequate, to initiate a float. When the rupiah continued to fall, the central bank adopted an extremely tight monetary stance—well before going to the IMF—in a bid to support the currency. This policy had severe consequences for the already-fragile banking sector.

Suharto's independence day speech in mid-August provided a sober assessment of the country's problems, and was followed by the creation of a special crisis management team headed by the widely respected technocrat Widjoyo Nitisastro. A wide-ranging set of policy measures followed in September (Soesastro and Basri 1998, 9-10).[20] In early October, two months after floating the rupiah, the government turned to the IMF. Although the negotiations were not without conflict, Indonesia was able to conclude an agreement much more rapidly than the Thai government.

The broad thrust of IMF advice with respect to macroeconomic policy was standard. But the Indonesian government also agreed to a wide

---

20. These included a tightened fiscal stance through the reconsideration of a number of costly infrastructure projects, the announced intention to address emerging problems in the financial sector, and tariff cuts.

variety of banking and structural adjustment measures, a number of which cut directly against crony and family interests. On 1 November, the government closed 16 small banks, several controlled by relatives or cronies.[21] On 3 November, major tariff cuts were announced in industries affecting crony firms. The government opened a number of previously closed sectors to foreign investors and lifted some restrictions on foreign participation in the stock market. The administration also promised a review of the strategic industries falling under the portfolio of technology minister B.J. Habibie and agreed to abide by the WTO's dispute settlement procedure with respect to its controversial national car project, controlled by one of Suharto's sons.

There is now a consensus that some elements of the early reform package, including the bank closings, suffered in their implementation if not their basic design. Yet whatever the wisdom of the policy course Indonesia charted in the early months of the crisis (see, inter alia, Radelet 1998; Radelet and Sachs 1998a; McLeod 1998a, 1998b; McLeod and Garnaut 1998; Hill 1999; Lane et al. 1999; World Bank 1998b, 1999b), it is impossible to explain the depth of Indonesia's economic difficulties without examining the political context. Uncertainty initially centered on the question of whether the government was in fact willing to confront crony privilege, but a range of more fundamental political problems subsequently arose, including uncertainty about Suharto's health, an (indirect) election, succession problems, and mounting political and social protest.

The difficulties with the international financial institutions began almost immediately after the Fund program was signed, as Suharto took rearguard actions to protect favored individuals. The first troubling signal came on 1 November, when amidst the flurry of IMF-related initiatives Suharto quietly signed a decree giving the green light to fifteen big-ticket investment projects that he had postponed in September in the name of fiscal restraint. Not only were a number of these projects of dubious economic rationality, but all of them involved relatives or close cronies (Soesastro and Basri 1998, 20).

The management of the bank closing and provision of liquidity support also called into doubt the government's commitment to reining in crony privileges. In a curious public relations event, the decision to close the 16 banks was challenged at a press conference by Suharto's second son, Bambang Trihatmodjo, and his half-brother, Probosutedjo. The two even

---

21. Given that these structural and banking sector reforms were later criticized heavily, it is important to underline that they conformed quite closely to the preferences of senior economic technocrats within the government. They both agreed with the Fund's overall diagnosis and saw in the crisis an opportunity to press forward with a number of reforms that they had sought for some time. More important, the policy measures sent an important *political* signal that Suharto was prepared to impose costs, even on crony and family businesses.

went so far as to file lawsuits against the minister of finance, Mar'ie Mohammed, and the governor of the central bank, Sudrajat Djiwandono. Given that these were close family members, their actions naturally raised questions about Suharto's intentions. The decision to close the banks was ultimately confirmed, but Bambang was able to circumvent the closing of his Bank Andromeda by acquiring the license of another bank, Bank Alfa, and shifting the assets of the closed bank to it. Probosutedjo persisted in his efforts to save Bank Jakarta, claiming that it was initially closed because of failure to pay adequate bribes to central bank officials (Economist Intelligence Unit, *Quarterly Report: Indonesia*, 1st Quarter 1998, 19, 27).

The integrity of the Bank of Indonesia was challenged further by the management of the central bank's special liquidity credit facility designed to support ailing banks. Not only did the facility undermine monetary policy, but crony banks consumed the bulk of the emergency liquidity credit. The Salim group's Bank Central Asia (BCA) soaked up Rp35 trillion (roughly US$7 billion in late 1997 prices) of support, equivalent to more than 500 percent of its capital (*Jakarta Post*, 1 October 1998). Crony banks not only borrowed disproportionately but also exchanged rupiah for dollars and siphoned them out of the country. The central bank was in effect financing speculative attacks against itself (Cole and Slade 1998, 64).

If the events of November and early December called the government's commitment to reform into question, the next 5 months raised deeper political problems. The question of succession, and the dependence of the entire economy on the person of Suharto, became painfully apparent in early December when rumors began circulating regarding the 76-year-old president's health. His office canceled a trip to Kuala Lumpur to attend an informal Association of Southeast Asian Nations (ASEAN) meeting of member heads of state scheduled for 14 December, purportedly because of fatigue, but in fact because of a stroke. Throughout December, the rupiah and stock market were both highly volatile in response to rumors about Suharto's health (Fisman 2000).

However, January proved the pivotal month. A series of events pushed Indonesia onto a trajectory that diverged sharply from those of the other crisis countries.[22] The year opened badly for all Asian currencies, but the president's presentation of the draft budget on 6 January again raised fundamental issues of credibility. In the week before the budget speech, pressure on the government was intense, between those seeing it as a key test of the government's commitment and a chorus of voices from the private sector pressing for a relaxation of fiscal policy (*Jakarta Post*, 4 January 1998). Social pressures were also beginning to mount.

The handling of the budget remains controversial, and some have criticized the IMF and the World Bank for undercutting the government by

---

22. Fisman (2000) shows that rumors concerning Suharto's health had particularly significant effects on the share prices of politically connected firms.

suggesting their unhappiness both with the budget and the implementation of the wider reform program (*Washington Post*, 8 January 1998). However, this criticism rests on the dubious assumption that the international financial institutions could have controlled the market reaction to the budget. The budget was not expansionary, but it rested on a number of unrealistic assumptions, particularly with respect to oil prices and the exchange rate, and projected growth and inflation rates that were wildly optimistic. The reaction was not limited to the foreign media and exchange markets. Ordinary citizens also lost confidence in the currency and began panic buying of basic foodstuffs and commodities.

The framework of the first IMF program clearly required reconsideration; negotiations for a new program began on 11 January. The IMF had already come to the conclusion that fiscal policy would need to be revised to accommodate the crisis. However, at the same time, the international financial institutions and creditor governments were increasingly concerned about Suharto's commitment, and believed that the only way it could be demonstrated was through a program that was highly comprehensive in its scope.

The second IMF program was signed by the president himself (the previous program had been signed by the central bank governor and minister of finance) and was widely circulated (the first program was held secret). The program included a 50-Point Memorandum of Economic and Financial Policies that covered virtually the entire structural adjustment agenda of the World Bank, including such controversial issues as an end of government support to the national car project and a gradual phasing out of subsidies on a number of basic foodstuffs. As if the public signing of the letter of intent was not enough—resulting in the now-infamous photograph of Camdessus appearing to stand over the president with arms folded—Suharto was also subject to intense foreign pressure through other channels. In January and February, Suharto received a succession of high-level delegations and telephone calls from a number of G8 leaders urging him to implement the program.

The ease with which the second program was negotiated should have itself given the international financial institutions pause. Even more than the first one, the program cut deeply into the patronage networks Suharto had built up; the government agreed to essentially all of the IMF's proposals. A number of critics of the program, including some Indonesian technocrats, felt that the international financial institutions had overplayed their hand and that the Fund should have concentrated more narrowly on the measures required to restore external balance. But these criticisms assume that some different policy package would have had a markedly different effect, when in fact the problem Indonesia faced was increasingly political as much as economic.

The first problem—too often discounted in authoritarian systems—was electoral. Although the outcome of the indirect presidential election in the People's Consultative Assembly in early March was never in doubt, the meeting became a focal point for diverse opposition forces. It was crucial for Suharto that this opposition and any divisions within the party be tightly controlled, and that he receive a mandate not only for himself but for his vice presidential running mate. The choice of Habibie, with his long history as an opponent of the technocrats and advocate of industrial policy, naturally created consternation among foreign investors; the rupiah sank to its lowest point to date the day after his candidacy was announced. But the choice also raised the prospect of a contested succession were Suharto's health to fail.

With opposition to the IMF mounting—from the private sector, academics, and increasingly vocal opposition politicians—it became important for Suharto to avoid any appearance that he was a tool of foreign interests. In speeches before the People's Consultative Assembly (MPR), he suggested that the Fund program was not working, that some of the measures might be unconstitutional, and that consideration should be given to instituting a currency board. Although the IMF was not opposed to currency boards in principle, the conditions for putting one in place in Indonesia were clearly absent. Fund officials feared that preoccupation with the idea would simply divert the president's attention from the program, which was already witnessing a number of areas of slippage (Johnson 1998, 28-29). On 6 March, the IMF suspended disbursement of the second $3 billion tranche and on 10 March, the day of Suharto's formal election, the Asian Development Bank and World Bank followed suit.

An important side effect of the political turn of events in February and March was a quite visible diminution of technocratic influence and independence, and an ever greater concentration of decision-making authority in the president. Central Bank Governor Soedrajat had been fired in mid-February, and in early March the head of the new bank restructuring agency was replaced, raising questions about its independence. However, the new cabinet announced on 14 March was a particular shock, including family members (daughter Tutut, as minister of social affairs, was seen as particularly influential; Schwarz 1999, 351) and cronies (Bob Hasan as minister of trade and industry, and Fuad Bawazier at the Ministry of Finance). Ginanjar Kartasasmisa was made the coordinating minister of the economy and subsequently developed a good relationship with the international financial institutions (IFIs) and creditors, but his reputation at the time was as an economic nationalist.

The importance of the election to the conduct of policy was revealed in its aftermath. Suharto quickly initiated efforts to mend fences with the IFIs, in part by dropping the currency board idea. The new negotiations began in mid-March and, unlike the finalization of the second letter of intent, involved more extended working group discussions between officials of the IFIs, Germany, the United States, Japan, and the Indonesian government.[23] The third IMF program included greater attention to the problems of banking and corporate restructuring and privatization, as well as greater emphasis on institutional questions, such as strengthening the capacity of the central bank, developing new bankruptcy laws and courts, and augmenting the mechanisms for monitoring the program (Johnson 1998, 30-34).

As before, the program faced slippage on several fronts, and as before many had to do with resistance from cronies and family (Johnson 1998, 33). But the government also began to face an increase in protest, not only against rising prices and shortages but also against Suharto's rule itself (Forrester and May 1999). The combination of increasingly organized opposition and widespread social violence gradually shifted the attention of government from the conduct of economic policy to political survival.

A first wave of social violence had come in January and February when panic over food prices and supplies was taken out on Chinese shopkeepers in a number of smaller towns in Northern Java and elsewhere. These actions were spontaneous, unorganized, and did not have an explicit political objective. Beginning in February, however, a student movement began to gain momentum, and by the time of the MPR meeting in March, a handful of prominent opposition politicians, including most notably Amien Rais, openly argued that the economic crisis could not be resolved without political change.

One important policy component of the third IMF program concerned subsidies. On 1 April, prices of sugar, wheat flour, corn, soybeans, and fish meal were increased, with the intention of lifting them altogether by 1 October. Subsidized prices for rice and soybeans, which weighed heavily in the consumption basket of the poorest, were also set to increase on that date. The management of fuel and electricity prices was left less precise; both were to increase gradually while allowing some differentials for rural and poor households. Yet quite inexplicably, the government announced a very steep increase in fuel and gas prices on 4 May. Although the price increases were partly reversed (with the IMF's blessing), they spurred spontaneous social violence in several parts of the country and led student protests to spill off the campuses to which they had previously been confined. The killing of four students outside Triskati University in Jakarta on 12 May triggered a wave of uncontrolled rioting. In addition to its social toll—over 1,000 dead—the events of 13-14 May led to another round of bank runs and a sharp fall in the rupiah. Indonesia under Suharto had become ungovernable.

---

23. Those discussions were structured around five sets of issues: monetary policy (in particular, developing some simple, credible rules for its conduct), banking reform, the budget, structural reform, and external debt restructuring. The inclusion of the last issue, which had previously been avoided by both the IFIs and the government on moral hazard grounds, was an important innovation of the new program.

Conclusion

Governments' policy choices cannot be held altogether blameless in explaining the depth of the crisis. But the critique of policy, and by extension of the IMF, typically makes one or more important mistakes: It assumes that the adjustment programs were in fact implemented; it attributes adverse economic developments to policy, when markets were responding directly to political developments; and it bases its critique on a counterfactual world in which the government enjoys the capacity to smoothly implement some alternative (presumably superior) program. In short, it assumes not only an alternative program, but an alternative government. Each of these assumptions are quite obviously problematic; collectively, they serve to underestimate the independent role that political factors play in the onset and initial aftermath of currency and financial crises.

A comparison of these four countries also allows us to isolate some differences in the initial response to the crisis. First, it is quite clear that Indonesia fared worse than other countries in the region. Much less attention has been given to the fact that Malaysia's economic decline was much worse than might have been predicted given initial conditions, which included a less fragile banking system and a more favorable external position than either South Korea or Thailand.

In both Malaysia and Indonesia, autocratic leaders exploited their discretion to isolate technocratic advisors and pursue policies that contributed to market uncertainty. In both countries, but particularly in Indonesia, favoritism and responsiveness to cronies undermined the credibility of policy. Over time, these problems were compounded by issues of political succession. Malaysia's more institutionalized political and party system made these problems manageable but in Indonesia they were debilitating. Protest over deteriorating economic conditions was gradually compounded by opposition to the regime itself.

Democracies also had difficulties in undertaking timely adjustments. In South Korea, these difficulties were primarily associated with the electoral cycle, but also with the apparent influence wielded by ailing *chaebol*. In Thailand, the problems appeared more deep-seated, as the party system generated yet another weak and unstable government that appeared captured by business interests. As will be seen in chapter 3, the Thai public also drew these connections between institutional arrangements and the crisis and supported passage of a wide-ranging constitutional revision as a result.

But as we will see in the next chapter, the democracies had the important advantage of broad social support and procedures that specified how failing incumbents could be replaced by governments with alternative programs. Despite its authoritarian features, the Malaysian political system also provided mechanisms through which the prime minister could organize party and electoral support. In Indonesia, by contrast, the crisis was deepened by fundamental political uncertainty that was only partly resolved by the transition to a new government. It is to these new governments, and the link between the crisis and political change, that we now turn.

Appendix 2.1
The Political Economy of Malaysia's Capital Controls

with Linda Low

The imposition of capital controls by Malaysia ignited a controversy over the merits of capital account liberalization (Krugman 1998c, 1998d; Bhagwati 1998a, 1998b; Wade and Veneroso 1998). As of mid 2000, the evidence on the economic effects of the Malaysian controls remained inconclusive. On the one hand, the controls gave the government some latitude with respect to macroeconomic and particularly interest rate policy. The country's export sector enjoyed advantages from the fixing of the ringgit as other currencies in the region began to appreciate in 1999. The stock market also responded positively.

On the other hand, Malaysia's recovery has been no more rapid than those of other countries in the region, and perhaps slower. The government appears to have paid a price for its ability to attract foreign investment, and over the course of 1999 it gradually backed away from the controls. Whatever the merits of selective controls as a means of limiting the destabilizing effects of short-term capital inflows, the Malaysian case does not provide convincing evidence that controls made a substantial difference as a tool for crisis management.

The controls also had a neglected political and foreign policy dimension. The controls followed a long-standing pattern of Prime Minister Mahathir using a nationalist foreign policy to consolidate political bases of support. The controls proved particularly costly for Singapore-based investors who had purchased Malaysian stocks in the offshore market, and generated a substantial controversy between Singapore and Malaysia on the issue. The ability to pursue the control option and avoid recourse to the IMF also rested on Malaysia's ability to secure alternative sources of international finance through an intense diplomatic effort. These dimensions of the controls raise interesting questions about their replicability.

The Control Package

The most dramatic elements of the Malaysian controls were the fixing of the exchange rate at RM3.80 to the US dollar[24] and the effort to end offshore trading of the ringgit. In 1994, Malaysia experimented with administrative regulations to control short-term capital flows. But the very effectiveness of the controls and additional restrictions imposed in August 1997 helped

---

Linda Low is associate professor in the Department of Business Policy, National University of Singapore.

24. More precisely, the rate was set in a trading band from RM3.77 to RM3.83.

spur the growth of the offshore ringgit market. The gross size of the offshore market, located primarily in Singapore, was between RM25 and RM32 billion (as much as $10 billion, depending on the exchange rate used), although these numbers exaggerate its size once short and long positions are netted out (*Straits Times*, 4 September and 21 October 1998; *Financial Times*, 7 October 1998).

The offshore ringgit market was not subject to direct controls or "window guidance" from the Bank Negara Malaysia (BNM). Rates on ringgit instruments could diverge substantially from those in the onshore market, creating both opportunities for speculation and difficulties for the conduct of Malaysian monetary policy just as some greater stimulus was needed. In May 1998, for example, hedge funds closed out substantial short positions in ringgit in Singapore, with the effect that 1-month offshore ringgit deposits were yielding up to 40 percent—in comparison with only 11 percent onshore (Economist Intelligence Unit, *Country Economic Report: Malaysia and Brunei*, 3rd quarter 1998, 20).

Following the imposition of controls, any ringgit outside the country after 30 September 1998 was no longer legal tender. The most immediate effect was to force firms and individuals holding ringgit to repatriate them.

Complementing the capital controls, the central bank injected liquidity into the financial system and relaxed prudential controls in the banking sector. The central bank urged commercial banks to meet certain lending targets (*Financial Times*, 14-15 November 1998) and limited the spreads that they could charge (*Financial Times*, 7 October 1998). A revision in the rules governing provisioning changed the definition of nonperforming loans from 3 to 6 months, reversing a reform that had been instituted in 1997 (*New Straits Times*, 2 September 1998). Prime Minister Mahathir explicitly argued that the controls would permit banks to show greater forbearance toward ailing corporates (*New Straits Times*, 2 September 1998).

Economic Effects and the Course of the Controls

Table A2.1 provides some evidence on the effects of the controls on interest rates and the stock market. Interest rates fell swiftly following the imposition of controls, and lending resumed, confirming the core macroeconomic objective of the controls. The controls also had a dramatic short-term effect on the stock market. The September package was announced as the Kuala Lumpur Composite Index (KLCI) was hitting new lows, suggesting that a strengthening of stock prices might have been at least one motive for the move. The stock market rose an astonishing 38 percent in the 3 days following the announcement of controls, although this might have resulted from strategic buying by government-controlled funds as well as from the return of offshore money. Since the controls, the KLCI index has steadily gained ground.

Table A2.1 Interest rates, exchange rates, and stock market index
(January 1997-March 2000)

	1-week interbank[a]	1-month interbank	3-month interbank	Exchange rate	KLCI
1997					
January	7.21	7.30	7.33	2.492	1,227.99
February	7.33	7.27	7.32	2.486	1,254.90
March	6.96	7.32	7.35	2.477	1,234.61
April	7.03	7.34	7.36	2.502	1,121.10
May	8.45	7.79	7.77	2.506	1,083.16
June	7.71	7.93	7.92	2.516	1,094.91
July	9.43	9.07	8.31	2.575	1,035.88
August	6.85	7.64	7.73	2.749	904.27
September	6.59	7.56	7.66	3.017	809.88
October	7.65	8.39	8.47	3.288	766.20
November	7.93	8.97	9.18	3.378	637.99
December	10.89	8.98	9.15	3.783	577.66
1998					
January	13.00	9.82	10.03	4.369	542.12
February	11.43	11.05	11.11	3.812	714.27
March	10.75	11.05	11.21	3.736	716.56
April	10.53	11.05	11.02	3.725	648.66
May	9.86	11.02	11.02	3.797	570.72
June	10.29	10.95	11.14	3.993	476.65
July	9.56	11.00	11.05	4.150	431.90
August	9.17	10.97	10.06	4.194	340.47
September	6.91	10.02	8.17	3.803	370.89
October	6.19	7.67	7.36	3.798	394.07
November	6.16	6.96	7.01	3.797	465.35
December	5.82	6.62	6.62	3.796	540.78
1999					
January	5.53	6.33	6.48	3.799	595.17
February	5.28	6.22	6.36	3.799	558.76
March	5.44	6.03	6.37	3.799	514.20
April	4.00	4.30	4.62	3.799	601.97
May	3.18	3.15	3.50	3.799	739.31
June	3.05	3.06	3.36	3.799	779.55
July	3.05	3.03	3.33	3.800	826.40
August	3.00	2.98	3.23	3.799	741.15
September	*	2.86	3.14	3.800	721.97
October	*	2.76	3.12	3.800	730.03
November	*	2.80	3.13	3.799	729.77
December	*	2.85	3.14	3.799	765.58
2000					
January	*	2.82	3.14	3.800	906.43
February	*	2.77	3.10	3.800	993.16
March	*	2.76	3.09	3.800	941.92

KLCI = Kuala Lumpur Composite Index

a. Not quoted with effect from September 1999.

Source: Reuters.

Table A2.2 Foreign investment in Malaysia: MIDA approvals, foreign direct investment, and net portfolio investment (RM million)

	MIDA approvals	FDI[a]	Net portfolio investment
1997			
July	n.a.	983	−3,932
August	n.a.	976	−5,347
September	n.a.	863	−7,038
October	n.a.	855	−3,158
November	n.a.	897	−4,198
December	n.a.	1,403	1,521
Total	n.a.	13,432	−29,067
1998			
January	n.a.	802	213
February	n.a.	642	4,092
March	n.a.	795	1,179
April	n.a.	884	−1,261
May	n.a.	866	−571
June	840	926	1,463
July	592	1,001	−1,382
August	392	991	−387
September	6,038	1,088	−1,899
October	1,214	2,777	−366
November	1,748	899	−398
December	424	1,003	43
Total	17,100	12,672	−2,206

n.a. = not available

a. FDI, foreign direct investment, is defined here as equity investment and purchase of real estate in Malaysia and abroad and loans drawn down from or to nonresidents, excluding retained earnings.

Sources: White Paper on Status of the Malaysian Economy, 6 April 1999, 45, 56; Malaysian Industrial Development Authority, *Annual Report 1998*.

Assessing the effects of the controls on capital flows has become more difficult as the government has become less forthcoming with data. Table A2.2 shows that investment approvals by the Malaysian Industrial Development Authority (MIDA) increased immediately after the controls were announced, but this reflected in part an effort to signal continued openness to foreign direct investment (FDI) by accelerating approvals. Actual investment seemed to surge, but these figures are also potentially misleading because much of the new investment could be traced to a small number of very large takeovers. For 1998 as a whole, Malaysia appears to have fared somewhat worse in attracting FDI than its counterparts, although this only partly reflects the effects of the controls, given that

Table A2.3 Flow of funds through external and special external accounts (15 February, 1999 to 2 June, 1999)

Date	Net flow* (RM million)
5 March	−21.7
10	18.5
17	21.2
24	37.3
31	74.2
7 April	62.4
14	398.1
21	424.0
28	554.1
5 May	1,089.3
12	1,436.3
19	2,063.7
26	2,372.5
2 June	2,831.3

a. Cumulative portfolio inflow.

Source: National Economic Action Council data, reported in *Straits Times*, 9 June 1999.

they were not introduced until September.[25] In the first half of 1999, MIDA increased its approval of foreign projects slightly over the previous year, but applications for the period were only 35 percent of total applications in 1998 (*Asian Wall Street Journal*, 25 August 1999). In mid-2000 MIDA again admitted that foreign direct investment for the first four months of 2000 had fallen relative to 1999 (from RM1.94 billion to RM1.64 billion) (*Reuters* report at http://business-times.asia1.com.sg/5/news/nmsia06.html).

As table A2.2 shows, net portfolio investment was strongly negative in the second half of 1997. It turned negative again after the middle of 1998, despite the controls, although at much reduced pace. According to NEAC data (table A2.3), the relaxation of the controls in 1999 reversed this trend (*Business Times*, 9 and 10 June, 23 August 1999). In the first

---

25. According to the United Nations World Investment Report, FDI in South Korea and Thailand increased dramatically between 1997 and 1998 (up 87 percent to $7.0 billion and 81 percent to $5.1 billion, respectively) in comparison with a decline in Malaysia from $5.1 to $3.7 billion (*Asian Wall Street Journal*, 24 September 1999). A World Bank source report offers somewhat different numbers for the same period—from $6.4 billion to $8.9 billion in Korea, $3.8 billion to $7.0 billion in Thailand, and $3.7 billion to $1.6 billion in Malaysia (Claessens, Djankov, and Klingebiel 1999, table 9). Even if the figures differ, the trends are in consensus.

Table A2.4 Malaysia's exit tax on foreign capital
(15 February, 1999)

Funds brought in before 15 February 1999	
Principal withdrawn	Tax (percent)
Within 7 months	30
Within 7 to 9 months	20
Within 9 to 12 months	10
After 12 months	0
Profits withdrawn	
During 12 month holding period	0
After 12-month holding period	10
Funds brought in on or after 15 February 1999	
Principal	No tax
Profits	
Withdrawn within 12 months	30
After 12 months	10

Source: Asian Wall Street Journal, 5-6 February 1999.

half of 2000, portfolio flows resumed in anticipation of Malaysia being reinstated into relevant regional stock indices. This development obliged portfolio managers to buy Malaysia stocks to rebalance index-based funds.

If the record with respect to capital flows is mixed, the government's own actions suggest a growing recognition of the costs of the controls. When the controls were first announced, the government exempted dividends. But large dividend payments by several foreign companies led the government to impose a cap on distributed profits. Not surprisingly, the foreign business community reacted negatively to this new restriction, and as early as December 1998 evidence began to surface of a reevaluation of the controls within the government (*International Herald Tribune*, 23-24 January 1999; *Asian Wall Street Journal*, 26 January 1999). In early February, the government instituted an exit tax in place of the earlier controls. The new measures included a graduated tax on capital gains designed to favor longer-term inflows (see table A2.4).

In August 1999, the government announced it would reduce the 10 percent exit tax on profits from portfolio investments made after 15 February 1999 (*Asian Wall Street Journal*, 13-14 August 1999). As the 1 September deadline approached, speculation mounted about how much foreign investment would choose to leave (*The Economist*, 21 August 1999, 63). On the first 2 days after the lifting of the controls, an estimated $400 million left the country—more than 40 percent of inflows since February— and the stock market fell more than 6 percent. But this outcome was below more apocalyptic estimates and had only a temporary effect on the recovery of the stock market (see table A2.1).

In sum, the controls, ushered in with great fanfare, appear to have had only ambiguous economic effects. On the plus side of the ledger, the controls did grant the government some leeway in the conduct of macro-economic policy. The fixing of the exchange rate arguably contributed to the amassing of a large current account surplus—nearly 14 percent of GNP for 1998 as a whole—and boosted reserves to $31.7 billion by August 1999 (*Business Times*, 23 August 1999). However, the path of Malaysia's recovery with controls does not appear substantially different than Thailand's, which pursued a more orthodox policy course. Interest rates in South Korea and Thailand have also fallen back to pre-crisis levels, and the exchange rates in both countries have stabilized and even appreciated since September 1998. Perhaps most telling in assessing the merits of the controls is the fact that the government itself found them constraining and finally relaxed them.

The Foreign Policy of Capital Controls

More than any other Southeast Asian political leader, Mahathir has used foreign policy as an instrument for consolidating domestic political support (Aziz 1997, Zainuddin 1994). One way of doing this is through nationalist gestures aimed at the West, including such measures as a short-lived "buy British last" policy, Mahathir's boycotts of the Asia Pacific Economic Cooperation (APEC) leaders' meeting in Seattle in 1993, and the threat to pull out of the Asia Europe Meeting (ASEM) over Europe's policy with respect to Burma. Mahathir has also attempted to forge alternative international coalitions and alignments. These include his long-standing overtures to the Islamic world, the "Look East" policy—which sought both to emulate Japan and South Korea and to forge deeper economic ties with them (Camroux 1994)—and the proposal for an East Asian Economic Caucus (EAEC), which would wield influence over the APEC agenda and develop a wider voice for developing Asian countries on the world stage.

The imposition of capital controls exhibited characteristics of both of these strategies. On the one hand, the controls targeted "speculators," including institutional and individual investors in Singapore. The capital controls created new bilateral issues between the two countries, exacerbated other conflicts of longer standing, and spilled over into intra-ASEAN relations. At the same time, Mahathir was crafting a new Look East policy in the wake of the crisis, seeking to put together a coalition of lenders, the most important being Japan, to provide an alternative to the IMF.

Singapore-Malaysia Relations: Financial De-coupling

Following the imposition of controls, banks and institutional investors had to manage outstanding ringgit positions, which had been contracted at exchange and interest rates prevailing before 1 September. Following guidelines set by the Singapore Foreign Exchange Market Committee, offshore banks netted out exposures with each other at the rate of RM4.00, instead of the pegged rate of RM3.80 to the dollar. Forward contracts were settled according to the forward curve prevailing at that time (*Asian Wall Street Journal*, 10 September 1998). Those with net positions in ringgit still ended up with losses, but this market solution did allow an orderly unwinding of contracts for those wishing to exit the ringgit.

The central objective at the controls was to close the foreign exchange market. The question of how to handle longer investments held by Singapore investors in offshore shares proved much more complicated; understanding it requires some exposition of how the offshore market evolved. While other institutions and firms were quickly separated following the end of Singapore's partnership with Malaysia (e.g., airlines), the Stock Exchange of Singapore (SES) continued share listings until 1989, when the Kuala Lumpur Stock Exchange (KLSE) ceased to allow joint listings of 180 Malaysian companies on the SES. This move was followed in 1990 by the creation of a Singapore over-the-counter (OTC) market in Malaysian shares, known as the Central Limit Order Book (CLOB).[26] Around the time capital and exchange controls were introduced in September 1998, there were about 200,000 CLOB account holders with some S$2 billion involved.

The existence of the CLOB had both advantages and disadvantages for the KLSE and for Malaysia more generally. On the one hand, the CLOB gave Malaysian shares a bigger market and more liquidity by providing a convenient way for Singaporeans to invest in the Malaysian market through their own brokers. Had the KLSE directed Malaysian companies not to accept transfers of Malaysian shares executed on the CLOB, it could have closed the market.[27]

On the other hand, the existence of the CLOB also had certain drawbacks for Malaysia. First, the arrangement enabled Malaysians to disguise their purchases and sales. Malaysians who bought stocks on the KLSE (in ringgit) and sold them on the SES (in S$) could keep those proceeds outside Malaysia, providing a relatively easy way to transfer money out of the country. This became an attractive option whenever there was pressure on the bilateral exchange rate between the two countries. There were also tax motives for Malaysians to hold their shares offshore.

---

26. The CLOB system maintained a computerized order book that matched buy and sell orders. Once the broker entered an order, it was recorded at the SES, which checked the order book and matched it with orders. The Malaysian stocks were not listed on the main SES board or the second board, Stock Exchange of Singapore Dealing and Automatic Quotation (SESDAQ).

27. The KLSE had the opportunity to close the CLOB on several earlier occasions, particularly after the SES went fully scripless in 1994. At that time, the KLSE could have stopped the plan that the SES had devised to register CLOB shares, which was to have Singapore investors hand their Malaysian share certificates to local brokerages, which would have deposited them with the Malaysian Central Depository (MCD) on investors' behalf.

Malaysia claimed that the CLOB also took business away from Kuala Lumpur brokers. The Malaysian White Paper of 6 April 1999 claimed that Malaysia had lost RM10.5 billion (S$4.8 billion) in forgone revenue since the CLOB was set up in 1990, a contention challenged by stockbrokers in Singapore. Nonetheless, it was true that the CLOB market was made up entirely of Singapore brokers, with Malaysian brokers simply agents with whom the shares were lodged. This practice ended with capital controls, because new rules prevented Malaysian brokers from dealing in securities on behalf of a client if there was reason to believe the transaction involved an exchange not recognized by the KLSE. As a result, both Malaysian and Singaporean investors were forced to take their Malaysian shares out of the CLOB and transfer them directly to a Malaysian stockbroker or open an account in Malaysia to deal directly; as we will see below, the terms of such a transfer became highly contentious.

A final issue was the Malaysian claim that the existence of the CLOB facilitated the short-selling of Malaysian shares, with implications for the currency. Malaysians moving profits out of ringgit, and downward pressure on the KLSE generated by selling in Singapore, had the effect of turning the market in equities into an additional source of pressure on the ringgit itself. The SES countered that CLOB investors were net buyers of Malaysian shares in the 20 months before 1 September 1998 (*Business Times*, 9 April 1999), and had doubled their holdings of Malaysian shares since the onset of the crisis. On each of the 15 days when the KLCI recorded dramatic falls between 21 August 1994 and 21 March 1999, SES figures showed low volumes of trading of KLSE stocks; the sell-off of KLSE stocks could not have been said to originate from Singapore. Moreover, the size of CLOB as a percentage of KLSE market capitalization had declined steadily since January 1990, falling to only 3 percent by the time the controls were imposed.

Singapore insisted that the closure of the CLOB was not a big loss to its financial sector, although the curbs constituted "a step backwards" in ASEAN's efforts to liberalize trade and finance (*Straits Times*, 13 October 1998). The actual cost of the controls, however, was not borne primarily by brokers but rather by the Singaporean investors holding frozen CLOB shares. Daim Zainuddin initially signaled his interest in a quick resolution of the issue, but concerns quickly centered on the possible effects of large sales on the KLSE. If Singaporeans were free to dispose of their shares as they wished, and decided to sell en masse because of heightened concerns about liquidity or the security of their shares, then prices in Kuala Lumpur would fall. The question of price also became politicized.

One suggestion was for the state investment arm, Khazanah Nasional, to buy over the shares at prices that prevailed in September 1998. A succession of such proposals, all effectively expropriations of Singaporean investors, followed. One of the first came from Malaysian-based Singapore businessman Akhbar Khan, an associate of Daim, who made a series of offers to CLOB investors. Each involved either freezing sales for some period or selling to Khan's new firm, Effective Capital, at a discount or with steep fees (*Asian Wall Street Journal*, 27 April 1999). Other offers followed, all effectively confiscatory.[28]

The issue quickly became politicized when Mahathir said Singaporeans should accept Akhbar Khan's offer (*Straits Times*, 4 May 1999). According to Mahathir, Singaporeans "were responsible for the fall in share prices" in 1998 and did nothing to help revive prices when they fell. It was therefore not morally right for them to benefit from price increases (*Asian Wall Street Journal*, 5 May 1999).

After consulting a queen's counsel, the SES broke its silence on the Akhbar Khan offer in May (*Business Times* and *Straits Times*, 6 May 1999), arguing that it lacked demonstration of financial ability, was not unconditional, and lacked relevant price information; in short, the offer document did not meet normal Singaporean or international standards (*Business Times* and *Straits Times*, 13 May 1999). Despite this finding, Deputy Prime Minister Lee Hsien Loong was explicit that the Singapore government had no responsibility for insuring CLOB shares (*Straits Times*, 7-8 May 1999). Lee further revealed that the Singapore government was unwilling to make the CLOB shares a sovereign issue between the two governments.[29]

The matter remained stalemated until February 2000, when the Singapore and Kuala Lumpur exchanges reached a "comprehensive solution" to the CLOB issue, which was based on two options for investors (table A2.5; *Straits Times*, 26 February 2000). The first option allowed a migration of the shares to individual accounts for trading, but on a staggered basis rather than all at once. The second option required that trading be frozen until 2003. Both solutions involved the payment of a substantial "transfer fee" (1.5 percent on assets released more than 13 months; 1 percent on those held until 2003), to which Singapore investors objected strenuously.[30]

Malaysia's nationalist response to the economic crisis has indirectly affected bilateral relations with Singapore on a variety of other historical issues as well (Ganesan 1998; Lee Kuan 1998). The most intractable remains

---

28. E.g., another Malaysian company owned by a Negri Sembilan prince proposed listing a unit trust outside of Malaysia (*Straits Times*, 22 May and 22 June 1999), and Telekom Malaysia and UEM, a firm with close links to the ruling party, also submitted proposals to the KLSE (*Asian Wall Street Journal*, 9-10 July 1999).

29. Mahathir had initially wanted to include the CLOB issue along with others in bilateral negotiations in December but changed his mind in March 1999 when the issue was left to the KLSE and SES to negotiate (*Straits Times*, 7 May 1999).

30. The Securities Investors Association of Singapore (SIAS), formed in 1999 with 50,000 members, argued that the Singapore Exchange should pay the transfer fee because investors were effectively assured by the exchange that the CLOB was legal.

Table A2.5 February 2000 solutions to the CLOB controversy

	Scheme A (amended effective capital)	Scheme B (agreement between central depositories of KLSE and Singapore Exchange)
Acceptance closing date	31 March 2000	Within 32 months of 31 March 2000
Plan	CLOB shares released to individual accounts on a staggered basis over 13 months from July 2000	CLOB shares released to owners for trading on KLSE over 9 months from January 2003
Fee charges to investors	1.5 percent transfer fee paid to Effective Capital based on 15 February 2000 closing price of repatriated shares	1 percent administrative fee to KLSE affiliate based on average closing prices of shares on last five trading days of October 2002.

CLOB = Central Limit Order Book
KLSE = Kuala Lumpur Stock Exchange
Source: *Asian Wall Street Journal*, 27 February 2000.

renewal of water contracts expiring in 2016, which Singapore tried to resolve with a loan offer that Kuala Lumpur turned down. Since the crisis, Malaysia has accused Singapore of seeking to discourage Malaysian cargo from going through Port Klang by offering rebates, and complained about differential treatment between East and West Malaysians with respect to Central Provident Fund contributions.[31] Even security issues—access to Malaysian airspace, including for search and rescue operations; military training and exercises; the Five Power Defence Arrangement (FPDA) exercises in 1998—were all affected by the crisis. Although these issues may subsequently be resolved, Malaysia's nationalist response to the crisis has weakened integration between the two countries and provided incentives for Singapore to reduce its dependence on Malaysia through whatever means possible.

Seeking Financial Support

The ability of Malaysia to sustain its capital controls without recourse to the IMF depended heavily on its capacity to tap other sources of funds; without these funds the current account adjustment would be that much larger. The government estimated that it needed to raise RM102 billion between 1999 and 2000 from domestic (RM81 billion) and foreign (RM21

---

31. The former were allowed to withdraw their Central Provident Fund savings when they left Singapore, whereas West Malaysians could not because they typically return regularly for employment.

Table A2.6 External sources of funds, 1998-2000

Source	Funds (millions US dollars)
Funds approved or disbursed	
World Bank	700
Japan Export-Import Bank (JEXIM) IA	300
JEXIM II	700
Islamic Development Bank	25
Sumitomo-Nomura Bank, Japan	665
OECF Phase I	1,100
Consortium of foreign banks in Malaysia	1,300
Total	4,690
Funds being negotiated	
Islamic Development Bank	50
JEXIM IB	200
JEXIM III	500
Total	**750**

Note: As of April 1999.

Source: White Paper on Status of the Malaysian Economy, 6 April 1999, 53.

billion) sources. Domestically, Malaysia enjoys not only high savings rates, but high public sector savings as well. In addition to being able to issue bonds, the government is able to tap the EPF, Petronas, and public insurance funds to meet short-term financing needs.

On the foreign front, the government's initial strategy of tapping the international financial markets had to be aborted; a planned $2 billion bond issue in mid-1998 ran into trouble immediately in the face of ratings agencies' downgrades. The imposition of controls certainly did not help with the international financial markets, either. Following the controls, the country's stock market was removed from several regional indexes, and in February 1999 ratings agencies complained about political intervention in the country's financial regulation and the reduced independence of the central bank (Straits Times and International Herald Tribune, 24 February 1999).

The government's response was to court a variety of sources of nonconditional or less conditional funding, including the World Bank and a consortium of foreign banks operating in Malaysia. However, the centerpiece of Mahathir's financial diplomacy was Japan. Mahathir was swift to endorse Japan's proposal for an Asian Monetary Fund, and has supported—in deeds as well as words—Japan's skepticism with respect to the IMF's approach to the crisis. As shown in table A2.6, Japan became a major patron.

Malaysia was one of the first beneficiaries of the Miyazawa Initiative, which falls under Japan's Overseas Economic Cooperation Fund. Japan has also supported Malaysia in trade financing and guaranteeing sovereign bonds raised through Japanese banking institutions. In sum, the crisis actually provided an opportunity for Mahathir to formulate a new Look East policy, reaffirming political as well as economic ties to Japan while eliminating the need to have recourse to the IMF. As the economy began to recover in 1999, it was able to once again tap international financial markets; ratings agencies upgraded the country, and the $2 billion bond issue aborted in July 1998 was successfully floated at the end of May 1999 (*Asian Wall Street Journal*, 27 May 1999; *Straits Times*, 28 May 1999).

Conclusions

Whatever gains the government received from short-term capital repatriation and the ability to stimulate the economy—and they are hard to judge—these effects were partly offset by the costs with respect to reputation, perceptions of the integrity of the policymaking process, and inflows of foreign direct investment. As will be argued in chapter 5, the controls were also part of an adjustment strategy that left close, discretionary relations between business and government in place.

These judgements do not speak to the wisdom of capital controls as a longer-run strategy to reduce vulnerability to short-term capital movements; however, they do suggest some complexities with respect to the timing of such policies. If modest prudential controls are maintained or imposed during periods of strong growth, they may moderate outflows during a crisis. However, if confidence falls sharply, investors might be willing to pay fairly stiff penalties to exit. During crises, the government is thus likely to have incentives to impose controls on outflows rather than inflows, which are more damaging to confidence; in short, incentives during crises may be perverse.

Finally, the crisis has a foreign policy dimension. As in the past, Prime Minister Mahathir has used foreign "threats"—particularly hedge funds— for domestic political purposes. As the case of the CLOB shows, the costs of the crisis are borne by foreigners, in this case CLOB shareholders and Singaporean investors. Moreover, the harsh way minority shareholders were treated in the CLOB episode does not speak well for Malaysia's treatment of foreign investors, and the strategy could have broader implications for intra-ASEAN cooperation.

3

Crisis, Political Change, and Economic Reform

Most analyses of the crisis (including in the last two chapters) are preoccupied with the question of causes. But economic crises can also have adverse political consequences: disaffected interest groups, protest, even riots and social violence. These problems can undermine support for reform, generate "backlash" against the market, and bring anti-reformist parties to power. Crises can generate changes of government, but also changes of regime: transitions to—but also from—democracy. To what extent were any of these patterns visible in East Asia?

The link between economic crises and political change begins with the obvious fact that severe economic distress is likely to decrease political support for incumbents. In democracies, the consequences of this disaffection are reflected in the appeals of interest groups, in protest, and most important in electoral outcomes. The worse the economic circumstances in the period before elections, the worse incumbents are likely to fare, ceteris paribus.[1] In South Korea, the crisis broke less than a month before the presidential election, and the typically conservative Korean electorate chose longtime dissident Kim Dae Jung as president by a narrow plurality. In Thailand, the crisis led to the replacement of the Chavalit government by a new coalition government led by the Democrat Party under Chuan Leekpai. However, the important point to underscore is that democracy in both countries proved resilient. Despite the severity of the crisis, there was little support in either country for a return to authoritarian rule.

---

1. The ceteris paribus condition referring primarily to possible differences in the quality and organization of the opposition.

Changes of authoritarian governments are less institutionalized and therefore somewhat more complex, but there are three main reasons why crises can be an important causal factor (Haggard and Kaufman 1995). First, the very absence of institutionalized political channels means that mass-based groups and social movements have little option but to resort to various forms of protest to express their grievances: strikes, protests, demonstrations. These protests typically have political objectives, such as political liberalization and democratization, but they attract adherents and gain momentum when they can also appeal to economic grievances.

Second, crises can lead private sector groups to lose confidence in existing political arrangements. If private-sector actors believe that authoritarian governments are unwilling or unable to manage economic challenges in a coherent way, they can quickly recalculate the costs of political change. Political reform and even democratization may be more attractive than a continuation of an uncertain status quo. This is particularly true when there are opportunities to ally with moderate oppositions that do not threaten basic property rights.

Third, crises can undermine the loyalty of the politico-military elite: the heads of the armed forces, key bureaucratic agencies, and the ruling party. The proximate cause for the fall of authoritarian governments can almost always be found in splits within this elite and the emergence of "softliners" amenable to political reform (O'Donnell and Schmitter 1986; Przeworski 1991). Economic crises can contribute to such splits in a number of ways, such as by reducing the ability of the authoritarian leaders to deliver material rewards to their followers.

However, the greatest challenge crises pose has to do with the problem of coercion. As crises generate political opposition and social protest, authoritarian leaders and their militaries have to make decisions about the use of force. At what point does repression breed more protest rather than quell it? Can officers be counted on to fire on their own citizens? If the military and police do respond with force, what affect does it have on the the military's integrity or on their future careers if the opposition wins? All of these questions can generate splits within the government and military that favor the process of political reform.

On each of these three dimensions, the challenges facing Suharto and his successor B.J. Habibie were more profound than those confronting Mahathir. This was due in part to the greater severity of the Indonesian crisis, but also to political factors. Mahathir did resort to force and other restrictive practices to curb antigovernment protest. Yet ironically, the greater openness of the Malaysian political system provided some channels for opposition action and served to ultimately *limit* the scope of antigovernment protest and demonstrations (Case 2000). Malaysia's parliamentary system is at best semi-democratic, but elections provided Prime Minister Mahathir a mechanism of securing support. When he called snap elections in November 1999, the economy had begun to rebound and he scored a substantial victory.

Second, the Mahathir government was particularly attentive to the interests of the Malay private sector, which saw little future in throwing its lot with opposition forces; this was true not only for Malays but for important segments of the Chinese business class as well. The private sector's loss of confidence in the Suharto regime, by contrast, was more profound. This loss of confidence did not reflect itself in overt political activity, particularly given the highly vulnerable position of the Chinese business community. But it did show up in massive and debilitating capital flight.

Third, the Malaysian military has long been firmly under civilian control, and as we have seen Mahathir also retained firm control over the party. By contrast, the depth of the crisis and mounting protest to the government created important splits within the Indonesian government, ruling party, and military that were the prelude to Suharto's fall.

Changes of government bring new political leaders and parties to office, but of what sort? One often cited fear is that increasing economic openness and exposure to shocks will generate "backlash"—the rise of parties and social movements that are radically opposed to the market or populist in orientation (Rodrik 1997; Friedman 1999). These political forces may find allies—or even be led by—private sector groups espousing ideologies that might be called "business nationalism."

Throughout the region, adversely affected groups signaled their distress in various ways, and governments responded by addressing the social dimensions of the crisis (see chapter 5). The organized private sector pressed the government for relief as well, particularly with respect to interest rates, and in every country some segments of business sought protection and subsidies and resisted reforms that adversely affected them.

Yet populist forces were partly offset by political leaders, parties, and movements reaching quite different conclusions about the crisis than a simple backlash hypothesis would suggest. This alternative diagnosis argued that the crisis was the result of political failures, including overly close business-government relations and the corruption of the policy process. These "market-oriented populists," such as Kim Dae Jung, advanced economic reform for political as well as economic reasons. Liberalization and reduction of the government's role in the economy would establish more arms-length relationships between business and government and reduce opportunities for favoritism and corruption. Greater attention to social issues was a component of this agenda, but a reform of the social contract did not necessarily undercut support for the market; to the contrary, it was increasingly seen as a necessary complement to greater openness. In addition to Kim Dae Jung, similar ideas were also visible in the resurgence of moderate Islam in Malaysia and Indonesia—for example, in the thinking of Anwar Ibrahim and Amien Rais—and had long been current among segments of the Chinese communities in both countries. In the Philippines, both Corazon Aquino and Fidel Ramos advanced similar ideas, despite other important differences between them (see appendix 3-1).

Moreover, these reformers were not simply interested in discrete policy changes; they also sought more fundamental institutional and even political reforms. These included greater emphasis on the rule of law, more accountability and transparency in government, and both increased independence and greater accountability in the regulatory process. In Indonesia, South Korea, and Thailand, these changes extended to a reexamination of the effects of electoral laws on the quality of governance and to pressure for more political and economic decentralization.

Even where reformist parties and politicians came into office, they differed in their ability to realize their policy objectives. These differences are related to the political constraints outlined in chapter 2—electoral and non-electoral challenges, decision-making structures, and links to private sector actors. Table 3.1 provides an overview. In South Korea, presidential and legislative elections are non-concurrent, and Kim Dae Jung initially confronted a divided government. But Kim finessed this constraint by working with the outgoing government to initiate a number of reforms before taking office. Kim Dae Jung's ties to, and dependence on, the private sector were much weaker than those of his predecessors, while his credibility with labor and the popular sector was high; this allowed him to use consultative mechanisms with business and labor to secure support for a reform agenda. The ability to maintain this momentum naturally declined over time, and as we will see in the following chapter, efforts at corporate reform continued to face resistance from the chaebol. But these limitations should not detract from what was achieved.

In Thailand, the Democrat Party historically had stood for similar reformist themes, but Chuan's six-party coalition faced many of the same constraints as its predecessor, and the Democrat Party itself was by no means unified on what to do. The combination of coalition government, weak ties between the Democrats and those most seriously affected by the crisis, and the continuing influence of business significantly constrained its ability to act in a decisive fashion. Decision making on a range of issues quickly stalled.

Indonesia and Malaysia also present interesting contrasts. In the face of a profound political as well as economic crisis, Habibie had strong incentives to remake himself as a reformer and instituted a number of extremely important institutional changes in Indonesia's political life, effectively overseeing a transition to democratic rule. Nonetheless, the incentives to economic reform were offset by ongoing ties to the remnants of the ruling party and favored segments of the private sector.

Table 3.1 Political constraints on crisis management: New governments

	Thailand	South Korea	Malaysia	Indonesia
Government, assumption of office	Prime Minister Chuan Leekpai, 11/1997	President Kim Dae Jung, 2/1998	Prime Minster Mohammed Mahathir (reelected 11/1999)	President B.J. Habibie (5/1998), President Wahid Abdurrahman (11/1999)
Political challenges				
Electoral	Seventh party added to coalition strengthen coalition, 4/98	Subnational elections 6/1998; legislative elections 4/2000	General elections scheduled 4/2000, called early for 11/1999	Parliamentary elections 6/1999; indirect election of president, 11/1999
Non-electoral and "backlash"	Some strikes and antigovernment demonstrations by opposition parties and NGOs, first half of 1998	Strikes, second half of 1998 and first quarter of 1999	Pro-Anwar demonstrations, 9-10/1998	Ongoing antigovernment and antimilitary demonstrations; rioting in Jakarta, 11/1998; increased secessionist pressures and social violence in provinces
Decision-making process	Parliamentary, six-party coalition; seventh party added, 11/1998	Presidential. Initially divided government; unified government from 8/1998	Parliamentary, coalition government, but UMNO Party dominant	Transitional presidential government, increasing parliamentary activism
Government links to business	Close links between legislators of all parties and business	Weaker links between Kim Dae Jung and *chaebols*	Close to politically favored groups	Continuing links with some favored groups and charges of corruption (Bank Bali scandal 7/1999)

Malaysia, finally, is the country where the crisis was most shallow, but also where political continuity prevailed. Not surprisingly, it was also the country in which the extent of political, institutional, and policy reform was the least pronounced.

Thailand

The crisis in Thailand contributed directly to a change of government that brought a reformist party to office. In contrast to South Korea, the new Thai administration faced a much more complex set of political constraints. But even before the fall of the Chavalit government, the crisis helped propel forward a wide-ranging constitutional reform process that had begun with the return to democratic rule in the early 1990s. The new constitution is of interest because its final passage was so clearly influenced by the crisis and the political and institutional weaknesses of the Banharn and Chavalit governments in managing it.[2]

The origins of constitutional reform date to the first Chuan government, which came to office following the return to civilian rule and the general elections of 13 September 1992. Neither the Chuan nor the Banharn government was able to complete the process.[3] As a result, the task of constitutional reform fell to the Chavalit government, which formed a Constitutional Drafting Assembly (CDA) composed of two indirectly elected groups: representatives from each of the country's 76 provinces; and 23 political, administrative, and legal experts. The CDA began its work in January 1997. Provincial representatives canvassed opinion in their districts, engaging a number of civil society groups in the process, and in April a first draft was passed by the CDA with only one opposing vote.

The CDA thus began to disseminate the draft of the new constitution just as the crisis was beginning to break, and the issues of political and economic reform became closely linked. The CDA revised the draft in August for submission to the National Assembly with a "fast track" provision: the National Assembly could only vote the document up or down. Very shortly after the revised draft was passed by the CDA, pressure mounted on the government to move the constitution toward consideration in the National Assembly.

---

2. The following account draws primarily on Klein (1998), Pasuk and Baker (1999), Suchit (1999), and Hicken (1998 and 1999) on the electoral system.

3. The first Chuan government established a Committee for Democratic Development that outlined a process for revising the 1992 constitution, but the government fell on charges of corruption. The Banharn government established a committee that recommended an official review of the constitutional reform process, but the Banharn government also fell on charges of corruption.

The forces arrayed against the document were powerful, including a range of institutions that would be politically checked, exposed to demands for greater transparency, or lose prerogatives: the police, army, judges, senators, subdistrict and hamlet chiefs (*kamnan*), and most political parties, including those in the ruling coalition. Opponents also banked on the conservatism and indifference of rural voters. An important set of allies in the fight against constitutional reform were the *kamnan*, the selection of whom was partly controlled by the powerful and centralizing interior minister. Under the new constitution, they would have to stand for election and would thus be excluded from *ex officio* positions in elected local government organizations.

However, support for the new constitution also came from diverse (and to some extent antagonistic) sources. Constitutional reform pulled support from a variety of reformist civil society groups and from the left, but also from the Bangkok middle class, which has played an important role in the restoration of democratic rule. The opposition Democrats also said that they would vote for the constitution, albeit with some reservations. The Bangkok business elite was initially skeptical about constitutional reform, but as Pasuk and Baker (1999, 9) point out, "The two cabinets in power through 1995-97 dramatically illustrated the danger of entrusting Thailand's fragile urban economy to the care of provincial business politicians." On the day before the vote on the constitutional revision, more than a thousand business executives gathered in the Silom Road district—the Wall Street of Bangkok—to demonstrate in favor of the reform (*Far Eastern Economic Review*, 9 October 1997, 20-21). On 27 September, the National Assembly approved the draft, with 578 votes for, 16 against, and 17 abstentions.

The constitution is a large and complex document, and the changes it promises to bring to Thai politics are profound. One of its objectives is to establish constitutional supremacy. The institution of judicial review and the establishment of a constitutional court reduce the ability of both laws and administrative decrees and regulations to take precedence over constitutional guarantees. In addition to the constitutional court, the new charter establishes a range of independent judicial and quasi-judicial institutions designed to protect particular rights and to act as a check on government. These include a new election commission, a human rights commission, an administrative court, an office of the ombudsman, and a strengthened National Counter Corruption Commission.

The constitution also overhauls the electoral system, and Parliament itself. The new constitution addresses the problem of party fragmentation by changing the electoral system to winnow the number of parties and make them stronger.[4] The constitution requires the Senate to be popularly

---

4. Representatives were previously elected from multi-member districts. The new system is two-tiered: 100 seats will come from nationwide party lists, which will enhance the power of party leaders; and 400 will come from single-member districts, thus reducing the number

elected for the first time, and seeks to disengage elected politicians both from the bureaucracy (e.g., by prohibiting senators from holding other administrative office) and from business (by prohibiting senators from being the beneficiary of government contracts, by requiring full disclosure of assets, and by requiring cabinet ministers to resign their parliamentary seats).

Finally, the constitution also includes a number of initiatives for decentralizing government and increasing direct citizen input. The most important of these are political and administrative decentralization and the guarantee that locales have a greater say in the management of resources. The latter issue pitted developers against small landowners and commons, and had become one of the most bitter and divisive during the boom of the 1990s. The constitution also allows for direct citizen participation in the law-drafting process (through ad hoc legislative committees with civil society membership) and establishes a referendum process.

The full implementation of this ambitious agenda would naturally take years and require changes in habit as well as law. Nonetheless, the change wrought by the constitutional revision was far-reaching, and it is highly doubtful that it would have occurred in the way it did in the absence of crisis circumstances.

Despite the expeditious passage of the constitution, economic policymaking by mid-October was in complete disarray. Even with a near complete collapse of confidence on the part of both the markets and the international financial institutions, Thai politics reverted to intercoalitional conflicts.[5] On 21 October, a cabinet meeting considered a declaration of a state of emergency, but in an important indicator of the strength of the new democracy, the proposal for a curfew and media censorship was blocked by the military (*Far Eastern Economic Review*, 6 November 1997, 20-21). Chavalit did succeed in putting together a cabinet that included nonpolitical appointees to key economic portfolios. However, after Chavalit resigned on 3 November, the coalition failed to find an alternative leader and the Democrat Party was allowed to form a government.

As in South Korea, the position of the new government was strengthened by the patent failures of its predecessor. Even though Chuan still required five additional parties to form a coalition (see table 3.2), the Democrat Party was the largest and he was able to insist that it occupy all of the top economic positions as a precondition for forming a government.

The ideological positions and even support bases of the parties in Thailand are difficult to pin down because of the fluidity of the system and

---

of parties per district. Party switching is also prohibited between elections, therefore increasing discipline.

5. A power struggle emerged between the New Aspiration Party (NAP) and its main coalition partner, Chart Pattana, over Chavalit's plan to bring in nonpartisan outsiders because it implied a reallocation of cabinet seats (*Bangkok Post*, 29 September 1997).

Table 3.2 Party composition of Thai governments and oppositions, 1996-2000

Chavalit government (11/1996-11/1997)		Chuan government (11/1997-11/1998)		Chuan government (11/1998-7/1999)		Chuan government (7/1999-1/2000)	
Government parties	Number of seats	Government parties	Number of seats	Government parties	Number of seats	Government parties	Number of seats
NAP	125	Democrats	123	Democrats	123	Democrats	123
Chart Pattana	52	Chart Thai	39	Chart Pattana	52	Chart Pattana	52
Chart Thai	39	SAP	20	Chart Thai	39	Chart Thai	39
SAP	20	Cobra faction	12	SAP	20	Cobra faction	12
Prachakorn Thai	18	Solidarity	8	Cobra faction	12	Solidarity	8
Muon Chon	2	Seritham	4	Solidarity	8	Seritham	4
				Seritham	4		
Percentage of seats	65	Percentage of seats	53	Percentage of seats	66	Percentage of seats	61

(continued next page)

Table 3.2 Party composition of Thai governments and oppositions, 1996-2000 (continued)

Chavalit government (11/1996-11/1997)		Chuan government (11/1997-11/1998)		Chuan government (11/1998-7/1999)		Chuan government (7/1999-1/2000)	
Opposition parties	Number of seats	Opposition parties	Number of seats	Opposition parties	Number of seats	Opposition parties	Number of seats
Democrat	123	NAP	125	NAP	125	NAP	125
Solidarity	8	Chart Pattana	52	Prachakorn Thai	5	SAP	20
Seritham	4	Prachakorn Thai	5	Palang Tham	1	Prachakorn Thai	5
Thai	1	Muon Chon	2	Thai	1	Muon Chon	2
Palang Tham	1	Palang Tham	1			Palang Tham	1
		Thai	1			Thai	1
Percentage of seats	35		47		34		39

NAP = New Aspiration Party
SAP = Social Action Party

Note: The Thai Party supported the government after 11/1997 but was not a coalition member. The Cobras were a faction of the Prachakorn Thai Party (PTP). When the Cobras left PTP in 11/97, one PTP member resigned, bringing the number of seats to 392. Chavalit reshuffled the cabinet in 10/1997, but there were no changes in party composition.

the need for all parties to compromise with regional power brokers to be effective at the national level. Nonetheless, the Democrat Party is the oldest party in the country, the most institutionalized, with the strongest ties to the Bangkok elite; it has also always had the easiest time attracting support from technocrats. To a substantial degree, Girling's (1981, 166) description of the party of nearly two decades ago still rings true: Democrat leaders are "people of wealth, standing and integrity: they were loyalists, supporters of a *laissez-faire* economy . . . and proponents of constitutional government and honest administration." In the more recent past, it had stood both for democracy against military rule (e.g., in the 1992 elections) and in favor of a technocratic, cautiously reformist approach to economic policy. Although the party suffered from its own corruption problems—indeed the party lost power over this issue in 1998—it generally was free of the more egregious patronage, pork-barrel spending, and corruption of a number of its opponents (e.g., in the 1996 elections). In the fall of 1997, the Democrat Party was the closest thing on the Thai political scene to a party of economic reform.

In some areas, particularly with respect to the management of the ailing finance companies, the new government moved with dispatch not only to address problems but to make needed institutional changes, such as increasing the independence of the Financial Restructuring Agency (see chapter 5). However, from the beginning, Chuan faced a more complex set of political constraints than in South Korea (see table 3.1). The government faced more diverse social protests and had to contend with business opposition to the government's (and the IMF's) macroeconomic policy stance that found reflection in important divisions within the Democrat Party's technocratic team itself. In seeking to pass reform legislation, these problems were compounded by the fact that the Senate contained a number of businessmen who would be adversely affected by proposed reforms and had the constitutional power to review, and thus delay, reforms.

As if these problems were not enough, Chuan had to continually contend with the problem of coalition maintenance. Despite the advantages the Democrat Party gained from the incompetence of the preceding government, its overall legislative majority was initially razor thin, and even that majority was sustained only by including two parties in the coalition that had participated in the failed Chavalit administration (see table 3.2). In combination, these factors contributed to a much more gradual reform process than that seen in South Korea, and one that yielded more modest results.

As early as January, the government faced the problem of how to deal with violent labor actions in the private sector (Hewison 1999). Problems with labor were later compounded by the announced intention to privatize a number of state-owned enterprises, a process that quickly stalled.

But the strongest social pressure on the government initially came not from the urban areas but from the rural Northeast. The Northeast was the poorest, most neglected region of the country and the one most heavily affected by the crisis. In February, a rural farmers' lobby assembled protestors in the Northeast in Chavalit's constituency and marched to the capital, and again in April farmers' groups organized demonstrations for relief of agrarian debt. The New Aspiration Party (NAP) had also built its appeal in the early 1990s as the representative of the region and made an effort (only partly successful) to tap into these concerns. The government made concessions on the debt issue that divided the different farmers' organizations, but social pressures did not abate. The NAP's new program, published in early 1999, emphasized help for the rural poor through decentralization and redistribution, and NGOs that had participated in the constitutional debate continued to place pressure on the government to implement the political reforms.

The self-evident failure of the opposition while in office limited its ability, at least initially, to capitalize on the crisis, and censure votes in early 1998 and early 1999 failed badly. More difficult for the government was the growing chorus of complaints from the private sector and the fact that the cabinet itself was quite sharply divided over economic policy (Pasuk and Baker 1998). Finance Minister Tarrin supported the IMF's approach, at least in its broad outlines, but Supachai (originally a deputy prime minister, minister of commerce, and senior economic cabinet member) argued publicly that the government should devote more attention to recovery.

As in all of the crisis countries, a major source of controversy was the conduct of fiscal and particularly monetary policy. In the third letter of intent of 24 February 1998, the IMF and the government reached an agreement on relaxing fiscal policy (although much too late in the eyes of some critics). But given that the baht was sinking to new levels, the program maintained a tight monetary stance (Ammar 1997). The core complaint of the business lobby and the pro-business wing of the cabinet centered on the question of interest rates and the priority that should be given to stabilizing the baht and reforming the financial sector, as opposed to addressing problems in the real economy. Throughout the spring of 1998, the government faced ongoing complaints over its high interest rate policy and pressure to relax them or devise other mechanisms to ensure an increased flow of credit.

Given the coalition nature of the government and the close links between all parties and the private sector, the government was more responsive to these pressures than in South Korea, and it made a number of concessions to private-sector demands.[6] The IMF sanctioned these

6. State-owned banks were used as vehicles to increase lending to adversely affected sectors, and in April the prime minister himself stated that the central bank should bring interest rates down. In May, Parliament passed important financial reform legislation that also

changed views to some extent in its fourth Letter of Intent (26 May 1998), which relaxed liquidity constraints while simultaneously laying out an ambitious timetable for financial restructuring and privatization.

But these divisions within the economic cabinet continued, usually surfacing in most visible form whenever new Letters of Intent were under consideration.[7] These divisions account for the failure of some legislation, including a much-needed liberalization of the rules governing foreign direct investment, and as will be seen in the next chapter, complicated the passage of bankruptcy legislation.

These various pressures both inside and outside the coalition naturally made it difficult to count on stable bases of support. In November 1998, Chuan bowed to his interior minister and party deputy to reach a deal with the 52 members of the opposition Chart Pattana (CP) that would bring them into the coalition, thus enlarging his political base (see table 3.2). The basic problem, as always in Thailand's fragmented party system, was that to bring Chart Pattana into the coalition not only meant compromises with politicians of less than sterling reputation, but granting them portfolios as well. The Democrat leadership managed to keep them away from most economic posts, but Chuan had to concede some.[8] As a result, a move that was designed to increase Chuan's margin and insulate him from opposition in fact resulted in a coalition in which the loyalty of the different parties and factions became even more dubious.

However, the opportunities for the opposition to capitalize on the weaknesses in the ruling coalition were limited by their own divisions and continuing doubts about their efficacy and probity. The recovery blunted the ability of the opposition to capitalize on the question of economic management, and the NAP's own history and reputation made it poorly positioned to make charges with respect to corruption.[9] A third censure

---

granted both the Financial Institutions Development Fund and the Ministry of Finance greater authority to borrow abroad in support of increased liquidity.

7. After the fourth Letter of Intent (LoI) in May, LoIs were signed in August 1998, December 1998, March 1999, and September 1999.

8. The inclusion of the CP also served to splinter both the Democrat and Social Action parties, and in July 1999 the Social Action Party withdrew from the government after the party finally broke up over the allocation of ministries.

9. On March 4, 2000, direct Senate elections were held for the first time. Candidates were prohibited by the new constitution from identifying themselves with political parties. As a result, the election results did not provide straightforward information on support for the government or the reform process. Some analysis suggested that reformers and candidates with links to civil society groups had done better than expected (*Bangkok Post*, 5 March 2000). However the elections also provided evidence of the difficulty of rooting out patronage politics and corruption. A total of 78 successful candidates were disqualified by the Electoral Commission for fraud. However, most of these candidates were allowed to run in a second round of balloting and 44 of the 78 were elected again.

motion in December 1999 failed decisively (229 to 125, with 12 abstentions).

In sum, the crisis in Thailand brought a reaction to the crony politics of the Banharn and Chavalit administrations and a return to rule by the Democrat Party, with its more reformist ambitions. The crisis also helped mobilize support for sweeping constitutional change. Nonetheless, a combination of social and business protest, the Democrats' reliance on more traditional parties for support, and the fractious nature of coalition politics made policymaking in Thailand difficult, slow-moving, and ultimately timid.

South Korea

Following Kim Dae Jung's election on 18 December, both international and domestic concern about South Korea centered on the management of the transition, and the danger that policymaking would drift. The IMF program signed in early December had failed to stabilize the won, and fears quickly centered on whether the Christmas Eve package would suffer a similar fate. With two months before the inauguration (25 February), a power vacuum at the center or conflict between the outgoing and incoming leaders would have had devastating consequences.

The conditions surrounding Kim Dae Jung's victory did not appear particularly auspicious for effective crisis management. Kim's margin of victory against ruling party candidate Lee Hoi Chang was extremely narrow (40.3 vs. 38.7 percent), and he was elected with only a plurality of total votes cast.[10] The non-concurrence of presidential and legislative elections raised the possibility of deadlock; from his first day in office, Kim Dae Jung's ruling coalition would face divided government.

Political circumstances appeared inauspicious for a second set of reasons as well. Because of his long history as an opposition figure and his identification with the poor, Kim Dae Jung appeared to be a populist. Both the international financial institutions and the United States viewed his election with some concern, particularly following his remarks about the need to reexamine the IMF program.

In fact, the international community had an extremely poor understanding of Kim Dae Jung. Kim's diagnosis of South Korea's problems was surprisingly orthodox and emphasized both the failures of state interven-

---

10. Kim Dae Jung's support was also geographically concentrated. In his home province, he received 95 percent of the vote; outside it, his average vote share was only 30 percent (Jaung 2000). Moreover, his victory was only possible because of an unlikely alliance between Kim Dae Jung's National Congress for New Politics (NCNP) and conservative Kim Jong Pil and his United Liberal Democrats (ULD)—a marriage of convenience that raised the specter of intra-coalitional conflict.

tion and the need for political checks on government. His analysis of the crisis in his book *DJnomics* (D. J. Kim 1999) notes the short-term problems of mismanaged liberalization and loss of confidence by foreign investors, but gives greater weight to the failure to develop "the rules and principles of a market economy [and] failing to implement structural reform policies consistent with changes in the international environment" (10). Kim strongly underlined the problems of moral hazard and corruption, and he traced them back to political factors that impeded the operation of the market: "one is unwarranted influence from political power figures and bureaucrats; the other is monopolistic and other anti-competitive behavior within the market" (31).

The solution to the first problem was to be found in more effective democracy. "Democracy supports the development of the market by preventing activities like corruption and collusive ties between the government and businesses . . ." (35). Problems of moral hazard, corruption, and collusion required regulation, but would also be addressed by making the economy more market-oriented: "opening and expanding competition within the market is critical for eliminating preferential treatment and irregularities that fundamentally distort the economic order" (32). In his often-used phrase, "democracy and the market economy are like two sides of the same coin" (35).

Kim Dae Jung was able to make substantial progress on his program by exploiting the crisis and his political assets wisely at the outset of his administration. Two days after the election, Kim Young Sam and Kim Dae Jung met and formed a joint 12-member Emergency Economic Committee (ECC). For the 2 months before the inauguration, this body, made up of six members from the outgoing and incoming governments but effectively under the president-elect's control, served as the de facto economic cabinet. Kim's coalition (NCNP and ULD) and the majority GNP also agreed to convene a special session of the National Assembly to deal with a series of reform bills required under both the original IMF program and its 24 December revision; two further special sessions followed (see table 3.3). As a result of these institutional agreements, Kim Dae Jung enjoyed an unusual executive and legislative position. Not only did he and his advisors effectively control the cabinet, but they also enjoyed a legislative majority because of the ability of Kim Young Sam and Lee Hoi Chang to deliver GNP cooperation in the National Assembly.

The importance of these arrangements for the course of South Korea's economic reform cannot be exaggerated. Table 3.3 suggests the range of the reforms passed during the special legislative sessions held during the transition. Of particular importance were financial reforms that had been stalled under the previous government. Although controversy continued to surround this legislation (see chapter 4), the government did succeed in creating a new financial regulatory agency and delegating substantial power to it.

Table 3.3 Reform legislation passed during the transition period, South Korea, 1997-98

Session	Legislation approved
186th (22-30 December, 1997)	Act Establishing Financial Supervisory Institution Bank of Korea Act (r) Bank Act (r) Act Concerning the Restructuring of Financial Industries (r) Security Exchange Act (r) Insurance Act (r) Mutual Trust Company Act (r) Depositor Insurance Act (r) Merchant Bank Act (r) Forward Business Act (r) Act concerning the Abolition of the Interest Rates Limits Special Consumption Tax Act (r) Act Concerning the External Auditing of the Corporation (r)
187th (15-21 January, 1998)	Session called to consider labor legislation, but defers to Tripartite Commission
188th (2-16 February, 1998)	Bankruptcy Act (r) Corporate Composition Law (r) Corporate Reorganization Law (r) Monopoly Regulation and Fair Trade Act (r) Foreign Investment and Foreign Capital Investment Act (r) Corporate Tax Act (r) Tax Reduction Act (r) Labor Standards Act (r) Employment Adjustment Act (r) Government Organization Act (r)

(r) = revised.
Source: Office of the Secretary, National Assembly.

But the Kim administration did not rely solely on legislation to initiate reform; it also created corporatist arrangements—albeit temporary ones—that permitted negotiation with business and labor. This strategy had a number of objectives, including placing pressure on the groups to make concessions and facilitating tradeoffs among them. The corporatist strategy also circumvented the legislative problems that would arise from working in a context of divided government; it would be hard for the now-opposition GNP to oppose reforms to which the major interest groups had already agreed.

Exploiting the unpopularity of *chaebol* management, their short-term financial weakness, and his relative political independence from them, Kim Dae Jung used an ad hoc meeting with the heads of the top 5 *chaebol* on 13 January, and on 6 February with heads of 30 others, to outline an agreement on five principles of corporate restructuring. The ambitious agenda of the early meetings (see table 3.4) reveals clearly that the govern-

Table 3.4 Five principles of corporate restructuring, South Korea

Objective	Measures	Schedule
Enhanced transparency	Adoption of combined financial statements	FY1999
	Adoption of international accounting principles	October 1998
	Strengthening voting rights of minority shareholders	May 1998
	Compulsory appointment of outside directors	February 1998
	Establishment of external auditors committee	February 1998
Resolution of cross-debt guarantees	Resolution of existing cross-debt guarantees	March 2000
	No new cross-debt guarantees between subsidiaries	April 1998
Improvement of financial structure	Agreement with banks to improve capital structure	April 1998
	Removal of restrictions of capital infusions	February 1998
	Introduction of asset-backed securities	August 1998
Streamlining business activities	Adoption of corporate-split system	June 1998
	Liberalization of foreign ownership of real estate	June 1998
	Full liberalization of mergers & acquisitions	May 1998
	Streamlining of bankruptcy procedures	February 1998
Strengthening accountability	Strengthen the legal liability of controlling owners	June 1998
	Introduction of cumulative voting systems	June 1998
	Allowing institutional voters rights	June 1998

FY = fiscal year.

Source: Reference Information: the Korea Forum, Ministry of Finance and Economy, October 1998.

ment's motives were political as well as economic; namely, to increase the transparency and accountability of the *chaebol*.

The political pressure to "do something" about the *chaebol* was closely related to another area of structural reform that was also to prove highly contentious: increasing the flexibility of the labor market while guaranteeing an adequate social safety net for adversely affected workers. To reach agreement on these issues, Kim Dae Jung resorted to a mechanism that Kim Young Sam had attempted without success (Kim and Lim 1999)— the tripartite commission.[11] The unions were aware from the beginning

---

11. The formation of the group was closely related to legislative politics. The government called a special session of the National Assembly (the 187th) to amend existing labor legislation to allow layoffs, but the GNP was reluctant to cooperate because of the potential political price; the National Assembly thus deferred to the tripartite commission.

that the objective of the commission was to extract labor concessions on the issue of layoffs. However, Kim Dae Jung's status with labor and the promise of political as well as economic compensation allowed the government to bring representatives from both labor federations (FKTU and KCTU) to the table.[12] Government-labor relations on social issues turned more stormy over time, but the tripartite mechanism did serve to secure some important reform legislation (see chapter 6).

In addition to his economic program, Kim Dae Jung also had an ambitious administrative reform agenda designed to create a "smaller but more efficient government." The central thrust of the administrative reforms (January-February 1998 and May 1999) was to reduce the size of the public sector by eliminating agencies and even whole ministries and to reallocate powers away from traditional ministries that had exercised substantial influence over economic policy in the past (E. Kim 1999). The Ministry of Finance and Economy was a particular target; it was stripped both of its budget powers (to a Planning and Budget Commission directly under the president and an independent Office of the National Budget) and most of its financial supervisory functions (to the Financial Supervisory Agency; see chapter 4). The Fair Trade Commission also saw its powers enhanced.

In sum, the period of transition was an extremely fertile one. Kim Dae Jung exploited the crisis and the unusual institutional circumstances to push through wide-ranging reform legislation, the most important part of which was the creation of a new supervisory agency, the Financial Supervisory Commission, which had substantial powers with respect to the management of the financial crisis. The president also exploited his stature and public opinion to strike agreements with both the *chaebol* and labor on wide-ranging adjustment measures, using concessions from each to gain concessions from the other in a kind of grand bargain.

Once this initial burst of reform activity was launched, the problems shifted from initiation to implementation, and the government began to face increasing political constraints. The greatest concern of the government was the high level of unemployment that accompanied the crisis; of the four most seriously affected countries, South Korea experienced the sharpest increase in unemployment.

But the government also faced important electoral constraints. Presidential, legislative, and subnational elections are non-concurrent in Korea. As a result, policymaking during the first 18 months of Kim Dae Jung's presidency took place under the shadow of elections that were cast as referenda on the government's reform efforts. The president's NCNP-

12. The tripartite structure included the major business associations (the Federation of Korean Industries and the Korean Employers' Federation), government officials (the Ministry of Finance and Economy and the Ministry of Labor) and representatives from each of the four major parties.

ULD alliance sought to use the elections to confirm public support for reform; the opposition GNP, by contrast, sought to discredit the government's efforts.

The results of early by-elections are difficult to interpret because of the powerful effect of region on voting behavior,[13] but the subnational elections of June 1998 were a nationwide contest and were read as a referendum on his government's performance in its first 6 months. The results outside of Seoul tracked regional bases of support to a large degree, but the president's victory in Seoul provided a mandate to continue and deepen the reform process. Shortly after the election, the government unveiled another round of reform measures (*Far Eastern Economic Review*, 18 June 1998, 24).

The June elections were also significant because of the effect they had on realignment within the National Assembly. After his inauguration, inter-party cooperation fell apart and the deadlock of divided government emerged.[14] This deadlock ultimately proved politically costly for the opposition (GNP), because divided government gave the president's (NCNP-ULD) coalition strong incentives to woo opposition legislators. The president was not above using the powers of his office, including prosecutorial powers, to persuade opposition legislators to defect (Diamond and Shinn 2000, 26). This effort finally proved successful in early September 1998, when the NCNP-ULD coalition won a majority. Another round of reform legislation followed.[15]

The survey data that we have from around this time (October 1998) suggest that the government was not wrong to believe it had a mandate to pursue reform, despite the depth of the crisis. Shin and Rose (1998) found that 32 percent of respondents ($n = 1,010$) were very or somewhat satisfied with the president's handling of the crisis, while 26 percent were somewhat or very dissatisfied; the remainder were neither satisfied nor dissatisfied (39 percent) or didn't know (3 percent). However, fully 63 percent believed that "economic reforms have to be pursued, even if it means significant hardship for people like you," and 45 percent believed

---

13. E.g., the 2 April by-election to fill four National Assembly seats was the first by-election under the new government, but the seats were contested in Kyongsang Province, where ruling party support was weak; the government coalition did not carry a single seat (*Korea Herald*, 4 April 1998).

14. The opposition in the National Assembly was unwilling to confirm Kim Dae Jung's appointment of Kim Jong Pil as prime minister; the president appointed him as acting prime minister and named his first cabinet on 3 March. Nonetheless, until August, when the GNP finally relented, every National Assembly session was dominated by unproductive controversy over the confirmation issue, blocking a number of other legislative initiatives (E. Kim 1999).

15. The coalition continued to expand thereafter, and as of August 1999, the NCNP held 105 seats, the UDL 55, and the opposition GNP 135, with 4 independents.

that the IMF had helped economic recovery either a lot (5 percent) or somewhat (40 percent), with another 33 percent saying "half and half"; only 12 percent believed that the IMF had hurt prospects of recovery.

Nonetheless, the second honeymoon provided by the June 1998 elections and the legislative majority also had limits. Kim Dae Jung reshuffled the cabinet in May 1999 to support a second round of administrative reforms (B-K. Kim 1999). But a series of corruption scandals broke in the middle of the year, and the opposition GNP capitalized on public resentment to soundly defeat the NCNP and ULD candidates in by-elections held on 3 June.[16]

The administration's attention increasingly shifted to political reform, and particularly to the question of how to reduce corruption and regionalism. Ongoing problems of corruption were linked to the rising costs of electoral politics, which in turn were attributed to the winner-take-all nature of single-member legislative districts. But the administration's efforts to sell multiple-member National Assembly districts were seen as self-interested by both the opposition and the NCNP's own UDL partners.[17]

By late 1999, the looming National Assembly elections of April 2000 made it difficult to initiate new economic or political reforms. Rather, Kim Dae Jung turned his hand to foreign policy with the dramatic announcement of the North-South summit just weeks prior to the election. The significance of the elections for the economic reform process is by no means straightforward. On the one hand, the elections were interpreted in Korea as a victory for the opposition GNP, which gained several seats, and a setback for Kim Dae Jung's coalition. The GNP had tried to capitalize on a number of unpopular policy reform measures including the privatization of state-owned enterprises and the sale of Daewoo to foreigners.

On the other hand, voting continued to be driven primarily by regional factors, the GNP did not secure a majority in the National Assembly, and

---

16. The scandals were for the most part small in scale, but undercut the administration's strong stance against corruption. Newly appointed Justice Minister Kim Tae Joung became embroiled in the "boutique scandal"; his wife had received expensive clothing from those seeking influence during his tenure as prosecutor general. Kim Dae Jung initially decided to retain him, but reversed his position following the by-elections in June. Longtime economic advisor North Cholla Governor You Jong Keun was forced to resign from his advisor position following a report that $120,000 in cash had been stolen from his house, leading to suspicion of corruption. The new environment minister, Son Sook, an actress, was forced to resign on 24 June after it was discovered that she had accepted $20,000 from Korean businesses (Economist Intelligence Unit, *EIU Country Report: Korea*, 3rd quarter 1999, 16; *Korea Herald*, 5 June 1999).

17. The ruling party's solution for regionalism was to form more broadly based political parties, in the first instance through a merger of the NCNP and UDL; however, this plan also fell through, and the NCNP was left to undertake a party reorganization on its own (*Newsreview*, 4 September 1999, 5).

the losses to Kim Dae Jung's coalition came not from his party—which actually gained seats—but from his smaller UDL coalition partner. Kim Dae Jung's new Millennium Democratic Party enjoyed the political benefits of economic recovery, and despite typical election posturing the two parties did not in fact divide sharply on issues of economic policy. In a post-election interview, GNP leader Lee Hoi even criticized the government for not being decisive enough in addressing problems in the financial sector (*Far Eastern Economic Review*, 18 May 2000, 22) and Kim Dae Jung immediately reconfirmed his commitment to completing the reform process. If not a resounding victory for the president, the elections provide little evidence of backlash either.

The crisis in South Korea brought a strongly reformist president to office. Kim Dae Jung aggressively (and sometimes controversially) exploited his powers and public support to push through a number of policy and institutional reforms early in his administration. In the face of divided government, he used consultative mechanisms to secure business and labor support, sometimes, as we will see, for measures of questionable legality (chapter 4). He sought to enhance the powers of independent regulatory agencies (e.g., the Fair Trade Commission and particularly the Financial Supervisory Commission) in support of his program. Kim Dae Jung's style raised important questions about the accountability of strong presidents, but dispels the notion that democratic governments are incapable of providing support for decisive policy action.

Malaysia

Malaysia is the one country of the four examined here where the crisis did not produce a change of government. If the crisis generated political change in Malaysia, it appeared to be in the direction of increasing concentration of authority in the hands of the prime minister and creeping authoritarianism. The dismissal of Anwar Ibrahim left Mahathir serving not only as prime minister, but also as home minister and finance minister, and provided him with the opportunity to appoint a close protégé who had headed the controversial privatization program to the position of central bank governor. Following Anwar's arrest, Mahathir purged the party of a number of Anwar supporters, and left the deputy prime minister position open, forcing loyalty on any who might have ambition to succeed him (*Far Eastern Economic Review*, 15 October 1998, 18). The government effectively contained the spread of protests and demonstrations, including through the use of force, and used a variety of both legal and legally questionable means to limit the growth of the opposition. Anwar's trial raised serious questions about the integrity of the judiciary and police in the country,[18] but it ended in a 6-year sentence that removed his most serious challenger from the scene. In November 1999, Mahathir called snap elections, and the National Front government was not only returned to office but also retained a substantial legislative majority.

Yet if the crisis did not lead to a change of government in Malaysia, economic developments nonetheless had an important bearing on politics after the fall of Anwar. Although the opposition was strongly motivated by the Anwar case and called for political reform, it also sought to highlight the government's economic failures, ongoing problems of business-government relations and corruption, and social inequality. Despite overwhelming odds, the opposition coalition (Barisan Alternatif, or Alternative Front) made gains in the 1999 election and is forcing important realignments in Malaysian politics.

The period under consideration here begins on 2 September 1998 with Anwar's dismissal from the government. Anwar did not go quietly; rather, he took his case to the public through a series of rallies in various parts of the country in the first three weeks of September 1998. Anwar's speeches during this period naturally focused on the political motivations behind his dismissal; but at the same time, he returned to broader themes that were very much related to the economic crisis, including misuse of UMNO funds, executive intervention in investigations by the Anti-Corruption Agency, the bailout of favored companies, and nepotism.[19]

On 20 September, Anwar was detained without trial under the Internal Security Act (ISA), and his wife, Wan Azizah, was prohibited from speaking in public or holding political gatherings in her home.[20] In the weeks

---

18. The initial charges against Anwar were twofold: first, that he had committed sodomy and adultery; and second, that he had abused his office by trying to cover up his behavior. However, shortly after the trial began, one of the witnesses for the prosecution, head of the police intelligence branch Mohamad Said Awang, testified that the sexual charges were "baseless" and that there was in fact a conspiracy to smear Anwar's reputation. A second prosecution witness retracted allegations that were key to the sexual misconduct case, and in December the prosecution was forced to drop those charges, leaving the allegations of abuse of office as the core of the first trial. The trial on sexual conduct was launched in June, but was suspended before the November 1999 elections. In January 1998, the attorney general was forced to admit that the police chief was responsible for Anwar's injuries while in custody. The presiding judge's use of contempt charges against the defense team raised concerns about intimidation, and led the bar association to issue a call in late 1999 for an inquiry into judicial independence; they were subsequently enjoined from even debating the issue in a ruling that suggested that such debate might even fall under the Sedition Act. The major documents of the first trial, including the judgments, are contained in *Malayan Law Journal 1999*. A useful chronology of the trial can be found on BBC Online at http://news.bbc.co.uk/hi/english/special report/1998/10/98/malaysia crisis.

19. See Anwar's speech of 20 September 1998, as translated in the Internet newsgroup at http://www.soc.culture.malaysia (this site may now be defunct).

20. During the next 10 days, 17 of Anwar's supporters were also detained, although all but 2 were subsequently released.

that followed, the loosely organized protest movement brought together a diverse set of political forces, from Muslims disaffected by the treatment of Anwar, to portions of the urban middle class, to social activists, grass-roots organizations, and NGOs seeking to capitalize on the crisis (Case 1999, 6-7). This movement crested with large antigovernment demonstrations in October.

The police broke up these demonstrations, on occasion with force. The government also made it clear that it would use its full battery of legal weapons to deter an expansion of antigovernment protests.[21] Demonstrations flared again in February (following the finding that Anwar had in fact been beaten by a police official while in custody), in April (when Anwar was sentenced), and in September (the first anniversary of Anwar's arrest). But these demonstrations were not of a magnitude or momentum to threaten the regime or produce the splits within the government or military and police visible in Indonesia. In each case, they were broken up by the police.[22]

Nonetheless, the combination of the crisis and political developments did contribute to the formation of a new opposition in Malaysia, and the strengthening of existing opposition parties. The first organized response to Anwar's dismissal was the formation of the Social Justice Movement (Pergerakan Keadilan Social, or ADIL) by Anwar's wife, Wan Azizah, in December 1998 and then the National Justice Party (Keadilan) the following April. The central thrust of the multi-ethnic, multi-religious movement and party was clearly political: to defend political and civil liberties and "to check the present dangerous slide towards one-man rule where all institutions of governance are directed towards preserving the power of a certain individual." However, these themes extended to the abuse of power, corruption, and the concentration of wealth. From jail, Anwar also continued to stress economic as well as political themes, including opposition to costly "megaprojects," such as the Bakun dam and Kuala Lumpur light rail system, lack of transparency in awarding privatization contracts, and the bailout of connected companies (*Far Eastern Economic Review*, 8 April 1999, 24-26).

The UMNO confronted an even more important challenge from the Islamic Party (PAS), with its stronghold in the northern part of the penin-

---

21. These weapons included denial of police permits (making rallies illegal), arrests, threatened use of the Societies Act (which permits up to 5-year imprisonment for those involved in managing unregistered groups), and the Universities and University Colleges Act (which prohibits students from engaging in opposition political activity).

22. Other forms of opposition activity were also attacked. Efforts to ferret out government and business malfeasance and corruption were countered with extraordinary lawsuits under the country's liberal libel laws, the press was subject to heightened scrutiny (and self-censorship), and even the efforts of opposition groups to use the Internet were frustrated by filters and blocks (Case 1999, 12).

sula.[23] The PAS embraced more fundamentalist Islamic positions in the first half of the 1980s. But this line reduced the party's electoral appeal, and it gradually swung back toward a more moderate line in the 1990s that resonated with a wider political audience, including urban Malay professionals and business people. The party did not shed its longer-run religious ambitions, but the platforms of the 1990s emphasized "questions of ethical values, greater egalitarianism, free and fair elections, governmental transparency, the preservation of the environment [and] the repeal of unjust laws (particularly the Internal Security Act). . . " (Hussein 2000, 30).

On 20 November 1999, Mahathir called snap elections (elections were required by April 2000). Calling the general elections early capitalized on increasing signs of economic recovery and the ability to exclude an estimated 600,000 younger voters who had registered but would not be eligible to vote until 2000. The National Front had a number of advantages, including superior financing, close ties with both Malay and Chinese business, and extensive grass-roots organization through the UMNO and its allied parties. The National Front effectively controlled the dominant broadcast and print media. Control of government also meant control of electoral districting and a highly disproportionate electoral system.[24] The ruling coalition enjoyed the cushion of a number of safe constituencies, so many in fact that they could lose more than half of the popular vote and still retain not only a legislative majority but also the supermajority (two-thirds) required to engineer constitutional changes.

The four opposition parties—PAS, DAP, the new Justice Party, and the small Malaysian People's Party—labored under a number of their own disabilities in forming an electoral coalition, the Alternative Front. The PAS had demonstrated strength in the northern states of Kelantan, Terengganu, Perlis, and Kedah, and controlled the state government of Kelantan, the only one of Malaysia's 13 states not run by the ruling coalition. A number of indicators, such as the sales of the PAS newspaper *Harakah*, indicated that the party was breaking into more middle-class urban Malay

---

23. The UMNO has always defined itself as a defender of Islam, but after the PAS left the ruling coalition in 1979, the party paid increasing attention to Islamic issues. Anwar, who had been the leader of a Muslim student organization (Malaysian Islamic Youth Movement, or ABIM) was invited to join the party in 1982, precisely to help the UMNO project an image that was both Islamic but at the same time progressive, moderate, and modern in its outlook.

24. Proportionality in electoral systems refers to the correlation between the share of the popular vote and the share of legislative or parliamentary seats; in a perfectly proportional system, the shares are identical. In disproportional systems, a given vote share is reflected in higher and lower share of seats, and can frequently result in "manufactured majorities," in which popular vote shares of less than 50 percent nonetheless produce legislative or parliamentary majorities. Virtually all electoral systems have some degree of disproportionality, although highly disproportional systems raise questions of basic fairness.

districts as well. Yet despite the gradual moderation of the PAS's rhetoric, the party had a minority fundamentalist wing to contend with and had only come recently to the idea of forming alliances and even having non-Muslim members. The National Front had the weapon of previous PAS party manifestos advocating the imposition of the *sharia* and other radical measures, a weapon that it did not hesitate to use.

The Chinese-dominated DAP had long criticized the government along lines strikingly similar to the PAS's and Anwar's, highlighting issues of creeping authoritarianism and corruption.[25] But at the same time, they had also long opposed ethnic favoritism; this was the key issue that differentiated them from the Malaysian Chinese Association (MCA), which was a member of the National Front coalition and continued to receive a majority of the Chinese vote. Yet despite these potential divisions, the four parties did agree on a common platform that downplayed religion and emphasized common political and economic themes: political reform, including of the state security apparatus, as well as reform of business-government relations and elimination of corruption.[26]

But on the crucial issues of ethnicity and religion, the DAP and the PAS were anything but natural allies, and the National Front exploited this point ruthlessly in its campaign. The ruling coalition raised the specter of Islamic fundamentalism, ethnic conflict, and even social violence. Some segments of the Chinese community recognized that Malay disaffection with the handling of the Anwar case and the economy enhanced their leverage vis-à-vis the National Front. In August, a group of important Chinese associations issued a list of 17 demands, which tracked the *reform-asi* agenda in important regards, including both political reforms (advancing democracy and human rights, restoring confidence in the police) and economic ones (making the privatization policy more transparent, reducing corruption) (*Straits Times*, 2 September 1999; *New Straits Times*, 24 September 1999). In the end, however, fears about the PAS outweighed whatever distaste some Chinese might have had for the National Front and UMNO, and the Chinese swing vote played a role in the National Front victory.

At one level, the election showed the continuing power of the National Front. Despite both the economic crisis and the handling of the Anwar case, the coalition still managed to secure 56 percent of the popular vote and 76 percent of legislative seats. But this was a long fall from its commanding performance in the 1995 elections, and only marginally better

---

25. The writings of Lim Kit Siang are exemplary; see Lim Kit Siang 1998.

26. Like the National Front, they also managed to coordinate electoral strategy within the coalition so that Alternative Front candidates from different parties did not contest the same districts: 152 of 193 parliamentary contests and 367 of 394 state seats were one-on-one contests between the National and Alternative fronts, the highest in history (*Straits Times*, 21 November 1999).

Table 3.5 Popular vote share of the National Front, Malaysia, 1969-99 (percent)

1969	1974	1978	1982	1986	1990	1995	1999
45	61	57	61	58	53	65	56

Table 3.6 Election results in Malaysia, 1995 and 1999

	Parliament		State assembly	
	1995	1999	1995	1999
Barisan Nasional	161	148	335	281
Parti Islam	7	27	35	98
Democratic Action Party	9	10	12	11
Semangat46	6	0	12	0
Parti Bersatu Sabah	8	3	0	0
Keadilan	0	5	0	4
Total	**192**	**193**	**394**	**394**
Barisan Nasional percentage of total	83.8	76.7	85.0	71.3
Opposition, percentage of total	16.2	23.3	15.0	28.7

Note: Includes one direct candidate in 1995 parliamentary with opposition.
Sources: Straits Times, 27 April 1995; 1 December 1999.

than in the elections of 1990, during which government and UMNO corruption had also been an issue (see tables 3.5 and 3.6).

Moreover, underneath the aggregates were some trends that called the UMNO's dominance into question. The National Front as a whole lost 13 seats, but the UMNO lost 16 seats, including no fewer than five ministers. Important regional shifts were also visible, particularly in the Malay heartland of the North (see table 3.7). The UMNO won no parliamentary seats in Trengganu (8 seats); only 1 in Kelantan (14 seats); and only 7 of 15 in Kedah, the prime minister's home state. This partisan and regional shift was even more evident in the battle for state-level assembly seats.[27]

Disaggregating the vote says something about the opposition as well. The new Keadilan Party managed to win five parliamentary seats, including the symbolically significant victory of Wan Azizah in Anwar Ibrahim's

---

27. The Barisan Nasional held 335 state assembly seats in peninsular Malaysia before the election but only 281 after. Virtually all of the losses came out of the UMNO. The PAS continued to hold the Kelantan state government, but the oil-rich state of Terenganu also fell to the PAS. Pahang and Perak saw sharp increases in the number of opposition seats in the state assembly.

Table 3.7 Election results in peninsular Malaysia by state, 1995 and 1999 (parliamentary seats)

State	Barisan Nasional		Opposition parties		Banisan Nasional as percentage of total	
	1995	1999	1995	1999	1995	1999
Perlis	3	3	0	0	100.0	100.0
Kedah	15	7	0	8	100.0	46.7
Kelantan	2	1	12	14	14.3	7.1
Trengganu	7	1	1	7	87.5	12.5
Pahang	11	11	0	0	100.0	100.0
Kuala Lumpur	6	6	4	4	60.0	60.0
Johor	20	20	0	0	100.0	100.0
Malacca	4	4	1	1	80.0	80.0
North Sembilan	7	7	0	0	100.0	100.0
Selangor	17	17	0	0	100.0	100.0
Perak	23	20	0	3	100.0	87.0
Penang	8	6	3	5	72.7	54.5
Total	123	103	21	42	84.8	71.0
State assembly						
Perlis	15	12	0	3	100.0	80.0
Kedah	34	24	2	11	94.4	66.6
Kelantan	5	2	38	41	11.6	4.7
Trengganu	25	4	7	28	78.1	12.5
Pahang	37	30	1	8	97.4	78.9
Johor	40	40	0	0	100.0	100.0
Malacca	22	21	3	4	88.0	84.0
North Sembilan	29	32	3	0	90.6	100.0
Selangor	45	42	3	6	93.8	87.5
Perak	51	44	1	8	98.1	84.6
Penang	32	30	1	3	97.0	90.9
Total	335	281	59	113	85.0	71.1

Note: One direct candidate in 1995 not allocated by state.

Sources: Straits Times, 27 April 1995, 1 December 1999.

old district. But the party struggled and was divided in the post-election period over the question of how to define an identity that transcended the issue of Anwar. The biggest gainer in the election was clearly the PAS, which displaced the DAP as the largest opposition party. The decline of the DAP can be traced directly to the difficulties of forging the Alternative Front. Malays who opposed the government might still vote against the Alternative Front if they were uncomfortable with either the DAP's nonracial stance or PAS's Islamic positions. Chinese voters forced to choose between the PAS and the National Front clearly preferred the latter, but many abandoned the DAP as well. In the days before the elections, peak Chinese and Indian business associations publicly backed the National Front, as did the main non-Islamic interfaith council (Malaysian Council of Buddhism, Christianity, Hinduism, and Sikhism) (*Straits Times*, 30 November 1999).[28]

The immediate aftermath of the election suggested continuity in Malaysian politics. If we return to the political factors highlighted in table 3.1, electoral pressures had passed, the government had contained antigovernment protest, and the private sector had signaled its support for the Barisan Nasional government. The new cabinet exhibited strong signs of continuity, for example in the inclusion of Daim Zainuddin. In the spring of 2000, Mahathir drew on the loyalty of party regulars to smother a leadership challenge within the UMNO, reconfirming both his personal dominance of the party and the status of his chosen successor, Abdullah Ahmad Badawi.

Over the intermediate run, the government would have to address the issues of race and religion raised once again by the election, perhaps by accommodating PAS's religious demands at the margin or by reinvigorating the ethnic preferences of the New Economic Policy. But a postmortem by a Malaysian politician, Abdullah Ahmad (1999), reveals an alternative, less sanguine interpretation of the election within some factions of the National Front government:

> [N]otwithstanding [the government's economic successes], old issues related to business and the economy must be re-addressed. Efforts must be redoubled to lessen corruption and wear away the links between business and politics . . . Moreover, the government and companies can do with greater transparency and a higher standard of governance—you can't have too much of either. This would go a long way in bettering citizens' quality of life and buttress their individual freedom. Indeed, Umno must be well aware that the latter has economic payback: Protecting freedoms creates conditions that allow innovation and creativity to flourish. . .(31)

Indonesia

If Malaysia provides a case study of a nondemocratic regime that survived the crisis intact, Indonesia shows how crises can, under different circumstances, have the opposite effect. We have already seen in chapter 2 how a sequence of political events—questions about Suharto's health and the succession, the emergence of the opposition, the presidential election, and increasing protest—complicated economic policymaking. Yet the causal arrows also work in reverse. Economic circumstances contributed to

---

28. An analysis of 144 electoral districts for which we have information on ethnic composition is revealing. The National Front carried 83 percent of the districts that were more than 30 percent Chinese (53 of 63), 75 percent of the districts that were more than 40 percent Chinese (31 of 41), and even managed to carry 63 percent of the districts that were more than 50 percent Chinese (15 of 24). In the aftermath of the election, both the DAP and the Keadilan expressed bitter disappointment about the defection of Chinese voters.

Suharto's fall and the initiation of a gradual process of democratic reform under Habibie. We begin with a brief analysis of the political consequences of the crisis and why it had such different effects in Indonesia than Malaysia, before turning to the achievements and failings of the Habibie government and the nature of the opposition that ultimately deposed it.

Indonesian politics under Suharto could never be construed as open or democratic, but in the late 1980s the government briefly signaled a political opening. Following the general elections of 1992 (in which support for Golkar slipped) and Suharto's indirect election in March 1993, politics turned back in a more authoritarian direction. Suharto centralized power within both the government and the ruling Golkar. He initiated an extensive purge of the military that both divided the organization more sharply into "red and white" (secular-nationalist) and "green" (Islamic) factions, while promoting loyalists, including his son-in-law Prabowo Subianto. One of the two opposition parties allowed to operate—the Indonesian Democratic Party (PDI)—was brought to heel in 1996 by purging its charismatic leader, Megawati Sukarnoputri, and her followers.[29] Increased labor activism, including efforts to form a new political party, was met with repression, and the country's most respected independent publication, *Tempo*, was closed.

As in Malaysia, Suharto reached out to "modernist" Islam,[30] which was undergoing a similar revival: through Habibie and his Indonesian Association of Muslim Intellectuals; through cabinet appointments; and through promotions within the army (Schwarz 1999, 327-31). As we have seen in Malaysia, however, modernist Islam was not necessarily hostile either to democracy or to market-oriented reform, and indeed found religious grounds for supporting both. Amien Rais, chairman of the mainstream modernist Muhammidiyah organization (approximately 28 million members and supporters) was among the first of major opposition leaders to argue that the economic crisis could not be overcome as long as Suharto remained in office. He was also a constant critic of the regime's authoritarianism, corruption, and lack of attention to social justice.

The crisis and government efforts to co-opt modernist Islamic forces contributed to a different ethnic and political dynamic than in Malaysia.

---

29. The PDI was the result of a forced merger of nationalist and Christian parties. The second nongovernment party allowed to operate in New Order Indonesia was the PPP (Partai Persatuan Pembanguan, or United Development Party), which appealed to an Islamic constituency.

30. "Traditionalist" Muslims, generally found in less affluent rural areas, are socially conservative, but also less sectarian, more pluralist, and even secular in their view of relations between Islamic organizations and the state. They were represented by the Nahdlatul Ulama (NU; approximately 40 million members and supporters), headed by Abdurrahman Wahid (Gus Dur), who was periodically critical of the Suharto government and ultimately succeeded Habibie as president. "Modernist" Muslims, by contrast, are more urban, wealthy, and

With the Chinese constituting between 25 and 30 percent of the Malaysian population, the National Front coalition headed by the UMNO had an interest in courting Chinese financial and electoral support and keeping a lid on ethnic polarization. In Indonesia, by contrast, some of the more radical Islamic groups and individuals that had gained access to the government in the 1990s were openly hostile to the Chinese, and went so far as to blame them for the crisis (Schwarz 1999, 345-48). The Chinese business community thus found itself in a much more vulnerable position vis-à-vis the government than in Malaysia. With no political channels through which to air grievances, they voted through massive capital flight.

A second major difference with Malaysia was the inability of the government to control the scope of protest. The most important actors in this regard were the students, but they were eventually joined by other opposition groups and proto-parties. The movement was diverse and fragmented into a number of competing organizations (Aspinall 1999), but it united around a number of simple themes: reduction in prices of basic commodities; elimination of *korupsi, kolusi,* and *nepotisme* (KKN); and political reform. At a minimum, students demanded that Suharto step down; "radicals" argued for constitutional change, a reduction of the military's political role in government, and complete democratization. Student protests gained force in February in direct response to the collapse of the economy, strengthened again before the People's Consultative Assembly (MPR) session in March that elected Suharto, and exploded in May following the announcement of price increases on fuel and a number of other commodities. The killing of four students outside Triskati University on 12 May marked a critical turning point in the political crisis. The funerals the next day brought even larger student protests and were followed by the riots and social violence on 13-15 May that ultimately brought the Suharto era to an end.

The third and critical difference with Malaysia is that the combination of economic collapse, mounting protest, and the riots began to split the political elite; Mahathir never faced defections on this scale.[31] On 18 May, the speaker of the Parliament, a close associate, called on Suharto to step down, threatening impeachment proceedings if he did not. An effort by Suharto to form a new reform cabinet found no takers. The military appeared divided on how to handle the challenge of mounting protests, and Chief of Staff Wiranto finally came to support a transition to Habibie after rejecting the suggestion that the military take over directly. On 21 May, Suharto resigned.

---

formally educated, but also harbor more explicit religious objectives and champion in varying degrees the Islamization of government and supports for the *pribumi.*

31. The most credible account of the endgame is Schwarz (1999, chap. 11), but for a flavor of the rumors and plotting of the last days, see Mann's (1998b) more sensationalist account.

If we simply list the political constraints under which the new Habibie administration operated, it would be quite easy to predict complete political and policy immobilism (see table 3.1). The economy had yet to hit its nadir, which arrived with another round of rice price increases in September. Habibie faced challenges from the military, the ruling party, students, and newly emergent opposition parties. Even some legislators elected or selected under Suharto had an interest in distancing themselves from the new government.

In the second half of 1998, the *reformasi* movement, which had been concentrated largely in Jakarta and other major urban centers, spread rapidly throughout the country. Local movements challenged provincial and local officials and elites who had benefited from the ancien regime, eroding both the government's and Golkar's hold on the country. The economic crisis and reaction against the political and economic abuses of the old regime unleashed a wave of armed secessionism, social violence of various sorts, political confrontations, and crime. Although estimates must be treated with the appropriate degree of caution, table 3.8 provides some rough sense of the magnitude and geographic scope of the problem. Such social violence could not be traced solely to the crisis; 1997 witnessed an upsurge of such conflicts before the crisis broke and the major trouble spots—East Timor, Aceh, West Kalimantan—were of long standing (see, e.g., *Inside Indonesia*, April-June 1997, 6-8). But there can be little question that the crisis exacerbated old conflicts and created new ones. More than in any other country in the region, the economic crisis in Indonesia threatened the integrity of the country and its very basic social fabric.

However, Habibie was not without his own bases of support. In the first several months of his administration, he managed challenges from within the military by elevating General Wiranto—who supported constitutional processes during the succession—sidelining General Prabowo, and sanctioning a purge of a number of Suharto and Probowo loyalists (Crouch 1998). Habibie's cabinet, appointed on 22 May, kept 21 members of Suharto's. But it also jettisoned Suharto's daughter and the cronies and reached out to modernist Muslims and to respected technocrats who could mend fences with the international financial institutions (Schwarz 1999, 373; *Far Eastern Economic Review*, 25 June 1998, 24-25). Drawing on support from Wiranto and provincial leaders, Habibie was able to narrowly defeat his opponents in Golkar and install his ally Akbar Tandjung as head of the party. In 1999, he engineered Golkar's nomination for the presidency as well. Habibie had managed to assert his authority over, or at least strike bargains with, the military, a cadre of reformist technocrats, and the ruling party.

Managing the opposition was a much more daunting task. Student demonstrations continued in the early days following the transition, but were partly neutralized by counter-demonstrations from modernist Mus-

Table 3.8 Major social violence in Indonesia, 1998-99

Province or region	Locale, nature of violence, and dates	Estimated deaths 1998 to Nov. 1999
Aceh	Armed secessionist movement (Gerakan Aceh Merdeka [GAM] or Free Aceh Movement); ongoing clashes with military and opponents; large-scale refugee problem (>10,000)	>200
East Java	Banyuwangi, killing of Muslim clerics, late 1998	>200
East Nusa Tenggara	Kupang, burning and vandalization of mosques, November 1998	
East Nusa Tenggara	Sumba, riots and killing triggered by bureaucratic corruption and communal tensions (Loli and Wewewa Timur), November 1998	23
East Timor	Armed secessionist movement; ongoing clashes with military and militias; large-scale refugee problem (>100,000)	>200
Irian Jaya	Independence demonstrations, clashes with military and riots, July and October 1998	5 to 50
Jakarta	Riots and anti-Chinese violence, 13-15 May, 1998	>1,200
Jakarta	Student protests, 13 November, 1998	15
Jakarta	Communal violence (Ketapang; Muslim-Christian), November 1998	14
Maluccas	Communal violence in Ambon and other villages (Christian-Muslim, indigenous peoples, antimigrant), January 1999 to present; large-scale refugee problem (>200,000)	>1,500
Riau	Batam Island, communal violence (Batak and Flores migrants), August 1999	14
South Sulawesi	Antimigrant communal violence, September 1998 to January 1999	25
West Java	Ciamis, vigilantism and contract murders, early 1999	>50
West Kalimantan	Communal violence (Malays, Dayaks, and Muslim migrants), early 1999	>300
Various locations	Anti-Chinese violence over price increases in a number of cities and towns, in Java Sumatra, Sulawesi, Nusa Tenggara, Lombok, Sumbawa, and Flores; extensive property damage, February-March 1998	>10

Sources: Author's estimates from *Jakarta Post* and *Far Eastern Economic Review*, various issues, and Human Rights Watch (2000); For the Maluccas, *The Economist*, 15 January 2000, 17.

lim students supporting Habibie. Perhaps the biggest test for Habibie was the convocation of the Special Session of the MPR in November 1998, called to validate his proposed electoral reforms. The body was made up entirely of politicians elected or appointed under Suharto. As a result, the special session became a lightning rod for the opposition. Antigovernment protests increased again, and the MPR session ended in a confrontation between protestors and the military, military-controlled gangs, and other Habibie supporters that left 15 dead. These events further weakened the reputation of both the army and Habibie. But plans to use the Special Session as the opportunity to remove the new president immediately and form some sort of interim government faltered when the main opposition leaders failed to support it.

Habibie not only survived his first 6 months, but made it clear quite early his desire to stay in office. Given the depth of the crisis, the growing strength of the opposition, and the discrediting of the old regime, it was impossible to achieve this objective by insisting on the constitutionality of serving his full term (until 2003). Habibie's only hope was to remake himself as a political as well as economic reformer. There will long be debate over whether Habibie deserves credit for the political reforms that followed, or whether he was simply bowing to the inevitable in order to position himself for the 1999 elections. In either case, the reforms were sweeping, including most fundamentally freedom of association and expression. The government released a number of political detainees and prisoners, guaranteed press freedom, and ended restrictions on the formation of political parties, unions, and other associations.

Habibie also acknowledged that his government was a transitional one and established a timetable for elections under new rules: general elections for Parliament (DPR) and subnational governments by the middle of 1999, followed by the indirect election of the president by a new People's Consultative Assembly (MPR) later in the year (Masters 1999). The electoral rules and design of the two national representative institutions retained several features that biased outcomes at the margin in Habibie's and Golkar's favor.[32] Nonetheless, the changes in the electoral system

---

32. The most significant and controversial of these was the continuing, albeit reduced, participation of appointed military representatives in the two legislative bodies (although in the end their loyalty Habibie proved uncertain). Military representatives were to make up 8 percent of the DPR, and those representatives also sat in the larger MPR that would choose the president (and constituted 5.7 percent of it). The government also retained disproportionate (although not exclusive) influence over the constitution of the all-important electoral commission and in the appointment of 65 functional group representatives to the MPR (representing 9.3 percent of the body). Because of its continuing organizational strength at the subnational level, Golkar also appeared to gain from the inclusion of 135 provincial representatives in the MPR (19.3 percent of the body).

were deeply democratizing, and the main opposition endorsed them in their broad outlines.[33]

On the economic front, Habibie's position as reformer was more ambiguous, reflecting the tension between the need to work with the IMF and project a reformist image and the need to build a support base in the private sector. One of the central demands of the opposition in the wake of the crisis was to address the problem of KKN. This would require not only legal reform to improve governance and increase transparency in the future (Lubis and Santosa 1998), but also an effort to right past wrongs through a thorough investigation of the wealth of the Suharto family and their cronies. Habibie showed much greater willingness to undertake the first task than the second, on which he dragged his feet until the very end of his term. This reluctance was not simply a matter of personal loyalty to Suharto; it also reflected his ongoing links to private-sector groups that were critical to financing his political ambitions and that were ultimately to embroil his presidency in scandal (see chapter 4 on the Bank Bali scandal).

At the same time, Habibie was also under pressure from a variety of political forces that sought to exploit the crisis to advance ethnic redistribution (Schwartz 1999, 414-19). The central source of this effort within the government was Minister of Cooperatives Adi Sasono. He wanted to see assets taken over from failing banks transferred to his ministry for distribution to the cooperatives, which constituted a wide-ranging patronage machine for Golkar (*Far Eastern Economic Review*, 3 December 1998, 14-16). Such ideas also received support from indigenous business groups that stood to profit directly from preferential distribution of seized assets.[34]

As we will see in chapter 4, the result of these conflicting political pressures was a reform process characterized by fits and starts, as well as a number of irregularities. But Habibie's support for economic reform cannot simply be dismissed. He publicly embraced the IMF in his very first statement as president, and worked quickly and successfully to restart the structural adjustment initiatives that had stalled under Suharto. Habibie retained Ginanjar as chief economic minister, despite the fact that he openly called for new elections, and strengthened the independence of the central bank and the Indonesian Bank Restructuring Authority (Kenward 1999; chapter 5 of the present volume).

---

33. Moreover, although the government did not seek to revise the 1945 constitution, important institutional changes checked the central government, including limiting the president to two terms in office, revoking a number of his extraordinary powers, and recognizing the need for greater political and economic decentralization.

34. These included the Indonesia Association of Young Businessmen and the Indonesian Chamber of Commerce and Industry, and even some newly mobilized labor groups, such as the Indonesian Muslim Workers Brotherhood.

Habibie's commitment to restoring the confidence of the Chinese business community was ringed with reservations and thus the cause of somewhat greater concern.[35] However, on this front there were also signs of rapprochement. The Special Session of the MPR adopted an ambiguous resolution on a "democratic economy," but the government deflected language that would have instituted a Malaysian-style redistributive program. In any case, some of the concerns of the Chinese constituted special pleading, because a number of reforms would also strike at privileges held by crony Chinese-Indonesian businesses.

The convergence between the government and the opposition on a number of important reform issues can be seen in the eight-point Ciganjur Declaration signed by the three leading opposition figures, Megawati, Amien Rais, and Abdurrahman Wahid, on 10 November 1998 (Young 1998, 96-97) before the Special Session of the MPR. The declaration underscored commitment to democracy, honest elections, and decentralization of government. The "Big Three" also called for an end to the military's role in government ("dual function," or *dwifungsi*), but to be achieved gradually during 6 years. Only in its insistence on a full investigation of Suharto's wealth would Habibie have found anything objectionable in the declaration.

Thus, despite the depth of the crisis, the parliamentary elections of 1999 did not appear to yield much support for radical or "backlash" parties and candidates; rather, the elections would be fought over the broad center of Indonesian politics. What did that center look like?

A total of 48 parties ultimately qualified for the June parliamentary elections. All the parties supported the rule of law, greater regional autonomy (although there were subtle divisions on this point), rooting out corruption, and good governance. All supported democratic political processes, and the overwhelming majority acquiesced to the new rules of the game drafted under Habibie. The parties divided on three different axes (MacIntyre 1998; *Van Zorge Report*, 23 April 1999). The first and most basic was between Golkar—the incumbents—and the opposition. Although Golkar clearly lost members with the transition, it could still draw on its roots in the subnational administration and portions of the military, from Habibie's appeal to some modernist Muslims, and as a haven for those seeking some continuity with the past. Nonetheless, the party quickly recognized the disabilities of incumbent status and quickly democratized its structure, shed its connections with Suharto, and attempted to project a reformist image.

A second cleavage divided the opposition on the question of religion. Megawati's PDI-P party dominated the secular-nationalist camp, emphasizing ethnic and religious diversity, a clear separation of religion from

---

35. See, e.g., the interview in *Business Week*, 3 August 1999.

government, and nationalist ideals that could be traced back to Soekarno. "Mega" was also popular among the urban poor and projected a populist image, but this did not mean that she adopted a populist or redistributive economic line. To the contrary, her chief economic advisor, Kwik Gian Kie, had leveled criticisms of the Suharto and Habibie governments that were quite orthodox in their implications.

The Muslim camp—if it could even be called that—was anything but homogeneous (Nakamura 1999). Eighteen of the 48 parties identified themselves as Islamic. This number included parties that might be labeled "fundamentalist" in the sense of vigorously asserting an Islamic identity, in being strictly exclusivist, or in calling for redistribution. But the larger Islamic parties were busy crowding the center on issues of political and economic reform. Amien Rais' National Mandate Party (PAN) was the party that emphasized most strongly issues of social justice and had close ties to the modernist Islamic Muhammidayah organization; he also went further on issues of decentralization, advocating federalism. But at the same time, Rais' was also the party that reached out to policy intellectuals and progressive business interests and formulated the most sophisticated, market-oriented policy platform. Wahid's National Awakening party (PKB), with ties to the traditionalist Nahdlatul Ulama (NU) organization, did not develop a distinctive identity on economic questions beyond support for the general *reformasi* themes such as eliminating KKN. The same could be said for most of the other Islamic parties, which primarily sought to differentiate themselves on religious issues.

The results of the June election confirmed Megawati and her PDI-P as the dominant voice of the opposition and thus the natural candidate to succeed Habibie (see table 3.9). But although Megawati received a third of the popular vote, this translated into just 30 percent of the seats in the DPR and just over 26 percent in the MPR, only marginally higher than Habibie's Golkar. Clearly she would have to forge coalitions in the MPR to win, but with whom? Aligning with Golkar or conservative Islamic parties would be impossible, and some parties found the idea of a woman as president anathema. Aligning with Wahid—a close personal friend— made the most sense. But Amien Rais used his political skills to forge a highly tactical "Central Axis" that advanced Wahid as an alternative to both Habibie *and* Megawati.

The complex drama of the MPR need not detain us. Outside the hall, Megawati's supporters were converging on Jakarta, fearing that she would be denied the presidency and threatening a rampage if she did. Inside, Golkar and the Central Axis reached an agreement that gave Amien Rais the speakership of the MPR and Akbar Tanjung the leadership of the DPR; this was the first concrete sign that things were not going Megawati's way. When Habibie was ultimately forced to withdraw his candidacy and Golkar did not nominate an alternative, it set the stage for a straight

Table 3.9 Indonesian parliamentary elections, 7 June 1999

Party	Key figures	Percentage share of valid votes cast	Seats won in DPR	Percentage share of seats in DPR	Percentage share of related faction in MPR
Indonesian Democratic Party of Struggle (PDI-P)	Megawati	33.7	154	30.1	26.4
Golkar	B. J. Habibie, Akbar Tanjung	22.4	120	24.0	25.9
National Awakening Party (PKB)	A. Wahid (Gus Dur)	12.6	51	10.0	8.1
United Development Party (PPP)	Hamzah Haz	10.7	39	7.8	10.0
National Mandate Party (PAN)	Amien Rais	7.1	35	7.0	6.9
Justice and Unity Party (PKP)		1.0	6	1.2	2.0
Indonesian Democratic Party (PDI)		0.6	3	0.6	*
Crescent Star Party (PBB)		1.9	2	0.4	2.0
People's Rule Party (PDR)		0.4	2	0.4	*
Other parties and factions		9.4	50	10.0	2.0
Military	General Wiranto		38	7.6	5.4
Functional group representatives					10.4
Regional representatives					Distributed among other factions

* = included under "other parties."

Note: The MPR calls for 135 representatives selected by provincial parliaments and 65 representatives of functional groups. The provincial representatives distributed themselves among the other factions in the MPR, which explains the differences in the seat shares in the two bodies. Of the 135 representatives, 1 elected member and the 5 representatives from East Timor did not attend, making for an effective total of 694 members. Seat shares are calculated on the basis of the statutory 700 members (the DPR does not have functional or regional representatives).

Sources: International Foundation for Election Systems, http://www.ifes.org; Thompson (1999).

fight between Wahid and Megawati, Wahid's victory (373 to 313), and the concession of the vice presidency to Megawati.

This brief outline of Indonesia's complex transition to democracy suggests two conclusions. First, the crisis was deeply implicated in the fall of Suharto: through its generation of protest, through the collapse of local as well as foreign private sector confidence, and ultimately through the split in the regime. Second, although the constraints that Habibie faced appeared daunting, the introduction of political competition in this transitional context pushed his hand in a strongly reformist direction.

If the crisis had several silver linings, they are more than offset by disturbing aspects of Indonesia's transition. As we have seen from the comparison of Korea and Thailand, not all democracies operate with equal efficiency, and Indonesian democracy is far less consolidated than in either of those two countries. If we look at the political constraints facing the new government, they do not augur well for its ability to manage the lingering problems associated with the crisis. *Electoral constraints* are temporarily alleviated, but *non-electoral political challenges* have become even more intense. Sectarian, ethnic, and secessionist violence have not abated with the transition to democratic rule but have become much worse. The religious war in the eastern Maluccas intensified following the transition, communal fighting has continued or escalated on the islands of Sulawesi, Bali, and Lombok, and the secessionist movements in Aceh and Irian Jaya have deepened.

Decision-making processes have rendered the government highly ineffective in the making of economic policy. Wahid's decision to form a "government of the whole" was reflected in the fragmentation of economic decision-making authority within the cabinet between a number of competing ministers and outside advisors, culminating in the embarrassing suspension of IMF support in late March 2000. Parliament is similarly fragmented into ten party factions, the second largest of which is Golkar, and the chairman of the assembly is Amien Rais, a direct political competitor to the president. Finally, with respect to *business-government relations,* the president did move to address issues of KKN, including the thorny issue of Suharto family wealth. But some in Wahid's entourage are not above such problems and the magnitude of financial and corporate distress is so great that it may be impossible to avoid some accommodation with beneficiaries of the old regime (see chapter 4). In sum, Indonesia's problems remain quite fundamentally ones of politics and institutions.

Conclusion

The Asian financial crisis set in motion complex political changes in all four countries. The first thing to note is the resilience of the democracies. Economic crises have not been kind to democracies in the past, particularly when they generate sharp political and social polarization. In the 1960s and 1970s, poor economic performance was the prelude to the installation of authoritarian governments in a number of Latin American countries, including Brazil (1964), Chile (1973), and Argentina (1973), as well as in South Korea (1961) and Indonesia (1965-66). Yet military intervention was never an issue during the crisis in Korea and was explicitly rejected by the military itself in Thailand in the fall of 1997. Democracies were also resilient in a second sense: Changes of government provided opportunities to initiate new programs and to change policy course. But all democracies are not created equal, and Thailand's fragmented party system and close business-government relationships continued to create problems for the reform process.

In both Indonesia and Malaysia, oppositions gained strength from economic grievances and sought to link them to the undemocratic nature of political rule. Yet all authoritarian regimes are not created equal either, and Malaysia's hybrid political system, with a number of democratic features, proved more resilient. Elections provided some channels for the opposition to operate, and Mahathir could draw support from the private sector and a well-organized party machine that occupied the political center on the most salient issues, particularly ethnic and religious ones. Indonesia lacked these advantages and proved surprisingly fragile in the face of concerted challenge.

A final conclusion concerns the nature of the opposition that emerged in the wake of the crisis. We have seen that business groups sought support and protection in the face of high interest rates and a reform agenda that threatened long-standing privileges. It would be wrong to dismiss their agenda as wholly self-interested. The IMF itself came to recognize the importance of relaxing fiscal and monetary constraints.

However, it is also important to be clear about the nature of the opposition that emerged in the wake of the crisis, because it was not wholly defined by business nationalism and social backlash. A consistent theme of a number of diverse opposition forces was that the crisis could be traced to insufficient democratic oversight, particularly of business-government relations: This was a theme of Kim Dae Jung's campaign, was visible in the Thai debate on constitutional reform, and was the centerpiece of the *reformasi* movement in both Indonesia and Malaysia.

Reformers urged not only discrete policy changes but also changing institutions of governance to increase both their independence (from narrow interests) and their accountability (to the public at large). Nor were oppositions necessarily hostile to market-oriented reforms. To the contrary, the idea that policy had been insufficiently market-oriented was a theme of a number of these reform forces as well. This can be seen by turning to the intimidating problems of financial and corporate restructuring that were a defining element of the crisis.

Appendix 3.1:
Two that Got Away—the Philippines and Taiwan Compared

The foregoing chapters have looked at both the longer-term vulnerabilities and short-term adjustment efforts of the most seriously affected countries in the region. However, the account suffers from a clear bias: the absence of discussion of those cases that did somewhat better than their counterparts, particularly Taiwan and the Philippines. Neither country completely escaped regional contagion; Taiwan's growth slowed from 6.8 percent in 1997 to 4.8 percent in 1998, whereas in the Philippines growth ground to a halt in 1998, falling from 5.2 percent in 1997 to –0.5 percent in 1998 before showing signs of recovery in 1999. However, the crisis in the two countries was clearly less severe than in the other countries in the region, and in Taiwan there is little basis for considering it a crisis at all. Why?

This appendix retraces the steps of earlier chapters, albeit in much condensed form. First, it is important to underline fundamental economic differences that might have made these countries less vulnerable to crisis in the first place. Taiwan's external position—perennially in surplus with virtually no foreign debt—was clearly very different from those of the other middle-income countries in the region. The Philippines, on the other hand, was not a small debtor, although its more recent reentry into international financial markets served to limit its exposure.

I then turn to the nature of business-government relations in the period before the crisis and the extent to which they alleviated or compounded risk. The two countries show somewhat different trajectories in this regard. The Philippines under the rule of Ferdinand Marcos (1969-86) resembled the Suharto regime in a number of respects, including the increasing weight of crony and family interests in economic policymaking. The transition to democratic rule certainly did not eliminate corruption in the Philippines, but it did reduce the grossest abuses. In Taiwan, by contrast, democratization has resulted in a marked increase in the role of business in politics and challenged the independence of the regulatory process. Taiwan exhibited a number of regulatory weaknesses that resembled in important respects those seen in other countries in the region. But their magnitude was less, and because of the absence of a foreign exchange and debt crisis they did not have the same consequences for the real economy that they did elsewhere.

Finally, I consider the political circumstances when the crisis hit, and how they created uncertainty that either facilitated or impeded the adjustment process; those conditions are summarized in table A3-1. In the Philippines in particular, political circumstances did contribute to the country's initial problems, but the president retained substantial political powers in addressing the crisis.

Table A3.1 Political constraints on crisis management in the Philippines and Taiwan

	The Philippines I	The Philippines II	Taiwan
Government, term in office	Fidel Ramos, 6/1992-6/1998	Joseph Estrada, 6/1998	Lee Teng Hui, 3/1995-3/2000 (last term)
Electoral	Impending presidential and congressional elections 6/1998	None	Continual pressures from nonconcurrent elections, including local (11/1997 and 1/1998), legislative (12/1998) and presidential (3/2000) elections
Non-electoral and "backlash"	Widespread public opposition to proposed constitutional amendment, mid-1997	Not significant	Not significant
Decision-making process	Strong presidential system with majority in lower (but not upper) house	Strong presidential system	Premier-presidential system with strong president, but narrow legislative majority; increasingly divided ruling party
Government links to business	Reduction of cronyism under Aquino and Ramos, although all parties dependent on business support	Increasing concerns of crony links	Increasing reliance by all parties on business support

127

The Philippines

The Philippines[37] presents the more interesting of the two cases because it would appear on initial inspection to be no less vulnerable to external shocks than Malaysia. The Philippines experienced a substantial debt crisis in 1983-84. The transition to the government of Corazon Aquino in 1986 and a Brady bond deal in 1992 permitted a gradual reduction of the external debt burden and a return to international capital markets. Following a stabilization and recession in 1990-91, the government was able to relax fiscal and monetary policy, and in the early 1990s the Philippine economy began to take off.

Thailand and the Philippines opened their capital accounts at roughly the same time. Although the Philippines' success in attracting capital was somewhat less than Thailand's, the country did experience real appreciation and a modest slowdown in export revenues. At the end of 1996, the total stock of external debt stood at just over $41 billion. However, the Philippines benefited from being a relative latecomer to the financial markets (Montes 1999; Hutchcroft 1999). New borrowing under Aquino and Ramos was relatively modest, and from 1992 to 1995 foreign direct investment, much of it associated with privatization efforts, dominated capital flows. Not until 1996 did the Philippines face the problematic surge of foreign borrowing and growth of portfolio investment visible in the other countries in the region; the country's ratio of debt to GNP fell every year from 1990 to 1996. Most important, the share of short-term debt in total debt was modest—peaking at 19 percent in 1997—and nearly half of that was trade-related. The Philippines was also less exposed to troubled Japanese banks than other Asian borrowers (Noland 2000b).

A second crucial factor for understanding the comparative performance of the Philippines lies in the banking sector. The Aquino administration spent most of its time in office trying to reestablish the integrity of the financial system, which had been the locus of cronyism and massive abuses during the Marcos years (Hutchcroft 1998). These efforts involved cleaning up the balance sheets of the major state-owned banks, at enormous cost to the central bank, and providing the major domestic banks with preferential access to high-return, low-risk government instruments. But these supports were accompanied by corresponding regulatory changes that included "strengthening prudential regulations in relation to minimum capitalization requirements; increasing compliance with the minimum capital to risk asset ratio, the single borrower limit, the limit on DOSRI [directors, stockholders, and related interests] loans, and the stipulations regarding interlocking directorships and management; making provision for loan losses or doubtful accounts, tightening audit and

---

37. This section draws on Lim (1998), Montes (1999), Hutchcroft (1999), Sicat (1999), Intal et. al. (1998), Lamberte (1999), MacIntyre (1999a), and Noland (2000b).

reporting requirements; and reviewing the bailout policy for problematic banks" (Intal et al. 1998, 147).

These reforms were carried forward by the Ramos administration, which pushed further liberalization of the banking sector through decontrol of interest rates, cautious opening to foreign banks, and relaxation of restrictions on bank activities. However, at the same time the administration secured congressional support for a new central bank law in 1993 that substantially increased the institution's independence and regulatory reach. The reforms of the central bank coincided almost exactly with the relaxation of foreign exchange controls (Satyanath 1999) and gave the bank new instruments to deal with the corresponding risks. For example, just before the crisis in the region broke, the central bank limited bank lending to the real estate sector. On the eve of the crisis, the Philippine financial sector was in relatively strong shape, and the corporate sector less heavily leveraged.

In sum, the Philippines' overall vulnerability to crisis was reduced by a conjuncture of fortuitous reasons, policy choices, and institutional reforms. First, the Philippines' prior debt problems delayed and limited the country's reentry into international financial markets. Second, the past crisis had set in train important regulatory changes in the banking sector. Hutchcroft (1999) argues that the Philippine banking system continued to show signs of collusive behavior; evident, for example, in high spreads between deposit and lending rates. But the potential for gross abuses and moral hazard was clearly reduced, and liberalization was undertaken in a cautious fashion, complemented by substantial strengthening of the government's regulatory capacity. When the government did face problems in the banking sector, as in the case of the failure of the Orient Bank, the central bank was firm that bailouts were not in order.[38]

Underneath these regulatory changes were more fundamental changes in business-government relations between the late-Marcos, Aquino, and Ramos periods, changes representative of the "market-oriented populism" outlined in chapter 3. Aquino did her share in reversing some of the worst crony abuses in the economy as a whole by selectively reintroducing market forces in a number of areas that had been dominated by monopolistic practices, protection, and various forms of subsidies (Dohner and Haggard 1994). These reforms included an important liberalization of foreign direct investment in 1991.

But it was the administration of Fidel Ramos (1992-1998) that pushed through some of the most substantial structural reforms in the Philippines' postwar history under the banner of "Philippines 2000." Ramos explicitly underscored the importance of reforming business-government relations

---

38. In addition to closing Orient Bank, the government also shut down about 50 small and weak thrift and rural banks (Satyanath 1999, 27).

for achieving these objectives (Lamberte 1999). In his inaugural address, he promised reform of an economic system that "enables persons with political influence to extract wealth without effort from the economy," and later argued that the reason for the Philippines' slow economic growth relative to the region was the political dominance of oligarchic groups (cited in Hutchcroft 1999, 165). The means of limiting these abuses combined a strengthening of regulatory capabilities already noted with liberalizing reforms: a quite dramatic liberalization of trade (average nominal tariffs fell from 23 percent in 1993 to just over 10 percent in 1999), deregulation of a number of cartels and monopolies (telecommunications, inter-island shipping, and the airlines), and a major privatization program.

These reforms did not insulate the Philippines from regional contagion. Immediately following the successful attack on the Thai baht in July, the peso also came under severe pressure. After seeking to defend it briefly, the Philippine central bank allowed the currency to depreciate while simultaneously pursuing a tight monetary policy, imposing some mild capital controls,[39] and substantially toughening prudential regulation of banks (Intal et al. 1999, 151-53).[40]

Yet despite the fact that the country was less vulnerable to external shocks than its regional counterparts, the extent of exchange rate depreciation was only slightly less than in Malaysia, South Korea, and Thailand. To what extent might this outcome be traced to politics?

On the one hand, a number of political developments appeared decidedly *inauspicious*, including important constitutional uncertainties and challenges to the government, a lame duck president, and a strongly contested but highly uncertain presidential race. Just before the onset of the regional crisis, the Ramos administration—operating nominally through its supporters—launched an initiative to amend the constitution to allow the president to stand for a second term. A petition drive collected 6 million signatures, a million more than required by law to put the issue to a referendum. A second proposal was to transform the Senate and House into a constituent assembly that would undertake the "charter change" ("cha-cha"). Ironically, these efforts gained momentum precisely because of the success of Ramos' economic reforms and fear that his achievements would be undermined if his populist vice president, former movie star Joseph Estrada, were to become president.

The petition drive was challenged in a series of lawsuits by its opponents, and both former president Aquino and the influential Catholic

---

39. The central bank placed a cap of $100,000 on over-the-counter sales of foreign exchange for non-trade-related purposes at the end of June, which was lowered to $25,000 at the end of July; this ceiling was partly lifted for residents in September.

40. These controls included further limits on lending to the property sector and a tightening of rules governing loan loss provisioning and lending to the property sector.

prelate Cardinal Sin weighed in against the change. Shortly after a massive demonstration against constitutional revision on 21 September, the Supreme Court ruled that the enabling law governing petitions for referenda was legally inadequate and Ramos abandoned his quest for a second term. These developments turned the Ramos administration into a lame duck and effectively signaled the onset of the presidential campaign that culminated in the elections of 11 May 1998.[41]

The presidential campaign constituted an additional source of uncertainty. The race engaged a number of aspirants, many motivated by the desire to stop the highly popular candidacy of Joseph Estrada. In his movies, Estrada often played Robin Hood-like characters, and one of his core campaign slogans was "Erap is for the poor." His lack of economic expertise and concerns about the potential for both cronyism and populism would all appear to be textbook ingredients for the generation of policy uncertainty.

Although counterfactuals are always risky, it is probable that the efforts of the Ramos government to lift the constitutional ban on term limits had the opposite effect from that intended. Rather than stabilizing expectations, the cha-cha movement unleashed widespread protest against the government, and this probably contributed to the peso's slide during the early months of the crisis. However, these adverse circumstances were partly offset by features of the presidential system that granted Ramos substantial legislative powers in addressing the crisis (MacIntyre 1999a).

If we were to look only at the party system, the Philippines appears to bear a number of similarities to Thailand. The party system is fragmented, with a shifting pool of six to eight parties capable of garnering some representation in the legislature at any time. Internally, Philippine parties are notoriously weak institutions, built around personalities and geographic bases of support rather than enduring programmatic lines. However, unlike Thailand, where such parties must form coalitions to rule, the Philippines has an unusually strong president with substantial powers to allocate resources to those who support him. As a result, presidents are typically able to build legislative coalitions fairly easily, despite electoral outcomes that appear to fragment legislative support. Indeed, it is quite common in the Philippines for legislators elected under one party label to switch to the president's party following elections. Ramos enjoyed a solid majority in the lower house as a result of this phenomenon, and shortly after Estrada's election in May legislators from other parties started to defect to him as well.

The ability of the president to control the legislative agenda provides an interesting contrast not only to Thailand but to South Korea under

---

41. These elections would also replace one-half of the Senate and the entire House of Representatives.

Kim Young Sam as well. As in those two countries, the policy challenges for the government centered on the legislation required to secure IMF support. Since 1962, the Philippines had had an uninterrupted succession of standby agreements with the Fund, the last of which was an Extended Fund Facility (EFF) agreement set to end in June 1997. However, the conclusion of the EFF program had been stalled by debate between the administration and Congress over a comprehensive tax reform; Congress had sought to apply tax exemptions to higher tax brackets than those proposed by the IMF and the administration, no doubt with electoral considerations in mind. The administration was unilaterally able to tighten fiscal policy through an across-the-board cut in expenditures, but passing tax reform and controversial legislation to assure the effective deregulation of oil prices required intense negotiation. Nonetheless, the president was able to prevail in both instances, albeit with a delay, setting the stage for the negotiation of a "precautionary" standby arrangement with the IMF that picked up following the termination of the EFF in early 1998.

The presidential election also proved somewhat less unsettling for confidence and the general direction of policy than it might have, in part because of Estrada's efforts to calm business and middle-class fears (*Far Eastern Economic Review*, 14 May 1998, 14-24). Despite his populist rhetoric, his policy pronouncements were surprisingly conservative and market-oriented. His approach to poverty alleviation emphasized job creation and greater spending on rural infrastructure rather than transfers. Estrada made strong efforts to alleviate concerns both about his populism and his connections to a variety of unsavory businessmen by announcing in advance an economic team that included respected business leaders, technocrats, and academics. He also promised to retain the central bank governor Gabriel Singson until the end of his term, and he "pre-announced" a successor who commanded wide respect.

The actual performance of the Estrada administration proved disappointing in a number of respects. By early 2000, his popularity had plummeted and his finance minister had resigned in protest at a growing "culture of corruption." A number of promised reforms had failed to materialize, and the president was forced to clean house by firing a number of appointees and seeking to initiate delayed reforms that would have carried on the Ramos legacy (see, e.g., *Asian Wall Street Journal*, 7-8 and 10 January 2000). However, these reform efforts subsequently ran into trouble in Congress (*Financial Times*, 13 April 2000)

A detailed evaluation of Estrada's performance would take us beyond the purpose here, which is to underline some of the key features of the onset and initial management of the crisis that are of comparative interest. First, it is important to reiterate that the Philippines was less vulnerable at the outset of the crisis. This different starting point was related in part to the later entry of the Philippines into the capital markets, or what Paul

Hutchcroft (1999) has called the country's "lower elevation": The country had less far to fall. However, this different starting point was not unrelated to important changes both in policy and in the nature of business-government relations, including particularly a reduction in cronyism and a strengthening of the regulatory environment.

In the short run, politics did contribute to the Philippines' troubles, particularly the campaign to extend Ramos' term. Moreover, the need for the president to buy support for reform proposals in Congress and legislative reticence about tax reform and the deregulation of oil prices did lead to some delays in legislation. But in contrast to South Korea, the president's powers held, and despite the rhetoric of the Estrada campaign there seemed little support for reversing any of his reforms; the larger risk seemed to be the reluctance to continue the forward momentum of the Ramos period. Estrada did not exploit his powers to initiate new reforms in the way Kim Dae Jung did, although he confronted a number of the same financial, corporate, and social issues. But this should perhaps not be surprising because the crisis proved less profound in the Philippines than in Korea as well.

Taiwan

As currencies in Southeast Asia began to depreciate after July 1997, the Central Bank of China (CBC) experienced strong selling pressure on the New Taiwan dollar (NT dollar). The difference was that Taiwan's[42] monetary authorities controlled reserves in excess of $93 billion (end-1996) and could mount a sustained defense; before the CBC gave up and let the NT dollar depreciate on 17 October, the central bank spent more than $7 billion on the effort. Once floated, the currency quickly fell from 28.6 to the dollar to 31.4 and then to 33 following the collapse of the won in November, where it remained before strengthening somewhat in late 1998. The stock market also fell victim to regional trends. After peaking in August, the market began a steady descent thereafter, losing roughly 20 percent of its value by the end of the year.

At one level, it is easy to explain why this sequence of events was not the prelude to a broader economic crisis. All the most seriously affected countries, as well as the Philippines, ran current account deficits in the 1990s, even if their magnitude was not particularly large. All four countries accumulated a corresponding amount of external debt, with a dangerous amount of it in Thailand and South Korea being short term. Taiwan, by contrast, had run a current account surplus for more than 20 years. Its average current account surplus—the excess of savings over investment—

---

42. The following draws on Kuo and Liu (1998); Noble and Ravenhill (2000b); and particularly Chu (1999a, 1999b).

from 1990-97 was 3.9 percent of GDP. As a result, the country did not increase its net foreign debt before the crisis. Government-guaranteed debt was less than 0.05 percent of GDP. The external liabilities of Taiwan's private sector totaled 10.6 percent of GDP, but this was less than the value of foreign assets held by domestic residents (Chu 1999a).

In 1998, Taiwan did feel the effects of the Asian financial crisis through two important channels: a decline in exports to the region and problems with foreign investments by Taiwanese firms in Southeast Asia; these factors contributed to the slowdown that we have already noted. But Taiwan was a net creditor to the rest of the world and as a result was simply not vulnerable to the rapid withdrawal of foreign funds and exhaustion of reserves that were the defining moment of the crisis elsewhere.

However, this explanation begs the deeper question of why Taiwan has pursued such conservative macroeconomic and exchange rate policies in the first place. As Chu (1999a, 190) summarizes, "The Nationalist government has invariably maintained a positive real interest rate, minimum public-sector foreign debt, small fiscal deficit, a fixed exchange rate pegged to the U.S. dollar, restrictions on the convertibility of the NT dollar, a rigorous regulatory regime over financial institutions, and a conservative ethos that permeated the entire banking sector." This discipline has eroded somewhat with the democratization process, particularly with respect to the conduct of fiscal policy (Cheng and Haggard 2000). But in the conduct of macroeconomic policy, in the design of financial liberalization and deregulation, and in the opening of the capital account, there can be little question that Taiwan has been relatively cautious.

The reasons can be traced to the political interests of the ruling Kuomintang (KMT) party, which dominated politics in Taiwan before the gradual transition to democracy in the late 1980s and early 1990s and continued to hold the presidency and a majority in the legislature until the presidential elections of March 2000 as well. For a series of historical reasons, political leaders have had a strong interest in the independence of the central bank, both in its conduct of macroeconomic policy and its role as regulator of the financial system (Cheng 1993). These reasons begin with the great Chinese hyperinflation of the late 1940s that contributed to the KMT's loss of the mainland. In the wake of that experience, the CBC was given a strong mandate for macroeconomic stability. The governorship of the bank became the senior economic post in the cabinet, and was always occupied by an individual with close political ties to KMT leaders.

The CBC's powers extended to regulatory authority over the banking system, which until the 1990s was overwhelmingly state-owned. State ownership of banking was seen as a way for the KMT—a party of exiled mainlanders, primarily government officials and employees—to control the commanding heights of the economy and to check the economic as well as political power of indigenous Taiwanese business (Cheng 1993). Credit from the state-owned banks tended to flow primarily to state-owned firms and a handful of larger private enterprises with collateral in land. Corruption was not altogether absent, and the highly conservative nature of the country's banking system was arguably a drag on its growth. But neither did the country develop the close bank-group relations, high levels of industrial concentration, or high corporate leveraging that constituted such a problem in other crisis countries, particularly South Korea (Noble and Ravenhill 2000b).

Over time, the CBC's role effectively extended into security issues. Taiwan's international position has become more rather than less exposed over time as a result of Beijing's efforts to isolate it and advance the cause of reunification. Taiwan is not a member of the IMF, and thus cannot count on its resources in times of crisis. Nor can it be assured that private investors would remain steadfast in the face of diplomatic shocks, economic sanctions, embargo, or actual military threats, such as the missile tests it endured before the presidential elections in 1995. Moreover, military support from its erstwhile ally, the United States, is the topic of ongoing controversy with China and remains purposefully ambiguous. These political vulnerabilities have undoubtedly influenced political leaders' preference for what otherwise would appear to be an excessively high level of reserves.

These same political considerations have also contributed to the government's hesitance to open the capital account. The CBC was highly resistant to the removal of foreign exchange controls, but the accumulation of massive surpluses in the mid-1980s (reaching nearly 20 percent of GNP), strong pressure from the United States, and the need to manage an emerging speculative bubble in equities and real estate led to a gradual liberalization process beginning in July 1987 (Kuo and Liu 1998). Foreign access to the securities market was also opened in stages beginning in 1991. Nonetheless, the central bank continued to intervene in a variety of ways to limit the internationalization of the NT dollar and to restrict the foreign assets and liabilities of banks. Some have suggested that this might have been a blessing in disguise, just as the timing of the Philippines' reentry into capital markets partly inoculated it against regional contagion. However even if capital movements had been completely free, it is doubtful that Taiwan would have experienced the problems of the most seriously affected countries; it was the country's external position, not capital controls, that provided the ultimate inoculation against crisis.

Nonetheless, political changes in Taiwan since the early 1990s, including the nature of business-government relations, have raised issues that are surprisingly similar to the difficulties seen in other countries in the region—even if their ramifications for the economy as a whole have been muted. During the period of authoritarian rule, the KMT encouraged the development of the indigenous Taiwanese private sector, but did not rely on it for political support: The government and party had substantial financial as well as administrative resources at their disposal, business was not organized, and there were fewer electoral incentives for the KMT to court business support. Moreover, the executive did not rely on legislative support to undertake policy initiatives, or to the extent that it did it was able to exercise strong control over legislators.

With the transition to democratic rule, however, these conditions changed quite dramatically. The party (and factions within it) had strong interests to reach out to business groups for political and financial support (Chu 1994). This tendency was reinforced by features of Taiwan's electoral system that bore surprising similarity to Thailand's. Electoral rules created strong incentives for candidates to pursue personal vote strategies that were heavily dependent on campaign contributions and thus on business support.[43]

And finally, the executive had to manage a contentious legislature. The KMT's share of votes in legislative elections dropped from 66.7 percent in 1986 to 46.1 percent in 1995, while its share of seats dropped from a commanding 83.1 percent to the narrowest of majorities—51.8 percent—during the same period. Not only did the government have to contend with the opposition, but legislators from within its own ranks also faced strong electoral pressures and the temptation to defect.

These political changes manifested themselves not only in upsurge of charges of corruption and "money politics" but also in broader changes in public policy. One way in which the government and ruling party could reach out to business was by engaging in deregulatory initiatives that benefited them (Chu 1999). Beginning in 1988, the government began to dismantle long-standing entry barriers in a range of sectors, including construction, mass transportation, airlines, segments of the petrochemical and power sectors, and, most important for our purposes, commercial and investment banking.

Beginning in 1991, the Ministry of Finance began to cautiously issue licenses for new banks while still exercising quite strict regulatory supervi-

---

43. Taiwan's electoral system is single nontransferable vote, or SNTV. Many legislators are elected from a single district, but each voter can only cast one ballot, and the votes a candidate gets cannot be transferred to other candidates of the same party. Under an SNTV system, any political party that has the potential to win more than two seats from a district faces the vote-division problem; parties may run too many or too few candidates in a district and may fail to equalize the votes among their nominees sufficiently. However, this issue is less significant than the politician's "product differentiation" problem: given intra-party competition, politicians must devise a strategy to distinguish themselves from candidates from their own parties seeking election in the same district. Numerous studies of SNTV in Japan and Taiwan have demonstrated how parties use pork, particularly public construction projects, to assist individual candidates in cementing personal support bases and securing campaign contributions. For an overview of the literature, see Haggard and McCubbins (2000).

sion over the sector, for example, in setting very high minimum capital requirements and sharply limiting the ownership share of corporate investors. The ministry also issued a series of directives limiting the amount of secured loans banks could extend to real property. In contrast to other countries in the region, the quality of portfolios and return on assets slipped only slightly with the liberalization (Noble and Ravenhill 2000b).

However, political pressures on the banking system of the sort outlined in chapter 1 were not altogether absent.[44] The provincial government of Taiwan, an artifact of the historical fiction that the KMT government ruled all of China, controlled three major commercial banks. With a widespread branch network on the island, these banks were periodically turned to patronage purposes before the central government—in a major constitutional revision in 1997—finally pushed through the elimination of the provincial level of government altogether. Local financial institutions, especially community credit cooperatives and credit bureaus for farmers and fisherman, "have been plagued by endemic problems of politicization, inefficiency and incompetence" (Noble and Ravenhill 2000b, 25), even though they accounted for only a small portion of the overall financial sector.

The liberalization of bills financing companies also shows some striking parallels to other cases in the region (Chu 1999a, 1999b; Noble and Ravenhill 2000b). Under strong political pressure, the Ministry of Finance opened the commercial-paper and unsecured-corporate-bond market in 1995, without putting in place an adequate regulatory system. When the regional economy began to contract in 1998, a number of export-oriented industries, such as steel, felt the effects. The stock market, which had rebounded during the first half of the year, underwent another sharp sell-off. The failure of a number of speculators to meet margin calls threatened to set of a chain reaction from the finance companies to stock and land prices. The government seized the opportunity to strengthen the regulatory framework. But with legislative elections looming in December, the government followed an earlier fiscal stimulus with a bailout plan that not only provided financial relief for particular firms but also specifically sought to stabilize the stock market.

Conclusion

This brief examination of these "two that got away" helps shed light on the other countries in the region. First, Taiwan makes abundantly clear that vulnerability to crisis depends in the first instance on a country's debt and reserve position; even when the NT dollar fell under attack, the

---

44. The following draws extensively on Chu (1999a, 1999b).

effects were muted by the absence of significant external debt and abundant reserves. The Philippines confirms this view. Later entry into financial markets and less reliance on short-term debt clearly reduced the government's vulnerability.

However, this observation does not obviate the importance of political factors; to the contrary, the comparison underscores the importance of both business-government relations and short-term political constraints on crisis management. One of the reasons why the external shock in the Philippines did not spread to the domestic economy to the same extent was precisely because of the cautious nature of the external liberalization and the prudential reforms that had been put in place as a result of a previous financial crisis. Monetary authorities in Taiwan have generally managed to maintain a strong regulatory framework. Nonetheless, changes in the business-government relationship have eroded regulators' independence at the margin; the costs of this erosion were real, but buffered by the strong external position the country enjoyed.

Finally, if a country—namely the Philippines—was vulnerable to external shocks, short-term political constraints, including protests against the administration and an election campaign, did have adverse consequences. However, these were partly offset by a strong presidency and at least some initial continuity between the Ramos and Estrada administrations.

4

The Politics of Financial and Corporate Restructuring

A defining characteristic of the Asian financial crisis has been systemic distress: the simultaneous insolvency of large numbers of banks and firms. Financial and corporate restructuring under such conditions pose a number of unresolved technical problems, but the issues are not simply technical. In the short run, the process of restructuring generates political conflicts over the recognition of losses and their allocation among interested parties—shareholders, management, workers, and taxpayers. In the long run, restructuring addresses even more fundamental issues, such as corporate governance and accountability, the transparency of business-government relations, the rule of law, and even the distribution of a society's assets.

Our knowledge of what constitutes best practice in managing systemic distress is still evolving, and the choices facing governments are typically bad. Nonetheless, government responses to such crises can be distinguished along two dimensions that are of particular importance to the success of the adjustment process: the *speed and decisiveness* of government and its *responsiveness to private interests*, particularly weak banks and firms. These two dimensions are clearly related. Banks and firms experiencing severe distress have strong interests in postponing the recognition of losses. Governments may have their own political reasons for delay as well. However, delay can also compound losses and increase uncertainty.

Government responsiveness to private interests is linked to the much-debated problem of moral hazard and the extent to which governments effectively guaranteed (ex ante) and "bailed out" (ex post) financial institutions and their corporate clients. Of course, there is no virtue in bankrupting potentially viable banks and firms. Moreover, it is misguided and even costly to think that governments can altogether avoid shouldering some of the costs of such crises.

But in periods of distress, all companies, regardless of their long-term viability, have an interest in making claims against the government, particularly the large ones that have political influence. To limit the public costs of such crises, governments require the political as well as administrative capability to distinguish among competing claims and to impose regulatory conditions on banks and firms that will limit future risks.

That capacity will clearly be influenced by the political factors outlined in chapter 2: the *security* of government, and the electoral and non-electoral challenges it faces; the *cohesiveness* of government decision-making; and the *degree of institutional and political access for private actors*. Governments facing electoral or non-electoral challenges, such as demonstrations and strikes, are more likely to delay and make concessions to stakeholders than those that are politically secure. The formal structure of decision-making also matters; policymaking processes with multiple veto gates are typically less decisive and more open to particularistic influences than are governments whose authority is more concentrated. But choices about financial and corporate restructuring will depend most on the nature of government-business relations. Moral hazard, bailouts, favoritism, and limited reform are more likely when top political leaders develop close, nontransparent political relationships with the private sector.

This chapter compares the politics of financial and corporate reform in the seven administrations that are the focus of this book—the Kim Young Sam and Kim Dae Jung administrations in South Korea, the Chavalit and Chuan governments in Thailand, the Mahathir government in Malaysia, and the Suharto and Habibie governments in Indonesia. Although we have seen how democratic politics in Korea and Thailand contributed to the initial mismanagement of the financial crisis, they also permitted new reformist governments to come into office. Under Habibie, democratic pressures also provided incentives for reform. In Indonesia under Suharto, more profound political uncertainties over succession made meaningful financial and corporate reform virtually impossible.

Yet all democracies are not created equal. Both the nature of decision-making structures and business access to government resulted in a more decisive, but also more interventionist, adjustment strategy in Korea than in Thailand. By contrast, close business-government relations weakened the ability of both the Suharto and Habibie governments to make decisions and undermined the credibility of the government when it did; we see these same problems operating in Malaysia as well, although to a lesser extent. These findings suggest that meaningful financial and corporate reform depend heavily on the broader institutional context, including the integrity of the legal and judicial process, independence of regulatory agencies, and the transparency of business-government relations.

Table 4.1 The politics of corporate and financial restructuring

Issue area	Political issues and conflicts
Limiting support to insolvent banks	Decisiveness of government in limiting liquidity support and guarantees to failing banks; allocation of losses among government, shareholders, depositors, and bank workers
Bank recapitalization	Decisiveness of government and provision of adequate resources; imposing conditions on banks; limiting costs to government of recapitalization by encouraging private recapitalization
Disposition of nonperforming loans (NPLs)	Decisiveness of government in identifying and financing "carve out" of NPLs; market pricing of asset purchases; timely rehabilitation or disposition of assets; maximizing value
Corporate debt restructuring	Facilitating timely restructuring; imposing conditions on corporates; limiting the cost to government
Encouraging foreign entry	Overcoming nationalist and protectionist pressures
Reform of corporate governance	Overcoming resistance from insiders to greater transparency, corporate accountability, and external monitoring

Five issues are central to the restructuring process in the short run: the management of illiquid and insolvent banks; bank recapitalization; the disposition of nonperforming loans (NPLs); the restructuring of corporate debt; and the operation, and reform, of bankruptcy procedures. Governments also took advantage of the crisis to pass reforms in an area of tremendous long-run significance—rules on corporate governance. A final issue that is also of great importance over the long run is the liberalization of rules governing foreign investment, which allow foreign banks and firms to play a greater role in the restructuring process; this issue is addressed in the conclusion. As table 4.1 suggests, each of these policy areas involves potential political conflicts.

The Political Economy of Financial Reform

The first task facing governments was to decide which banks and other nonbank financial institutions (NBFIs) were insolvent and nonviable and to stop the flow of public credit to them. It is extraordinarily difficult for any government to impose the costs of bank failures on small depositors, even if a formal insurance mechanism is not in place. The political challenge, rather, is dealing with shareholders, large creditors, managers, and bank workers. Once a bank is insolvent, managers have few incentives to run it on a commercial basis, and looting can set in. Moreover, insolvent banks will pressure the central bank to provide liquidity support, with adverse implications for monetary and fiscal policy. Stopping the flow of credit to insolvent institutions does not necessarily mean banks should be suspended or closed immediately, but delay in recognizing and accepting bank insolvency can be extremely costly.

The next task is triage: To develop a rehabilitation plan for those institutions that are viable but require support and to deal with those that are nonviable and will ultimately need to be closed. These decisions crystallize around two related policy issues—recapitalizing the banks and disposing of nonperforming loans. In severe financial crises such as those in Asia, the extent of distress and risk to the overall financial system is so great that injections of public money to recapitalize the banks is unavoidable. The key political question is the nature of the conditions attached to any support. Governments can limit the costs to taxpayers as well as future moral hazard by insisting that share prices be diluted or written down completely, by requiring banks and shareholders to raise matching capital, by limiting deposit insurance extended to large creditors, and by displacing management. Governments can also reduce the risks of future crises by improving the quality of regulation with respect to crucial variables such as capital adequacy requirements, loan classification and provisioning, disclosure, and exposure to different sorts of risk.

The disposition of nonperforming loans constitutes a third policy area in which there are potential conflicts of interest between the government and banks and debtors. Governments have typically intervened either through a liquidation agency or through more ambitious rehabilitation agencies that seek to manage and restructure the assets before sale (Klingebiel 1999). The purchase price of the assets, and the extent to which they approximate fair market value, is a good indicator of the cost to taxpayers and the extent of the bailout.

But even if assets are purchased at a steep discount, their management is equally if not more critical to the final resolution process. If the assets are transferred to a weak asset management company and simply "warehoused," bank balance sheets are cleaned up and borrowers can reestablish relations with their creditor banks, but neither may have incentives to meet their obligations. By contrast, the government can manage acquired assets aggressively to maximize value: by swapping debt for equity, taking an active managerial role in turning the company around, or foreclosing on collateral. Undertaking such actions requires not only an unusual degree of technical capacity, but also substantial political independence. The restructuring agency must have an unambiguous mandate to maximize returns to the government—even when it involves conflicts with powerful debtors.

The performance of asset management companies has led a number of analysts to favor more market-based solutions, in which the assets are sold to private agents, including foreign ones, who can manage or foreclose on them (Klingebiel 1999). But this strategy also requires substantial political capabilities. Selling assets, particularly to foreigners, and guaranteeing that foreclosure and bankruptcy processes are functioning can involve the same conflicts with debtors as do more active strategies of asset management.

Comparisons of national strategies for managing bank failure, recapitalization, and disposal of assets across countries are of necessity difficult because initial conditions and the magnitude of problems varied. Nonetheless, the indicators in table 4.2 and the case studies that follow suggest that political factors played a crucial role in the restructuring process. National differences emerge quite clearly in paired comparisons between South Korea and Thailand, the two democracies, and between Malaysia and Indonesia. Not surprisingly, business-government relations played a particularly crucial role in the pace of reform. All governments faced the problems associated with the high concentration of private assets noted in chapter 1: the difficulty of imposing reforms on powerful private actors. But governments did differ in their political connections with business. The closer the political relationship between political leaders and the banks and debtors undergoing restructuring, the more the government deferred to private interests, and the more limited and costly the private restructuring process proved to be.

The Kim Young Sam government supported the banking system following several major corporate failures in 1997 and nationalized two major banks before leaving office, but (as we have seen in chapter 2) political circumstances precluded a coherent strategy. Following Kim Dae Jung's election, however, the government moved quickly to address financial sector distress through a new regulatory agency that gave the government a powerful position in the financial sector. All banks were subject to thorough review, on the basis of which five were shut down and merged with others under government direction. A large number of nonbank financial institutions were also shut down, although many weak ones were left open. Korea's record in disposing of acquired assets seems weak, but it moved more aggressively than Indonesia, Malaysia, or Thailand.

The Thai government under Chavalit initially supported weak finance companies. The Chuan government, by contrast, moved quickly to close a number of them and dispose of their assets. But it did not recapitalize the banks or purchase NPLs from them directly. Rather, it sought to induce banks to recapitalize on their own by enforcing capital adequacy and loan loss provisions. This strategy failed, and the government finally committed itself to bank recapitalization. But few banks participated in the voluntary program because of its tough conditions and the government's lack of capacity to enforce them. As a result, the government was forced to manage the crisis through regulatory forbearance and an extraordinarily high level of NPLs (still above 40 percent in mid 2000).

Table 4.2 Managing bank failure and recapitalization

	South Korea	Thailand	Malaysia	Indonesia
Managing bank insolvency				
Institutional framework	Financial Supervisory Authority, 4/1998; Korea Deposit Insurance Corporation	Financial Restructuring Agency, 10/1997 (Finance companies only); Financial Restructuring Advisory Committee	Danamodal, 7/1998	Indonesian Bank Restructuring Authority. 1/1998, authority expanded 2/1999
Banks closed and/or merged (percentage of financial sector assets)	5 closed and merged	1 of 15 closed (2 percent)	None closed, 9 banks and 2 merchant banks merged to create 4 new commercial banks	64 of 237 closed (18 percent); 4 of 7 state-owned banks to be merged into 1 bank (54 percent)
Other financial institutions closed or merged (percentage of financial sector assets)	17 merchant banks and over 100 nonbank financial institutions (with bank closures, 15 percent)	57 of 91 finance companies closed (11 percent)	6 mergers of finance companies and banks (2 percent)	
Nationalizations (percentage of financial sector assets)	4 commercial banks (25 percent)	7 commercial banks (13-15 percent) and 12 finance companies (2.2 percent)	1 bank, 1 merchant bank, and 3 finance companies (12 percent)	12 commercial banks (20 percent)
Bank recapitalization strategies				
Initial plan and timing	$8 billion injected into 9 commercial banks, 1/98.	$8.9 billion for private banks and $11.7 billion for state banks, plan announced, 8/1998	$1.6 billion injected into 10 financial institutions, 7/1998	$41 billion plan announced 3/1999 for 9 private banks; all state-owned banks to be recapitalized.

Total amount disbursed for recapitalization, 10/1999 plus estimated remaining fiscal costs (as share of GDP)	13 percent + 4 percent	16 percent + 8 percent	4 percent + 6 percent	11 percent + 48 percent
Share of financial assets held by state-owned and nationalized banks, 8/1999	58 percent	45 percent	18 percent	78 percent
Financial assets held by state-owned and nationalized banks as share of GDP (8/1999)	124 percent	127 percent	62 percent	79 percent
Asset resolution				
Asset management company and assets, 8/1999	Korean Asset Management Company, $37 billion	No asset management unit for banks. Financial Restructuring Agency for finance companies	Danaharta. $2.13 billion	Indonesian Bank Restructuring Authority. $28 billion
Assets transferred, mid-1999	26 percent of NPLs, 10 percent of GDP	All assets of closed finance company assets, 2 percent of GDP	50 percent of NPLs, 14 percent of GDP	66 percent of NPLs, 35 percent of GDP
Assets sold as share of those transferred, mid-1999	4.7 percent	100 percent of core assets of finance companies, but some to government Asset Management Unit	0.1 percent	0.7 percent

NPLs = non-performing loans

Sources: Claessans, Djankov, and Klingebiel (1999); World Bank (2000b); author's calculations and assessments.

Comparing Malaysia to the other three poses some difficulties because the extent of its banking problems were substantially less than those in the other countries. The government moved swiftly to undertake a bank recapitalization scheme, developed an institution for managing nonperforming assets, and proposed a massive bank consolidation that would have substantially reduced the number of players in the financial sector. However, the government also engaged in costly bailouts of several financial institutions that had played political roles in the past.

Indonesia appeared to respond decisively to its banking crisis, but (as we saw in chapter 2) the initial closing of 16 banks was badly handled, which contributed to the onset of the crisis, and this was followed by support for a number of politically connected banks. Although the Suharto government established a bank restructuring authority, its efforts were undermined by deepening political uncertainty. The Habibie government initiated a strategy for recapitalizing the banking sector, but implementation was subject to delay and political interference, and the state-owned banking sector remained largely unreformed. By the end of 1999 when a new government came into office, Indonesia's problems were clearly greater than those of the other countries. But it had also made the least progress in addressing them.

The Political Economy of Corporate Restructuring

Closely related to these issues of financial restructuring are questions of corporate restructuring. As with the banks, corporations may have an interest in delaying financial and operational restructuring, and can collude with banks to do so at public expense. The government can solve this problem in one of two ways. First, it can enforce capital adequacy and loan loss provisions rigorously, while providing incentives for banks to engage in out-of-court settlements; this is the so-called London Rules approach. This approach, however, depends heavily on the structuring of incentives, and in particular the capacity of the government to credibly commit to its hands-off stance.

An alternative strategy is for the government to play a more active role in the corporate restructuring process. This role may range from coordinating intra-creditor and creditor-debtor relations and monitoring and enforcing agreements, to using various instruments to enforce financial and operational restructuring objectives, such as the extent of leveraging, the nature of business portfolios, and corporate governance.

The incentives for corporate restructuring are powerfully affected by foreclosure and bankruptcy laws, the final area of potential conflict among the government, banks, and corporations. If implementation of foreclosure and bankruptcy laws are overly favorable to debtors, firms have incentives to delay debt and operational restructuring and even repayment. Reform of the bankruptcy process and clear enforcement of bankruptcy and foreclosure laws are not only important for managing actual firm failures, but also for providing incentives for creditors and debtors to reach out-of-court settlements.

Table 4.3 outlines some indicators that are relevant to understanding the corporate restructuring process in the four countries. Bankruptcy laws were stronger in South Korea and Malaysia when the crisis hit. Bankruptcy reform was delayed in Thailand. Despite legal reforms, Indonesia's bankruptcy processes in fact remain weak. In all cases, governments established agencies to facilitate out-of-court settlements.

However, Korea's approach differs somewhat from the other cases. We have seen how firms in Korea manipulated bankruptcy procedures in 1997, but under Kim Dae Jung these loopholes were shut down. Despite the nominal embrace of a market-oriented, London Rules, process, the government in fact played a strong role in pushing corporate debt restructuring and linking it to operational restructuring and reforms of corporate governance. Indeed, the question in Korea was whether the government had become *too* activist and directive in leading the corporate restructuring process.

In Thailand and Indonesia, for the political reasons already outlined, debt and corporate restructuring have been much slower and have had much weaker links, if any, to the reform of corporate governance. In Malaysia, the government designed an asset management company with a mandate to engage in active corporate restructuring. But the government simultaneously engaged in several controversial bailouts of private firms.

South Korea

The key reform of the early Kim Dae Jung presidency was the passage of the financial reform legislation stalled under Kim Young Sam and the creation of the Financial Supervisory Commission (FSC) out of other regulatory agencies.[1] With strong support from the IMF and the United States, Kim Dae Jung intervened to shift control over the agency away from MOFE and the bureaucracy to the Prime Minister, and thus effectively to the Blue House. The FSC consolidated financial supervision across all financial entities and markets and played a role in developing a new regulatory and supervisory framework. However, the power of the FSC

---

1. The agency was formed through the consolidation of the office of the financial inspector of the Ministry of Finance and Economy (MOFE), Office of Bank Supervision under the Bank of Korea (BOK), Securities Supervisory Board, Insurance Supervisory Board, and Credit Management Fund Agency.

Table 4.3 Corporate restructuring

	South Korea	Thailand	Malaysia	Indonesia
Corporate restructuring				
Agency and mandate	Financial Supervisory Commission, 4/1998; nominally London Rules, but through control of financial system, linked to reforms of corporate governance	Corporate Debt Restructuring Advisory Committee, 6/1998. Initially strict London Rules, some increase in coordinating function in 1999; no link to corporate governance	Corporate Debt Restructuring Committee, 8/1998; largest debtors only	Jakarta Initiative Task Force, 9/1998, supported by Indonesian Debt Restructuring Agency, 4/1998; no link to corporate governance
Ratio of out-of-court debt restructured to total debt, 8/1999	40 percent	22 percent	32 percent	13 percent
Bankruptcy				
Bankruptcy law	In place at time of crisis, reformed, 4/1998	Reformed, 4/1998 and 4/1999	Satisfactory British legacy of common law	Reformed, 4/1998
Efficiency of judicial system index (from 1 = worst to 10 = best)	5.3	5.2	9.0	2.2
Foreclosure	Possible	Difficult, reformed, 4/1998	Possible	Difficult
Ratio of in-court debt restructured to total debt, mid-1999	8 percent	7 percent	—	4 percent

Sources: Claessans, Djankov, and Klingebiel (1999); World Bank (2000b); author's calculations and assessments.

arose not only from its routine supervisory functions,[2] but also from the central role it was to play in restructuring the financial sector in the wake of the crisis. This role involved a range of highly contentious responsibilities, from making judgments about which banking institutions were viable to closing or merging those that were not and disposing of their assets. The FSC oversaw the recapitalization and restructuring plans of the banks and assisted in the disposition of nonperforming loans.

The creation of the FSC both reflected and permitted a strategy for the financial sector that emphasized speed, even if at some substantial short-run cost. The government quickly set aside W64 trillion ($49.2 billion, or roughly 15 percent of GDP) to resolve the financial crisis, with half allocated to the Korean Deposit Insurance Company (KDIC) for recapitalization and coverage of losses, and half to finance the Korean Asset Management Corporation (KAMCO), which was assigned the task of purchasing and disposing of nonperforming loans.[3]

Operating through the FSC, the government moved swiftly and in a highly directive fashion to address the problems of the banking sector.[4] At the end of 1997, only 12 Korean banks out of 26 satisfied the international capital adequacy standard of 8 percent. In early December, the Kim Young Sam government nationalized the two banks in the worst condition, Korea First Bank and Seoul Bank.[5] The next task was to make decisions about the remaining undercapitalized banks; these were made after the elections. The FSC acted quickly to order the 12 unsound banks to submit rehabilitation plans by late April 1998. No bank plans were approved outright; 5 of the 12 plans were disapproved, and immediately following local elections in June, the FSC shut down these banks down and ordered the transfer of their assets into 5 healthy banks. To compensate the solvent banks, the KDIC undertook a series of injections that totaled W8.04 trillion ($6.7 billion) by the middle of 1999; that total rose to around 10 trillion by the end of the year. To solve the problem of the NPLs, the FSC devised a purchase and assumption (P&A) method: the viable assets were transferred to the acquiring banks, with promises of compensation against further losses for one year, while the NPLs were purchased by

---

2. Some of these powers, such as strengthened Prompt Corrective Action (PCA) to ensure that banks met capital adequacy requirements, were substantial.

3. KAMCO quickly acquired W12 trillion of assets in 1998, but at relatively high prices (62.6 percent of book value) *Newsreview*, 3 July 1999, 30.

4. The government also acted swiftly in dealing with the merchant banks; 16 of 30 were closed outright. However, the nonbank financial institutions (NBFIs) continued to pose challenges to the government through mid-2000; this issue is addressed in more detail below.

5. After the election, the plans for these banks were toughened to include the write-down of shareholder capital to below a 10 percent ownership stake and recapitalization in preparation for sale to international bidders.

the Korean Asset Management Corporation (KAMCO), to be sold later through auctions.

Assessments of Korea's achievements in the banking sector are generally positive. The government exploited the powers enjoyed by the FSC to move swiftly, albeit at some substantial cost to the government. The FSC also used its powers to impose international standards with respect to capital adequacy, as well as high standards of transparency and disclosure and increasingly stringent loan classification and provisioning requirements (OECD 1999, 84-87). The question of foreign entry did pose political dilemmas for the government. The sale of the two nationalized banks, Korea First and Seoul Bank, stalled because of differences over valuation but also faced criticisms over the cost to the public of rehabilitating the banks and from self-interested borrowers who feared that foreign banks would take a more strict stance with borrowers.

The heavy leveraging of Korean corporations and the government's effective control over the banking system gave it a powerful instrument in seeking corporate restructuring, but the very meaning of that term was the subject of quite substantial controversy (Woo-Cumings 1999; Yoo 1999). One position, associated with some economists and the *chaebol* themselves, was that the *chaebol* form per se was not at fault. What was required in the short run was an orderly process of debt rescheduling, to be negotiated between the banks and the corporations, and some reforms of corporate governance to make firms more transparent and accountable to shareholders.

However, Kim Dae Jung, who lacked close personal connections to the *chaebol*, brought with him a number of close political advisors who had a much more hostile attitude toward them. Believing that the *chaebol* would never willingly reform themselves, and that the moment was tactically auspicious given the *chaebol*'s financial weakness, these advisors advocated a more command-and-control style of corporate restructuring, and even an effort to break up the *chaebol* groups. In the first 2 years of his presidency, these two lines coexisted in an uneasy mix.

The program of corporate reform was first outlined when Kim Dae Jung used ad hoc meetings with top *chaebol* leaders to present an "agreement" on five principles of corporate restructuring (see table 3.4). Some elements of the agreement were amenable to legislation, including in the areas of corporate governance and competition policy.[6] Changes in the listing requirements to the Korean Stock Exchange strengthened minority shareholders' rights and required listed firms to have at least one outside director. These legal changes, in turn, encouraged the formation of public interest groups that pressed the rights of minority shareholders. Revisions

---

6. For example, to increase transparency, revisions of the External Audit Law required that the financial statements of companies in business groups be prepared on a consolidated basis and toughened penalties against both external auditors and corporate accounting officers.

of the Securities Investment and Trust Law relieved financial intermediaries of the obligation to vote with management and facilitated the exercise of shareholder rights on the part of institutional investors. Removing barriers to mergers and acquisitions served as a check on management, as did liberalization of rules governing foreign direct investment (FDI) that opened the way for 100 percent foreign ownership of publicly traded companies, including through hostile takeovers.

Under noncrisis circumstances, the implications of these legal changes would be felt over time as they worked through corporate organization and strategy. However, the government had to contend with a more fundamental threat of large-scale corporate failure and extraordinarily high corporate leverage. During the course of 1998 and 1999, the government used the FSC and ultimately its de facto control over the banking system to achieve objectives that were not specifically legislated, and even of questionable legality.

The government's approach was a three-tiered one. The first tier consisted of the Big Five—Samsung, Daewoo, Hyundai, and the LG and SK groups. These *chaebols* were both economically and politically important, and the government sought to deal with them through the negotiation of informal, "voluntary" agreements. The three most contentious issues with the Big Five were the elimination of mutual payment guarantees, the reduction of excessive indebtedness, and the operational restructuring of business portfolios. The first issue centered on the common *chaebol* practice of subsidizing loss-making units, contributing to weak overall performance and low productivity growth. A revision of the Fair Trade Law during the transition period prohibited the issue of new guarantees from 1 April 1998, and required all *chaebol* to phase out existing ones by March 2000.

The government's efforts to reduce the level of overall debt were particularly controversial. Early in 1998, the FSC urged the top 30 *chaebol* to lower their debt-equity ratios from an average of 519 percent at the end of 1997 to 200 percent by the end of 1999. For the Big Five, this commitment was embodied in Capital Structure Improvement Plans (CSIP), agreements with their banks on a variety of restructuring measures—asset sales, including to foreigners; issuance of new equity; debt-equity swaps; and operational restructuring.

Although these plans were to be formulated by the firms themselves, one important element of operational restructuring came directly out of the Blue House: the so-called Big Deals. Under the program, the Big Five would swap major lines of business among themselves to consolidate excessive and duplicative investments while simultaneously achieving greater economies of scale (see table 4.4). A number of premises behind the Big Deal concept were dubious, including the assumption that they would necessarily realize efficiencies or reduce surplus capacity. The

Table 4.4 Status of the Big Deal plan (as of January 2000)

Sector	Before restructuring	After restructuring	Status
Semiconductors	Samsung Electronics Hyundai Electronics LG Semiconductor	Samsung Electronics; Hyundai + LG to merge	Hyundai Electronics acquired LG Semi for won 2.6 trillion
Petrochemicals	Samsung Chemical Hyundai Petrochemical	Merger, with foreign capital	No agreement
Aircraft components	Samsung Aerospace Daewoo Heavy Industry Hyundai Space & Aircraft	Joint venture, including a foreign partner	Subject to commercial arrangements with a foreign strategic partner
Automobiles	Hyundai Motor Daewoo Motor Samsung Motor	Hyundai acquired Kia	Swap of Samsung Motors for Daewoo Electronics canceled. Samsung Motors in receivership
Rolling stock	Hyundai Precision Daewoo Heavy Industry	Joint venture	Commercial terms, with some bank assistance
Ship engines	Korea Heavy Industry Samsung Heavy Industry	Korea Heavy Industry to acquire Samsung Heavy Industry	Acquisition, no financing
Power generation	Samsung Heavy Industry Hyundai Heavy Industry Korea Heavy Industry	Korea Heavy Industry to be privatized	Acquisition by Korea Heavy Industry

Source: Mako and Jung (2000), table 3.

negotiations over them were plagued by sharp differences about the valuation of assets, a variety of questions about how quite different operations would in fact be integrated, and uncertainty about the final corporate form the new entities would take. Politics also entered into the process; both the government and the *chaebol* managers appeared to believe that the Big Deals could be consummated without closing facilities and shedding labor, which seemed to undercut one central rationale for the program. Nonetheless, the Big Deals became a litmus test of corporate commitment to the restructuring process, and were indicative of the government's directive approach to corporate restructuring.

Throughout 1998 and the first half of 1999, the government engaged in an ongoing public relations battle with the Big Five, in which it repeatedly claimed that the large *chaebol* were not being aggressive enough in introducing restructuring plans and reducing their indebtedness. The call for explicit CSIPs was the first step in this process; it continued with the government decision to halt credit to a number of small Big Five subsidiaries in June and a revision of the companies' initial Big Deal proposal, and it culminated in the public signing of financial pacts between the Big Five and their banks in December 1998.

Coming almost a full year after the corporate restructuring principles were first announced, the pacts included four elements: Specific commitments to reduce the number of affiliates by target dates, including through the Big Deal mechanism; specific targets for the reduction of debt-equity ratios; an acceleration of the elimination of cross-guarantees between affiliates; and a reiteration of the commitment to reforms in corporate governance. The groups also submitted to a quarterly review process, under the threat that failure to comply would be met by higher interest charges or even a suspension of credit (*Korea Money*, December-January 1999, 25-27).

The new agreements differed from the principles of a year earlier in their specificity and the monitoring that went along with them. The reduction of debt-equity ratios by a particular date had the most far-reaching implications, since it appeared to necessitate dramatic asset sales. Yet by April, the president was again publicly chiding the *chaebol* for reneging on their promises to sell assets, raise capital, and cut their debt (*Korea Insight*, May 1999). Data released in April 1999 showed that much of the improvement in the financial positions of the Big Five had been achieved through asset revaluations as well as new rights issues.

Moreover, both Hyundai and Daewoo had openly defied the government by taking on more debt in 1998, primarily by circumventing the banks and placing high-yield bonds with nonbank financial institutions.[7]

---

7. My thanks to Sandra Eccles for this analysis.

This practice was explicitly aimed at confounding the government's efforts to limit *chaebol* control of financial institutions and the extent of corporate leveraging. Between March 1997 and March 1999, the combined market share of the 33 nonbank financial institutions owned by the Big Five increased from 18.6 percent to just over 30 percent (*Korea Herald*, 6 December 1999). The growth in the investment trust sector was even more spectacular (from 5 percent of the market to over 30 percent), and generated a whole new round of moral hazard problems in late 1999 and the first half of 2000.

In Daewoo's case, the gambling was particularly flagrant, amounting to a strategy of "invest recklessly on an international scale and use borrowed money to do it"(Graham 2000, 93). During the spring, it became increasingly clear that the government was headed toward a showdown with one or both of the two firms.

Daewoo proved the test case. In mid-July 1999, Daewoo Motors admitted to liquidity problems. The firm had been involved in prolonged negotiations over one of the most controversial of the big deals: the swap that would transfer Samsung's ailing automobile operations for Daewoo's increasingly profitable electronics business. However, Daewoo's global auto operations were also weighed down with debt. On 17 July, the chairman was forced to pledge personal properties to secure rollovers of short-term debt. In a "final" effort to secure support, the firm offered a restructuring plan on 20 July that would sell off all but nine affiliated firms, and even those would be largely divested to foreign partners in order to focus the core of the new group on Daewoo Corporation and Daewoo Motors.

The creditor group, and behind them the FSC, responded by rolling over W10 trillion in short-term debt and extending W4 trillion more in new credits. But the market reaction to both the restructuring plan and the government's decision to support Daewoo was strongly negative and gradually pushed the government toward the position that Daewoo should be dismantled. When due diligence was finally done on the group, it was revealed that its net worth was negative W17 trillion (more than $14 billion). The final reorganization plan agreed to with creditors in mid-August allowed for six units to be kept, but only on the condition that a number of profitable ones would be sold. By early 2000, the precise details of Daewoo's complex workout plan were still being negotiated and finalized.

The fall of Daewoo will undoubtedly be seen as an important event in Korea's postwar economic history. The government did not altogether avoid a bailout of the firm, because debt was rolled over and ultimately converted to equity and the core firms were not liquidated. Moreover, in September and October, the government was forced to establish massive funds to bail out the investment trust companies, which were big purchasers of Daewoo bonds. But the conditions were tough, and in his Liberation Day speech on 15 August, Kim Dae Jung even signaled an interest in breaking up other *chaebol* into independent units. Although the president retreated from this position (*Korea Herald*, 16-17 August 1999), he took advantage of Daewoo's crisis to press a restructuring of the Federation of Korean Industries itself, the peak organization that had long represented *chaebol* interests and which under the leadership of Daewoo's Kim Woo-Chang had actively opposed the government's corporate restructuring plans. The Daewoo action, the Liberation Day speech, the attack on FKI, and yet another round of public agreements with the Big Five sent strong signals that brinkmanship would have high cost.

The second tier of the corporate restructuring effort centered on the so-called "6-64" *chaebol*, and gained momentum after the June 1998 elections (Lieberman 1999; Mako and Jung 2000). On 18 June 1998, the FSC declared that 55 companies, including 20 subsidiaries of the Big Five, would no longer have access to bank credit (*Far Eastern Economic Review*, 2 July 1998). On 24 June, 236 financial institutions signed and entered into the Corporate Restructuring Accord, which defined the informal workout procedure for troubled firms. Eight major creditor banks, identified as lead banks, would take responsibility for negotiating workouts of problem debts with the 6-64 corporate groups. These workouts were nominally organized around so-called London Rules, but the process was closely overseen by the FSC through its Corporate Debt Restructuring Committee (CDRC).[8]

Although the speed of the process is noteworthy when compared to other countries, it is also the case that a degree of forbearance is visible in the fact that the principal restructuring method has been interest rate reductions, and that the contribution of new equity, whether local or foreign, has been minimal. This suggests that another round of restructuring might be required in the future, and in September 1999 the administration moved to reach more expansive operational restructuring agreements with the firms in this second group as well (*Newsreview*, 11 September 1999, 26).

The restructuring of small and medium-sized enterprises (SMEs) had particular political significance in Korea. Kim Dae Jung came to office with a longstanding belief that SMEs had been slighted by government policy, and employment, equity, and political considerations thus pushed the administration to address their problems aggressively. The administration's approach resembled a kind of corrective industrial policy. Initially, SME debts to the banks were rolled over for 6 months and for a

---

8. The CDRC is empowered to act as an arbitration committee in the case that the banks cannot agree on a workout strategy among themselves or the lead bank and the debtor fail to come to an agreement. If a CRA signatory fails to comply with an approved workout agreement or arbitration decision, the CDRC can impose penalties (Lieberman 1999).

subsequent 6 months, and in 1999, the banks began to restructure SME debts. But the government has also shown a concern for restoring liquidity to the sector, and has done so through a variety of means, including credit insurance funds, a central bank credit line, funding for trade finance, and four SME restructuring funds. To date, Korea is the only one of the crisis countries to aggressively address small business restructuring.

The Kim Dae Jung government initiated a broad financial and corporate reform process, facilitated by his status as an outsider with fewer connections with, or dependence on, the *chaebol*. The government was able to legislate quickly because of the unique political position enjoyed by the president in the period immediately following the election. In other areas where legislation proved more contentious or impossible, the president used direct negotiations with *chaebol* leaders and public pressure to secure business concessions. The creation of a powerful new statutory body with a clear mandate for reform expedited implementation.

However, the strongly directive elements of the Korean restructuring process also raise important questions about policy tradeoffs among speed, accountability, and the extent of government intervention. The speed with which the Korean government moved was bought by an exercise of directive powers that rested on a dubious legal foundation and lacked democratic safeguards (Mo and Moon 1999). For example, the Big Deals and the setting of quantitative targets and deadlines for achieving arbitrary debt-equity ratios are both of questionable legality as well as merit, as was the suggestion that *chaebol* should be broken up into individual business units. Moreover, these measures carried an important irony: They involved the Korean government even more deeply and directly in the economy than it had been before the crisis. Formulating an exit strategy now looms as a crucial task; I return to this question in the conclusion.

Thailand

The initial financial sector strategy of the Chuan government was two-pronged. The Financial Restructuring Authority (FRA) would evaluate the rehabilitation plans of the suspended finance companies and make judgments about whether they should be left open, while simultaneously devising a strategy for liquidating failed ones built around the "good bank-bad bank" model. In early December, the FRA recommended that all but 2 of the 58 finance companies be closed permanently, quickly resolving a problem that had been lingering for months (*Bangkok Post*, 19 December 1997). In June, 5 additional finance companies were shut down, bringing the total to 63.

For the 33 finance companies that initially remained open and the 15 banks, the government's strategy was to limit access to liquidity credit through the FIDF while substantially tightening loan classification and provisioning rules and capital adequacy requirements. These regulatory measures would force recapitalization, and serve the additional purpose of diluting the control exercised by a small number of families that effectively controlled the Thai banking system. At the same time, the Bank of Thailand relaxed rules governing foreign ownership, sending the message that domestic banks should consider taking on partners. The government also agreed to a tight timetable for the passage of other legislation that would facilitate the financial and corporate reform process.[9]

A number of banks responded to these new incentives (*Asiamoney*, September 1998, 15). The Thai Farmers Bank and Bangkok raised new equity through share issues, and Thai Danu Bank, Thai Farmers Bank, and the Bank of Asia took on foreign partners. However, a number of banks stood little chance of meeting the recapitalization requirements and were effectively insolvent.[10] The size of these banks—which collectively accounted for 20 percent of banking-sector assets—made them difficult to close outright, and the problems of negotiating sales in a timely fashion as well as the absence of buyers seemed to foreclose the option of selling them quickly. Through its recapitalization efforts, the FIDF became the effective owner of all four, although without clear plans for their disposition. With the combination of its equity injections, recapitalization, and earlier liquidity support, the losses of the FIDF in the early part of the year reached 20 percent of GDP.

In sum, the initial stance of the new government toward the resolution of the financial sector's difficulties appeared quite decisive in some respects. The government closed down a number of ailing finance companies. In a series of 11 auctions ending in August 1999, the FRA sold off their assets, although some ended up in the hands of the government's Asset Management Company. The government faced substantial political criticism from interested parties over the low sales prices, but it rode out the resistance and realized nearly $4 billion on them, equal to 25 percent of face value.

With respect to insolvent banks, the government took a tough stance with their shareholders, although it backed away from closing the banks outright and absorbed very large losses as a result. But this pattern is not

---

9. These include new standards for disclosure and auditing, a revision of the bankruptcy and foreclosure laws, liberalization of rules governing foreign direct investment, and the privatization of a number of state-owned enterprises, designed in part to help finance the costs of bank restructuring (*Bangkok Post*, 26 November 1997).

10. The Bangkok Bank of Commerce (BBC) came under public control in December 1997, and the capital of the bank was dramatically written down. In February 1998, the government took over three more ailing banks: Siam City Bank (SCIB), First Bangkok City Bank (FBCB), and Bangkok Metropolitan Bank. In the case of the last two banks, capital was written down to practically nothing, again sending a strong signal to shareholders.

untypical in crises of this magnitude. With respect to viable banks, the government's strategy sought to limit public expense by forcing private recapitalization, and thus implicitly breaking the hold that a small number of banks and families had on the financial system.

However, the government's restructuring plans quickly faced political as well as economic obstacles. The political problems, as we have seen, centered on the splits within the cabinet and the growing chorus of complaints from the Thai private sector against the government's macroeconomic policy. The economic problems centered on the gradual deepening of the crisis, which cast further doubt on the balance sheets of the banks and their ability to recapitalize on their own.

Moreover, the government's initial strategy did not directly address the underlying question of corporate debt restructuring, which had important implications for how losses were distributed. When the government did finally address the issue in June 1998, through the creation of a Corporate Debt Restructuring Advisory Committee (CDRAC), the approach was modeled on the London Framework. The government did provide an important incentive to restructure in May by allowing banks to maintain nonperforming loans off their books if debts were being restructured. But because the reform of bankruptcy and foreclosure laws and laws governing foreign direct investment were delayed, banks and particularly corporate debtors had only weak incentives to engage in serious restructuring efforts. To the contrary, the regulatory forbearance extended in May and the absence of a strong foreclosure law encouraged "shallow" restructurings that later proved of questionable value (*Thailand Economic Monitor*, 2nd quarter 1999, 15).

The fourth letter of intent formulated a new reform timetable to speed up the pace of reform of the financial and corporate sectors. Among the key elements of the new timetable were that the banks and finance companies sign memoranda of understanding (MOUs) outlining their plans to meet the new provisioning and loan-loss standards. As the mid-August deadline for these MOUs approached, it became apparent that the government's effort to handle the banking crisis by relaxing liquidity and inducing private recapitalization was failing. Large banks that were unwilling or unable to recapitalize early, including Krung Thai and Siam Commercial, faced severe distress.

On 14 August 1998, the government unveiled a new initiative for the banking sector. The first element of the new plan was to deal with problem institutions more forcefully.[11] The second element of the program was

---

11. Two more banks and five finance companies were effectively nationalized pending resolution strategies, while the government also clarified its strategy to deal with the previously nationalized banks. BBC was to be closed, First Bangkok City Bank to merge with Krung Thai Bank, and Siam City and Bangkok Metropolitan to be privatized, with the government guaranteeing buyers' potential losses.

regulatory forbearance; to reduce Tier 1 capital requirements from 6 to 4.5 percent. The centerpiece of the new strategy, however, was a complex, and voluntary, recapitalization scheme, backed by only implicit threats if recapitalization targets were not met.[12] But the conditions for financial support were onerous. Not only would the government have to approve the banks' restructuring plans, but banks would have to adopt end-2000 provisioning requirements immediately; given NPLs of 30-40 percent of total portfolios, this would imply an immediate write-off of shareholder capital. Moreover, the government retained the right to displace existing management.

Not surprisingly, banks showed little interest in the program, turning rather to a number of innovative, but high-cost, short-term instruments to meet capitalization targets.[13] By relying on these instruments, bank owners effectively sidestepped the need to raise "real" capital and bought time. Although the government set aside Bt300 billion for the program, it had to be modified in June 1999, and by September only 13 percent of the funds set aside for the program had been used (*Thailand Economic Monitor*, 2nd quarter 1999, 15). In effect, the policy of the government toward the financial sector had become one of forbearance: In August 1999, nonperforming loans stood at 47 percent of total outstanding loans, only marginally below their peak in May, and they didn't drop below 40 percent until mid 2000 (*Thailand Economic Monitor*, June 2000, 24).

The second component of the August scheme was to support Tier 2 capital and to provide incentives for the banks to begin debt restructuring. The problem with this second pillar of the program is that, while attractive to banks, the scheme was not necessarily attractive to debtors, who continued to delay payment; this in turn had to do with the absence of a legal framework that would support the corporate workout process under CDRAC.

In late 1998, the politics of reform came to center on a group of 11 reform bills that were conditions of the fifth Letter of Intent with the IMF.[14] Failure to pass these laws, and particularly those governing the bankruptcy and foreclosure process, were adversely affecting the financial and corporate restructuring process. But the existence of multiple veto gates and the influence of interested parties served to further delay the reforms.

---

12. For Tier 1 capital, the government would recapitalize up to 2.5 percent by swapping tradable bonds for preferred shares, and match any private capital up to 4.25 percent on a one-to-one basis, also granting the banks buy-back options.

13. In particular, Stapled Limited Issuance Preferred Stocks (SLIPS) and Capital Augmented Preferred Shares (CAPS).

14. The bills included bankruptcy, bankruptcy court, and foreclosure; state enterprise capital; real estate property leasing, land and condominiums; civil justice procedures; and foreign investment.

Reform of the bankruptcy process had been a condition of the second Letter of Intent with the IMF in November 1997, but legislation proposed by the government immediately ran into strong objections from senators who would be adversely affected by the legislation, including particularly the heads of two heavily indebted groups, Thai Petrochemical and NTS Steel.[15] When bankruptcy reform was first vetted in early 1998, objections centered on the relative powers granted to creditors and debtors in the new process, including the ability to appoint administrators who would influence the restructuring plan, and the absence of provisions that would allow debtors to remain in possession. Opponents feared that the lack of Thai insolvency experts would lead foreign creditors to appoint foreign insolvency professionals, who would have less of an interest in reviving the company.

The changes introduced by the Senate contributed to a bill that discouraged its use; moreover, critical accompanying legislation governing foreclosure was not passed. Between May, when the bill was passed, and August only five business rehabilitation plans had been filed with the courts (*Bangkok Post*, 25 August 1998). As the chairman of the Senate blue-ribbon committee argued when reviewing the amended legislation, "the introduction of the business rehabilitation plan, intending to minimize judicial reviews on bankruptcy cases, has now been associated with the refinancing of the business community rather than debt-restructuring as commonly understood before the passage of this new law" (*Bangkok Post*, 27 November 1998).

When the amended bills were reintroduced in the fall, the criticism in the Senate widened to include a range of new issues and changes that would have dramatically weakened the legislation.[16] The Senate also sought similar dilutions of the bankruptcy court law.[17] In the end, the bankruptcy and foreclosure law reform had taken the Chuan government more than 15 months to complete, and even then concerns remained that procedural concessions with respect to the appeals process made the

---

15. The Senate has the power to review and amend legislation; if the House objects to the Senate's changes, they are mediated through a joint committee. If the joint committee fails to reach agreement, the House can nonetheless pass its version. But the review process and the publicity surrounding it provided an opportunity for senators opposed to the bill to secure concessions favorable to debtors.

16. These included raising the minimum debt limits, a prohibition on filing bankruptcy against holders of personal guarantees, a common way to "secure" lending, and even a provision that would have prohibited bankruptcy suits in cases where the value of the collateral matched the amount of debt outstanding *on the day the loan was made* (*Bangkok Post*, 12 March 1999)!

17. These included reducing the power of the court to declare a firm bankrupt if its rehabilitation plan were not approved, stripping the new courts of their powers to handle criminal aspects of bankruptcy, and keeping a cumbersome appeals process that had been a major factor in slowing the bankruptcy process.

bankruptcy process unwieldy. Creditors and debtors proved unwilling to settle disputes in court. In 1999, only 37 business reorganization petitions were filed with the Central Bankruptcy Court, although the pace increased in the first half of 2000 (*Thailand Economic Monitor*, June 2000, 33). Rather, private innovations through CDRAC provided the basis for an increase in the number of debt restructuring agreements.[18]

To summarize, politics in Thailand exerted a powerful influence over policymaking with respect to the financial sector and corporate restructuring. Under Chavalit, there are clear signs of moral hazard related to the way the FIDF interpreted its mandate (Nukul Commission Report 1998, para. 329-40), but the problems ran deeper. Politicians with direct interests in regulated financial institutions were able to influence the government's decision-making, delaying an effective response to the problem. Both intracoalitional and intraparty conflict frustrated the efforts of reformers. These political failings directly contributed to the onset of the crisis by weakening confidence in the Thai financial sector, and deepened it once the devaluation occurred by further delaying adjustment until the change of government.

As with the Kim Dae Jung government in South Korea, the Chuan government demonstrates how a new democratic government can exploit a crisis to extend the reach of the technocrats over policy. The decisiveness of the government was particularly visible in the handling of the finance companies, the establishment of the FRA, the disposition of assets, and the intervention of the four insolvent banks.

However, the government's action toward the finance companies proved the exception rather than the rule, and the government ended up being much less decisive in other areas. In recapitalizing the banks, the government made a large sum of money available and devised a scheme that would have imposed strong conditions on the banks. But the scheme was voluntary, not used extensively, and in the end rested on substantial forbearance toward bank owners. The government was slow to move on the issue of corporate debt restructuring and in passing bankruptcy and foreclosure laws. These delays had a powerful influence on the distribution of losses among groups. The burden of financial restructuring was borne largely by taxpayers and bank shareholders, although their losses were limited by government forbearance. However, the weak legal and administrative regime for bankruptcy benefited debtors and even created

---

18. Of particular importance were the development of debtor-creditor agreements and intercreditor agreements that defined an expedited process that allowed for information sharing and negotiations; 75 percent majority voting approval; and a mechanism for enforcement, including an expanded role for the Bank of Thailand in the process. As of April 2000, 2,682 "target debtors" had been identified, but full restructuring agreements had been completed in only 266 cases, although accounting for over 20 percent of total debt. (*Thailand Economic Monitor*, June 2000, 34).

perverse incentives for them to continue to avoid repayment. It was ultimately left to the private sector to devise a more coherent strategy.

Why does the Thai recovery strategy look very different than Korea's— less decisive and more prone to forbearance toward the private sector? The answers can be found in the political constraints outlined in chapter 3. The combination of parliamentary rule and the dependence on coalition partners meant that legislative support for reform was always fragile. As the case of the bankruptcy reform shows, Thailand also had legislative processes that substantially slowed decision making, certainly when compared with the early days of the Kim Dae Jung administration. Although such deliberation is a legitimate function of democratic government, many of the objections to the reform process reflected the interests of large debtors, some of whom actually sat in the Senate.

Finally, the political circumstances just described fed into a third factor; the government's political relationship with the private sector. From the outset, the Chuan cabinet and the Democrat Party were divided over a range of policies between those around Tarrin, who defended the IMF line and sought to limit government commitments to private actors, and those around Supachai and in the Senate, who sought a macroeconomic stimulus, greater government intervention in support of business, and a cautious approach to reform. The very existence of this split provided an important entry point for the private sector.

Malaysia

Malaysia was somewhat slower than the other countries in devising an institutional structure to handle the financial and corporate restructuring process, in part because the depth of the problems in its banking sector was substantially less. It was not until mid-1998, following the issue of the National Economic Action Council (NEAC) report, that the government established three new institutions to deal with the problems of nonperforming assets in the financial system, bank recapitalization, and corporate debt restructuring. In general, the design of these institutions mirrored best practice and they subsequently moved with great speed, even if the government ran some risks in adopting an active asset management strategy.

But the operation of the formal institutions did not constitute the full scope of the government's approach to financial and corporate distress; the government also engaged in a small number of controversial bank and corporate bailouts. The extent of these bailouts should not be exaggerated, and some were modified and partly reversed in response to political pressures. Nonetheless, they shed light on continuities in the nature of business-government relations in Malaysia.

The first to be established, Pengurusan Danaharta Nasional Bhd, or Danaharta, was set up on 20 June 1998 under the Ministry of Finance to acquire nonperforming loans from banks.[19] Unlike the asset management companies in South Korea and Thailand, Danaharta (1999, 3) is neither a rapid disposition agency nor a warehouse agency. Rather, it was granted a wider range of restructuring options, with the only stipulation being that recovery value was maximized. Danaharta could take legal action to recover security through the bankruptcy process and could sell the loans to a third party, but it could also take a more active role in rehabilitating companies. Given the risks associated with such a strategy, Danaharta outlined strict loan restructuring guidelines to avoid problems of moral hazard.[20]

As of 30 June 1999, Danaharta had a portfolio of RM39.3 billion of nonperforming loans, 17.7 billion acquired at an average discount of 57 percent and another RM21.5 billion in assets from two failed banks— the Sime Bank Group and Bank Bumiputra—that fell under Danaharta management (Danaharta 1999, 1).[21] Sixty-six financial institutions sold loans to Danaharta, but the majority of acquired NPLs were concentrated in fewer than 10 financial institutions, with the Sime Group and Bank Bumiputra the largest offenders.[22] This suggests that, although the banking system was generally sound, there were pockets of serious regulatory and institutional weakness (*Business Times*, 17 March 1999); as we will see, these weaknesses had political roots.

The most important test for an asset management company is its ability to maximize value, either by turning assets around or disposing of them judiciously. By the end of 1999, Danaharta had initiated recovery with 88 percent of borrowers in terms of value and over one-third of debt had undergone loan restructuring, asset restructuring or outright disposal (Thillainathan 2000, 13). Given Danaharta's ambition of restructuring companies, its performance should not necessarily be measured by asset sales.

---

19. With paid-up capital of RM250 million (approximately $59 million), Danaharta raised RM25 billion in working capital in zero-coupon government-guaranteed bonds.

20. These included the ability to displace management and appoint "special administrators" to manage distressed companies, insistence that shareholders take disproportionate "haircuts" in any loan rescheduling, and the provision that borrowers are provided only one opportunity to implement a restructuring plan (Thillainathan 2000, 12).

21. The largest sectors in Danaharta's portfolio (as of June 1999) were the property sector (31.9 percent); purchase of securities (18.6 percent); finance, insurance, and business services, particularly investment holding companies (15.2 percent); and manufacturing (12.7 percent). These numbers underline that risk was concentrated in the nontradable goods sector. The variation around the mean discount of acquired assets was wide. Danaharta acquired unsecured nonperforming loans for a flat 10 percent of the principal outstanding, while construction and real estate loans, which constituted more than half the portfolio, had an average discount of approximately 30 percent.

22. Those banks that chose not to sell nonperforming loans to Danaharta were required to write down their values immediately to Danaharta's valuation (20 percent discount to market value).

Nonetheless, it is noteworthy that its first sale of physical property did not take place until November 1999, and the sale was extremely modest.[23] It is even more difficult to judge the success of Danaharta's operational restructuring efforts, but as of early 2000, the agency had appointed administrators for 53 companies. But the risk with Danaharta is that its relatively long life span may result in the effective warehousing of assets, with high costs for the government and taxpayers (Thillainathan 2000).

The second institution for managing the crisis was the bank recapitalization agency, Danamodal Nasional Bhd, incorporated on 10 August 1998 with an anticipated life span of 5 to 7 years.[24] With assistance from two foreign investment banks, Salomon Smith Barney and Goldman Sachs, Danamodal moved very quickly to identify 14 institutions in need of recapitalization. By October, it had recapitalized 9, in March 1999 a 10th (for a total of RM6.2 billion), and had worked out arrangements with the remaining 4 to recapitalize privately. To address problems of moral hazard that are inherent in such an exercise, Danamodal operated on the first-loss principle, under which losses arising from past credit decisions are born by shareholders. Danamodal also appointed nominees to the banks' boards and a monitoring process to assure the operational restructuring that constituted the quid pro quo of the restructuring.

Danamodal's recapitalization efforts were only part of a wider restructuring of the financial sector. In contrast to other countries in the region, the government did not move to close financial institutions directly; rather, it sought to consolidate the sector through a merger plan. Mergers would cut the number of domestic banks from 22 to 16, and merchant banks from 12 to 9, increasing the degree of concentration. The plan also envisioned a substantial reduction in the number of finance companies (*Straits Times*, 9 March 1999). But somewhat contradictory factors resulted in a number of institutions resisting the pressure for merger. On the one hand, the recession made merger partners less attractive; on the other hand, the recapitalization effort and purchase of NPLs allowed a number of smaller institutions to survive without assistance. The merger plan stalled.

In July 1999, a central bank (Bank Nasional Malaysia, or BNM) decree outlined an even more radical restructuring plan designed to increase the size and competitiveness of the financial sector: To cut the number of commercial banks from 21 to 6, finance companies from 25 to 6, and merchant banks from 12 to 6, with each class of institution built around a small number of "anchor" institutions. (*Straits Times*, 31 July 1999; *Asian*

---

23. Of 44 properties with a face value of RM122.6 million (0.3 percent of Danaharta's total assets), 24 were sold to successful bidders at an average 8 percent over their indicative value.

24. Danamodal fell under the central bank (Bank Nasional Malaysia, or BNM), and was to be funded by capital raised in the form of equity, hybrid instruments, or debt, in both the domestic and international markets, to minimize the use of public funds. The central bank provided the initial seed capital of RM3 billion, and another RM2 billion on a standby basis.

Wall Street Journal, 2 August 1999). The plan was highly directive: The BNM itself identified the likely anchor institutions, how they would be built, and the generous incentives they would receive. Also noteworthy is the fact that as many as 4 of the 6 new banks would continue to have significant government equity, maintaining the government's presence in the financial sector, and even increasing it in relative terms.[25]

The merger plan naturally set off a political scramble, as banks lobbied to be designated one of the anchor banks (*Straits Times*, 11 October 1999). But the most contentious political issue was the effect the consolidation would have on Chinese banks. Under the New Economic Policy, the Malay presence in the banking sector had grown dramatically, primarily at the expense of foreign and to a lesser extent Malaysian-Chinese banking institutions.[26] Because they have been smaller and weaker institutions, the proposed consolidation would have had an important effect on the Chinese presence in the sector. The number of Chinese-controlled banks would have been reduced to two. Hong Leong and Phileo Allied, two institutions affiliated with Anwar and his supporters, also emerged as losers out of the plan as well. The political significance of the bank consolidation plan was made apparent in early October when Mahathir himself signaled that the number of anchor banks was arbitrary and the plan might be modified; protests from the Chinese community and electoral calculations clearly had a bearing on this decision. The minister of finance and the central bank quickly fell in line, and the plan was modified to allow for a larger number of anchor institutions (*Asian Wall Street Journal*, 21-23 October 1999; *Straits Times*, 15 February 2000).

In the final piece of its restructuring efforts, the government moved to address the underlying problems in the corporate sector through the formation of a Corporate Debt Restructuring Committee in October 1998 under BNM. The purpose of the committee, like its counterparts in Indonesia, South Korea, and Thailand, is to minimize losses to creditors, shareholders, and other stakeholders through voluntary coordinated workouts that sidestep the formal bankruptcy procedure, particularly for larger debtors. Existing insolvency legislation in Malaysia was clearly more institutionalized than in either Indonesia or Thailand. Nonetheless, it was unpopular with creditors and did not provide the range of solutions to preserve value for other stakeholders in complex corporate groups with multiple creditors. The purpose of the committee was thus to persuade

---

25. Rules for bank valuations would be set by BNM, and shareholders of acquired banks in the scheme would have the option of being paid either in cash or in shares of the merged entity (*Straits Times*, 11 August 1999).

26. Foreign banks have had a significant presence in the Malaysian banking system— accounting for roughly 30 percent of assets and lending. But unlike in other countries in the region, the crisis in Malaysia has not spurred efforts to further open the system, and the current cap of 30 percent on the foreign stake in local banks has remained in place.

financial institutions not to precipitate insolvency, while simultaneously keeping companies from running for the cover of court protection (Section 176).[27] As of the end of 1999, the CDRC had managed to oversee only 16 restructurings, but they were very large, with a total value of RM13 billion (Thillainathan 2000, 15).

Although the Malaysian government did move to establish strong institutions for managing bank and corporate restructuring, not all interventions took place through these institutions. In contrast to other countries in the region, a distinguishing feature of the Malaysian response to the crisis has been to extend support directly to a number of firms. These interventions do not exhibit a single pattern. Not all were straightforward bailouts; some involved indirect forms of support. In others, a proposed bailout was either rejected or modified, suggesting some of the checks that operate on the government. Others, however, suggest the socialization of private risk and the presence of moral hazard, including forbearance toward shareholders and management of ailing firms. Some actions could have been predicted by government efforts to use companies to fulfil social and foreign policy objectives. But others appear to stem from political and even family connections to recently privatized companies.

Projects initiated directly by the government and state-owned enterprises always pose dilemmas for governments; the temptation to use budgetary resources to support them during times of distress is high. The Proton national car project provides an example. As we saw in chapter 1, the Proton project was initially undertaken by a state-owned enterprise, Heavy Industries Corporation of Malaysia Holdings Bhd (HICOM), but by late 1995, the government had divested itself of majority control of Hicom by selling its remaining 32 percent interest to Yahya Ahmad's publicly held Diversified Resources Bhd, a holding company involved in assembling motor vehicles among other things (*Far Eastern Economic Review*, 2 May 1996).[28] Proton was badly affected by the crisis, but the firm also faced longer-term challenges, including the elimination of tariffs by 2002 under the ASEAN Free Trade Area (AFTA) agreement. The firm informed the government in early 1998 of the need for substantial capital investments to compete internationally.

Although the government had relinquished ownership, the prime minister remained closely involved with, and committed to, the national car project. Petronas, the state-owned oil company that falls directly under the control of the prime minister, was tapped to assist the ailing project,

---

27. A CDRC workout includes initial meetings of debtors and creditors, appointment of consultants, an initial review of the viability of the business, a formal standstill among creditors if the restructuring exercise proceeds, and oversight of restructuring plans. For details, see Thillainathan 2000, 13-18).

28. Hicom Holdings owned 32 percent of Perusahan Otomobil Nasional Bhd (Proton) and 27.2 percent of its distributor Edaran Otomobil Nasional Bhd (EON).

while Chinese-owned private companies with prior experience in the auto industry were excluded from participation in the restructuring of Proton-EON.[29] Petronas has vigorously denied that its involvement constitutes a bailout and insists that it would pay "fair market value" for its stake based on "due diligence." However, the prima facie evidence is strong that the transaction constitutes a "reverse privatization" of an ailing company and had the indirect effect of assisting Diversified Resources as well. (*Far Eastern Economic Review*, 12 August 1999, 13).

The management of Bank Bumiputra's financial problems provides a second example of the dilemmas governments face in dealing with loss-making state-owned enterprises. "Bank Bumi" started in 1965 to help ethnic Malays and was bailed out in 1984 and again in 1989. After injecting fresh capital in 1998, the government arranged a merger with another state-owned institution, Commerce Asset-Holding Bhd (CAHB) (*Asian Wall Street Journal* and *Straits Times*, 9 February 1999).[30] With assets of some RM65 billion, BCB will be Malaysia's largest banking group after Malayan Banking. To ensure the new bank is free of encumbrances, it was granted an option to sell some RM5 billion of Bank Bumiputra's nonperforming loans to Danaharta at face value; as the opposition was quick to point out, this favorable but costly arrangement was not made available to other banks.[31] CAHB will get a clean bank at a good price, while the government will avoid the problem of retrenchment of bank workers by spinning off a new Islamic bank that will continue to pursue the objectives previously pursued by Bank Bumiputra. During periods of systemic distress, it is typical for banks to get relief through recapitalization and purchase of nonperforming loans, but the terms on which CAHB and BCB were managed clearly differed from those of other private or state-owned banks.

The most visible and controversial case of government support for private companies is the complex saga of Renong and its affiliates, which shows—at a variety of points—how close business-government connections can generate high social costs. Fleet Holdings was UMNO's holding

---

29. The two-stage transaction, involving RM1 billion, has Proton first acquiring Hicom's other auto businesses, including a 32 percent stake in EON and several automotive-component manufacturing companies. Second, Hicom would sell its equity interest in Proton to Petronas, netting enough through the two transactions to settle its debts (*Asian Wall Street Journal*, 7 July 1999).

30. The share-swap deal reduced the government's 100 percent stake in CAHB to 30 percent, and gave CAHB 99 percent of the new Bumiputra Commerce Bank Bhd (BCB). Swapping RM334.2 million in new shares for the government's entire RM1.4 billion shares in Bank Bumiputra, CAHB will also pay up to RM560 million in cash or other instruments pending final valuations, for a total of approximately RM1.6 billion.

31. See the statement by Lim Kit Siang on Danaharta's purchase of Bank Bumiputra's NPLs at http://www.malaysia.net/dap/sg1680.htm.

company in the 1970s and in 1991, "through a complicated series of share swaps, takeovers and mergers" (Gomez and Jomo 1997, 52), Renong became its main corporate instrument. Renong was one of the success stories of the Mahathir strategy of privatization. By the early 1990s, its well-connected *bumiputra* management had benefited from privatization and established an extensive network of holdings in media, construction, and finance.

The controversy surrounding Renong involves several different transactions. The first dates to 1996, when the company's chief executive officer, Halim Saad, rescued the debt-laden National Steel Corp of the Philippines from Wing Tiek Holdings, which in turn was controlled by a Malaysian member of Parliament.[32] Wing Tiek's holding in the troubled company was sold to a shell subsidiary of Renong, Hong Kong-based Hottick Investment Ltd. The transaction was financed by a consortium of Malaysian banks. Danaharta took over the RM3.09 billion loan to Hottick Investments Ltd., albeit at a deep discount, thereby limiting losses to parent Renong. This single loan, not initially included in Danaharta's balance sheet, was equal to more than 15 percent of all of its purchased loans (*Asian Wall Street Journal*, 17 March 1999).

The next controversy was the government's decision to allow United Engineers Malaysia Bhd (UEM), a subsidiary of Renong, to undertake a reverse takeover of its ailing parent. Three issues were involved in the UEM-Renong case, the first being the waiver of the requirement to make a mandatory general offer. This waiver was opposed by Anwar, who attempted to revoke it in Parliament on 25 November 1997, but with Daim's support the waiver was reinstated on 12 January 1998. The reinstatement of the waiver raised questions of who held ultimate decision-making authority within the government. The second related issue was whether the reverse takeover of Renong was at the expense of minority shareholders, a long-standing criticism of Malaysia's weak rules on corporate governance (Gomez 1990).[33]

The third issue was whether the government would come to Renong's assistance more directly. As a major beneficiary of Mahathir's privatization program, Renong had gained interests in building and operating toll

---

32. Wing Tiek was controlled by a Malaysian member of Parliament, Joseph Chong, and had initially acquired National Steel at government urging as a gesture of support to the Ramos government. Wing Tiek faced financial problems in 1995, and Fidel Ramos personally sounded out Mahathir on whether other Malaysian investors could take over Wing Tiek's stake; Wing Tiek held 87.5 percent of the firm. Renong stepped in at that point.

33. On 17 November 1997, UEM bought 32.6 percent of Renong from eight different shareholders. The question was raised whether Halim was the actual purchaser of the eight tranches. With an existing personal stake of 23.3 percent in Renong, he would then come to own 55.9 percent of the company, exceeding the 33 percent trigger at which point it becomes mandatory to make general offers to minority shareholders.

roads, including the North-South Highway. The company had also gained exclusive rights to build a new telecommunications systems along the highway, as well as a variety of other concessions (motels, rest areas, restaurants, petrol stations, and toll collection itself). However, the company sustained a loss for the financial year ending 30 June 1998 of RM818 million, and its debts as a group amounted to 5 percent of total outstanding loans in the entire banking system! Initially, the government contemplated an outright bailout for the firm through the issue of RM10.5 billion in zero-coupon bonds (*Straits Times*, 28 October 1998). In the face of criticism from the opposition, subsequent plans moved to tap the group's subsidiary, Projek Lebuhraya Utara-Selatan (PLUS), which holds the toll concession on the North-South Highway.[34] Beyond the question of whether Renong should be directly or indirectly bailed out was the further question of whether Renong should be allowed to retain ownership of PLUS at all (Jomo 1998b).

The state-owned enterprise Bakun Hydro-Electric Corporation (BHEC) in Sarawak also demonstrates a number of the political and contractual complexities surrounding Malaysia's privatization program. BHEC was co-owned by a consortium of private and government entities, and was involved in a project that would transmit electricity to Peninsular Malaysia via a submarine cable (*Straits Times*, 10 July 1996).[35] The revival of the project was controversial because it involved Malaysia's largest build-operate-own (BOO) contract—RM15 billion—but was awarded without tender to Ekran's Chinese executive chairman Ting Pek Khiing, who was closely connected with Sarawak Chief Minister Abdul Taib Mahmud, Daim, and Mahathir (Gomez and Jomo 1997, 110-16).

As the crisis began, Ekran threatened to break a RM13.6 billion contract with Asea Brown Boveri (ABB), Ekran's main subcontractor. ABB refused to absorb cost overruns associated with the project, and announced in April 1997 that all subcontract work would be awarded competitively (*Straits Times*, 1 August 1997). ABB's announcement ran counter to the intentions of Ting Pek Khiing to give four of his listed companies some RM9 billion in subcontract work. ABB was not willing to concede control over subcontracting. The government took over BHEC from Ekran at a cost of RM290.2 million (*Straits Times*, 21 November 1997),[36] not only

---

34. PLUS, rather than the government, would issue the bonds in exchange for the sale of undisclosed assets by Renong. But the government would extend PLUS's toll concession and still forgo future tax payments by PLUS as a way of providing indirect support to Renong.

35. BHEC's owners: Ekran (32 percent), the Sarawak government (19 percent), Tenaga Nasional (25 percent), Malaysian Mining Corporation (5 percent), EPF (10 percent), and Sarawak Electricity Supply Corporation (9 percent).

36. The government also compensated Ting RM390 million for work done, but stopped short of his request to be compensated for "foregone profits" and other expenses (*Far Eastern Economic Review*, 23 April 1998, 75-6; *Straits Times*, 6 May 1999).

compensating Ting for a contract secured through less-than-transparent means, but effectively saving the firm from a dispute generated by its desire to channel business to related firms.

Finally, although nepotism has not been anywhere near as pronounced in Malaysia as in Indonesia, there are several troubling examples. A visible bailout involved the prime minister's eldest son, Mirzan Mahathir, and his Konsortium Perkapalan, a transportation conglomerate with debt of RM1.6 billion ($412 million) (*Far Eastern Economic Review*, 19 March 1998). The bailout again involved the government using Petronas to purchase Perkapalan's shipping assets. Both father and son have denied charges of nepotism, and Mirzan Mahathir subsequently sued Dow Jones Publishing for what he believed was a defamatory article about his growing business empire (*Asian Wall Street Journal*, 13 February 1999). But Mirzan is not the only son of Mahathir to be the beneficiary of government largesse.[37]

A common pattern in these cases is for the government to initiate projects, either directly through state-owned enterprises or through policy decisions, and then to privatize those efforts in whole or in part to favored private partners. It is impossible to say whether these partners were selected on the basis of political criteria alone; all had some prior experience in business. But it is possible to say that the discretionary and non-transparent means of allocating assets and contracts, as well as the personal connections to government officials, created risks. Because the projects in question served some broader political and policy purposes—diversification of the economy (Proton); supplying credit to *bumiputra* borrowers (Bank Bumiputra); advancing foreign policy goals (Hottick); and supplying infrastructure (Renong, Ekran)—the government had strong incentives to intervene to keep the projects afloat when they experienced distress. In some of the cases, this occurred by tapping various resources over which the executive had discretionary control, including the reserves of the Employees' Provident Fund and Petronas (*Far Eastern Economic Review*, 12 August 1999, 11). In others, such as the Bakun project, direct fiscal outlays were involved. In yet others (UEM-Renong), regulatory forbearance appears key. Yet, in all cases, the government's private partners or their creditors have been shielded to some extent from losses they might have otherwise incurred.[38]

---

37. The privatization of hospital support services for the southern region was awarded to Tongkah Medivest Sdn Bhd, in which the prime minister's second son, Mokhzani Mahathir, had a 13.19 percent stake; Mokhzani was also UMNO Youth treasurer (*Straits Times*, 22 June 1999).

38. It should be underlined that the group of politically favored private actors is by no means limited to *bumiputras*, but includes a number of Chinese (Gomez 1999). It is also interesting to note that firms with ties to Anwar also realized advantages before the crisis, but were not recipients of similar government largesse once it struck; indeed, their failure marks a reduction of that faction's economic as well as political capabilities. Multi-Purpose Holdings faced its problems unaided (*Asian Wall Street Journal*, 12-13 March and 9 April

The Malaysian government's strategy toward financial and corporate restructuring appears to have two faces. On the one hand, the government established institutions with clear mandates and professional staff to address the problems of bank recapitalization, nonperforming loans, and corporate debt restructuring, and launched an aggressive plan of mergers in the banking sector. On the other hand, the government's strategy has relied heavily on an interventionist approach to asset restructuring that runs the risk of shifting losses onto Danaharta and the government. Moreover, the government also intervened directly in support of a number of public and private firms. Although Daim has publicly deemed it "politically unacceptable to use public funds to bail out businessmen who have made mistakes in judgement" (*Far Eastern Economic Review*, 30 April 1998, 62), in fact such government involvement remains a central theme of the opposition.

Indonesia

Of the four countries discussed here, the challenges of financial and corporate restructuring are clearly the most daunting in Indonesia. The government's program for the rehabilitation of the banking sector was unveiled under Suharto on 27 January 1998, and while it contained a number of important reform initiatives, we saw in chapter 2 how its implementation was affected by a variety of political constraints. The Indonesian Bank Restructuring Authority (IBRA), charged with overseeing the financial restructuring process, had little room for independent maneuver, and was in fact subjected early to turnover of high-level personnel.

The political pressures on Habibie would appear nearly as daunting as those that operated in the first half of 1998, but these pressures were not all counterproductive. In his 16 August Independence Day speech, Habibie announced that his four economic priorities would be cleaning up the banking sector, resolving the debt problem, eliminating monopolies, and increasing transparency. Given the further deterioration that occurred as a direct result of the political crisis, addressing the problems in the banking sector was primary among these four objectives; and in August, the government outlined a major package of banking legislation.

The package included a number of measures, but its central feature was a program that combined recapitalization with more aggressive action against weak banks and their clients. The audits ordered by Bank Indonesia—to be completed by October—were used to divide the banks into three categories: Category A banks, with a capital adequacy ratio above

---

1999) and other Chinese groups associated with Anwar, including Malaysian Resources Corp. Bhd (newspapers and a television station, once owned by UMNO), Hong Leong Bhd (from construction to finance), Phileo Allied Bhd (financial group), and Promet (a diversified conglomerate) also received no assistance (*Asian Wall Street Journal*, 7 April 1999).

4 percent (62 mostly small banks); B, for those below 4 percent and above –25 percent (66 banks); and C, for those under –25 percent (38 banks). Banks in group A were deemed temporarily sound, but called upon to raise capital to 8 percent in 3 years. B banks were eligible to participate in the recapitalization program.[39] But the government also exercised some conditionality; banks seeking recapitalization were required to submit a business plan showing that the owners were capable of meeting their share of the initial recapitalization and a schedule for higher capital-adequacy ratios. The plan also required that the banks' owners fully absorb the losses arising from loans extended to affiliated parties and that all bank obligations obtained from central bank liquidity support be transferred to IBRA, which would convert them to equity or subordinated loans.

The presumption was that some of the category B banks and most of those in category C faced closure, and thus many private banks had very strong interests in seeing the implementation of the program delayed.[40] The big exception to the rule, however, was the government's continuing commitment to 6 state and 15 provincial banks. Although all fell into category C, all were to be recapitalized. The key political issue with respect to the state banks was not only whether they would be retained or privatized, but whether the government and IBRA could collect on nonperforming loans or seize assets in compensation for them. The state banks had become a central means for channeling resources to politically favored parties and projects under Suharto, and the rate of nonperforming loans in them was extraordinarily high.

The recapitalization program would incur high costs for the government in the form of bond issues of Rp350 trillion, approximately 90 percent of GNP, and that figure excluded liquidity credits and in any case had to be revised upward to accommodate the tremendous cost of recapitalizing the state-owned banks. On the other hand, the plan did require owners to demonstrate their capacity to raise capital and contained the implicit threat that if they failed to do so, the banks would be taken over and sold or liquidated.

The key question was whether IBRA had the political as well as administrative capacity to design and execute the recapitalization program. With losses mounting, the negotiation of a new letter of intent with the IMF in November 1998 committed the government to announce the result of the audits on the banks and to move forward with the recapitalization program by the end of January.

---

39. The government would inject up to 80 percent of the capital required to reach the stipulated capital adequacy requirement of 4 percent in the form of government bonds.

40. C banks were required to raise their capital adequacy ratio (CAR) above –25 percent within a month of completion of due diligence and would be required to produce a business

The program immediately ran into a series of delays, reversals, and irregularities—all of which centered on the question of whether the marginal group B and C banks would gain access to government money. It was later revealed that at least one of the banks that had been categorized as Category B had a capital-asset ratio of minus 210 percent with 99 percent of its loans questionable (*Far Eastern Economic Review*, 19 August 1999, 12). In January, Habibie also signed a presidential directive authorizing government participation in the recapitalization of 12 banks before the scheduled release of the full list. This interim directive covered 10 regional development banks, which played an important political role for the government, but also two private ones, including Lippo Bank owned by the Riady family, which was close to Habibie.[41]

On March 13, the government finally announced that it was closing down 38 domestic private commercial banks (21 Category B, 17 Category C), nationalizing 7, and recapitalizing 9, subject to their ability to raise adequate capital by 21 April; 8 of the 9 made the deadline. The plan was hailed by the international financial institutions as a breakthrough. Some cronies and Suharto family members lost their banks, and the government initiated a process of investigation into whether the bank failures were the result of irregularities. However, questions were raised not only about those banks that the government chose to recapitalize, but about the closed and nationalized banks as well.[42]

The fate of the 7 larger banks that came under IBRA management proved even more complex.[43] The owners of 4 of the larger banks, which accounted for the overwhelming share of all liquidity assistance—BCA, Danamon, BDNI, and Bank Umum Nasional—expressed a willingness to strike deals with the government by providing funds and other assets and stretching out the deadline for repayment of liquidity credits. Given that much of the banks' bad lending was to affiliated companies,[44] the

---

plan bringing their share of intergroup lending to less than 20 percent of capital and their CARs to 8 percent by the end 1999.

41. Lippo had raised the required 20 percent share through a rights issue and brought its CAR up to 4 percent, but it was scheduled to receive almost all of the allocated funds (3.75 trillion of 4.2 trillion) under the special directive.

42. The government had not proved effective in resolving the banks that it had previously closed. The assets of the 10 banks that had been "frozen" in April 1998 and the 7 smaller banks suspended in April 1999 were to be transferred to the Asset Management Unit for liquidation, but well into 1998 the licenses of the first 10 had not been revoked nor had all assets been successfully transferred due to conflicts over pricing and taxes.

43. Of the 7, 3 were suspended (BDNI, Bank Umum Nasional, and Bank Modern) while the other 4 (Bank Danamon, Bank PDFCI, Bank Tiara, and Bank BCA) were to be retained by the government with the intention of restructuring their capital (Economist Intelligence Unit, *Country Report: Indonesia*, 4th quarter 1998, 33).

44. Bank Dagang Nasional Indonesia, owned by the Nursalim family, was one of the worst offenders, with 91 percent of all lending to affiliated groups. But the situation was similar

government set a condition that the funds and assets provided must cover both central bank liquidity support and all credits extended to their groups. But given the limited administrative resources of IBRA, the deals held out the possibility that owners might continue to control both their banks and their pledged assets.

The nationalization list was also controversial.[45] Nationalization was justified on the grounds that closure of the banks would have adverse effects on the payments system, and it implied that owners would lose control over their assets. The boards of a number of the banks were purged. But liquidation would have arguably led to a faster unraveling of the troubled banks' loans and seizure of collateral.

However, the biggest test for IBRA was whether it could recover on the accumulating portfolio of assets it held. After the announcement of the recapitalization plan, these holdings included a bewildering variety of assets: Those pledged as a result of negotiations with seven major groups over repayment of liquidity credits; bad debts from state banks; and assets from private banks either closed, nationalized, or recapitalized. By the end of 1999, estimates of IBRA's assets (at face value) ranged as high as Rp500 trillion ($85 billion and well over half of Indonesian GDP; Hufbauer 1999).

In February, Habibie signaled his commitment to recover assets by extending the life of IBRA for 4 years and placing it on a more firm legal footing. The agency was also granted quite substantial quasi-judicial powers to seize assets and even to cancel commercial contracts that were seen to impose losses on IBRA; when the significance of these powers became fully apparent, they generated quite substantial controversy among foreign investors and banks (*Asian Wall Street Journal*, 20 May 1999; *Jakarta Post*, 12 May 1999). But the question was whether these and other powers could be exercised.

In the period before and after the June 1999 elections, the government came under increasing pressure from the opposition to aggressively pursue bad debtors (*Jakarta Post*, 2 June 1999). The process began with an effort to identify the largest 20 debtors to the state-owned banks, which accounted for more than half of those banks' NPLs, and to initiate a debt restructuring program with them. These debtors included well-connected businesspeople and some of Suharto's children. IBRA and the banks also

---

at the others: e.g., 78.4 percent of Bank Umum Nasional's portfolio was intergroup, and 43.8 percent of Bank Danamon's was intergroup, according to Forum Keadilan.

45. Among those nationalized were Bakrie Group's Bank Kusa Nasional (BNN), owned by Aburizal Bakrie, head of the Indonesian Chamber of Commerce and a member of Habibie's board of advisors; and Bank Duta, majority-held by one of Suharto's foundations. Both banks had heavily exceeded related-party credit limits, and both were expected to have negative returns on equity and CARs by the end of 2001 (*Far Eastern Economic Review*, 25 March 1999, 65).

began releasing lists of the largest debtors from the nonstate banks and held a high-level meeting with the largest debtors to exploit their political vulnerability—including their identity as Chinese[46]—and to pressure them to sign "letters of commitment" by 22 June. These letters would include an agreement to be transparent, to allow IBRA audits, to propose a restructuring plan, and to agree to divestments when debtors lack the cash to make repayments. If such agreements were not reached by 30 August, the government threatened to take "unpopular steps." By 22 June, 173 of the 200 had signed the letters, and the government was threatening litigation against the rest.

But the signed letters of commitment were only the first step in the recovery process (*Jakarta Post*, 13 and 25 June 1999). An even more challenging task was how to move from the restructuring of the banks to the task of corporate restructuring. IBRA's mandate extended only to bank restructuring and loans made by banks; most large corporations had borrowed from foreign or domestic creditors as well, and those obligations were not being serviced either. Beyond this narrow sense of debt restructuring was the larger issue of how to push forward the *operational* restructuring process.

One positive effect of the change of government from Suharto to Habibie was the establishment of a framework for the workout of corporate foreign debt. Following the successful conclusion of negotiations with foreign creditors, on 2 July 1998 the government established the Indonesian Debt Restructuring Agency (INDRA), which would allow debtors to covert their foreign-denominated obligations into rupiah ones—thus removing exchange risk—and shifting the burden of foreign exchange payments to INDRA.[47] The framework to facilitate and encourage voluntary corporate debt restructurings was announced on 9 September 1998. The so-called Jakarta Initiative was designed to provide a framework for out-of-court negotiations, overseen by a Jakarta Initiative Task Force (JITF).[48] The government tried to jump-start the process by making the Indonesian government's investment banking arm, PT Persero Danareksa, a test case by restructuring $438 million (*Asian Wall Street Journal*, 21 April 1999); but by late 1999, only three other major cases were moving through the process.

As in Thailand, the progress of the private restructuring exercise was partly influenced by the bankruptcy process. Unlike in Thailand, the

---

46. Interview with IBRA chairman Glenn Yusuf, *Asiaweek*, 28 May 1999, 91.

47. For an outline of the how INDRA works, see Johnson (1998, 53).

48. The JITF had the ability to obtain and develop information on companies to be restructured; help design restructuring action plans; facilitate negotiations and encourage participation of creditors and debtors; and speed regulatory approvals for restructurings in progress. The JITF could also recommend that the public prosecutor file bankruptcy proceedings against particular debtors if they were deemed to be stripping assets or showing a lack of good faith.

problems in the process did not arise in the legislation of the reform; the new law was passed quickly under the Suharto government and contained all the features that the IMF had sought when making it a condition of the third Letter of Intent (Johnson 1998). The problem, rather, was in the weakness of the courts. In the first 6 months, the bankruptcy court consistently ruled in favor of insolvent business groups in a series of decisions that were highly confusing to lawyers; fewer than a third of the 50 petitions filed with the Jakarta Commercial Court in that period actually led to bankruptcies. In a number of cases, the results appeared to rest on a weak understanding of the law, but others appeared to reflect political judgments about the undesirability of liquidation and foreign acquisitions

Despite the potential importance of both the courts and informal mechanisms over the longer run, the major vehicle for corporate restructuring would perforce be the government itself, for it had come to control approximately 80 percent of the banking sector's total assets. But therein lie a host of unresolved political problems and conflicts over precisely how IBRA should exercise its power, particularly given the diversity of the assets IBRA controls. To manage the assets pledged against unpaid liquidity credits, IBRA set up 5 holding companies "managing" 200 companies (*Asian Wall Street Journal*, 9-10 July 1999). IBRA exercises shareholders' rights until debts are repaid, but owners continue to manage the companies on a day-to-day basis. However, it is far from clear that this model can be extended to the variety of other assets that IBRA effectively owns, which are in general very inferior to the pledged assets.

Moreover, until the change of government in November, serious disagreements continued within and outside the government over the fundamental nature of IBRA's mandate. As with Malaysia's Danaharta, an inherent contradiction existed between the objectives of getting the best price for foreclosed assets or the best settlements with debtors, and acting swiftly to dispose of assets both to reduce the short-term liquidity constraints on government and the wider uncertainty surrounding the process.

But both strategies faced fundamental political as well as economic and administrative constraints. Those emphasizing the first path argued that IBRA should follow the Malaysian model and get into the asset rehabilitation business, including through offering debtors "haircuts" (and leaving them in control of businesses) and swapping debt for equity (which implies haircuts, in any case). At the extreme, this strategy could involve more ambitious operational and even industrial restructuring efforts.[49] But this would have required that IBRA have both the political indepen-

---

49. One idea circulating in Jakarta in late 1999 was for IBRA to effect a major consolidation of the entire petrochemical sector through a combination of mergers, asset sales, and supporting industrial policies.

dence and administrative capacity to undertake such an ambitious strategy.

The alternative—to dispose of assets quickly—is the favored route of those critics who see problems in any form of government intervention in the rehabilitation process. They see the barrier to a swifter resolution of the crisis in the emergence of a new "iron triangle" of IBRA technocrats and corporate owners and managers aligned against a group of willing buyers, both domestic and especially foreign. The main piece of evidence for the prosecution is that by August 1999, less than 1 percent of all of the assets IBRA had acquired had been sold (*Business Times*, 2 October 1999).

But as in Thailand, the sale of assets is limited precisely by the absence of a credible resolution process. Without a process that permits buyers to get access to collateral, the problem visible in Thailand recurs: Firms do not have incentives to reach meaningful settlements. Not surprisingly, those wanting to see more rapid asset sales naturally focus on expanding, or simply using, IBRA's extrajudicial powers.

When compared with the other countries under IMF programs, it is clear that Indonesia lags the other countries in bank restructuring and recapitalization, in corporate debt restructuring, and in restructuring or disposing of acquired assets. This is in part a result of the fact that Indonesia's problems have been much more severe than in the other countries, but the depth of the country's difficulties can also be traced in part to politics. Passing and implementing reforms have been affected by elections and non-electoral challenges, and particularly by the ability of private-sector actors to exploit generalized political uncertainty to evade reform.

The Bank Bali scandal of August 1999 also demonstrated that old patterns of business-government relations died hard. The scandal revolved around the alleged illegal transfer of about $80 million from the bank to an Indonesian firm as a commission for helping the bank recoup interbank claims on banks suspended but guaranteed by IBRA. But precisely because such claims are guaranteed, there should be no rationale for such a payment, and certainly not one of this size. Rather, the transfer, which involved government officials from both the executive and IBRA, was used to help finance Golkar's election campaign.

In the wake of Bank Bali, it was abundantly clear that political change and reform was a necessary condition for effective financial and corporate restructuring. However, it was not clear that it was a sufficient condition.[50] The Wahid administration replaced the existing IBRA leadership and the new team quickly pushed through the important sale of one of Indonesia's largest groups, Astra International, over substantial political resistance. However, IBRA has not received consistent support from the courts for

---

50. The following draws on *Van Zorge Report*, 22 May 2000, 5-13.

its actions and the president has intervened directly in several important restructuring cases in ways that undermined IBRA's independence and even appeared to bail out dubious enterprises and projects associated with the old regime. As in all of the crisis countries, the ability to undertake effective corporate restructuring ultimately hinges on a combination of consistent political support from the executive and a legal foundation for forcing the hand of recalcitrant debtors.

Liberalizing Foreign Investment

Despite strong political resistance, all four governments have not only launched short-term restructuring programs but initiated regulatory reforms that will affect the evolution of the financial and corporate sectors for some time to come. One of the most important of these reforms centers on the rules governing foreign direct investment.

Well before the crisis, all the countries discussed here had already begun to liberalize their rules governing FDI. This was particularly true in the three Southeast Asian countries, which took advantage of the sharp appreciation of the yen in the mid-1980s to position themselves as major sites for manufacturing investment—not only from Japan, but from the other newly industrializing countries, the United States, and Europe as well. However, the rules governing FDI were often ringed with exceptions, for example, emphasizing export-oriented industries; shielding the non-tradable goods sector, and particularly finance, from foreign entry; and continuing to impose equity requirements.

In all four countries, the crisis dramatically accelerated the liberalization of foreign investment, often with the explicit objective of facilitating the restructuring process.[51] In Thailand, the Chuan government eased restrictions governing land ownership; and after an initial delay, a difficult political fight in the Senate, and some restrictive amendments, it replaced the Alien Business Law of 1972 with a new Foreign Investment Law in October 1999. The new law retains a restrictive negative-list system and still requires firms to seek approval for investment in a number of sensitive sectors. But it opened domestic transport, retail trade, and legal services to foreign ownership. In the manufacturing sector, the Board of Investment substantially liberalized the criteria required for firms to receive investment incentives, particularly with respect to equity requirements, and even set up a mergers and acquisitions unit. Foreign firms responded quickly by expanding their stake in joint ventures or buying out partners entirely. In 1999, a review of Board of Investment incentives went farther,

---

51. The following discussion on Indonesia, Malaysia, and Thailand draws extensively from Felker and Jomo (1999).

proposing an elimination of all equity requirements and the move toward complete national treatment.[52]

Finance Minister Tarrin was also explicit in his desire to use foreign investors to facilitate the financial restructuring process. Foreign parties were major bidders in the asset sales organized by the FRA—again over political objections—and the government encouraged Thai banks to seek foreign equity partners and approved foreign takeovers of four failed banks in 1998.

Of the middle-income Asian countries, South Korea was historically one of the most restrictive in its approach to FDI. Under Kim Young Sam, the government had already launched a comprehensive investment liberalization in anticipation of OECD membership which left only 40 of 1,148 industries either partly or completely closed. Kim Dae Jung placed particular emphasis in changing Koreans views of foreign investment (D.J. Kim 1999, chap. 9). Liberalization of portfolio investment and direct investment in banking was a part of the IMF program and in May, the new government liberalized hostile takeovers by foreigners. In November 1998, the government passed legislation that replaced the entire legal framework governing FDI with a new Foreign Investment Promotion Act. The legislation was based on the principle of national treatment, and reorganized Korea's notoriously cumbersome application and approval process.[53]

But the most innovative administrative component of the reform, no doubt growing out of Kim Dae Jung's interest in expanding investment to poorer regions of the country, was to decentralize the management of incentives governing FDI to the provincial level. Local bodies can obtain financial assistance for the formation of Foreign Investment Zones, which extend additional tax and trade privileges and facilitate the leasing of land for larger investors. Provinces are also granted some discretion over the setting of relevant tax rates, thus spawning competition among provinces to attract investors. The new law substantially extended the tax holidays previously given to "high technology" activities and expanded the number of industries eligible.

Of the Southeast Asian countries, Malaysia was the most aggressive in courting export-oriented foreign investment prior to the crisis, but a number of domestically-oriented and import-substituting industries, such as autos, were restricted. Following the crisis, the government eliminated sectoral restrictions on new manufacturing projects, allowed foreign joint-venture partners serving the domestic market to increase their sharehold-

---

52. With the exception of some continuing incentives to deconcentrate investment away from Bangkok and to induce technology transfer.

53. A summary of the new law can be found at http://www.kotra.or.kr/kti/issues/1999/1-2/focus.html.

ings, and permitted wholly owned foreign firms to expand their local sales (from 20 to 50 percent). The imposition of the capital controls in September 1998 explicitly guaranteed convertibility on current account transactions and "free flows of direct foreign investment and repatriation of interest, profits, and dividends and capital" *(New Straits Times,* 2 September, 1998, 23); the controls clearly sought to minimize disruption to ongoing foreign operations.

In one respect, however, Malaysia did take a more restrictive stance than the other most seriously affected countries, and one that is consistent with the adjustment strategy outlined above. Wholly foreign-owned banks licensed in the past continue to occupy an important position in the financial system, but the government has retained the 30 percent equity cap on new investment in the financial sector. Nor was foreign purchase of assets seen as a central component of the restructuring process.[54]

Like that of South Korea, Indonesia's investment regime has historically been relatively restrictive. Following the decline of oil prices in the early 1980s, the government renewed efforts to court manufacturing investment in order to diversify away from dependence on natural resource exports. The government relaxed complex sectoral, equity, and trade and sales restrictions and opened its first export-processing zone, which allowed 100 percent foreign ownership. A major liberalization in 1994 partially opened nine previously closed "strategic" sectors to foreign participation,[55] although the brokering of foreign entry into these sectors provides an example of how liberalizing measures can be captured by private actors; many became the locus of new Suharto business enterprises.

The crisis resulted in a commitment to privatize a number of state-owned enterprises and to open or further open a number of sectors to foreign investment: petroleum, infrastructure, mining, utilities, retail trade, plantation agriculture, finance, and other nontradable sectors. In October 1998, Habibie introduced and passed legislation allowing 100 percent foreign ownership in the banking sector as a component of the financial sector restructuring effort. Felker and Jomo (1999) conclude that by 1999, Indonesia's investment regime was the most liberal and neutral in the Association of Southeast Asian Nations.

Conclusion

This chapter has identified the main policy challenges associated with systemic distress and explained some of the differences that have emerged

---

54. The government has also not been aggressive in seeking foreign buyers for Danaharta's acquired assets, but neither has it been aggressive in seeking *any* buyers to date.

55. The new activities included ports, electricity, telecommunications, shipping, air transport, railways, and mass media, but were subject only to a minimum 5 percent Indonesian ownership.

across the four crisis countries in trying to manage it. The first set of conclusions has to do with how democracies and non-democracies fare. Delays caused by electoral and non-electoral pressures, decision-making processes, and rent-seeking are certainly not absent from democracies. Thailand demonstrates these problems most clearly. But democracy gives competing politicians incentives to monitor corrupt business-government relations and for the public to bring new reformist governments to office. The differences between the Kim Young Sam and Kim Dae Jung governments in South Korea and between the Chavalit and Chuan governments in Thailand are clear.

The experiences of Indonesia and Malaysia suggest that whatever problems democracies have in undertaking reforms of business-government relations, the problems are equal if not greater in undemocratic systems. Indeed, because of the high level of discretion and low level of transparency, these governments are particularly prone to weaknesses in financial regulation and corporate governance. Government commitments to private-sector actors have strong implications for how firms behave; without the capacity to monitor those business-government relations, the public is likely to pay the cost of rent-seeking, weak regulation, moral hazard, and forbearance.

A second set of conclusions concern the role that independent agencies can play in the reform process, and particularly the assumption that they can reduce the problems caused by multiple veto gates and private-sector resistance. However, it is important not to confuse cause and effect; the power of the FSC in South Korea was ultimately grounded in some base of political, legislative, and party support. By contrast, the relative weakness of IBRA in Indonesia or the declining regulatory efficacy of the Bank of Thailand in Indonesia is not just administrative, but also political.

A final set of conclusions center on the question of how to make an overall assessment, particularly of a target that is moving quickly. The task of financial and corporate restructuring during a crisis is a daunting one, and even relatively positive assessments recognize that there is much to be done (Claessens, Djankov, and Klingebiel 1999); more critical ones have pointed out the risk of continuity and a reversion to old ways of doing business (Mann 1999). There is certainly much in the accounts just outlined to buttress the skeptics. But in drawing up a balance sheet, it is important not to make a simple but important error: to discount the longer-term consequences of legal and regulatory changes spawned by the crisis that will take some time, perhaps a decade, to have effects at the level of the firm and particular markets. Two important examples already noted in our case studies are the development of bankruptcy and foreclosure laws and reforms of corporate governance. A third reform—born of financial constraint and pushed by the IMF but also championed by reformers—were the rules governing foreign direct investment.

The concluding chapter addresses the question of how and whether such longer-term legal and regulatory changes are affecting business-government relations. To fully address that theme, however, it is important to first understand the social dimensions of the crisis.

5

The Social Fallout: Safety Nets and Recrafting the Social Contract

with NANCY BIRDSALL

Before the spread of democratic rule in developing East Asia, governments denied citizens effective political voice and offered only limited social insurance.[1] But they pursued policies that increased household incomes and minimized or prevented the increasing inequality frequently associated with the development process. East Asia's growth lifted millions of households out of poverty and generated not only a class of the newly rich, but upwardly mobile urban middle and working classes that might be called the "striving class."

Even before the economic crisis of 1997-98, this approach to social issues was coming under pressure. Secular changes, including aging populations, urbanization, greater openness to trade and investment, and demands arising out of the democratization process in a number of countries called into question the adequacy of informal social insurance mechanisms. However, the financial crisis of 1997-98 demonstrated clearly that reliance on growth and informal mechanisms to provide social insurance had left governments badly equipped to respond to large-scale social distress. The problem was not just one of the poor, although they too were adversely affected by the crisis. The crisis struck hardest precisely

---

Nancy Birdsall is senior associate at the Carnegie Endowment for International Peace and director of the Economic Reform Project in the Global Policy Program. She was formerly the executive vice-president of the Inter-American Development Bank.

1. A more extended version of the arguments presented here can be found in Birdsall and Haggard (2000).

at the urban "striving class," thus calling into question the social mobility of the past.

The first response of governments and the international financial institutions to the social dimensions of the crisis was to relax fiscal policies that were initially too tight and to protect public spending on education, health, and other social investment programs. The second was more direct: To craft policies and programs that would protect the poor and vulnerable groups through targeted transfers and public employment, and to create or substantially upgrade social insurance for the working and middle classes.

Each of the four countries in the region instituted short-term social safety net programs: food, emergency employment, and in some cases income supplements to ensure minimum consumption levels among the poor. These efforts helped alleviate the social costs of the crisis, even if they were limited in varying degrees by the institutional weakness of the government in the social policy area, and in some cases by corruption.

But governments proved resistant to suggestions for targeted transfers and institutionalized social insurance. Their doubts stemmed in part from weaknesses in administrative capacity, particularly in the ability to target the poor, and legitimate concerns about the fiscal burden on the state and corruption.

But the nature of the response to the social fallout from the crisis also had its politics. On the one hand, conservatives both inside and outside the government harbored a deep-seated political resistance to Western models of the welfare state. They argued that such measures were not only ill-timed and expensive, but would fit poorly with long-standing cultural traditions of work, discipline, and family responsibility—traditions and values they view as central to the region's past achievements. Whatever the merits of these arguments, they also masked material concerns: that private sectors operating in increasingly competitive environments, both in international markets and at home, not be burdened with additional costs.

On the other hand, the countervailing political forces that have historically been the carriers of a widened social agenda—organized labor and social democratic parties (Esping-Anderson 1990)—have generally been weak throughout the region (Goodman, White, and Kwon 1998). The poor are rarely well-represented politically, but the configuration of political parties and interest groups did not provide strong representation for the urban "strivers" either. The backlash that was visible in the region was less a result of organized social resistance to reform than of the weakness of affected groups and of their lack of institutionalized, organized channels of representation.

Opportunities for national debate on social insurance and the broader social contract were greatest where such forces had managed to gain greater political voice. The conditions for this occurring were partly struc-tural; for example, South Korea is more urbanized and industrialized than its Southeast Asian counterparts and thus better able to institute more formal social insurance mechanisms. But the conditions were also more purely political and paralleled in important ways an important condition for reform already noted in chapters 1-3. New social contracts were more likely from governments less beholden to business interests and conserva-tive social groups and more attentive to broader publics and those most seriously exposed to the uncertainties of the market.

The Economics and Politics of Growth with Equity

Before the crisis, countries in East and Southeast Asia did have a strategy of social protection, but it was highly implicit.[2] Its central component was healthy rates of per capita GDP growth that were broadly shared through rapid expansion of employment, increasing participation in the formal labor market, and rising real wages. Even if East Asian growth was primarily the result of sheer factor accumulation, that is, high rates of savings and investment rather than growth of total factor productivity (Young 1995; Krugman 1994), households nonetheless enjoyed steady and reliable increases in real annual income.

What was behind this growth-with-equity model? First, the East Asian approach did not solely emphasize labor-intensive manufacturing for exports, although that was certainly a distinctive feature. Rather, it was a relatively balanced development model that avoided the implicit and explicit taxes on agriculture seen in other regions and addressed rural poverty through land reform (in South Korea and Taiwan) and substantial public investments in rural infrastructure and agricultural technologies.

Second, public spending on human development increased with rising GDP per capita, and was generally concentrated on programs that bene-fited the poor, such as primary and secondary education and basic curative and preventive healthcare. Education policy was particularly important. The combination of a greater supply of basic education with the greater demand for educated workers associated with the export-led growth strategy created a virtuous cycle: Rapid growth and good returns to education made it rational for households and individuals to invest in it. The result was a dramatic increase in average levels of schooling, and equally impressive, a rapid decline in the inequality of schooling.[3] Public

---

2. This discussion is based on Birdsall, Ross, and Sabot (1995), and World Bank (1993).

3. Birdsall and Londoño (1998) compare East Asia and Latin America. The coefficient of variation of schooling in East Asia declined from over 1.6 to above 0.9 between 1960 and 1990.

and private investment in education, particularly primary education, also had the effect of lowering inequality by minimizing the wage premiums scarce educated labor captured in other regions.

A third component of the growth with equity strategy was a minimal government role in providing a social safety net (Goodman, White, and Kwon 1998; Tyabji 1993). Governments invested in people but did not necessarily protect them directly against risk. Outside of some protections extended to civil servants, public-sector workers and the military (e.g., in Indonesia, South Korea, and Thailand), social insurance was generally private and informal and rested on high levels of household savings, strong traditions of family support, and private transfers (e.g., from urban workers to rural households; between generations). In some countries, notably South Korea, larger enterprises had begun to provide social insurance, but this was the exception rather than the rule.

The fourth and final component of the East Asian model was political—the prevalence of authoritarian governments that served to dampen social demands. A number of commentaries have emphasized the "shared" nature of East Asia's growth or emphasized the fact that high growth itself served to limit political pressures for formal safety net programs (Campos and Root 1996, chapter 3; World Bank 1993). But this language is subtly misleading. Such "agreements" were not achieved through democratic political processes—and indeed were not "agreements" at all. Before the democratic transitions of the 1980s and 1990s, they resulted from authoritarian or semi-democratic paternalism. Social democratic political parties were weak; labor movements were weak, repressed, or both; and interest groups and nongovernmental organizations (NGOs) had only the narrowest space in which to operate.

These political features of the Asian model had several second-order consequences for the nature of the social contract. The truncated nature of the political spectrum, limitations on interest groups, and outright repression meant that any nascent political demand for state-run social safety nets was attenuated. During periodic political or economic crises, such as the ethnic riots in Malaysia in 1970 or the oil shocks of the 1970s, governments responded to social pressures by instituting new programs. But they did so as Bismarck had over a century before: preemptively and on terms set by the government and its conservative political allies. The result was formal mechanisms that limited direct state expenditure, relied on schemes funded by business and labor, and, with the exception of Malaysia's ethnic affirmative action policies, shunned redistributive objectives.

The effect of authoritarian politics on industrial relations was also important (Deyo 1989; Frenkel 1993; Frenkel and Harrod 1995). By allowing labor markets to clear relatively freely, East Asian economies avoided the labor-market dualism visible in Latin America and Africa. This may have had positive implications for efficiency and equity, but at the cost of direct and indirect controls over the labor movement. Governments could not push wages below market-clearing levels; they could, however, guarantee that labor had little say either in the wage-setting process or in the rules governing the shop-floor. In some cases, government paternalism did introduce some rigidities. For example, in South Korea, the system of industrial relations established under Park Chung Hee made it difficult for firms to fire workers in larger enterprises, and all governments typically faced pressures from workers in state-owned enterprises. On the whole, however, labor markets in East Asia were relatively flexible.

The Limits of the Model in the 1990s

A number of secular trends posed new challenges to the implicit social policy of the high growth period, even before the onset of the crisis. First, long-term demographic changes were altering the age composition of countries in the region. Between 1995 and 2025, the share of the economically active working-age population in northeast Asia is projected to edge down from 61.6 to 59.3 percent, while the share of those over 65 will more than double from 7.2 to 17.6 percent of the population (Asian Development Bank 1998). The implication is not only slower overall rates of per capita growth, but new questions about the adequacy of the pension and health-care systems.

A second demographic trend with important implications for the social contract is the continuing process of urbanization. South Korea is the most urbanized of the group (81 percent urbanization rate in 1998), and not surprisingly has moved farthest in extending unemployment insurance to its urban workforce, although as we will see below, coverage and benefits are far from generous. Malaysia was also more than half urban: 57 percent in 1998; projected to increase to 70 percent by 2025. Urbanization rates in 1998 were only 31 percent in Thailand and 37 percent in Indonesia, in comparison with rates above 50 and even 60 percent in countries of comparable per capita income in Latin America (United Nations 1999). But by 2025, urbanization rates will increase to a still-low 36 percent in Thailand and 58 percent in Indonesia. The inexorable trend of urbanization and a relative decline in agricultural employment implies the weakening of the informal social insurance that exists as a result of mobility between the urban and rural sectors.

A third concern is rising inequality of income and wealth. The much touted "growth-with-equity" model was not in fact based on substantial reductions in inequality; in the 1970s and 1980s, Indonesia, South Korea, and Malaysia saw modest reductions but by international standards inequality in Malaysia and Thailand remained high. Rather, the characterization was based on the region's success in achieving rapid growth

Table 5.1 Gini coefficients, for selected countries of East Asia, 1978-96

	High-inequality countries				Low-inequality countries		
	Malaysia	The Philippines	Thailand		Indonesia	South Korea	Taiwan
1978				1978	38.6		28.4
1979	51.0			1979			27.7
1980				1980	35.6	38.6	28.0
1981			43.1	1981	33.7		28.2
1982				1982		35.7	28.5
1983				1983			28.5
1984	48.0			1984	32.4		28.8
1985		46.1		1985		34.5	29.2
1986			47.4	1986			29.3
1987				1987	32.0		29.7
1988		45.7	47.4	1988		33.6	30.0
1989	48.4			1989			30.4
1990			48.8	1990	33.1		30.1
1991		45.0		1991			30.5
1992			51.5	1992			30.8
1993				1993	31.7	31.0	30.8
1994				1994			
1995	48.5			1995			
				1996	36.5	29.5	
Average	48.9	45.6	47.6	Average	34.2	33.8	29.3

Note: Ginis are based on household distributions of income per capita, except for Indonesia, where Ginis are based on hosehold distribution of expenditure per capita.

Source: Deininger and Squire (1996).

without the increases in inequality hypothesized by Kuznets (1955; Birdsall, Ross, and Sabot 1995). Yet new evidence suggests that may be changing. Even before the crisis, increases in inequality were marked in Thailand and were visible in Indonesia as well (see table 5.1 and figure 5.1). In South Korea, the Gini coefficient of inequality of urban wage income rose between 1993 and 1996 from 26.3 to 28.2, a substantial increase, though from a very low level.[4] Although East Asia in the 1980s and 1990s was much more equal than Sub-Saharan Africa and Latin America, it was no more equal than the Middle East and North Africa and less equal than South Asia or the advanced industrial states (Ahuja et al. 1997, table 3.1).

Even where inequality of income has not increased dramatically, the potential for conflict over the distribution of wealth is high. Before the crisis, booms in the stock and property markets in the 1990s generated large and visible gains for the very top of the income distribution, creating

---

4. Based on the data made available by Nicholas Prescott of the World Bank, calculated from the household income and expenditure survey reported monthly by the Korean National Statistical Office, which covers household and urban wage and salary workers only.

Figure 5.1 Gini coefficients in high- and low-inequality East Asian countries, 1978-96

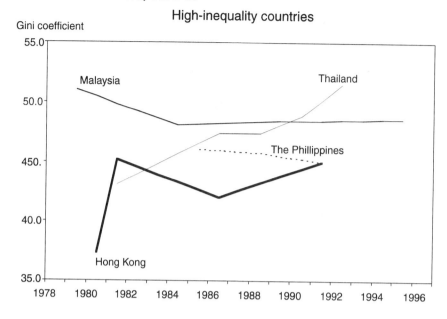

High-inequality countries

Gini coefficient

Malaysia

Thailand

The Phillippines

Hong Kong

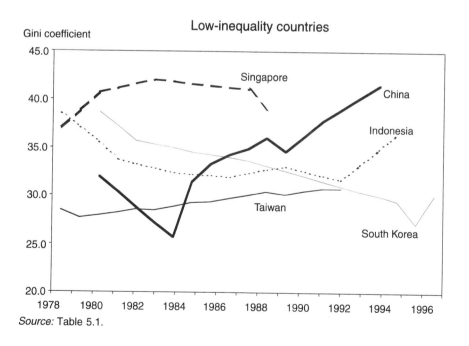

Low-inequality countries

Gini coefficient

Singapore

China

Indonesia

Taiwan

South Korea

Source: Table 5.1.

a class of the newly rich. As argued in chapter 1, the subsequent collapse revealed that some of these gains were the result of insider dealing, cronyism, and corruption. The steep losses imposed on urban workers and their households, the efforts of corporate owners and managers to secure bailouts, and the high fiscal costs of the crisis are all potential sources of political resentment.

A fourth concern is related to the process of globalization. Whatever the advantages of an outward-oriented growth strategy, continued reliance on exports coupled with increased openness to trade and investment have also produced a new set of insecurities. As the middle-income countries of the region developed, light, labor-intensive manufacturing activities are coming under pressure at home, or are shifting offshore, creating new adjustment problems. In Thailand, for example (where export growth collapsed completely in 1995-96), the demand for the skilled labor required to adjust to shifting comparative advantage is outstripping supply because of lagging secondary enrollment rates, complicating the adjustment process and contributing to that country's trend of increasing inequality.

Finally, as we have seen, the political context was also becoming more contentious. South Korea and Thailand underwent democratic transitions beginning in the late 1980s. These political transitions were not spearheaded by populist forces and typically had a quite conservative cast (Haggard and Kaufman 1995). In South Korea, the first transitional election was won by a protégé of the outgoing dictator. In Thailand, gradual democratization in the 1980s occurred under military auspices and was interrupted by a coup and brief military interregnum. Yet in both countries, political changes reinforced incentives for politicians to address social issues in some form, and encouraged mobilization of new social groups. Nor, as we have seen in chapters 2 and 3, were the nondemocratic systems of Indonesia and Malaysia immune from these pressures.

Who Got Hit?

The capital flight and devaluations with which the crisis began combined with the initial policy response of tight monetary and fiscal policy brought layoffs, declining demand for new entrants into the labor market, real wage declines, and a resultant squeeze on the informal sector.[5] Real incomes were also affected by price increases associated with devaluation,

---

5. We would expect that labor markets would respond differently to such shocks, depending on institutions. Labor markets characterized by wage rigidities would experience the effects primarily in the form of layoffs, while more flexible labor markets would see less unemployment but declines in real wages, potentially to very low levels. Although countries do in fact vary in the mix of these two effects, most combined both, suggesting that concerns about labor market rigidities in countries such as South Korea were, at least in the aggregate, exaggerated.

Table 5.2 Indicators of economic activity and social welfare pre- and post-crisis

	Indonesia	Thailand	Malaysia	South Korea
Annual per capita GDP growth				
1990-96	5.7	7.0	7.0	6.3
1998	-14.4	-10.8	-9.3	-6.6
Annual inflation (consumer price index)				
1990-96	8.8	5.0	4.2	6.0
1998	57.6	8.1	5.3	7.5
Annual per capita growth of private consumption				
1990-96	6.8	6.4	5.4	6.5
1998	-4.7	-15.1	-12.6	-10.2
Unemployment				
1996	4.9	1.8	2.5	2.0
1998	5.5	4.5	3.2	6.8
Poverty incidence				
1996	11.3	11.4	8.2	9.6
1998	20.3	13.0	n.a.	19.2
Percentage change	79.6	14.0		100

n.a. = not available

Source: World Bank (2000b), 116. World Bank staff estimates based on household surveys, national accounts, and labor force surveys. Poverty incidence is derived from national poverty lines, which are based on consumption in Indonesia and Korea and income for Malaysia and Thailand. Data for Korea are urban areas only. Data for Malaysia are for 1997.

particularly in Indonesia, where inflation for 1998 exceeded 50 percent. Table 5.2 shows the effect of the crisis on several indicators of aggregate economic activity and household welfare.

When the crisis hit, countries also undertook highly controversial fiscal adjustments.[6] The resulting fiscal stance, in addition to compounding the demand contraction, had the potential to directly affect those households most reliant on public spending for basic social services. In fact, as the depth of the recession became apparent, fiscal targets in the three countries with IMF programs were adjusted to allow for larger deficits (Lane et al. 1999). Malaysia's tight fiscal stance was also reversed in the summer

6. From previous plans of modest fiscal surpluses (less than 0.5 percent of GDP in Indonesia, South Korea, and Thailand), the initial IMF-supported programs called for increases in the surpluses of 2.1 percent of GDP in Thailand in the first full fiscal year of the program; 1.1 percent in Indonesia, and 0.6 percent in Korea (all including bank restructuring carrying costs) (Lane et al. 1999). In Malaysia, the government also undertook a controversial fiscal tightening in late 1997.

of 1998. In addition, fiscal spending was augmented by a relatively rapid increase in lending from the World Bank and the Asian Development Bank and major donors, including particularly Japan. The new loan packages typically included agreements by governments to maintain spending for social programs, including education, health, and emergency employment, and to encourage better allocation of such spending to the most effective programs.

Although debate about the appropriateness of the IMF's adjustment strategy is likely to continue for some time, we can now see with the benefit of hindsight that the crisis did not generate the degree of social distress initially feared. Nonetheless, for affected households the crisis was a wrenching event, calling into question the more-or-less sustained income growth and upward mobility of the recent past. How effectively did governments respond to the social dimensions of the crisis? To what extent were the new policies and programs short term, and to what extent did they constitute the core of a new social contract?

Before we can address these questions, we need to know more about who was affected. Across the four countries, the poor—and especially the urban working poor—were of course particularly vulnerable. But a much broader group, not easily distinguished at the bottom from the working poor, was also hit very hard: the class of urban strivers with reasonably good jobs or thriving small businesses but with relatively limited education and accumulated physical assets.

This group is more easily defined in terms of absolute income and education than in terms of their relative income or education status within each country. Figure 5.2 compares absolute income by quintiles of the population for Indonesia, Malaysia, South Korea, and Thailand. Note that in absolute terms, the average income per capita of the richest quintile of households in Indonesia, at about $7,000, is slightly below the average of the middle quintile in South Korea. All households except the richest in Indonesia have income per capita below $5,000; that is more or less the income level of the second poorest quintile of households in South Korea and the middle quintile in Thailand. It is around this income level, of about $5,000, that households are likely to be in the new urban striver class, although in Indonesia this group is near the top of the distribution, in Thailand in the middle, and in South Korea near the bottom.

Indonesia

The social risk of the crisis was greatest in Indonesia, because about 11 percent of the population, or about 22 million people, were living in poverty when the crisis struck. During the first half of 1998, poverty projections became highly politicized. Initial World Bank estimates suggested that poverty would rise to 17 percent (Poppele, Sumarto, and Pritchett 1999, 5-6). But government estimates in June put the number of

Figure 5.2   Average per capita income (1997 PPP dollars) by quintile: Indonesia, Malaysia, South Korea, and Thailand

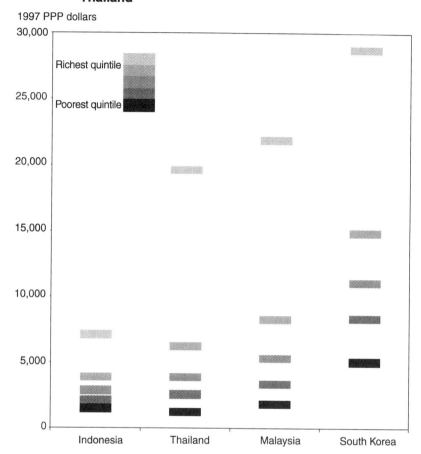

PPP = purchasing power parity
Source: Pettinato (1999).

people living in poverty at 40 percent, and the international media ran stories suggesting the possibility of widespread malnutrition and even starvation (see, e.g., *Washington Post*, 1 September 1998, A1). Subsequent studies have shown convincingly that these initial projections were wildly out of line and that the World Bank estimates were surprisingly accurate (Poppele, Sumarto, and Pritchett 1999; Suryahadi et al. 1999).

Who was affected? The crisis—initially an urban one, concentrated in the formal economy—did not generate a substantial increase in aggregate unemployment. But certain sectors, particularly construction and industry, were very hard hit. Given that unemployment in such an economy is not an option, the number of self-employed expanded rapidly, as did employment in agriculture; the informal and rural sectors played the role of shock absorbers, but with an increase in underemployment.

That people were working does not mean they were necessarily doing well. Household per capita expenditures fell an alarming 33.9 percent in urban areas, in comparison with 17 percent in rural areas (Poppele, Sumarto, and Pritchett 1999, 6).[7] Increases in poverty were also more marked in urban areas.[8] When we look at the decline in median expenditures (5.0 for urban households and 1.6 for rural ones), they are much more modest, suggesting that expenditures of the better off fell most sharply.[9] In contrast to the other crisis countries, the less well educated also fared better than the educated, and by a substantial margin.[10] These findings suggest why the effects of the crisis on poverty and other key social indicators, such as school dropout rates, were somewhat less than anticipated. Many of those most seriously affected by the crisis were among the relatively well off to begin with.

Another way of capturing the highly uneven nature of the social crisis is to look at the regional picture (Poppele, Sumarto, and Pritchett 1999, 9-11; Suryahadi et al. 1999, 34-38). Those parts of Java with closer links to the formal economy—and therefore higher incomes to begin with—were the hardest hit. The effort of the government to dampen rice prices meant that farmers did not initially reap the advantages that should have accrued from their rise; in any case, many small-producer households are net consumers of rice. But the Maluccas, Sulawesi, and Sumatra have been minimally affected or have actually gained because of the effect of

---

7. Wage data show a similar "urban bias" in the Indonesian crisis. For rural men (22-65 years old), real daily wages decreased about 6 percent from 1997 to 1998, but urban daily wages fell by 20 percent (Beegle, Frankenburg, and Thomas 1999, 52; see also Suryahadi et al. 1999, chap. 3).

8. The urban headcount index increased from 9.7 percent in February 1996 to 15.4 percent in December 1998, while the rural headcount increased from 12.3 percent to 17.6 percent (Manuelyn-Atinc 1999).

9. Real per capita expenditures of the top quintile fell much more dramatically (from February 1996 to February 1999) than for the lower two quintiles (-23.3 percent vs. -9.2 for the first quintile, and -11.4 for the second; Suryahadi et al. 1999, 8; Poppele, Sumarto, and Pritchett 1999, 12-13), although the fall in expenditures at the very bottom of the income distribution contributed to the increase in the poverty rate (Thomas, Frankenberg, and Beegle 1999, 10, and fig. 2).

10. Other data also point to the conclusion that relatively better off households in urban areas were hard hit. Enrollment in junior secondary school in 1998 relative to 1997 fell more in urban (6.3 percent down) than rural areas (1.3 percent down); urban enrollment declines at this level were very high for girls (19 percent). Use of both public and private health care fell most among middle-income households. Spending on food rose for all households, but rose most for the poorest and, controlling for income, the best-educated (Thomas, Frankenberg, and Beegle 1999).

the depreciation on export crop earnings. Subsequently rice prices also rose, and rice was in any case protected.[11]

Thailand

Thailand shows a number of differences from Indonesia, most notably in how the poor fared (Brooker Group 1999; World Bank Thailand Office 1999a, 1999b). Unemployment doubled from just under 2 percent in 1997 to a peak of about 5 percent in May 1998, before the seasonal demand for labor lowered unemployment in August 1998 to 3.4 percent (although a year earlier, August unemployment was under 1 percent). The greatest losses in the year following the onset of the crisis were in the construction sector (-32 percent), where the boom had been concentrated, and to a much lesser degree in commerce (-3 percent) and manufacturing (-2.4 percent); by contrast, employment in the service sector grew by 5.6 percent, suggesting again the role of the informal sector in absorbing the unemployed. Small and medium-sized firms were responsible for the bulk of unemployment.

Real wages fell 6 percent from February 1997 to February 1998, with the fall greater in urban areas (8.3 percent) than in rural areas (4.7 percent). But again, differences across sectors were pronounced; for example, men working in urban construction saw real wages fall 24 percent, and women in urban manufacturing also saw larger-than-average losses. In sharp contrast to Indonesia, the declines in both employment and welfare were heavily concentrated among those whose education did not go beyond the primary level (World Bank Thailand Office 1999a, 8-9).

The role of the rural sector in the Thai crisis appears to be somewhat different than in Indonesia, because unemployment was concentrated in the rural areas of the Northeast, where poverty is also highest; of the total unemployed in February 1998, more than 40 percent were in the Northeast. However, this is probably an artifact of a significant migration out of the cities to the countryside. In general, agricultural households fared somewhat better than the average household if we compare 1996 and 1998. Urban-rural migration was later reversed when agricultural wages fell and it became apparent that rural areas offered fewer opportunities than urban ones (Brooker Group 1999, chaps. 2, 6).

Both poor rural and urban households witnessed real income declines; fully 18 percent for poor rural households and 14 percent for poor urban households. However, increases in poverty between 1996 and 1998 were relatively contained, rising from 14.9 to 16.9 percent in rural areas (but a worrisome 19.3 to 22.7 percent in the Northeast) and from 3.8 to 4.4

---

11. In a number of rural areas outside Java that did poorly, it is difficult to disentangle the effects of droughts and fires unrelated to the crisis.

percent in urban areas. Inequality also remained constant (World Bank Thailand Office 1999a, 12-13).

As in Indonesia, region also mattered. One of the reasons the crisis was not more severe was the differential effects of rising prices across households. Net producers of agricultural products—fully 25 percent of Thai households—saw an increase in earnings due to the effect of the El Niño drought on rice prices (World Bank Thailand Office 1999a, 10). Nonetheless, at an income level below the average and closer to our $5,000 marker, household welfare almost certainly declined, and took the form of employment and wage losses in urban sectors such as construction.

Malaysia

Of the Southeast Asian countries, Malaysia was least hard hit by the crisis (see Haflah, Johan, and Abubakar 1999; Jomo and Lee 1999). Unemployment was more modest, although the increases were large, going from 2.7 percent in 1997 to 3.9 percent in 1998, and 4.5 percent in March 1999. Nominal wages grew 4 percent in 1998—well below past trend and just a bit below the increase in the consumer price index for the year (5.3 percent). As we will show below, labor market flexibility was an important explanation for this outcome. However, a second reason for the modest effects is that many of the workers in the hardest hit sectors, most notably construction, were foreign and simply left the country; in effect, Malaysia exported a substantial part of its unemployment.

Data on retrenched workers show that 54 percent were in manufacturing (concentrated overwhelmingly in production workers), followed by 27 percent in services and 11 percent in construction (despite the fact that the construction sector contracted by nearly 25 percent in 1998). More detailed information on who was affected by the crisis is still unavailable, but what we know suggests the importance of the groups we have highlighted in Indonesia and Thailand: the urban working class as well as the poor.[12] Using Malaysia's poverty line, poverty edged up from 6.1 to 7.0 percent from 1997 to 1998 (Jomo and Lee 1999, 27). But the urban-rural income imbalance and overall income inequality may have improved slightly in 1998 in comparison with the widening gap experienced during 1996-97, again suggesting the concentration of the effects of the crisis in the urban areas.

South Korea

South Korea, the richest, most urbanized, and most industrialized of the four countries examined here presents an apparent contrast to Indonesia,

---

12. The mean income of urban and top 20 percent of households fell slightly in 1998, while the mean income of the bottom 40 percent of households, especially in the rural areas, remained stable owing in part to higher agricultural prices.

Malaysia, and Thailand. In fact, somewhat similar groups were at risk, but they occupied different positions in the economic and social structure.

The most striking difference with the Southeast Asian countries is the sharp rise in overall unemployment, from 2.1 percent in October 1997 to 8.7 percent in February 1999, near its peak. The loss of employment was concentrated in manufacturing (13.3 percent) and particularly construction (21.3 percent); as in the other Asian countries, agricultural and fishing picked up some of the slack (4.2 percent growth) although informal sector growth did not to the same extent (Park 1998). Contrary to the argument that the South Korean labor market showed major rigidities, rising unemployment was accompanied by sharply falling real wages, 12.5 percent from mid-1997 until the end of 1998 (Manuelyn-Atinc 1999).

Employment losses were heavily concentrated in semi-skilled workers and laborers, and initially came overwhelmingly from small and medium-sized firms, many of which relied heavily on temporary and day laborers (Park 1998). Professional, managerial, technical, and administrative workers saw no declines in employment through 1998; the numbers employed in these categories actually rose. Workers at large firms initially saw only slight declines. Data on education are also revealing; as in Thailand, those with less than secondary schooling bore the brunt of employment losses (Moon, Lee, and Yoo 1999).

In contrast to Indonesia, the fall in income in South Korea was most serious for the poorest 20 percent (-23.7 percent versus -2.5 for the top 10 percent), with corresponding consequences for poverty (Park 1998).[13] Again, this group in South Korea corresponds quite closely to similar groups affected by the crisis in the other countries, even though their relative economic status in South Korea is lower.

In sum, the financial crisis cut across broad swaths of the population in each country; its effects were by no means limited to the poor. These findings are consistent with a broader analyses of financial crises by Diwan (1999). Examining 53 financial crises from 1975 to the mid-1990s, Diwan finds that the share of labor in GDP falls sharply following a crisis—5.5 percentage points—and only partly recovers after. We have seen that in addition to the poor, the newly vulnerable included workers in the formal urban sector, particularly in construction and to a lesser extent manufacturing, and those with less than secondary education. Workers and owners of small and medium-sized enterprises were hit particularly hard.

---

13. As with all countries, poverty measures are always arbitrary, but the Korean headcount measure among urban workers doubled from 3 percent in the fourth quarter of 1997 to 7.5 percent in the third quarter of 1998, and this measure excludes the unemployed (Moon, Lee, and Yoo 1999, table 4-3). More differentiated analysis suggests that the ranks of the poorest of the poor—those with incomes less than 80 percent of the poverty line—increased more rapidly than the poor as a whole or the near poor (Manuelyn-Atinc 1999).

The crisis, in short, affected precisely those emergent, transitional, weakly organized "striving classes" to which the growth-with-equity model had historically granted social mobility, pushing them back, at least temporarily, into the urban informal sector or the countryside. The social consequences of the crisis were partly mitigated because this group was able to draw on personal savings, rely on intrafamily transfers, shift employment, work longer hours, migrate, and reallocate expenditures to protect investments, including in human capital. In this sense, the outcome could be seen as vindicating the region's reliance on informal mechanisms and a relatively limited government role. However, it could also be interpreted as revealing the severe limitations of the formal social contract in East Asia.

The Policy Response: The Political Economy of Social Policy

If governments were not immediately aware of all the details just outlined, the social response to the crisis—including strikes, demonstrations, riots, and deeper social violence—signaled the depth of the problem. Given their lack of experience with social safety nets and the acute need for external financial support, governments turned to international financial institutions, which subsequently played a major role in the definition of the social policy agenda.

Table 5.3 summarizes the main outlines of government policy in the most seriously affected countries. In some areas, such as maintaining levels of health and education expenditure in the short run or launching public works programs, outside intervention supported governments' own inclinations and buttressed fundamental components of the growth-with-equity model. However, in varying degrees across countries and programs, ideas for a broadening of the policy response beyond temporary measures to a reconsideration of the social contract ran into institutional and political difficulties.

The problems facing the East Asian governments were in the first instance administrative. In all cases, and particularly in Indonesia, the large size of the informal and self-employed sectors posed daunting administrative problems for reaching the poor and even more so for constructing a broader system of social insurance. However, the very reliance on informal social safety nets also meant that lines of bureaucratic responsibility were not clear. Agencies with responsibilities for social issues lacked detailed information on the poor and vulnerable. Bureaucracies not only lacked the capacity to respond in a timely fashion, but were poorly positioned to act as political advocates for those affected as well. As a result, delays in responding to the social dimensions of the crisis were a common feature of all cases.

Table 5.3 Social safety net programs in East Asia during the crisis

Country	Food security	Cash transfers	Social funds	Health and education	Workfare programs	Unemployment assistance, insurance, and severance pay	Active labor market policies
Indonesia	New program of targeted cheap rice distribution		Community based programs	Back-to-School Program launched (provided scholarships for the poorest students and school grants for schools in the poorest communities) Subsidies to maintain prices of essential drugs		Existing *padat karya* programs expanded and subsequently redesigned	
Thailand		Social pensions for the elderly and cash transfers to needy families expanded	Community based programs (new)	Low-income healthcare for the poor and voluntary health insurance for the near poor expanded Scholarships and educational loan program expanded Allowing fees to be paid in installments; fee waivers; provisions for free uniforms to students School lunch program expanded	Public workfare scheme (new)	Severance payments increased New Employee Welfare Fund set up to partially finance unpaid severance claims for workers from bankrupt firms	Training for skills development for unemployed expanded Self-employment loans

(continued next page)

Table 5.3 Social safety net programs in East Asia during the crisis (continued)

Country	Food security	Cash transfers	Social funds	Health and education	Workfare programs	Unemployment assistance, insurance, and severance pay	Active labor market policies
Malaysia							Training for unemployed expanded
South Korea		Temporary non-contributory means-tested livelihood protection program (new) Social pension for the elderly (new)			Public workfare scheme (new)	Unemployment insurance program expanded	Active labor market programs (vocational training, wage subsidies, job placement) expanded

Source: World Bank (2000b).

200

Table 5.4 Aspects of social protection, 1997

Country	Unemployment insurance	Severance pay (months of salary)	Ratio of social security coverage to total employment (percent)
Indonesia	No	4	12
Thailand	No	6	16
Malaysia	No	n.a.	48
South Korea	Yes	n.a.	38

n.a. = not available
Source: Lee, E. (1998), table 3.1.

A second problem was that a number of Asian policy makers, as well as political oppositions and NGOs, were wary of the new social agenda because of the potential for leakage not to the nonpoor (always a legitimate technical concern with social welfare subsidies) but to local politicians and corruption. These concerns were present in Thailand but particularly acute in Indonesia, where controversy about corruption in antipoverty programs engulfed initial World Bank efforts.

In addition to these administrative problems, the design of social programs faced more fundamental political barriers, particularly in efforts to institutionalize more explicit forms of social insurance. Governments in Malaysia, South Korea, and Thailand expressed concern about taking on the spending and transfer programs of the Western welfare state. As tables 5.4 and 5.5 show, social insurance commitments are relatively modest in the countries in question. Malaysia's Employees' Provident Fund is the most comprehensive, but covers just under half of all employees and involves no direct government commitments.

This skepticism combined legitimate doubts about the European model with a traditionalist rhetoric that emphasized reliance on family and community and past success in harnessing work, discipline, and responsibility at the individual level. The idea of social welfare programs that included entitlements to government transfers faced strong resistance from conservative forces, who argued that such programs were costly to business and undermined the roots of past economic success.

Governments in Indonesia, South Korea, and Thailand all faced various forms of social protest. With the partial exception of South Korea, however, none of the political systems had strong parties representing the interests of those most seriously affected by the crisis in an ongoing, institutionalized way. European-style social democratic parties are alto-

Table 5.5 Compulsory contributions to social insurance schemes in Asia (percent)

		Old age, disability, death	Sickness and maternity	Work injury	Total
Indonesia	Employees	2.0 of earnings	None	None	2.0
	Employers	4.0 of payroll	3.0 percent or 6.0 of payroll[a]	.24 to 1.74 percent of payroll	7.24 to 11.74
	Government	None	None	None	0
	Total				9.24 to 13.74
Thailand[b]	Employees	1.0 of earnings	Included in 1st column	None	1
	Employers	1.0 of payroll	Included in 1st column	0.2 to 1.0 of payroll	1.2 to 2.0
	Government	1.0 of payroll	Included in 1st column	None	1
	Total				3.2 to 4.0
Malaysia	Employees	11.5 of earnings	Included in 1st column	0.5	12 percent
	Employers	12.5 of payroll	Included in 1st column	1.75 of payroll	14.25
	Government	None	Included in 1st column	None	0
	Total				25.25
South Korea	Employees	3.0 to 4.5 of earnings	1.0 to 4.0 (average) 1.64	None	4.0 to 8.5
	Employers	4.5 of payroll	1.0 to 4.0 (Average) 1.64	0.3 to 31.9[c] (Average) 1.65	7.15 to 10.15
	Government	Subsidy as needed	Subsidy as needed	Subsidy as needed	
	Total				12.68 to 18.68[d]

a. Contribution for singles is 3 percent and married 6 percent.
b. Pension benefits payable starting in 1998 with an additional 3 percent contribution by employees and 3 percent contribution by employers.
c. Varies by industry and amount of predetermined risk in that industry.
d. The "Total" was calculated using the average Work Injury contribution by the employer (1.68 percent).
Source: US Social Security Administration (1999).

gether absent in the region, and links between parties and civil society are generally weak. Where opposition parties did seek to exploit social issues, it was often through appeal to other political identities, such as Islam in Indonesia and Malaysia or region in Thailand (the Northeast) and South Korea (the Cholla provinces before the Kim Dae Jung presidency).

The organized groups that are historically most associated with the advance of the social agenda, namely labor, were either controlled by the government (as in Malaysia), weak (in Indonesia) or concentrated in sectors where they did not necessarily speak for the interests of those most seriously affected by the crisis (e.g., state-owned enterprises in Thailand). South Korea, again, is a partial exception. Kim Dae Jung's presidency did allow organized labor to influence the social agenda. Although divisions within the labor movement and cross-cutting pressures on the government ultimately led to the dissolution of his corporatist experiment, the partisan orientation of the Kim Dae Jung presidency and the inclusion of labor allowed a substantial broadening of the social contract in South Korea.

Indonesia

We begin again with Indonesia, where the crisis was most severe and the political problems most daunting. In January and early February 1998, the food supply seemed threatened by drought and an inability to import due to difficulties securing letters of credit. The combination of political uncertainty and the collapse of the rupiah generated panic buying, hoarding of food, and riots in a number of provinces, compounded by the initial hesitancy of the government-controlled distribution system (BULOG) in releasing adequate stocks. In early May, an ill-managed price increase in a number of basic foodstuffs—whose design was wrongly attributed to the IMF—generated another round of rioting and protest which, as we have seen, contributed to the fall of the Suharto government.

Before the fall of Suharto, the government's social policy efforts were concentrated overwhelmingly on seeking to ensure supplies of basic foodstuffs by stabilizing prices and by placing strong pressure on suppliers and middlemen. This pressure had a political dimension. Private rice distribution was largely in the hands of Chinese merchants. The anti-Chinese rhetoric that periodically tinged statements by government officials and military officers and the large-scale violence in Jakarta in May generated short-term political uncertainties in the rice markets. This pressure continued after the fall of Suharto as certain political forces, grouped around the Ministry of Cooperatives, sought to expand their role in the rice distribution system. The country faced another spike in rice prices in August and September 1998, due once again to BULOG's reluctance to play its stabilization role and perhaps to fears by large Chinese traders of further violence at the time of Habibie's Independence Day address.

The response of massive subsidization proved inefficient. Not only did the subsidy flow to all consumers regardless of income level, it also had the perverse effect of encouraging rice exports exactly as the government was fearing shortage. After the price spike in August-September, however, the international community developed a more effective relationship with

BULOG, and the more aggressive release of stocks contributed to an easing of prices.

Only after Habibie assumed the presidency and the political situation was temporarily stabilized could the government and the donor community begin to formulate a more coherent social strategy. The background to these new efforts was an important IMF policy shift toward support for a more accommodative fiscal stance. Again, a top priority was achieving food security through a targeted program of distribution of rice to poor families; this program expanded rapidly from 150,000 families to nearly 10 million by early 1999. Although considered reasonably successful, the nature of the poverty data available to the government, inertial pressures from rural districts, and the weak organization of labor and—as always—the urban poor, limited the expansion of the program to households in the cities. Only 5 percent of recipients were urban (World Bank 1999c).

The two other core government programs for alleviating the effects of the crisis were the effort to maintain education and health spending and to generate public employment. With support from external agencies, the new government quickly committed to maintaining social expenditures at past levels and even increasing them and re-allocating spending to focus on the poorest groups.[14] But the World Bank was also stung in mid-1998 by the "revelation" that some Bank-supported programs were subject to political leakage, a fact that could hardly have been surprising given the nature of the country's political system and the ongoing control of the bureaucratic apparatus by Golkar. A loan document outlining a comprehensive social safety net program approved in mid-1999 refers to "implementation delays, fund leakage, budget allocation issues, and inadequate or inappropriate design" (World Bank 1999a, ii), euphemisms for corruption and the political use of funds. Opposition groups also latched onto this critique, claiming that the World Bank and donor community were effectively supporting Habibie's efforts to extend his stay in power.

These criticisms generally fail to distinguish between those programs that worked relatively effectively given administrative constraints, those that faced serious administrative problems, and those that had more fundamental political flaws. In the first category belong the "cheap rice" program and efforts in the education area. In fiscal 1998-99, the government increased the budget for primary education by more than 55 percent, primarily to finance crisis-relief programs providing scholarships and school block grants. A massive "back to school" program provided block grants to the poorest schools and fellowships (direct transfers) to the poorest students. Although this program no doubt suffered from adminis-

---

14. These programs faced a number of problems in implementation, some of them administrative. Government expenditures for the first 9 months of fiscal 1998-99 on social safety net programs were only 37 percent of the annual budgeted amount (World Bank 1999c, 6).

trative problems and some leakage, it was consistent with the broadly based approach to education of the growth-with-equity model and appeared to have helped stem the dropout problem.

The political and administrative problems associated with the variety of employment generation programs—labor-intensive public works programs, demand-driven community funds, and credit schemes to small and medium-sized enterprises—were somewhat more acute. As with the rice program, a common problem was the lack of crisis-responsive geographical targeting. Provincial leaders from better off areas were resistant to efforts to redirect spending from past patterns. Many of the employment creation programs (*padat karya*) were to be carried out by ministries and agencies with no experience in running social policy, and thus little means of measuring whether or not they were effective in meeting social objectives.

However, the continuities in the political system outlined in chapter 3 also created strong incentives and opportunities for abuse. Golkar continued to exercise substantial influence over provincial, local, and community institutions; subnational elections did not take place until June 1999. After the fall of Suharto, these governments became political battlefields as the *reformasi* movement spread out from the cities to the provinces and countryside (Budiman, Hatley, and Kingsbury 1999). The range of social protest was wide, ranging from demonstrations against corrupt officials, to strikes, land seizures, and outright looting of various commodities (*Indonesia Update*, July 1998). In a political setting characterized by a weak transitional government, impending elections, and a proliferation of political challengers from both inside and outside the government, the risk that funds would be diverted to political and electoral uses or outright corruption was high. The effort to rapidly increase social spending and the emergence of strong populist pressures in the system compounded these risks. Prominent among these were calls from Minister of Cooperatives Adi Sasono to use his patronage-laden bureaucracy as the vehicle for an ethnic affirmative action program.

The government's self-assessment of earlier antipoverty efforts recognized the importance of expanding consultation beyond existing provincial and local leaders, but the transitional nature of the government made it difficult if not impossible to institutionalize such checks. The $600 million World Bank Social Safety Net Loan devised a complex governance structure that attempted to increase accountability, in part by engaging NGOs directly in monitoring disbursements in the hope of "less misuse of funds . . . better targeting and design, and less delay" (World Bank 1999a, iii). Even with these controls, the World Bank chose to temporarily suspend some loan disbursements before the elections of June 1999 to avoid charges by the opposition that they were indirectly supporting the government (*Asian Wall Street Journal*, 13 April 1999). Little could be done with respect to a longer-term social agenda until the new democratic government came into office in November 1999.

Thailand

In Thailand, the effort to respond to the social dimension of the crisis was similarly delayed by politics. The social consequences of the crisis were not fully apparent in the last months of the Chavalit government, but even if they had been it is doubtful that it could have responded effectively. After the Chuan government came into office, it immediately faced a variety of social pressures, particularly from the stronghold of the opposition NAP, the rural Northeast, and to a lesser extent from organized labor and other grass-roots organizations.

Before finalizing negotiations with the Asian Development Bank and World Bank for social sector loans, a variety of ad hoc efforts emerged that were driven in part by efforts of competing ministries (and their ministers) to protect budget shares.[15] By the summer of 1998, however, the overall context for the formulation and implementation of social policy had changed. Thailand completed negotiations with the Asian Development Bank for a large social loan in March, and the negotiations over the fourth letter of intent with the IMF in May codified a substantial relaxation of fiscal policy, with some of the loosening explicitly directed to social policy.[16]

Given the weakness of existing machinery for managing the social safety net, the loans generally supported or expanded existing programs rather than launching altogether new ones, and did so relatively effectively (World Bank Thailand Office 1999a, 1999b). For example, the health program expanded funding for the poor, and the education component increased a student loan program to keep children in school. The World Bank loan supported existing government programs designed to provide jobs to the poor, as well as core social services.

To what extent did the crisis generate longer-term changes in the design of the social contract? The most innovative dimension of the World Bank loan was its emphasis on decentralization and local community development through the creation of a Social Investment Fund (SIF), whose objectives were broadly in line with the new constitution's emphasis on devolu-

---

15. Many of these efforts ran into serious opposition, either from management (such as repatriation of foreign workers who were important in the milling industry) and labor (such as the introduction of flexible work rules) or proved impractical (such as encouraging workers with few rural connections to return to the countryside or increasing the labor intensity of production by discouraging the use of machinery).

16. Negotiations with the World Bank were more protracted but were completed by November.

tion of power to lower levels of government.[17] Both the Asian Development Bank and World Bank loans also included decentralizing initiatives, such as shifting Ministry of Health staff to rural areas, granting universities greater autonomy, and encouraging both provincial and local governments to expand their capacity to devise projects and monitor and track the poor in their jurisdictions.

But the opportunity provided by the social funds for patronage, particularly given the coalition nature of the cabinet, made both the government and the international financial institutions (IFIs) cautious in approving projects. Less than 10 percent of all project money had been allocated by April 1999, in part because of concerns on the part of the Democrat Party that the projects would be diverted to political uses and corruption (*Bangkok Post*, 3 April 1999). Despite the constitutional changes, the development of effective local government remained a long-term project that faced resistance from within the central government bureaucracy.

The government also appeared reluctant to undertake new social insurance commitments. When the crisis hit, Thailand had a social security system that provided benefits to workers in the private sector and self-employed professionals. But the program covered only 6 million workers and its benefits were limited to sickness, childbirth, death, and disability benefits; it did not provide unemployment benefits (Sauwalak and Intaravitak 1998). The strongest safety net for urban workers has been severance pay. Under pressure from labor, the government extended the length of severance payments from 6 to 10 months, and launched a special program to provide free health care to laid-off workers and their families as well as job placement services. Not only were these benefits temporary; they were limited to workers in the formal sector.

The Chuan government was openly resistant to expanding the social security program, including a prior government commitment to the development of the pension system (*The Nation*, 5 August 1998), arguing not only that it would have high fiscal cost but that transfers raised issues of moral hazard and entitlement. In the words of one government official, "the reason behind giving them such a tiny amount of money is to create an incentive for them to look for jobs; otherwise they may want to live on social security for the rest of their lives and take advantage of others" (*Bangkok Post*, 7 June 1998).

This reluctance can be traced in part to fiscal constraints, but also to important features of Thai politics. Despite the significance of greater Bangkok in the Thai economy, the country remains largely rural. As a result, the urban-based parties such as the Democrats need to accommo-

---

17. The SIF would provide grant support for small scale subprojects proposed by local governments, NGOs, or community groups (which requires a 10 percent counterpart contribution) and a Regional Urban Development Fund to provide on-lending support to larger, revenue-generating projects in selected municipalities (25 percent counterpart contribution).

date rural interests, as they did, for example in devising a rural debt-forgiveness scheme and micro-lending programs that fell outside the ambit of multilateral financing. At the same time, the nature of organized labor interests reflected relatively privileged segments of the working class, such as workers in the state-owned-enterprise sector. As a result, the government has resisted calls from both the IFIs and domestic political opponents for a formal safety net. Rather, the Chuan administration has favored temporary measures, such as increased attention to education and training—which has lagged in Thailand—and various forms of local self-help.

Malaysia

The politics of social policy in Malaysia initially had less to do with an overt social reaction, as in Indonesia and Thailand, as it did with the policy debates within the government outlined in chapter 2. Anwar initially identified himself with a tough fiscal stance; the announcement of the 1998 budget in October 1997 anticipated a surplus of 2.7 percent of GNP. As the work of the National Economic Action Council unfolded in the spring of 1998, and the depth of the crisis became apparent, Anwar's position became untenable. Fiscal targets were relaxed to a 0.5 percent surplus in March 1998, and finally to a deficit of 3.7 percent.

One reason for the revised fiscal stance was to defend higher social spending. The succession of UMNO-led governments in Malaysia has had a strong record in providing education and health care, motivated in part by their pro-*bumiputra* policies. Both primary and secondary education are heavily subsidized in Malaysia, and initial cuts in the education budget for these levels were quickly restored, as was money for fellowships; as a result, the country experienced no significant problem with respect to school dropouts (World Bank 1999c, 8; Jomo and Lee 1999, 24). Health expenditure, also in the public domain, was cut in 1998 but increased in 1999, as were expenditures by ministries involved in agriculture and rural development. Roughly half of Malaysia's poor are concentrated in three states—Kelantan, Trengganu, and Sabah—that are more predominantly rural and in the first two cases highly susceptible to appeals from the PAS as well.

The distinctive features of Malaysia's approach to the social dimensions of the crisis was in its strong emphasis on maintaining labor market flexibility. One of the most important set of policies had to do with guest workers. The Malaysian government was the first in the region to announce plans to repatriate large numbers of workers: approximately 200,000 migrant workers who were likely to be laid off from the construction sector and 700,000 migrant workers whose permits would be denied renewal after expiry. The plan generated heated political debate, and was ultimately scaled back in part due to employer resistance (Haflah, Johan, and Abubakar 1999, 43-45). Nonetheless, the Home Ministry estimated that more than 200,000 illegal foreign workers returned to their home countries between January and August 1998, and this almost certainly underestimates the number returning: Approximately 80 percent of construction workers were migrants, and employment in this sector was estimated to have dropped by as much as 600,000 workers in 1998 alone (Jomo and Lee 1999, 12, 15).

Maintaining a flexible labor market was also a key policy objective with respect to domestic workers. Trade unions in Malaysia have never been particularly influential political actors, in part because of the low level of unionization (approximately 10 percent of the workforce), in part because of various legal restrictions and formal and informal government controls over their organization and activities (Navamukundun 1998). In August 1998—after the party congress of that year—the government undertook a number of labor market reforms that included closer links between wage settlements and productivity and encouraging management to use pay cuts, reduced working hours, and temporary and voluntary layoffs rather than outright retrenchment.[18] Labor—in a weak bargaining position both politically and economically—went along with these adjustments and negotiated more modest wage settlements than in previous years.

A second pillar of the government's approach was the creation of a variety of special loan funds designed to lift the income of targeted groups; a number of these initiatives were announced by Anwar at the UMNO general assembly in mid-1998. Yet the problem with such funds paralleled the problems we have seen in Indonesia and Thailand with government employment programs; the administrative capacity to move funds efficiently was lacking, substantially diminishing the programs' short-term effects.[19]

A final feature of the government's approach to the social contract was particularly strong resistance to the use of transfers, despite urging from the World Bank about the effects of the crisis on the low-income urban self-employed. Malaysia's Employees' Provident Fund is more comprehensive in its coverage than similar schemes in Indonesia, Thailand, and even South Korea, despite the fact that it is yet to be extended effectively to the self-employed and agricultural workers. But in line with the Asian

---

18. Worker exit was to be supported by both government and firm-level retraining and search schemes, but extremely few workers—in the hundreds—appear to have benefited from the government training program (Jomo and Lee 1999, 17).

19. In 1998, the Fund for Food Program, which provides low-interest loan to farmers and the Farmers' Association, approved only RM199 million worth of loans out of a RM700 million allocation. The Special Scheme for low- and medium-cost housing approved RM241 million out of the RM2,000 million allotted, and the Small-Scale Entrepreneur Fund approved RM882 million out of RM1,500 million approved (Haflah, Johan, and Abubakar 1999, 51).

welfare model, the fund is financed entirely by mandated contributions from employers and workers and direct transfers are minimal. Only 1 poor household in 10 receives a government transfer, and they account for only about 1 percent of the poor's gross income (World Bank 1999c, 4).

Comments made by Prime Minister Mahathir are worth citing at length, because they summarize well a resistance to certain forms of social insurance visible elsewhere in the region, including in both Thailand and South Korea. Referring to social safety nets in the form of unemployment benefits, Mahathir argued that

> this method will only wreck the economy. When the unemployed is [sic] paid an allowance, then many will choose not to work. The Government will need to allocate money for dole which can only be done through raising taxes on the employed ... Of course the production costs for goods will increase, so will the cost of living. So each time dole is raised, taxes follow suit and the cost for manufacturing goods will only reduce our competitiveness in the world market. (*New Straits Times*, 11 June 1999)

South Korea

On coming into office, the Kim Dae Jung government faced a particular dilemma: On the one hand, the unemployment problem in South Korea was serious—the most serious of the four countries—with fewer opportunities for the rural and informal sectors to absorb displaced workers from small and medium-sized firms. On the other hand, the high degree of concentration had resulted in fairly strong and militant unions. Unions represented only 12-13 percent of wage and salary workers, only marginally higher than the unionization rate in Malaysia. But unions were dominant in large firms and public enterprises that enjoyed greater bargaining power; whereas 76 percent of workers in firms with 15,000 or more workers are unionized, only 0.9 percent are unionized in small firms with 10-29 workers. Moreover, South Korean unions operated in a newly democratic context that provided them much wider freedom of action than enjoyed by their Malaysian counterparts.

These differences in unionization had important effects on the ability of firms to lay off workers. Large-scale firms maintained long-term secure employment on a seniority-based wage and promotion system and had difficulty firing workers.[20] These factors meant that while small firms faced little resistance to layoffs and could adjust to redundancy illegally, large firms had to resort to early retirement, voluntary leave, and, where possible, wage restraint. Such measures were not likely to be adequate to encourage the corporate restructuring envisioned by the government.

---

20. In principle, the legal framework concerning labor adjustment was quite strict; only in the case of "emergency managerial needs" would extensive layoffs be allowed, and the supreme court had ruled that such layoffs required consultation with the unions.

Moreover, remaining labor market rigidities could act as a deterrent to foreign investment across a range of sectors.

To secure labor agreement to greater labor market flexibility, Kim Dae Jung resorted to a mechanism not used in South Korea with any success before (Kim and Lim 1999): the tripartite commission. The purpose of forming the group was related in part to legislative politics. The government called a special session of the National Assembly (the 187th) to amend existing labor legislation to allow layoffs, but the opposition in the legislature was reluctant to cooperate because of the political price; the National Assembly thus deferred to the tripartite commission.

The unions were aware from the beginning that the objective of the commission was to extract labor concessions on the issue of layoffs. Kim Dae Jung's status with labor and the promise of political as well as economic compensation allowed the government to bring representatives from both labor federations (FKTU and KCTU) to the table, in addition to the major business associations (the Federation of Korean Industry and the Korean Employers' Federation), government officials (the Ministry of Finance and Economy and the Ministry of Labor), and representatives from each of the four major parties. After weeks of intense debate, and promises from the administration that it would also extract concessions from the *chaebol* as well, a bargain was struck. In return for agreement to permit layoffs when "urgently" needed or in case of takeovers, and to allow the formation of a manpower leasing system for both specialized professions and laborers, the government made a number of political and policy concessions. These included the establishment of a W5 trillion unemployment fund, but many of the concessions to labor were political and procedural: the right for public servants to form a labor consultative body, for teachers to unionize, and the reversal of a long-standing prohibition on labor involvement in political activities. The agreement also recognized the right of labor to participate both in the policymaking process with respect to labor issues and in management decision-making. More vaguely, "all parties" would work to minimize layoffs and seek alternative solutions such as work-sharing.

As Song (1999) has pointed out, the two sides saw the agreement very differently. Management believed it had gained greater freedom to retrench, whereas labor immediately believed that the terms of the bargain were not being enforced. The first serious test of the tripartite agreement with labor came on 31 July 1998, when the Hyundai Motor Company laid off 1,538 workers for "emergency managerial reasons," becoming the first *chaebol* subsidiary to undertake extensive layoffs. The union refused to accept management's layoff plan, and as the dispute dragged on, the government decided to mediate it. After marathon talks, labor and management reached a compromise on 24 August (*Korea Herald*, 25 August 1998), which resulted in layoffs of only 277 workers (with 7- to 9-month severance payments), with another 1,261 placed on an 18-month unpaid leave.

The Hyundai Motor labor dispute was widely regarded at the time as a critical test of the tripartite agreement, and one that the government had failed. Not only had the government become involved in the dispute, but it appeared to broker a deal that signaled that large-scale layoffs were impossible (*Business Week*, 7 September 1998, 48; *Business Korea*, September 1998, 12). In fact, the government moved quickly to dispel this conclusion. In the banking sector, the government stared down financial sector workers and extracted large concessions on downsizing. In a series of confrontations in the fall and spring, the government intervened with force to break strikes (see, e.g., *Korea Herald*, 4 September 1998).

The government's policy shift was apparent to labor, and led the more independent KCTU to pull out of the second tripartite process in late February 1999 on the grounds that the government had failed to implement a number of the committee's accords. Although the KCTU's hopes for forcing the government's hand through the mounting of a general strike proved misplaced, by the spring the tripartite process had clearly broken down.

Despite the administration's stormy relations with labor, the government in fact moved quite vigorously to expand the social safety net.[21] As in other countries, some initiatives were temporary. Because the majority of workers in the country were uncovered by unemployment insurance, the government initiated a workfare program in May 1998 that supported 437,000 workers by February 1999 and was extended through the entire year by the supplementary budget of May 1999. The government also expanded its social assistance to the poor through a temporary livelihood program that added 310,000 newly poor recipients in April 1998 and increased this to 750,000 with the supplementary budget of May 1999.

But the distinctive aspect of South Korea's response to the crisis was the ability of the Kim Dae Jung government to move beyond short-term measures to address the broader social contract. We have noted above the efforts, albeit only partly successful, to remove a range of political restrictions on labor's freedom to organize and participate in politics. With assistance from the World Bank and the Asian Development Bank, the government entered into a series of commitments to expand eligibility and coverage of its unemployment insurance (Korea Labor Institute 1998). Such insurance was late in coming to South Korea; introduced only in 1995 under Kim Young Sam, it had initially covered only workers in firms of 30 or more employees. Under Kim Dae Jung, this was expanded to firms with 5 or more employees, as were mandatory contributions to

---

21. In 1998, the government budgeted 1.3 percent of GDP for social safety net and unemployment program spending; in 1999, the budget allocation for these programs rose by 34 percent (Moon, Lee, and Yoo 1999, 43).

training and wage subsidy schemes. The Kim Dae Jung government also initiated a reform of the pension system, and offset the low coverage and benefit levels by increasing the allocation for the noncontributory means-tested social pension.

From the perspective of the advanced industrial states, these efforts might be seen as little more than catch-up; moreover, implementation was not without difficulties. As of June 1998, for example, among the 1.5 million unemployed, only 7 percent had received unemployment benefits. The extension of benefits to day laborers, formerly set in October 1998, had not been implemented a year later due to lack of administrative capacity (Park 1999, 205). Minimum benefits are low: 70 percent of the minimum wage, which is itself just 25 percent of average earnings. As in Malaysia and Thailand, these benefit levels reflect concern with incentive effects and the risks of "welfare disease" (Park 1999, 206). Public assistance for the poor is less than 9 percent of average earnings, probably not enough to cover basic expenses.

Nonetheless, the South Korean government, headed by a democrat and outsider who appealed to and sought to incorporate labor, clearly went farther than governments in the other crisis countries. Not only did the government move quickly to provide a social safety net, but it initiated broader reforms of the social contract that expanded social insurance and improved labor's participation in both government and management decision-making.

Conclusion

The crisis made clear that the next generation of poor people could not necessarily count on unremitting growth to lift them out of poverty. However, despite the quite justified emphasis of the multilateral organizations on the poor, those vulnerable to the social fallout from financial crises constitute a much larger group that encompasses segments of the urban working and even middle classes. This group includes precisely those who are the most recent beneficiaries of the growth-with-equity model, but who are also lacking in financial, physical, and often educational assets and are not far removed from poverty.

As the crisis unfolded, both governments and the IFIs quickly acknowledged the need to deal with the social consequences of the crisis. In all cases, governments instituted a variety of temporary programs, but the speed with which they could move was limited precisely by the lack of administrative experience in providing a social safety net.

However, the problems of devising social policy are not limited to the administrative; social policy also engages broader political interests. We can see the contours of these political interests by reviewing some of the potential risks that are believed to arise in recrafting the social contract under democratic circumstances.

The first risk is that democratic politics would place demands on government that politicians would attempt to meet at the cost of fiscal and macroeconomic stability. The East Asian cases provide very little evidence for such an eventuality. Democratization has been accompanied by changes in the composition of government spending, but in no East Asian case —including, notably, Indonesia—has political reform been accompanied by an unsustainable expansion of government. The reasons for this are multiple, but include not just the crisis or the involvement of the IMF but the conservative nature of the democratic transitions and the absence of the yawning social deficits and inequalities that generate populist politics.

Rather, the risk is almost exactly the opposite: changing tax and expenditure patterns that are increasingly regressive in their structure. A sound social contract would have at its core either near-neutrality in the incidence of government or biases in favor of the structurally poor rather than the middle classes or rich; by and large, the countries in the region achieved this enviable feat in the early years of their growth.

In the aftermath of the financial crisis, however, the situation is less pretty. As we saw in chapter 1, the opening of capital markets in the 1990s led to collusion between the corporate and banking sectors in which the rich used the banks to accumulate debt-financed wealth. As was detailed in chapter 4, a substantial portion of the resulting liabilities in the form of nonperforming loans has now been assumed directly or indirectly by government. This socialized debt will ultimately be paid off by the taxpayers, as the increasing share of debt servicing in government expenditures already demonstrates. In short, the risk to a new social contract comes not from populist demands, but from the threat that the cleanup of the financial crisis involves fiscal commitments that will squeeze out social expenditures; this threat is particularly real in Indonesia, where the burden of the crisis is heaviest.

A second, related risk is that democratization will allow newly freed interest groups, and particularly labor and the "popular sector," to launch an assault on market-oriented policies. We have already seen in chapter 3 that these risks were muted by parties and movements that advanced market-oriented reforms as well as social ones. But the review in this chapter suggests again that the risks are very much the opposite, namely the weakness of countervailing political forces. Outside of some isolated sectors, labor is relatively weak in the region. Moreover, the most coherent social response to the crisis came in the country, South Korea, where labor was best organized and integrated into the policy process. South Korea's tripartite experience may not be applicable in all other settings, and it had its own limitations. Nonetheless, it did permit the government to solve a number of thorny political problems and ultimately served to advance the cause of a more coherent, comprehensive social policy. Responses to the crisis in Indonesia, Malaysia, and Thailand, by comparison, appear relatively short-term and limited by comparison.

A third, more troublesome risk stems from various forms of corruption to which the programs we have outlined might be subjected. These take a bewildering variety of forms, from the expropriation of individual retirement accounts by unscrupulous financial agents (as in Albania), to the political use of fiscal resources to benefit cronies or advance narrow electoral aims. It is important to recognize that such risks exist in any system, but they appear more egregious in nondemocratic settings where the closed, nontransparent nature of government provides ample, and in some cases virtually unlimited, opportunities for political manipulation of the budget.

A final risk is that the new democratic politics and the new social contract would do little to protect the very poor. For their own reasons, authoritarian governments in the region had incentives to pursue policies from which the poor benefited, even if that was not necessarily their initial design. Under democratic rule, however, the poor are seldom well-represented politically, and their interests may be pushed aside in the interests of business, the middle class, or even the somewhat better off strivers on whom we have placed so much emphasis.

Again, these fears appear misguided, and although it is not a foregone conclusion, the prospects for social protection of the poor seem more, rather than less secure under democratic rule, which seeks to incorporate urban middle- and working-class interests. First, political entrepreneurs do have incentives to appeal to the poor wherever they can be counted on to vote; the strong showing of Megawati in the Indonesian elections was based in no small measure on her implicit appeals to the urban disadvantaged. Second, where the poor have benefited from programs of social protection, it is often because the middle or working classes endorse program designs that in effect provide help to all who face some risk of falling into poverty under well-defined circumstances; South Korea under Kim Dae Jung provides evidence of this fact.

These findings do not address the issue of what a new social contract in Asia might actually look like; that issue, among others, is taken up in the concluding chapter.

6

Conclusion: A New Asian Miracle

If the preceding chapters have not already made the point abundantly clear already, it bears reemphasis that there was, and is, no single "Asian model." Generalizations across cases of such diversity are necessarily risky and must acknowledge enduring differences in resource endowments, level of development, history, culture, and politics. Nonetheless, a common geostrategic setting and some political and policy similarities do provide the starting point for more refined comparisons.

For several decades, the middle-income countries of East and Southeast Asia pursued successful, outward-oriented growth strategies, propelled by high levels of investment in both physical and human capital and an emphasis on exports. The extent and nature of government intervention across these countries by no means followed a common pattern. Yet outside of Hong Kong, an orientation toward exports was by no means equivalent to laissez-faire. In differing degrees, governments employed a variety of instruments—selective protection, subsidies, state-owned enterprises, and a host of other interventions—to achieve their investment, export, and industrial objectives.

The political systems in the region were characterized by authoritarian or semi-democratic rule and close, nontransparent, and sometimes corrupt business-government relations. Curiously, both critics and defenders of the model saw these political characteristics as contributing to high growth, whether through the discipline and social order strong states could impose or the assurances—and rents—close business-government relations gave to investors. In either case, these were *regimes of accumulation*—political systems geared to generating high levels of investment.

Leaders did not maintain power simply by coercion alone, although many were not averse to using it. Government also delivered high growth, upward social mobility, and a reduction of poverty. Defenders of "Asian values" argued that these systems were held together and given legitimacy by the glue of a common Confucian, or Asian, value system that prized social order and rested on a strong ethic of individual responsibility and work. Whatever the merits of these arguments—which I believe are rightly seen as ideological justifications for authoritarian rule—there can be little question that political systems limited the participation of the public, opposition parties, and interest groups.

Well before the financial crisis of 1997-98, this "model" had undergone important changes of two sorts. On the economic front, governments in the region had, albeit from very different starting points, begun to liberalize trade and investment, deregulate markets, and reduce and reposition the state's role in the economy. In politics, a number of countries underwent transitions to democratic rule, which meant not simply the staging of elections but the emergence of new parties and interest groups, including labor, and the freeing of intellectuals and the media.

Looking forward, the big questions arising out of the crisis are easily posed. What effect will the Asian financial crisis have on these larger trends toward the market and democracy? But more important, what type of market-oriented economies and democracies will they be? Are they converging on Japanese, Anglo-Saxon, or European varieties of capitalism, or breeding some altogether new hybrid? What sorts of democratic institutions will countries develop? To answer these questions, I first look back, recapping briefly some of this book's findings and how they might complement other work being done on the origins and management of financial crises and on processes of political change. I then turn to the question of whether a new Asian model is emerging and what it might look like, focusing particular attention on possible outcomes of the financial and corporate restructuring process and debates about a new social contract that are beginning to emerge.

The Political Economy of Financial Crises

Goldstein, Kaminsky, and Reinhart (2000) underline neatly the lacuna in economic analyses of financial crises that this study seeks to address:

> Because these exercises concentrate on the macroeconomic environment, they are not capable of capturing the kind of political triggers and exogenous events— the Danish referendum on the European Economic and Monetary Union (EMU) in 1992, or the Colosio assassination in 1994, or the debacle over the Suharto ouster in 1997-98, for instance, which often influence the timing of speculative attacks. In addition, because high frequency data are not available on most of the institutional characteristics of national banking systems—ranging from the extent

of "connected" and government-directed lending to the adequacy of bank capital and banking supervision—such exercises cannot be expected to capture some of these longer-term origins of banking crises. (17)

Among these longer-term sources of vulnerability, the most frequently invoked with respect to the Asian financial crisis was moral hazard; yet surprisingly little work has gone into tracing the actual sources of moral hazard or why governments would allow themselves to be exploited. Chapter 1 showed that industrial policy, in the sense of targeting particular industries, was not a major source of moral hazard, at least in Thailand and South Korea. But continuing government involvement in the financial sector did create the "risk of socialized risk" in all four countries. Despite purported financial liberalization, politicians in Indonesia, Malaysia, and South Korea still used the banking system as an instrument not only of policy but of politics. In Thailand, owners of financial institutions were able to influence the regulatory process to their benefit. In all cases, these arrangements generated both high social costs and perverse incentives for the managers of financial institutions.

One solution to these problems is for the government to credibly commit to liberalize financial markets, thus eliminating the problems of moral hazard and capture. But liberalization processes can be captured too. Both privatization and deregulation of entry into the provision of financial services have occurred in ways that favored connected firms and individuals or invited outright fraud. The weak prudential regulation, which many have underlined as a cause of the crisis, was not simply the result of inadequate bureaucratic capacity but of more deep-seated political problems centered on the relationship between politicians and private actors.

The channels through which such influence was exercised varied depending on the political system. In Indonesia, it was centered on the executive and highly personalized and clientelistic. In South Korea, it involved campaign contributions and in some cases bribes to legislators. In Thailand, the interested parties were in some cases themselves legislators. It should be underscored that enumerating these risks is not simply an ex post facto rationalization or 20-20 hindsight. The underside of close business-government relations has been a central topic of intellectual controversy in every single country in the region for some time (see, e.g., MacIntyre 1994a; Kim 1997 on South Korea; Gomez and Jomo 1997 on Malaysia; Pasuk and Sungsidh 1996 on Thailand; Robison 1986 and MacIntyre 1991, 1994b on Indonesia, among many others). When the crisis broke, the political debate about its causes quickly homed in on these factors in each of the countries (chapter 3).

These sources of vulnerability do not necessarily translate into crises or losses of confidence, however; there is still the question of how crises start and are transmitted to the real economy. During periods when governments are challenged by economic pressures (e.g, on the exchange rate), market participants react not only to economic fundamentals but to how they expect governments to respond. Once crises break, expectations will have similarly powerful effects on agents' economic behavior. Such expectations are, in turn, based on assessments of political factors: electoral and non-electoral challenges, the decision-making process, and the nature of business-government relations.

Chapter 2 reexamined the period before the crisis—not from the perspective of the economic changes that were occurring, but to reconstruct the policymaking environment. Much has been made of the fact that the crisis was unanticipated and that few foresaw the problems that would subsequently emerge. But an examination of the cases suggests that there was political uncertainty about the capacity of the government to manage the economy *at the time*.

These uncertainties had several sources. Electoral pressures were an important component of the story in South Korea, and Indonesia's indirect presidential election and the party elections in Malaysia also affected policy in those two countries. Particularly in Indonesia, and to a lesser extent in South Korea and Thailand, governments had to contend with non-electoral political challenges in the form of antigovernment protests, demonstrations, or strikes; in Indonesia, these protests raised the highly unsettling issue of succession. The decision-making processes of government played an important role in framing expectations in South Korea (stalemated government), in Thailand (weak coalition), and in Malaysia (divided decision-making authority).

However, one political constant across the cases was the difficulties governments faced in managing their commitments to private-sector allies. Hill (1999), a leading authority on the Indonesian economy, is worth quoting at some length:

> Thus, corruption was a serious problem, but it is difficult to advance the argument that it was a key precipitating variable. More plausible is the thesis that the particular forms corruption, and the political system in general, had assumed by the 1990s rendered the Suharto government unwilling—indeed unable—to move decisively and swiftly once the crisis had hit . . . corruption deserves great emphasis at this stage of the process, rather than as an initial precipitating factor. (69-70)

If we extend Hill's focus on corruption narrowly conceived to cover the broader problem of business-government relations, it captures perfectly the spirit of the argument advanced here. Reducing East Asia's vulnerability is therefore not simply a question of changing policies, but of reconsidering the privileged political position domestic business has enjoyed during the high-growth period, and subjecting business to greater regulatory restraint and accountability.

A legitimate criticism of this analysis is that the sources of political uncertainty have been cast fairly widely, and that virtually all political systems are subject to political uncertainty, some, if not all, the time. Moreover, these political factors were significant only because countries had already entered a "zone of risk" with respect to other early warning indicators of crisis (Goldstein, Kaminksy, and Reinhart 2000). Clearly, the hypotheses suggested here about the role of politics and financial crises require further testing against a wider array of cases, and some statistical work along those lines has begun (Fisman 1998; Leblang 1999; Mei 1999). However, even within the small number of cases examined here, there is compelling evidence that changes of political circumstance can result in changes both in economic policy and in market sentiment. The transition to new governments in South Korea and Thailand, and to a lesser extent in Indonesia, provided the opportunity for new policy initiatives and a stabilization of expectations. The consolidation of authority under Mahathir in the fall of 1998 also brought an end to internal divisions over economic policy.

These observations suggest a final, crucial point about the political economy of the Asian financial crisis, and that has to do with the relative performance of democratic and nondemocratic systems. Since the late 1980s, an important transPacific debate has occurred on the relative merits of different political forms, usually referenced as the controversy on Asian values. The arguments have many strands, and have to do with the role of culture (Zakaria 1994), with whether human rights are universal or culturally bound (Bauer and Bell 1999), and with the value and meaning of democracy. However, the defense of nondemocratic regimes by political leaders such as Senior Minister Lee Kuan Yew of Singapore, Prime Minister Mahathir of Malaysia, President Suharto, and the Chinese Communist Party leadership has always had a strongly utilitarian dimension. Asian political systems were able to deliver economic growth to their citizens and to lift them out of poverty and should therefore ultimately be judged for their performance in securing various "economic rights" as well as human and political ones.

The dubious ethical foundations of these propositions have been eloquently picked apart by Sen (1999, chap. 10), but recent economic history, including but not limited to the recent financial crisis, also calls their empirical foundations into question. Well before the crisis, South Korea, Taiwan, and Thailand made transitions to democratic rule without any noticeable change in their economic performance, while in the Philippines economic performance improved markedly with the fall of Marcos and the transition to democratic rule. For every high-growth authoritarian country in the region, there are dictatorships that have imposed mind-numbing hardship on their citizens—Cambodia, Myanmar, North Korea, and China itself during the Great Leap period and the Cultural Revolution. At a minimum, we should be agnostic about the relative economic performance of democratic and nondemocratic regimes over the long run.[1]

---

1. There is a growing body of cross-national empirical work on this subject. Some studies suggest that democratic governments perform less well than autocracies (Barro 1996). Clague et al. (1997) find that long-lived autocracies outperform short-lived autocracies and short-

However, the cases reviewed here provide at least some support for the more hopeful proposition—now strongly ensconced as the new received wisdom of both international financial institutions and US foreign policy—that democracy, the market, and growth can go together in developing and transitional economies. The contrast between South Korea and Thailand on the one hand and Indonesia on the other shows the advantages that democracies can enjoy. Democracy benefits from popular support, which itself stabilizes expectations, provides the basis for monitoring government and private-sector malfeasance, even if imperfectly, and has a crucial self-corrective mechanism, in the form of elections, through which failing governments can be changed.

Malaysia presents a challenge to these ideas, as Prime Minister Mahathir has not hesitated to point out. The country has enjoyed phenomenal economic success in the past and appeared to escape from the crisis no worse off than the democracies or those that were forced to go to the IMF. However, the analysis offered here suggests a somewhat less charitable interpretation. The Malaysian government has convinced a substantial international audience that it has done well pursuing its unorthodox policy course, but this begs an important question of what the counterfactual should be. Should Malaysia have in fact experienced the shock that it did, or should we have expected its performance to look more like the Philippines', Singapore's, or Taiwan's? A review of the events of 1997 and 1998 makes it hard to escape the conclusion that whatever the role of international capital movements in Malaysia's difficulties, some portion of them were self-inflicted.

Crisis and Political Change

Well before the crisis, the Asian region (and the world more generally) had seen a historic shift toward more democratic forms of governance. South Korea, the Philippines, Taiwan, and Thailand all made transitions to democratic rule beginning in the 1980s. What effect, if any, did the crisis have on this regional trend? A first point, and one that should not be taken for granted, was that the crisis did not lead to *reversals* of democratic rule. Only in Thailand at the end of the Chavalit government did there appear to be any question of the military reentering politics, and that discussion was flatly quashed by the military itself. The new democracies in Asia all proved robust in the face of quite substantial economic and social distress.

---

lived democracies, but stable democracies perform best of all. However, a wide review of the evidence suggests that there is probably no significant relationship between economic performance and regime type one way or the other and that variations within each type are more important (Przeworski and Limongi 1993; Helliwell 1994).

The role of the crisis in the transition to more democratic rule in Indonesia has already been spelled out in chapter 3, but the Malaysian case again requires some further discussion. It is clear that the crisis, both at home and in Indonesia, spurred Anwar to issue a more pointed challenge to Mahathir's leadership, and that challenge included references to the creeping authoritarian tendencies in the system. It is also clear that the crisis as well as the handling of the Anwar case contributed to increasing support for the opposition after Anwar was sacked and that political demands—for a freer press, for greater judicial and police independence, for an end to the political use of the Internal Security Act—were a component of these opposition efforts.

Yet Mahathir survived, suggesting that the relationship between crisis and regime change is not straightforward (Haggard and Kaufman 1995). Much depends on the nature of political institutions. Malaysia exhibits a number of features that gave it advantages when compared to Suharto's New Order in Indonesia. Among these are first and foremost a strong political party, which serves as a means of co-opting political support and contesting elections. Indonesia's Golkar was a much weaker instrument; nor did the channels of electoral representation and opportunities for the opposition—however circumscribed in Malaysia—exist to the same degree. Such findings are sobering for understanding the prospects for change in other countries in the region that may be vulnerable to economic crises in the future, such as China and Vietnam. As the North Korean case shows in most appalling fashion, strong political parties with military backing can survive the worst economic crises, even if at extraordinary cost (Noland 2000a, chapter 5).

The nature of political change is of course not limited to the question of whether regimes fall. In democracies, governments change as the result of elections, and in all systems, economic decline is plausibly associated with a variety of other political changes: increases and decreases of political support for existing parties, the formation of new parties, demonstrations, protests, riots, and other forms of social violence.

A motivating question in the discussion in chapter 3 was the question of backlash: To what extent did the crisis give rise to parties and movements that were populist and anti-market in their orientation? These political forces cannot be dismissed; in each country, business groups sought to maintain existing privileges or extend them, organized labor was rightly concerned about job loss, and NGOs at the grass roots sought to deal with localized social distress.

Yet although the reaction against incumbent governments was ubiquitous, it did not simply reflect populist backlash. Reformers in each country gained adherents through programs that targeted the exact same political problems identified in chapter 1: weak regulation and regulatory institutions, lack of transparency, overly close business-government relations, and corruption. These particular actors were not necessarily associated with the right or conservative wing of the political spectrum; indeed, such characterizations confuse the nature of political cleavages in the region. Rather, they made appeals precisely on populist grounds of greater democracy, fairness, and equity. At the same time, these appeals are poorly understood in terms of traditional populism either. Reformers did argue for the necessity of disciplining concentrated private power. However, they saw the introduction of greater market forces as a means for achieving that objective.[2]

This brand of progressive, market-oriented policy is extraordinarily important in understanding not only the politics of the crisis, but the politics that has surrounded its interpretation. There can be little question that external constraints, including both market pressures and the operations of international financial institutions, were crucial to the political economy of reform; these pressures are well known. But contrary to the assertions of some analysts (Wade and Veneroso 1998)—as well as a variety of self-interested parties in East Asia—the reforms that accompanied the crisis were not simply an imposition of outside forces. Nor was support for them limited to technocrats. In each case, they had important domestic proponents and bases of support as well.

Looking Forward I: The Reform of Business-Government Relations

Chapter 4 outlined the initial management of systemic distress in the four Asian countries, and underlined some of the differences that had emerged across the countries. But financial and corporate restructuring involve longer-term institutional and organizational changes, and thus the final resolution of these problems remains far from clear. As of mid-2000, a number of short-term problems—now already of some duration!— continued to weigh on the region. A number of banks in each country remain weakly capitalized (particularly if they were required to fully provision against loan losses) and nonperforming loans remain extremely high, nearly 40 percent in the Thai banking system. A curious result of the crisis is an inadvertent change in the state's role in the economy. Through the end of 1999, more than 20 banks in the four countries had been nationalized. Through these nationalizations, recapitalization, and purchase of nonperforming loans, the government has acquired substantial ownership claims over corporations as well. Again, the problems in Indonesia are the most daunting; by early 2000, the Indonesian Bank Restructuring Authority held assets equal to approximately 40 percent of

---

2. A useful historical parallel to this mix of ideas can be found in the American progressives of the early twentieth century.

GDP at face value. Devising an appropriate exit strategy remains an important issue.

If we attempt to see through the dense fog of these problems, the basic political issue is how and in what way to restructure the relationship between the government and the private sector, and more specifically, among the government, banks, firms, and other relevant stakeholders.

A first possibility is that the crisis will in fact have very little effect on the nature of business-government relations, regulation, and corporate governance. This might occur for four reasons. First, the region began to witness a strong recovery in 1999. As a result, incentives to restructure fell as waiting appeared to be a more rational strategy and banks and firms grew out of their problems. Second, even the most reformist governments cannot sustain the pace of policy and institutional change as reform fatigue sets in and adjustment costs rise. Third, private actors, including private banks and particularly debtors, remained politically powerful and were able to resist regulatory and institutional changes that would make them more accountable and responsible. They sought to shift the burden of the crisis onto the shoulders of the taxpaying public while escaping with their assets unscathed.

Finally, as Hamilton (1999) has argued eloquently, it is important to recall that not all Asian firms fell into the financial difficulties associated with the crisis. And even if they did, many had already adjusted to the changed policy environment of greater openness and competition, in part through tight integration into cross-border production networks. The crisis may have accelerated these firm-level adjustment strategies, but they have been going on for some time.

This scenario contains important elements of truth, but it underestimates the political as well as policy change that has occurred as a result of the crisis. Taxpayers have paid and will continue to pay dearly for the crisis, a number of banks and debtors have been bailed out, and private actors have resisted both reform legislation and its implementation. But we have also seen important legislative and regulatory reforms and the emergence of political support for a restructuring of business-government relations as well.

A second possible outcome is that the crisis would lead to rapid convergence not only on "Western" standards of financial regulation and corporate governance, but also on "Western" patterns of corporate finance (i.e., with greater reliance on capital markets and less reliance on bank financing) and bank and corporate forms of organization (assuming that such a common model exists). This position can also not be dismissed out of hand. For example, the trend in financial markets away from bank-based systems toward capital-market based systems has been going on for some time and appears to have accelerated with the crisis. But in other areas, the legal framework that would force such convergence is not yet in place, assuming again that there is in fact a common "Western" model. And even if the legal and regulatory framework for such convergence were adopted quickly, it would take some time for those changes to generate convergence at the level of particular markets and firms.

The intermediate view is that both politics and market forces are already pushing toward some reorganization of the business-government relationship in the region. At the most basic level, the central task is to establish a more healthy, balanced relationship between the government and large private-sector actors. This requires a system in which the private sector enjoys strong guarantees of property rights and is capable of airing its views and influencing the political and policy process. But the system must also be one in which the exercise of private economic power is checked by countervailing interests, there is greater transparency both in business-government relations and in corporate governance, and the inevitable social risks and negative externalities associated with private risk-taking are subject to regulation. This outcome can be achieved in part by the strategic use of the market, but it also involves a variety of institutional and ultimately political capacities.

These problems can be introduced by considering several outstanding issues in the reform of financial markets and corporate governance. With reference to the financial sector, a first step is to reduce the government's ownership of banks. The existence of financial market failures is well known, and there may be some limited role for specialized banks or preferential credit programs to address those problems. But the case studies show repeatedly that public ownership of banks poses a range of political economy problems, including the temptation on the part of politicians to use banks for political ends and the corresponding incentives for private firms to lobby state-owned banks and to shift risk to them.[3]

With respect to the private banking sector, the core of the new political bargain involves recognition of the need to develop franchise value and provide incentives for banks to develop reputational capital. This might require some forbearance in the short run with respect to reaching international capital adequacy requirements or regulating entry. (Of course, the public has already made a huge down payment in the form of recapitalization and purchase of nonperforming assets.) But in return, the financial community needs to be exposed to more rigorous prudential regulation and to greater competition. The latter can be achieved by permitting the entry of foreign banks and by developing capital markets and reducing reliance on bank financing; as noted, the latter trend is already under way and is likely to accelerate. The core elements of a new regulatory

3. La Porta, Lopez-de-Silanes, Schleifer and Vishney (2000) present cross-national evidence that government ownership of banks has adverse effects on growth. On the difficult institutional requirements for avoiding capture and moral hazard problems, see Haggard and Lee 1995.

regime, including the emphasis given to disclosure, have been dealt with elsewhere in detail, including in the work of the Basel committee and other international reform proposals (Bank for International Settlements 2000); they need not detain us here.

However, two particular problems bear underlining because they were central to Asia's difficulties. The first has to do with the licensing of banks. As we saw in chapter 1, the problems in the financial sector were not limited to the public sector. Weakness or outright capture of the bank licensing process contributed powerfully to Indonesia's banking-sector difficulties, and is visible in the licensing of merchant banks in South Korea and finance companies in Thailand as well. A second problem is that regulators need to be alert to the ways that banks with ties to nonfinancial enterprises within a group structure can transfer risks to themselves in order to exploit the safety net. Regulators need full disclosure of these relationships with respect to ownership, portfolio, and risk structure.

The financial risks associated with the group structure point to a second cluster of policy issues surrounding the public-private divide—the need to reform corporate governance. The manifest success of the East Asian firm, even in national settings where the rule of law was weak, have led some analysts to downplay the significance of legal rules and to celebrate the advantages of informality, private enforcement of contract and the personal connections known in Chinese as *guanxi*. However, evidence is now accumulating that legal rules matter (see Johnson and Shleifer 1999 for a review). For example, countries with less protection for minority shareholders have smaller equity markets, firms in countries with weaker investor protection use less outside finance, and countries with weaker corporate governance can also suffer larger collapses when hit by adverse shocks.

But for our purposes there are additional political reasons to be attentive to corporate governance. An important parallel exists between an accountable, transparent political system and accountable and transparent systems of corporate governance. Just as accountability of government serves to check the abuse of public authority, so accountability and transparency of firms serves to prevent the abuse of private power in the form of expropriation, insider dealing, fraud, and corruption.

Principles of corporate governance differ across advanced industrial countries in important ways, and promotion of improved corporate governance does not necessarily imply the wholesale rejection of existing Asian models. But the principles drafted through the Organization for Economic Cooperation and Development[4] are indicative of the central objectives of any system of sound corporate governance. These include:

---

4. Available at http://www.oecd.org/daf/governance.htm.

- Guaranteeing shareholder rights;

- Guaranteeing the equitable treatment of all shareholders, including minority and foreign shareholders;

- Recognizing the role of other stakeholders in the firm, including workers and suppliers;

- Ensuring transparency and full disclosure;

- Guaranteeing that the board exercises effective monitoring of management.

Given the dominance of family ownership in a number of Asian countries and the lack of transparency in corporate operations, these rules challenge prerogatives long enjoyed by majority shareholders, managers, and insiders that have allowed them to expropriate wealth. One strategy for addressing this problem would be to directly attack the group form per se, and require firms to be broken up or to change their ownership structure; the Kim Dae Jung administration flirted with this strategy, and in cases where firms are in fact insolvent it is wholly justified. However, it is not clear that such a strategy makes sense for firms that are viable and have demonstrated their competitive powers. Rather, the emphasis (as with financial regulation) needs to be placed on changing incentives.

Such a strategy involves at least three distinct components: the market, direct negotiations with firms, and encouraging countervailing private actors with incentives to monitor the firm. The governments in the region have all substantially liberalized rules governing foreign investment, including allowing foreign firms to participate actively in the market for corporate control through mergers and acquisitions, even hostile ones. Trade liberalization is also gradually changing the competitive landscape across the region and will continue to do so. External liberalization is an important solvent against domestic collusion. However, it will have to be complemented by a strengthening of competition policy and antitrust law, including a shift from reliance on administrative enforcement, which remains vulnerable to capture, to judicial enforcement that can encourage monitoring by affected parties (Bollard and Vautier 1998).

A second component of such a strategy is more directive and involves more explicitly negotiated quid pro quos with the largest firms and their representative organizations. Government support for restructuring of corporate debt, including the granting of haircuts, can be exchanged for commitment to principles of good corporate governance and operational restructuring, using the government's short-run advantage as a bank shareholder as a lever. Finally, governments can assist in the development of other agents with an interest in corporate accountability, including shareholders' movements and more aggressive monitoring of firms by pension funds, mutual funds, financial analysts, think tanks, and the media.

The core question with all of these reforms centers on implementation and enforcement. As has been emphasized throughout this book, these problems are not simply ones of administrative capacity; they also involve avoiding problems of capture of the regulatory process, particularly with respect to the core agencies for financial regulation and the oversight of monopolistic and collusive practices.

The formal independence of these entities is no doubt important. In South Korea, the Kim Dae Jung administration transferred most, but not all, regulatory and supervisory responsibilities out of the Bank of Korea and the Ministry of Finance and Economy into a new Financial Supervisory Commission (FSC). In the short run, such agencies can serve to reduce the problems caused by the existence of multiple veto gates and private-sector resistance. However, as argued in chapter 4, it is important not to confuse cause and effect. The differential capabilities of the FSC in South Korea and the Indonesian Bank Restructuring Authority (IBRA) in Indonesia are not simply administrative; indeed, the IBRA has a strong reputation for the quality of its management. Rather, the weaknesses have been political.

Ultimately, the regulation of the private sector requires support from political coalitions willing to check private power and hold themselves accountable for their relationships with private actors. As Schedler (1999, 17) argues, "A is accountable to B when A is obliged to inform B about A's past (or future) actions and decisions, to justify them, and to suffer punishment in the case of eventual misconduct"; accountability involves information, justification, and punishment. In a number of countries in the region, political reforms of government itself may be necessary to achieve this goal of horizontal accountability.

Information is clearly the cornerstone of accountability at both the corporate and governmental levels. A first step of great importance is to increase the transparency of relations between politicians and their financial supporters. How tightly campaign contributions can or should be regulated remains a topic of substantial debate in the advanced industrial states, but again the principle of transparency and the provision of information are minimum first steps. If such contributions are transparent, voters at least have the ability to reach judgments about the political commitments of their legislators and can vote accordingly.

Other institutions of accountability can also help solve informational problems by monitoring the government, including public interest associations and the media, which has itself been captured and dominated by business interests in a number of countries in the region. But these institutions are not adequate to achieve a healthy business-government relationship unless buttressed by "justification"—a set of rules clarifying the boundaries of the public and private spheres—and institutions for punishing malfeasance, such as independent corruption agencies and ultimately the courts.

In drawing up a balance sheet and looking forward, it is important once again to underline a particular fallacy: to discount the effects of legal and regulatory changes that have been put in place by the crisis but have not had a chance to fully take hold. These measures include bankruptcy and foreclosure laws, the liberalization of foreign direct investment, the strengthening of rules on corporate governance, and financial regulation. In Thailand they include a new constitution. But these reforms cannot hold unless backed up by institutions of accountability, in short by a deepening of democracy itself.

Looking Forward II: Toward a New Social Contract

If the relationship between business and government constitutes one cornerstone of a new Asian model, the other is the nature of the social contract.[5] The financial crisis accelerated changes that were already undermining the implicit social contract of the pre-crisis model of growth with equity. The crisis made clear that the next generation of poor people could not necessarily count on unremitting growth to lift them out of poverty, and also that the achievements of the nascent working and middle classes were more fragile than thought. With the aging of populations, urbanization, more open economies, and the recurring risk of financial shocks, the holes in the social safety net became more apparent, leading to new insecurities. Ideally, a new contract would continue to address the problem of poverty alleviation that was so effectively managed through high growth. But at the same time, it would begin to address the insecurities faced by the growing urban working and middle classes.

What might such a social contract look like? Again, it is possible to consider several limiting cases. One possibility might be called "conservative reaction." During the crisis, governments in both Malaysia and Thailand outlined a conservative critique of the European welfare experience, citing the traditional reliance on family and community in Asia, and their past success in harnessing work, discipline, and responsibility at the individual level to produce high growth. The idea of "social welfare" programs (including entitlements to government transfers), they argued, contradicted the roots of past success based on productivity-enhancing investments in health, education, and performance-based small-credit programs. Business groups also expressed skepticism about any further extension of the safety net on the grounds that it would adversely affect recovery in the short-run and competitiveness in the long run.

A danger of this sort is already present. Because of the large real devaluations that have occurred and the corresponding fall in unit labor costs,

---

5. This section draws on Birdsall and Haggard 2000. See also Manuelyn-Atinc 1999.

governments might be tempted to revert to a growth strategy relying on low-cost labor. Of course, exchange rate adjustments are designed precisely to promote expenditure switching. But relying on real wage adjustments as a solution to problems in the manufacturing and services sectors seems self-defeating in the long run, particularly given the presence of a number of labor-abundant economies in the region, including both China and India, and the increasing importance of knowledge-intensive economic activity. Such a strategy would deflect attention from the fact that tight labor markets caused by economic booms often masked weaknesses in the *quality* of the workforce that need to be addressed through upgrading; this was particularly true in Thailand.

It is at least possible that political forces could arise that would push in the very different direction of a European-style welfare state. The one country in which this might happen would be South Korea, where the labor movement is strongest. Kim Dae Jung did use his credentials with labor to convene a tripartite committee in early 1998, and in the process both extended unemployment insurance to a broader group of workers and also increased benefits. But the Korean exercise was relatively modest, and was aimed in no small part at extracting concessions from labor with respect to labor market flexibility. Labor fully understood the downside of this bargain, and the more progressive of the two peak union organizations ended up boycotting subsequent tripartite meetings. The exercise casts doubt on the viability of the welfare state option in the absence of strong, unified labor movements and social democratic parties, and nowhere in the region do such political forces currently exist.

Some sort of middle way remains that builds on the strengths of East Asia's past growth strategy while addressing the new requirements of those vulnerable to external shocks. Political debate on these issues is likely to revolve around five central policy areas: the provision of social insurance, the reform of industrial relations and labor market issues, education, decentralization, and how to address persistent or structural poverty.

Of the four areas, the provision of social insurance of various sorts is likely to be the most contentious, encompassing issues as diverse and complex as health insurance and pensions. One type of social insurance that should be particularly salient to the "striving class" has to do with employment.[6] In addition to its social insurance function, unemployment

---

6. Such programs are of two sorts. The first provide income support for the unemployed, financed either by the budget or preferably by some form of earmarked "contributions" made by employers and employees. Even when these contributions are, for all practical purposes, payroll taxes, they are typically understood to provide "insurance" rather than unearned transfers. Even when employers contribute, it is not clear who bears the real costs of the payroll tax. Employers can pass on the costs to consumers in the form of higher prices, as long as the demand for their product is not too price-elastic. In open economies, this will be difficult in the tradable sectors. The more flexible wages are, the more employees

insurance has other benefits, the first of which is playing a macroeconomic policy role as a countercyclical Keynesian stabilizer. Reform of social insurance (and particularly of pensions) can also deepen and "democratize" capital markets by creating an increased supply of long-term financing, providing alternative sources of financing to commercial banks, and giving individuals a greater stake in the economy. Unemployment insurance can encourage job mobility—an advantage to economies undergoing needed structural change—and reduce resistance to temporary layoffs, often a more efficient step for firms than reducing wages or firing workers.

The economic conditions for launching initiatives in this area are in some ways more propitious in Asia than in other developing countries. Household savings is already high in the region, and formal insurance schemes would simply channel some portion of these savings through new institutional mechanisms. Moreover, most middle-income Asian countries have good records with respect to the conduct of fiscal policy.

Conversely, the politics of such insurance programs is by no means clear cut. What political bargains would support such a system? For both political and administrative reasons, social insurance is likely to emerge earlier in the more developed countries—South Korea and Malaysia—in which a substantial portion of the workforce is in the formal sector; such a system is already highly developed in Singapore (Low and Aw 1997). Thailand, the Philippines, and particularly Indonesia are likely to follow more slowly. In this second group of countries, emphasis might be placed initially on improving the design and administration of public works programs and institutionalizing them to ensure they are automatically triggered in response to crises.[7]

In the first group of countries, conservative biases and the absence of either strong encompassing unions or social democratic parties suggest that such schemes should avoid emphasizing strong redistributive objectives and instead focus on an ethic of individual responsibility. For insurance schemes, this would imply an emphasis on prior contributions and, in the case of other forms of insurance such as pensions and health, the maintenance of individual accounts.[8] Gaining political support for such

---

will indirectly bear the costs of employer contributions. However, as we note below, it may be politically sensible to charge employers anyway. A second kind of insurance, employed on an ad hoc basis during the crisis, addresses employment and income losses through labor-intensive public works programs.

7. This would include wage-setting below the prevailing market to avoid the work disincentives that have plagued European unemployment insurance programs. More generally, unemployment programs financed by general revenues can be made more politically palatable, as well as efficient, if the macroeconomic conditions under which they kick in are transparent and automatic.

8. Such programs can also reduce risk by giving individuals defined rights to borrow against their insurance accounts—not only during spells of unemployment, but also for housing, children's education, and small business investments (Stiglitz 1999).

programs will still require overcoming financing concerns. Smaller businesses are most likely to complain about the cost of employee contributions, and the support of larger export-oriented firms facing stiff cost pressures is by no means guaranteed.

The South Korean experience suggests that the optimal political sequence for initiating insurance schemes should begin with workers in larger firms. This approach is vulnerable to the criticism that it addresses the needs of the best organized first. But if successful, the program will generate its own demand for expansion to other categories of workers, including smaller firms and even the self-employed.

But gaining political support for such programs is not simply a question of financing; it also depends critically on their governance structures. These structures must guarantee effective oversight of funds and prevent theft and diversion. This can be done by ensuring the political independence of fund managers or their regulators, while simultaneously insisting on high degrees of transparency and opportunities for citizen oversight through participation on boards or panels.[9]

The formulation of these programs is related to a second component of the social contract: a new approach to labor relations. The traditional social bargain in East Asia rested on an authoritarian approach to labor relations in which unions were simply repressed or more typically brought under various forms of government control (Deyo 1989). Democratization made such arrangements anachronistic; and in all the newly democratic countries, old unions sought to remake themselves and new competing federations and unions entered the political fray.

A wide array of factors will influence the nature of the new union structure and its relationship with government,[10] but some simple principles can guide a new political deal for labor in the region, and thus contribute indirectly to advancing the cause of the new social contract. The first task is to get government out of the union business and to recognize the right to form unions, engage in collective bargaining, and strike. In return, the government should insist on its right to guarantee that unions themselves are organized and run in a democratic, transparent fashion and to mediate disputes that cannot be settled between management and labor directly.

---

9. The problem of government involvement in public works programs is more difficult. In Indonesia, the *padat karya* programs were welcomed by incumbents and bureaucrats but hotly contested by opposition groups, which saw them as little more than traditional patronage. However, the World Bank is working with the Indonesian government to devise a system of oversight that would involve participation by NGOs and other groups as well.

10. These include industrial structure and the size of the informal economy, political factors such as the nature of the authoritarian status quo, the party system and the partisan identity of incumbents, and current economic conditions (see, e.g., Deyo 1989; Frenkel 1993; Frenkel and Harrod 1995).

Once such broad frameworks are in place, it is difficult to predict what political role labor will play; a variety of patterns are possible. Where union organization is relatively concentrated, governments may draw labor into broader tripartite discussions, as in South Korea. However, South Korea is likely to be an exceptional case, and the assessment of this experiment also requires a dose of skepticism. Kim Dae Jung was able to do what he did because of his stature as a champion of labor, crisis conditions, and the temporary cooperation of the two union federations; in the end, one of those balked at continuing the process. Elsewhere in developing Asia, labor's overall influence has been small, in part because of the newness of democratic rule, in part because of structural factors such as the size of the small-firm and informal sectors and the emphasis on export-oriented manufacturing. This may change over time, but we must look beyond labor to lead the debate on the new social contract.

A third issue that is likely to have strong cross-class appeal and build strongly on Asia's past development record is education. An obvious ingredient of a post-crisis social contract is a guarantee that public spending on primary and secondary education will not be cut in the event of future economic downturns. Moreover, direct support for poorer students, as in stay-in-school subsidy programs in Indonesia and Thailand, was a noteworthy crisis-induced innovation.

The biggest challenge will come at the tertiary level. Political pressures for increased public spending on university education will inevitably mount as the emergent middle class seeks upward mobility for its children.[11] The key principle for a post-crisis social contract on higher education should be to channel public spending on universities primarily into research and other public goods while avoiding across-the-board support, which can contribute to overbuilt, inefficient public university systems. Misguided spending on tertiary education can be highly costly, particularly in poorer countries, draining human and administrative as well as financial resources from other levels of education and ultimately making public spending on education highly regressive.

A fourth element of the social contract is the greater decentralization of social programs. The arguments in favor of decentralization of service provision—as well as the risks—have been examined in detail elsewhere and need not be fully rehearsed here. Greater decentralization is a critical part of the new social contract, because education and health services that are publicly financed will only continue to be efficient and effective

---

11. The demands of a number of technology-intensive sectors will require that the middle-income countries of Asia, while maintaining incentives for private research and development, also ratchet up public investment in basic and applied research. Larger firms are likely to support public-private partnerships with universities.

if providers, whether public or private with public financing, are accountable to immediate consumers.[12]

The central political dilemma of decentralization of services is that it requires not only the ceding of greater functions to lower levels of government, but the institution of electoral accountability, local revenue-raising capacity, and the involvement of local community groups and NGOs in the decision-making and implementation process. These changes are clearly not just administrative; rather, they involve a replication of the national level process of democratization at the local level, including the formation of responsible, accountable governments, the formation of local party organizations that can recruit leaders and politicians, and the institutionalization of accountable, transparent government. There is clearly strong support for such measures. Given the barriers to entry at the national political level, oppositions in particular tend to favor political decentralization. Decentralization was a central feature of Thai constitutional revision and has become a burning political issue in South Korea and particularly in Indonesia. Yet there is great resistance at the center among both politicians and bureaucrats to ceding power to lower levels of government, and reform on this dimension is likely to be strongly contested.

The final component of the social contract has to do with the needs of the poor. During the crisis, the attentions of international financial institutions were very much focused on the needs of the structurally poor, but there is some question about whether their gradual departure will result in diminished attention to poverty questions. Even in mature democracies, the poor are unlikely to command a political voice consistent with their numbers. Poverty programs are vulnerable to the political critique that they generate moral hazard—that programs designed for the poor will induce the very behavior that leads to poverty—and that programs meant for the truly poor will end up benefiting the nonpoor (always a legitimate technical concern with social welfare subsidies) or, worse, will end up as a source of patronage and corruption of local politics.[13]

Despite these political problems, there is cause for cautious optimism about the prospects for social protection of the poor. When the poor have benefited from programs of social protection, it has often been because the middle class has endorsed program designs that in effect provide help to all who face some risk of falling into poverty under well-defined

---

12. Decentralization does not eliminate the possibility of some redistributive transfers, but these should not be the only—nor in most cases the major—source of financing.

13. Strict targeting of social expenditures on the poorest minimizes the financial burden on middle-class taxpayers but implies a limited number of beneficiaries, who by definition will not be politically powerful and also may carry a social stigma.

circumstances. Indeed, the poor may gain more from a small portion of a large program than from a large portion of a targeted but underfunded one (Nelson 1999). Second, politicians do have some incentives to appeal to the poor wherever they can be counted on to vote; the strong showing of Megawati in the Indonesian elections was based in no small measure on her implicit appeals to the urban disadvantaged.[14] Finally, there is the relevance of social solidarity and moral impulses. Historically, it seems to be the case that once citizens act collectively through government to provide social protection in some form, the moral imperative of including the poor is likely to receive at least some attention. In politics, it is too narrow to rely only on the play of interests without some understanding of reciprocal obligations that have deeper social roots.

A New Asian Miracle

The quest for the taproot of East Asia's extraordinarily rapid economic ascent has been a major preoccupation in the social sciences for more than two decades. Among economists, a dominant strand of thinking is the idea that Asia's remarkable growth is in fact not remarkable, but can be traced to rapid capital accumulation (Krugman 1994). Given the inexorability of declining marginal returns, as well as long-term demographic changes now in train, Asia's rapid growth will necessarily fall back to earth. Of course, the crisis of 1997-98 can in no way be taken as a confirmation of that prediction, but it is nonetheless probable that past rates of growth cannot be replicated.

But the past is not a relevant benchmark; what we want to know is how the region—given these fundamental constraints—is likely to do. Moreover, an assessment of the region's performance needs to look beyond economic indicators to other features of the development process, including political and social developments, and the advance of human freedom.

This study provides the basis for some substantial optimism. First, many of the fundamentals that have long been highlighted by analysts of the region remain in place, including high rates of savings and investment, strong commitment to education, openness to learning from abroad, and exposure to international competition. Despite a number of worrying problems in the financial and corporate sector, in three fundamental ways the crisis has strengthened the institutional framework for growth in the future. First, it has given rise to demands for reforms of economic governance both at the level of the state and of the firm. Second, the crisis

---

14. Graham and Kane 1998 show that politically "opportunistic" social expenditures may benefit the poor (and help build the case for economic reform), but at the risk of inefficiency and misuse.

has generally strengthened rather than reduced countries' commitment to engagement in the international economy. Third, these two developments have occurred under auspices that are more and more—although not yet uniformly—accountable and democratic. The crisis also initiated debate on social contracts to make those democracies better able to withstand shocks in the future. Taken together, these developments constitute a silver lining to an otherwise costly episode in the region's economic history.

References

Ahmad, Abdullah. 1999. What UMNO Must Now Do. *Far Eastern Economic Review*, 9 December: 31.

Ahuja, Vinod, Benu Bidani, Francisco Ferreira, and Michael Walton. 1997. *Everyone's Miracle?* Washington: World Bank.

Alba, Pedro, Leonardo Hernandez, and Daniela Klingebiel. 1999. Financial Liberalization and the Capital Account: Thailand, 1988-97. Unpublished manuscript. Washington: World Bank.

Alesina, Alberto. 1994. Political Models of Macroeconomic Policy and Fiscal Reforms. In *Voting for Reform*, eds. Stephan Haggard and Steven B. Webb. New York: Oxford University Press.

Alesina, Alberto, Nouriel Roubini, and Gerald D. Cohen. 1997. *Political Cycles and the Macroeconomy*. Cambridge, MA: MIT Press.

Ammar Siamwalla. 1997. Can a Developing Democracy Manage its Macroeconomy? The Case of Thailand. In *Thailand's Boom and Bust: Collected Papers* (no editor), (December). Bangkok: Thailand.

Amsden, Alice. 1989. *Asia's Next Giant: South Korea and Late Industrialization*. Oxford: Oxford University Press.

Anek Laothamatas. 1992. *Business Associations and the New Political Economy of Thailand*. Boulder, CO: Westview Press.

Arndt, H.W., and Hal Hill, eds. 1999. *Southeast Asia's Economic Crisis: Origins, Lessons and the Way Forward*. Singapore: Institute of Southeast Asian Studies.

Asian Development Bank. 1998. *Key Indicators of Developing Asian and Pacific Countries 1998*. New York: Oxford University Press.

Aspinall, Edward. 1999. The Indonesian Student Uprising of 1998. In *Reformasi: Crisis and Change in Indonesia*, eds. Arief Budiman, Barbara Hatley, and Damien Kingsbury. Clayton, Australia: Monash Asia Institute.

Athukorala, Premachandra. 1998. Malaysia. In *East Asia in Crisis: From Being a Miracle to Needing One?*, eds. Ross H. McLeod and Ross Garnaut. London: Routledge.

Aziz, Ahmad. 1997. *Mahathir's Paradigm Shift: The Man Behind the Vision*. Taiping, Perak (Malaysia): Firma Malaysia Publications.

Backman, Michael. 1999. *Asian Eclipse: Exposing the Dark Side of Business in Asia*. Singapore: John Wiley and Sons (Asia).

Baig, Tamur, and Ilan Goldfajn. 1999. *Financial Market Contagion in the Asian Crisis*. IMF Staff Papers 42, no. 2 (June): 167-195.

Bank for International Settlements. 2000. *Compendium of Documents Produced by the Basel Committee on Banking Supervision*. Basel, Switzerland: Bank for International Settlements.

Barro, Robert. 1996. Democracy and Growth. *Journal of Economic Growth* 1, no. 1 (March): 1-28.

Bauer, Joanne R. and Daniel A. Bell, eds. 1999. *The East Asian Challenge for Human Rights*. Cambridge: Cambridge University Press.

Beegle, Kathleen, Elizabeth Frankenberg, and Duncan Thomas. 1999. *Measuring Change in Indonesia*. RAND Report to the World Bank (May). Washington: World Bank.

Bhagwati, Jagdish. 1998a. The Capital Myth. *Foreign Affairs* 77, no. 3 (May/June): 7-12.

Bhagwati, Jagdish. 1998b. *Why Free Capital Mobility May Be Hazardous to Your Health: Lessons from the Latest Financial Crisis*. http://www.columbia.edu/~jb38/papers/NBER comments.pdf.

Bhanupong Nidhiprabha. 1998. Economic Crises and the Debt-Inflation Episode in Thailand. *ASEAN Economic Bulletin* 15, no. 3: 309-18

Biddle, Jesse, and Vedat Melor. 1999. Consultative Mechanisms and Economic Governance in Malaysia. Unpublished manuscript. Washington: World Bank, Private Sector Development Department, Business Environment Group.

Bird, Kelly. 1999. Concentration in Indonesian Manufacturing. *Bulletin of Indonesian Economic Studies* 35, no. 1 (April): 43-73.

Birdsall, Nancy, and Stephan Haggard. 2000. *After the Crisis: The Social Contract and the Middle Class in East Asia*. Washington: Carnegie Endowment for International Peace.

Birdsall, Nancy, and Juan Juis Londoño. 1998. No Tradeoff: Efficient Growth Via More Equal Human Capital Accumulation in Latin America. In *Beyond Trade-Offs: Market Reforms and Equitable Growth in Latin America*, eds. Nancy Birdsall, Carol Graham, and Richard Sabot. Washington: Brookings Institution and Inter-American Development Bank.

Birdsall, Nancy, David Ross, and Richard Sabot. 1995. Inequality and Growth Reconsidered: Lessons from East Asia. *World Bank Economic Review* 9, no. 3: 477-508.

Bollard, Alan, and Kerrin Vautier. 1998. The Convergence of Competition Law Within APEC. In *Business, Markets, and Government in the Asia Pacific*, eds. Rong-I Wu and Yun-Peng Chu. London: Routledge.

Bowie, Alasdair. 1988. *Crossing the Industrial Divide: State, Society and the Politics of Economic Transformation in Malaysia*. New York: Columbia University Press.

Bresnan, John. 1993. *Managing Indonesia: The Modern Political Economy*. New York: Columbia University Press.

Brooker Group. 1999. *Socioeconomic Challenges of the Economic Crisis in Thailand*. Report Submitted to the Asian Development Bank and the National Economic and Social Development Board under an Asian Development Bank Technical Assistance on Capacity Building for Social Reform (July). Bangkok: Brooker Group.

Budiman, Arief, Barbara Hatley, and Damien Kingsbury, eds. 1999. *Reformasi: Crisis and Change in Indonesia*. Clayton, Australia: Monash Asia Institute.

Calvo, Guillermo. 1999. *Contagion in Emerging Markets: When Wall Street Is a Carrier*. http://www.bsos.umd.edu/econ/ciecrp8.pdf.

Campos, Jose Edgardo, and Hilton L. Root. 1996. *The Key to the Asian Miracle: Making Shared Growth Credible*. Washington: Brookings Institution.

Camroux, David. 1994. *Looking East and Inwards: Internal Factors in Malaysian Foreign Relations During the Mahathir Era, 1981-1994*. Asia Working Paper 72. Brisbane, Australia: Griffith University.

Caprio, Gerald. 1998. Banking on Crises: Expensive Lessons from Recent Financial Crises. Unpublished manuscript (June). Washington: World Bank, Development Research Group.

Caprio, Gerald, and Daniela Klingebiel. 1997. Bank Insolvency: Bad Luck, Bad Policy, and Bad Banking. In *Annual World Bank Conference on Development Economics 1996*, eds. Michael Bruno and Boris Pleskovic. Washington: World Bank.

Case, William. 1996. *Elites and Regimes in Malaysia: Revisiting a Consociational Democracy.* Clayton, Australia: Monash Asia Institute.

Case, William. 1999. Politics Beyond Anwar: What's New? *Asian Journal of Political Science* 7, no. 1 (June): 1-19.

Case, William. 2000. Malaysia's General Elections in 1999: A Consolidated and High-quality Semi-democracy. Unpublished manuscript. Canberra: Australian National University.

Casserley, Dominic, and Greg Gibb. 1999. *Banking in Asia: The End of Entitlement.* Singapore: John Wiley & Sons (Asia).

Chang, Ha-joon. 1994. *The Political Economy of Industrial Policy.* London: Macmillan.

Chang, Ha-joon. 1998. Korea: the Misunderstood Crisis. *World Development* 26, no. 8 (August): 1555-61.

Chang, Ha-joon. 1999. The Hazard of Moral Hazard: Untangling the Asian Crisis. Paper presented at American Economic Association Annual Meeting, New York (3-6 January).

Chang, Ha-joon, Hong Jae Park, and Chul Gyue Yoo. 1998. Interpreting the Korean Crisis: Financial Liberalisation, Industrial Policy and Corporate Governance. *Cambridge Journal of Economics* 22: 735-46.

Cheng, Tun-jen. 1993. Guarding the Commanding Heights: the State as Banker in Taiwan. In *The Politics of Finance in Developing Countries*, eds. Stephan Haggard, Chung Lee, and Sylvia Maxfield. Ithaca, NY: Cornell University Press.

Cheng, Tun-jen, and Stephan Haggard. 2000. Democracy and Deficits in Taiwan. In *Presidents, Parliaments and Policy*, eds. Stephan Haggard and Mathew McCubbins. New York: Cambridge University Press.

Chinn, Menzie. 1998. *Before the Fall: Were the East Asian Currencies Overvalued?* NBER Working Paper 6491. Cambridge, MA: National Bureau of Economic Research.

Cho, Yoon Je. 1998. *Financial Crisis of Korea: Causes and Challenges.* Working Paper 98-05. Seoul: Sogang Graduate School of International Studies, Sogang Institute of International and Area Studies.

Choi, Byung-Sun. 1993. Financial Policy and Big Business in Korea: The Perils of Financial Regulation. In *The Politics of Finance in Developing Countries*, eds. Stephan Haggard, Chung H. Lee, and Sylvia Maxfield. Ithaca, NY: Cornell University Press.

Cho Kap Che, and Pu Chi Yŏng. 1998. IMF Sat'aeüi Naemak (The Inside Story behind the IMF Situation), March. *Wolgan Chosun* [in Korean].

Chu, Yun-han. 1994. The Realignment of Business-Government Relations and Regime Transition in Taiwan. In *Business and Government in Industrializing Asia*, ed. Andrew MacIntyre. Ithaca, NY: Cornell University Press.

Chu, Yun-han. 1999a. Surviving the East Asian Financial Crisis: The Political Foundations of Taiwan's Economic Resistance. In *The Politics of the Asian Financial Crisis*, ed. T. J. Pempel. Ithaca, NY: Cornell University Press.

Chu, Yun-han. 1999b. Surviving the East Asian Financial Crisis: The Political Foundations of Taiwan's Economic Resistance. Paper presented at the American Political Science Association annual meeting, Atlanta (2-5 September).

Chua, Eng Kee. 1998. Time to Ring the Changes. *Malaysian Business*, 1 March: 36-40.

Clifford, Mark, and Pete Engardio. 2000. *Meltdown: Asia's Boom, Bust, and Beyond.* New York: Prentice Hall Press.

Claessens, Stijn, Simeon Djankov, and Daniela Klingebiel. 1999. *Financial Restructuring in East Asia: Halfway There?* Financial Sector Discussion Paper 3. Washington: World Bank.

Claessens, Stijn, Simeon Djankov, and Larry Lang. 1998. East Asian Corporates: Growth, Financing and Risks over the Last Decade. Unpublished manuscript. Washington: World Bank.

Clague, Christopher, Philip Keefer, Stephen Knack, and Mancur Olsen. 1997. Institutions and Economic Performance: Property Rights and Contract Enforcement. In *Institutions and Economic Development: Growth and Governance in Less-Developed and Post-Socialist Countries*, ed. Christopher Clague. Baltimore: Johns Hopkins University Press.

Cole, David. 1999. Rebuilding the Indonesian Financial System: Lessons from the Past and Suggestions for the Future. *Journal Hukum Bisnis* 9: 7-12.

Cole David, and Yung Chul Park. 1983. *Financial Development in Korea, 1945-1978.* Cambridge: Harvard University Press.

Cole, David, and Betty Slade. 1996. *Building a Modern Financial System: The Indonesian Experience.* Melbourne, Australia: Cambridge University Press.

Cole, David, and Betty Slade. 1998. Why Has Indonesia's Financial Crisis Been So Bad? *Bulletin of Indonesian Economic Studies* 34, no. 2 (August): 61-66.

Corden, Max. 1998. *The Asian Crisis: Is There a Way Out?* Singapore: Institute of Southeast Asian Studies.

Corsetti, Giancarlo, Paolo Pesenti, and Nouriel Roubini. 1998. *What Caused the Asian Currency and Financial Crisis? Part I: A Macroeconomic Overview.* http://www.stern.nyu.edu/~roubini–asia–AsiaHomepage.html.

Crouch, Harold. 1996. *Government and Politics in Malaysia.* Ithaca, NY: Cornell University Press.

Crouch, Harold. 1998. Wiranto and Habibie: Military-Civil Relations since May 1998. In *Reformasi: Crisis and Change in Indonesia,* eds. Arief Budiman, Barbara Hatley, and Damien Kingsbury. Clayton, Australia: Monash Asia Institute.

Danaharta. 1999. *Operations Report: Period from 20 June 1998 to 31 December 1998.* Kuala Lumpur: Danaharta.

Deininger, Klaus, and Lyn Squire. 1996. A New Database for Income Distribution in the World. *World Bank Economic Review* 10, no. 3 (September): 565-91.

Dekle, Robert, Cheng Hsiao, and Siyang Wang. 1998. Do High Interest Rates Appreciate Exchange Rates During Crisis? The Korean Evidence. Unpublished manuscript (December). University of California, Berkeley.

Delhaise, Philippe. 1998. *Asia in Crisis: The Implosion of the Banking and Finance Systems.* Singapore: John Wiley & Sons (Asia).

Deunden Nikomborirak. 1999. Market and Corporate Governance in the New Environment: The Challenge Facing Thai Companies. Unpublished manuscript. Bangkok: Thailand Development Research Institute.

Deyo, Frederick. 1989. *Beneath the Miracle: Labor Subordination in the New Asian Industrialism.* Berkeley, CA: University of California Press.

Diamond, Larry, and Don Chull Shinn. 2000. Introduction: Institutional Reform and Democratic Consolidation in Korea. In *Institutional Reform and Democratic Consolidation in Korea*, eds. L. Diamond and D.C. Shin. Stanford, CA: Hoover Institution Press.

Diwan, Ishac. 1999. Labor Shares and Financial Crises. Unpublished manuscript. Washington: World Bank.

Dohner, Robert, and Stephan Haggard. 1994. *The Political Economy of Adjustment in the Philippines.* Paris: Organization for Economic Cooperation and Development.

Doner, Richard, and Ansil Ramsay. 1998. Thailand: From Economic Miracle to Economic Crisis. In *Asian Contagion: the Causes and Consequences of a Financial Crisis*, ed. Karl D. Jackson. Boulder, CO: Westview Press.

Doner, Richard, and Daniel Unger. 1993. The Politics of Thai Economic Development. In *The Politics of Finance in Developing Countries*, eds. Stephan Haggard, Chung H. Lee, and Sylvia Maxfield. Ithaca, NY: Cornell University Press.

Edwards, Sebastian. 1999. Financial Reform in Emerging Markets: Lessons from Latin America and East Asia. Paper prepared for National Endowment for Democracy Conference on Latin America and East Asia, Santiago, Chile (11-13 November).

Elliott, Kimberly Ann, ed. 1997a. *Corruption and the Global Economy*. Washington: Institute for International Economics.

Elliott, Kimberly Ann. 1997b. Data Sources for Cross-Country Analysis of Corruption. In *Corruption and the Global Economy*, ed. Kimberly Ann Elliott. Washington: Institute for International Economics.

Emmerson, Donald K. 1999. A Tale of Three Countries. *Journal of Democracy* 10, no. 4 (October): 35-53.

Esping-Anderson, Gosta. 1990. *The Three Worlds of Welfare Capitalism*. Cambridge: Cambridge University Press.

Evans, Peter. 1995. *Embedded Autonomy: States and Industrial Transformation*. Princeton, NJ: Princeton University Press.

Evans, Peter. 1997. Transferable Lessons? Re-examining the Institutional Prerequisites of East Asian Economic Policies. In *East Asian Development: New Perspectives*, ed. Yilmaz Akyuz. London: Frank Cass Publishers.

Feldstein, Martin. 1998. Refocusing the IMF. *Foreign Affairs* 77 (March-April): 20-33.

Felker, Greg, and Jomo K.S. 1999. New Approaches to Investment Policy in the ASEAN 4. Unpublished manuscript. Kuala Lumpur: University of Malaysia.

Fischer, Stanley. 1998. The Asian Crisis and the Changing Role of the IMF. *Finance and Development* 35, no. 2 (June) at http://www.imf.org/external/pubs/ft/fandd/2000/06/index.html.

Fisman, Raymond John. 2000. *Estimating the Value of Political Connections*. Unpublished manuscript. New York: Columbia University School of Business.

Forrester, Geoff, and R.J. May. 1999. *The Fall of Suharto*. Singapore: Select Books.

Frenkel, Stephen, ed. 1993. *Organized Labor in the Asia-Pacific Region: A Comparative Study of Trade Unionism in Nine Countries*. Ithaca, NY: ILR Press.

Frenkel, Stephen, and Jeffrey Harrod, eds. 1995. *Industrialization and Labor Relations: Contemporary Research in Seven Countries*. Ithaca, NY: ILR Press.

Frieden, Jeffry A. 1997. The Politics of Exchange Rates. In *Mexico 1994: Anatomy of an Emerging Market Crash*, eds. Sebastian Edwards and Moises Naim. Washington: Carnegie Endowment for International Peace.

Friedman, Thomas. 1999. *The Lexus and the Olive Tree*. New York: Farrar, Straus, and Giroux.

Fukuyama, Francis. 1995. *Trust: the Social Virtues and the Creation of Prosperity*. New York: Free Press.

Furman, Jason, and Joseph E. Stiglitz. 1998. Economic Crises: Evidence and Insights from East Asia. Unpublished manuscript. Paper prepared for Brookings Panel on Economic Activity, Washington.

Ganesan, N. 1998. Malaysia-Singapore Relations: Some Recent Developments. *Asian Affairs* 25, no. 1 (Spring): 21-36.

Gill, Ranjit. 1998a. *Anwar Ibrahim: Mahathir's Dilemma*. Singapore: Epic Management Services.

Gill, Ranjit. 1998b. *The UMNO Dilemma*. Singapore: Sterling Corporate Services.

Girling, John L.S. 1981. *Thailand: Society and Politics*. Ithaca, NY: Cornell University Press.

Goldfajn, Ilan, and Taimur Baig. 1998. Monetary Policy in the Aftermath of Currency Crises: the Case of Asia. Unpublished manuscript. Washington: International Monetary Fund.

Goldstein, Morris, Graciela L. Kaminsky, and Carmen M. Reinhart. 2000. *Assessing Financial Vulnerability: An Early Warning System for Emerging Markets*. Washington: Institute for International Economics.

Gomez, E.T. 1990. *Politics in Business: UMNO's Corporate Investments*. Kuala Lumpur: Forum.

Gomez, E.T. 1991. *Money Politics in the Barisan Nasional*. Kuala Lumpur: Forum.

Gomez, E.T. 1994. *Politics in Business: Corporate Involvements of Malaysian Politics*. Townsville, Australia: James Cook University of North Queensland.

Gomez, E.T. 1999. *Chinese Business in Malaysia: Accumulation, Ascendance, Accommodation*. London and Honolulu: Curzon and University of Hawaii Press.

Gomez, E.T., and K.S. Jomo. 1997. *Malaysia's Political Economy: Politics, Patronage and Profits*. Cambridge: Cambridge University Press.

Goodman, Roger, Gordon White, and Huck-ju Kwon. 1998. *The East Asian Welfare Model: Welfare Orientalism and the State*. New York: Routledge.

Gourevitch, Peter. 1991. *Politics in Hard Times*. Ithaca, NY: Cornell University Press.

Graham, Carol, and Cheikh Kane. 1998. Opportunistic Government or Sustaining Reform? Electoral Trends and Public-Expenditure Patterns in Peru, 1990-1995. *Latin American Research Review* 33, no. 1: 67-104.

Graham, Edward M. 1998. Korea and the IMF: What Went Wrong During the First Weeks Following the Bailout? *Cambridge Review of International Affairs* 11, no. 2 (Spring): 31-54.

Graham, Edward M. 2000. The Reform of the Chaebol since the Onset of the Financial Crisis. The Korean Economy in an Era of Global Competition. *Joint US-Korea Academic Studies* 10. Washington: Korea Economic Institute.

Haflah, Mohd. Musalmah bt. Johan, and Syarisa Yanti Abubakar. 1999. The Social Impact of the Asian Crisis: Malaysia Country Paper. Unpublished manuscript. Kuala Lumpur: Malaysian Institute of Economic Research.

Haggard, Stephan. 1990. *Pathways from the Periphery*. Ithaca, NY: Cornell University Press.

Haggard, Stephan. 1994. Business, Politics and Policy in East and Southeast Asia. In *Business and Government in Industrializing Asia*, ed. Andrew MacIntyre. Ithaca, NY: Cornell University Press.

Haggard, Stephan, Richard Cooper, Susan Collins, Ro Sung-tae, and Kim Chungsoo. 1994. *Macroeconomic Policy and Adjustment in Korea, 1970-90*. Cambridge, MA: Harvard University Press.

Haggard, Stephan, and Robert Kaufman. 1995. *The Political Economy of Democratic Transitions*. Princeton, NJ: Princeton University Press.

Haggard, Stephan, and Mathew McCubbins, eds. 2000. *Presidents, Parliaments and Policy*. New York: Cambridge University Press.

Haggard, Stephan, and Andrew MacIntyre. 2000. The Politics of Moral Hazard: the Origins of Financial Crises in Korea, Thailand and Indonesia. In *Tigers in Distress: the Political Economy of the East Asian Crisis*, eds. Francisco L. Rivera-Batiz and Arvid Lukauskus. London: Edward Elgar Publishers.

Haggard, Stephan, and Jongryn Mo. 2000. The Political Economy of the Korean Financial Crisis. *Review of International Political Economy* 7, no. 2: 197-218.

Haggard, Stephan, and Chung-in Moon. 1990. Institutions and Economic Policy: Theory and a Korean Case Study. *World Politics* 42 (January): 210-37.

Haggard, Stephan, and Steven B. Webb, eds. 1994. *Voting for Reform: Democracy, Political Liberalization, and Economic Adjustment*. New York: Oxford University Press.

Haggard, Stephan, and Chung Lee, eds. 1995. *Financial Systems and Economic Policy in Developing Countries*. Ithaca, NY: Cornell University Press.

Hamilton, Gary. 1999. Asian Business Networks in Transition: Or, What Alan Greenspan Doesn't Know About the Asian Business Crisis. In *The Politics of the Asian Economic Crisis*, ed. T.J. Pempel. Ithaca, NY: Cornell University Press.

Hamilton-Hart, Natasha. 1999. Indonesia: Reforming the Institutions of Financial Governance? Unpublished manuscript. Canberra: Australian National University.

Handley, Paul. 1997. More of the Same? Politics and Business, 1987-96. In *Political Change in Thailand: Democracy and Participation*, ed. Kevin Hewison. New York: Routledge.

Harwood, Alison, Robert E. Litan, and Michael Pomarleano, eds. 1999. *Financial Markets and Development*. Washington: Brookings Institution.

Harymurti, Bambang. 1999. Challenges of Change in Indonesia. *Journal of Democracy* 10, no. 4 (October): 69-83.

Helliwell, J.F. 1994. Empirical Linkages Between Democracy and Economic Growth. *British Journal of Political Science* 24, no. 2: 225-48.

Hewison, Kevin. 1999. *Localism in Thailand: A Study of Globalisation and Its Discontents.* University of Warwick, Working Paper 39/99 (September). Coventry, United Kingdom: Centre for the Study of Globalisation and Regionalisation.

Hicken, Allen. 1998. From Patronage to Policy: Political Institutions and Policy Making in Thailand. Paper presented at the Midwest Political Science Association Annual Meeting, Chicago (23-25 April).

Hicken, Allen. 1999. Parties, Politics and Patronage: Governance and Growth in Thailand. Unpublished manuscript. San Diego: University of California.

Hill, Hal. 1998. Southeast Asia's Economic Crisis: Origins, Lessons, and the Way Forward. Paper presented to the ISEAS 30th Anniversary Conference, Singapore (30 July-1 August).

Hill, Hal. 1999. *The Indonesian Economy in Crisis: Causes, Consequences and Lessons.* Singapore: Institute of Southeast Asian Studies.

Hufbauer, Gary C. 1999. Cleaning up the Financial Wreckage: An Eight Point Program for Indonesia. Paper prepared for the Conference on The Economic Issues Facing Indonesia, Jakarta (18-19 August).

Human Rights Watch. 2000. *Moluccan Islands: Communal Violence in Indonesia.* http://www.hrw.org/press/2000/06/indo-back0629.htm.

Hussein, Syed Ahmad. 2000. Muslim Politics and the Discourse on Democracy in Malaysia. In *Democracy in Malaysia: Discourses and Practices,* eds. Loh Kok Wan and Khoo Boo Teik. London: Curzon.

Hutchcroft, Paul. 1998. *Booty Capitalism: the Politics of Banking in the Philippines.* Ithaca, NY: Cornell University Press.

Hutchcroft, Paul. 1999. Neither Dynamo nor Domino: Reforms and Crises in the Philippine Political Economy. In *The Politics of the Asian Economic Crisis,* ed. T.J. Pempel. Ithaca, NY: Cornell University Press.

Il Nam, Chong, Joon-Kyung Kim, Yongjae Kang, Sung Wook Joh, and Jun-Il Kim. 1999. Corporate Governance in Korea. Paper presented to the OECD Conference on Corporate Governance in Asia: A Comparative Perspective, Seoul (3-5 March).

Indonesia Corruption Watch. 1998. *Statement No. 051/SK/ICW/X/98: Proof of Criminal Act (sic) in the Form of Abuse of Power by Former President Suharto.* Jakarta: Indonesia Corruption Watch.

Institute for International Finance. 2000. *Capital Flows to Emerging Market Economies.* Washington: Institute for International Finance.

Intal, Ponciano Jr., Melanie Milo, Celia Reyes, and Leilanie Basilio. 1998. The Philippines. In *East Asia in Crisis: From Being a Miracle to Needing One?* eds. Ross McLeod and Ross Garnaut. London: Routledge.

Ito, Takatoshi. 1999. *Capital Flows in Asia.* NBER Working Paper 7134. Cambridge, MA: National Bureau of Economic Research.

Jaung, Hoon. 2000. Electoral Politics and Political Parties. In *Institutional Reform and Democratic Consolidation in Korea,* eds. L. Diamond and D.C. Shin. Stanford, CA: Hoover Institution Press.

Jesudason, James V. 1989. *Ethnicity and the Economy: the State, Chinese Business and Multinationals in Malaysia.* Singapore: Oxford University Press.

Johnson, Chalmers. 1983. *MITI and the Japanese Miracle: The Growth of Industrial Policy, 1925-1975.* Stanford: Stanford University Press.

Johnson, Chalmers. 1999. The Developmental State: Odyssey of a Concept. In *The Developmental State,* ed. Meredith Woo-Cumings. Ithaca, NY: Cornell University Press.

Johnson, Colin. 1998. Survey of Recent Developments. *Bulletin of Indonesian Economic Studies* 34, no. 2 (August): 3-60.

Johnson, Simon, and Andrew Schleifer. 1999. Coase and Economic Freedom. Paper prepared for the Mitsui Conference on Economic Freedom, Tokyo, 17-18 June.

Jomo, K.S. 1986. *A Question of Class: Capital, the State, and Uneven Development in Malaya.* Singapore: Oxford University Press.

Jomo, K.S. 1994. *U-Turn? Malaysian Economic Development Policies after 1990.* Cairns, Australia: Centre for Southeast Asian Studies, James Cook University.

Jomo, K.S., ed. 1995. *Privatizing Malaysia: Rents, Rhetoric, Reality.* Boulder, CO: Westview Press.

Jomo, K.S. 1998a. Malaysia: From Miracle to Debacle. In *Tigers in Trouble: Financial Governance, Liberalization and Crises in East Asia,* ed. Jomo K.S. London: Zed Books.

Jomo, K.S. 1998b. Malaysia Props Up Crony Capitalists. *Asian Wall Street Journal.* (21 December).

Jomo, K.S. 1998c. *Tigers in Trouble: Financial Governance, Liberalization and Crises in East Asia.* London: Zed Books.

Jomo, K.S., and Lee Hwok Aun. 1999. Social Consequences of the Economic Crisis. Unpublished manuscript. Report to the Thai Development Research Institute, University of Malaysia, Bangkok.

Jomo, K.S., with Chen Yun Chung, Brian C. Folk, Irfanul Haque, Pasuk Phongpaichit, Batara Simatupang, and Mayuri Tateishi. 1997. *Southeast Asia's Misunderstood Miracle: Industrial Policy and Economic Development in Thailand, Malaysia and Indonesia.* Boulder, CO: Westview Press.

Kahler, Miles, ed. 1998. *Capital Flows and Financial Crises.* Ithaca, NY: Cornell University Press.

Kahn, Haider. 1999. The Problem of Transition from Family-Based Corporate Governance in East Asia. Unpublished manuscript. Manila: Asian Development Bank Institute.

Kaminksy, Graciela A., and Carmen M. Reinhart. 1998. The Twin Crises: The Causes of Banking and Balance-of-Payments Problems. *American Economic Review* 89, no. 3 (June): 473-500.

Kenward, Lloyd R. 1999. What Has Been Happening at Bank Indonesia? *Bulletin of Indonesian Economic Studies* 35, no. 1 (April): 121-27.

Kim, Byung-Kook. 1999. Electoral Politics and Economic Crisis, 1997-98. In *Consolidating Democracy in South Korea,* eds. Larry Diamond and Byung-Kook Kim. Boulder, CO: Lynne Rienner.

Kim, Byung-Kook, and Hyun-Chin Lim. 1999. Labor Against Itself: A Fundamental but Contentious Labor Movement and Structural Dilemmas of State Monism. In *Consolidating Democracy in South Korea,* eds. Larry Diamond and Byung-Kook Kim. Boulder, CO: Lynne Rienner.

Kim, Eunmee. 1997. *Big Business, Strong State: Collusion and Conflict in South Korean Development, 1960-1990.* Albany: State University of New York Press.

Kim, Eunmee. 1999. Crisis of the Developmental State in South Korea. *Asian Perspective* 23, no. 2: 35-55.

Kim Dae Jung. 1999. *DJnomics: A New Foundation for the Korean Economy.* Seoul: Korean Development Institute for the Ministry of Finance and Economy, Republic of Korea.

Klein, James R. 1998. The Constitution of the Kingdom of Thailand, 1997: A Blueprint for Participatory Democracy. Asia Foundation Working Paper 8 (March). San Francisco: Asia Foundation.

Klingebiel, Daniela. 1999. The Use of Asset Management Companies in the Resolution of Banking Crises: Cross-Country Experiences. Unpublished manuscript. Washington: World Bank.

Knowles, James C., Ernesto M. Pernia, and Mary Racelis. 1999. Assessing the Social Impact of the Financial Crisis in Asia: Overview Paper. From the conference, Assessing the Social Impact of the Financial Crisis in Selected Asian Developing Economies. Asian Development Bank, Manila (17-18 June).

Korea Labor Institute. 1998. *Korean Labor and Employment Laws.* Seoul: Korean Labor Institute.

Krause, Lawrence. 1998. *The Economics and Politics of the Asian Financial Crisis of 1997-98.* New York: Council on Foreign Relations.

Krugman, Paul. 1979. A Model of Balance of Payments Crises. *Journal of Money, Credit, and Banking* 11: 311-25.

Krugman, Paul. 1994. The Myth of Asia's Miracle. *Foreign Affairs.* 73, no. 6 (November/December): 62-78.

Krugman, Paul. 1998a. A Letter to Malaysia's Prime Minister. *Fortune,* 28 September: 35-36.

Krugman, Paul. 1998b. Malaysia's Opportunity? *Far Eastern Economic Review,* 17 September: 32.

Krugman, Paul. 1998c. Saving Asia: It's Time to Get Radical. *Fortune,* 7 September: 74-80.

Krugman, Paul. 1998d. *What Happened to Asia?* http://www.mit.edu/people/krugman/index.html.

Krugman, Paul. 1999. *Analytical Afterthoughts on the Asian Crisis.* http://www.mit.edu/people/krugman/index.html.

Kuo, Chengtian, Shangmao Chen, and Zonghao Huang. 1999. The Politics of Taiwan's Credit and Stock Markets. Paper presented at the Annual Convention of the American Political Science Association, Atlanta (2-5 September).

Kuo, Shirley A.Y., and Christina Y. Liu. 1998. Taiwan. In *East Asia in Crisis: From Being a Miracle to Needing One?*, eds. Ross H. McLeod and Ross Garnaut. London and New York: Routledge.

Kuznets, Simon. 1955. Economic Growth and Income Inequality. *American Economic Review* 45, no. 1: 28.

Lamberte, Mario B. 1999. The Philippines: Challenges for Sustaining the Economic Recovery. Paper presented at the conference on The Post-Financial Crisis: Challenges for Progressive Industrialization of Asian Economies, Seoul (15-17 December).

Lane, Timothy, Atish Gosh, Javier Hamann, Steven Phillips, Marianne Schulze-Ghattas, and Tsidi Tsikata. 1999. *IMF-Supported Programs in Indonesia, Korea and Thailand: A Preliminary Assessment.* IMF Occasional Paper 178. Washington: International Monetary Fund.

La Porta, Rafael, Florencio Lopez-de-Silanes, and Andrei Schleifer. 1999. Corporate Ownership Around the World. *Journal of Finance* 45: 471-517.

La Porta, Rafael, Florencio Lopez-de-Silanes, Andrei Schleifer, and Robert Vishney. 2000. Government Ownership of Banks. Unpublished manuscript. Department of Economics, Harvard University.

Leblang, David. 1999. Political Uncertainty and Speculative Attacks. Unpublished manuscript. University of North Texas, Denton.

Lee, Eddy. 1998. *The Asian Financial Crisis: The Challenge of Social Policy.* Geneva: International Labor Organization.

Lee, Hock Lock. 1987. *Central Banking in Malaysia: A Study of the Financial and Monetary Management.* Singapore: Butterworths.

Lee, Kuan Yew. 1998. *The Singapore Story: Memoirs of Lee Kuan Yew.* Singapore: Singapore Press Holdings, Times Editions.

Leipziger, Danny. 1998. *Public and Private Interests in Korea: Views on Moral Hazard and Crisis Resolution.* Economic Development Institute Working Papers. Washington: World Bank.

Lieberman, Ira. 1999. Korea: Corporate Restructuring. Paper presented to the Korea Economic Institute, Korean Economic Working Group, Washington (8 June).

Lim, Joseph Y. 1998. The Philippines and the East Asian Economic Turmoil. In *Tigers in Trouble: Financial Governance, Liberalization and Crises in East Asia,* ed. Jomo K.S. London: Zed Books.

Lim Kit Siang. 1998. *Economic and Financial Crisis.* Selangor Darul Ehsan, Malaysia: Democratic Action Party, Economic Committee.

Lin See-Yan and Tin Fah Chung. 1995. Money Markets in Malaysia. In *Asian Money Markets,* eds. David C. Cole, Hal S. Scott, and Philip A. Wellons. New York: Oxford University Press.

LoGerfo, James, and Gabriella R. Montinola. 1999. Thailand: Episodic Reform, Regulatory Incapacity and Financial Crisis. Unpublished manuscript. Davis, CA: University of California.

Low, Linda, and Tar Choonn Aw. 1997. *Housing a Healthy, Educated and Wealthy Nation through the Central Provident Fund.* Singapore: Times Academic Press for the Institute of Policy Studies.

Lubis, T. Mulya, and Mas Achmad Santosa. 1998. Economic Regulation, Good Governance and the Environment: an Agenda for Law Reform. In *Reformasi: Crisis and Change in Indonesia*, eds. Arief Budiman, Barbara Hatley, and Damien Kingsbury. Clayton, Australia: Monash Asia Institute.

MacIntyre, Andrew. 1991. *Business and Politics in Indonesia.* Sydney: Allen & Unwin.

MacIntyre, Andrew. 1993. The Politics of Finance in Indonesia: Command, Confusion and Competition. In *The Politics of Finance in Developing Countries*, eds. Stephan Haggard, Chung Lee, and Sylvia Maxfield. Ithaca, NY: Cornell University Press.

MacIntyre, Andrew, ed. 1994a. *Business and Government in Industrializing Asia.* Ithaca, NY: Cornell University Press.

MacIntyre, Andrew. 1994b. Power, Prosperity and Patrimonialism: Business and Government in Indonesia. In *Business and Government in Industrializing Asia*, ed. A. MacIntyre. Ithaca, NY: Cornell University Press.

MacIntyre, Andrew. 1998. Whither Indonesia? What America Needs to Know and Do. Unpublished manuscript. University of California, San Diego.

MacIntyre, Andrew. 1999a. Institutions and Investors: The Politics of the Financial Crisis in Southeast Asia. Paper presented at the annual meeting of American Political Science Association, Atlanta (2-5 September).

MacIntyre, Andrew. 1999b. Political Institutions and the Economic Crisis in Thailand and Indonesia. In *The Politics of the Asian Economic Crisis*, ed. T. J. Pempel. Ithaca, NY: Cornell University Press.

McKendrick, David. 1992. Obstacles to Catch Up: The Case of the Indonesian Aircraft Industry. *Bulletin of Indonesian Economic Studies* 28, no. 1 (April): 39-66.

McLeod, Ross. 1998a. Indonesia. In *East Asia in Crisis: From Being A Miracle to Needing One*, eds. R. McLeod and R. Garnaut. London: Routledge.

McLeod, Ross. 1998b. The New Era of Financial Fragility. In *East Asian in Crisis: From Being a Miracle to Needing One*, eds. R. McLeod and R. Garnaut. London: Routledge.

McLeod, Ross, and Ross Garnaut, eds. 1998. *East Asia in Crisis: From Being a Miracle to Needing One?* London: Routledge.

Mahathir, Mohamad. 1998. *Currency Turmoil.* Kuala Lumpur: Prime Minister's Department.

Mahathir, Mohamad. 1999. *A New Deal for Asia.* Kuala Lumpur, Malaysia: Pelanduk.

Mako, William. 1999. Thailand Case. Unpublished manuscript. World Bank, Washington.

Mako, William, and Young Seok Jung. 2000. Korea: Financial Stabilization and Initial Corporate Restructuring. Unpublished manuscript. World Bank, Washington.

Mann, Richard. 1998a. *Economic Crisis in Indonesia: The Full Story.* Toronto: Gateway Books.

Mann, Richard. 1998b. *Plots and Schemes that Brought Down Suharto.* Toronto: Gateway Books.

Mann, Catherine L. 1999. Progress and Prospects: A Simple Framework and Review of the IMF Programs of Brazil, Indonesia, Republic of Korea, Thailand. Testimony before the Senate Subcommittee on International Trade and Finance (March 9) at http://www.iie.com/testimony/imframe.html.

Manuelyn-Atinc, Tamar. 1999. Towards a New Social Contract. Unpublished manuscript. Washington: World Bank.

Masson, Paul R. 1999. Multiple Equilibria, Contagion and the Emerging Market Crisis. Unpublished manuscript. Washington: Research Department, International Monetary Fund.

Masters, Edward. 1999. Indonesia's 1999 Elections: A Second Chance for Democracy. *Asia Society Asian Update.* http://www.asiasociety.org/publications.

Mauro, Paolo. 1995. Corruption and Growth. *Quarterly Journal of Economics* CX 2, no. 441 (August): 681-712.

Maxfield, Sylvia, and Ben Ross Schneider, eds. 1997. *Business and the State in Developing Countries*. Ithaca, NY: Cornell University Press.

Mei, Jinping. 1999. Political Election, Financial Crisis and Market Volatility. Unpublished manuscript. Princeton University, Princeton, NJ.

Milne. R.S., and Diane K. Mauzy 1999. *Malaysian Politics under Mahathir*. London: Routledge.

Mo, Jongryn, and Chung-in Moon. 1999. Korea after the Crash. *Journal of Democracy* 10, no. 3 (July): 150-64.

Mody, Ashok. 1999. Financial Distress: After the Party, the Cleaning Up. Unpublished manuscript. Washington: World Bank.

Montes, Manuel F. 1998. *The Currency Crisis in Southeast Asia*. Singapore: Institute of Southeast Asian Studies.

Montes, Manuel F. 1999. The Philippines as an Unwitting Participant in the Asian Economic Crisis. In *Asian Contagion: The Causes and Consequences of a Financial Crisis*, ed. Karl D. Jackson. Boulder, CO: Westview Press.

Moon, Chung-in. 1994. Changing Patterns of Business-Government Relations in South Korea. In *Business and Government in Industrializing Asia*, ed. Andrew MacIntyre. Ithaca, NY: Cornell University Press.

Moon, Chung-in, and Jongryn Mo. eds. 1999. *Democratization and Globalization in South Korea*. Seoul: Yonsei University Press.

Moon, Hyungpo, Hyehoon Lee, and Gyeongjoon Yoo. 1999. The Social Impact of the Financial Crisis in Korea: Economic Framework. Unpublished manuscript. Seoul: Korean Development Institute.

Moten, Abdul Rashid. 1999. The 1999 Sabah State Elections in Malaysia: The Coalition Continues. *Asian Survey* 39, no. 5 (September/October): 792-807.

Nakamura, Mitsuo. 1999. Prospects for Islam in Post-Suharto Indonesia. *Asia-Pacific Review* 6, no. 1(May): 89-108.

Nasution, Anwar. 1999. The Financial Crisis in Indonesia. In *East Asia's Financial Systems*, eds. Seiichi Masuyama, Donna Vanderbrink and Chia Siow Yue. Toyko and Singapore: Nomura Research Institute and Institute of Southeast Asian Studies.

National Economic Action Council. 1998. National Economic Recovery Plan at http://thestar.com.my/archives/neac/.

Navamukundun, A. 1998. Industrial Relations. Paper presented at the Malaysian Institute of Economic Research 1998 National Outlook Conference, Kuala Lumpur (1-2 December).

Nelson, Joan. 1999. Possible Allies: Overlapping Interests of the Poor and Not-so-Poor. In *Creating Commitment: Politics and Poverty Reduction Policies*, eds. Peter Houtzager, Mick Moore, and James Putzel.

Noble, Gregory W., and John Ravenhill, eds. 2000a. *The Asian Financial Crisis and the Structure of Global Finance*. Cambridge: Cambridge University Press.

Noble, Gregory W., and John Ravenhill. 2000b. The Good, the Bad and the Ugly? Korea, Taiwan, and the Asian Financial Crisis. In *The Asian Financial Crisis and the Structure of Global Finance*, eds. Noble and Ravenhill. Cambridge: Cambridge University Press.

Noland, Marcus. 2000a. *Avoiding the Apocalypse: The Future of the Two Koreas*. Washington: Institute for International Economics.

Noland, Marcus. 2000b. *How the Sick Man Avoided Pneumonia: The Philippines in the Asian Financial Crisis*. Working Paper 00-5. Washington: Institute for International Economics.

Noland, Marcus, Li-Gang Liu, Sherman Robinson, and Zhi Wang. 1998. *Global Economic Effects of Asian Currency Devaluations*. Washington: Institute for International Economics.

Nukul Commission Report 1998. *Analysis and Evaluation on Facts Behind Thailand's Economic Crisis* [English language edition]. Bangkok: Nation Publishers.

Obstfeld, Maurice. 1996. Models of Currency Crises with Self-Fulfilling Features. *European Economic Review* 40, no. 3-5: 1037-47.

Ockey, James Soren. 1992. Business Leaders, Gangsters and the Middle Class. Unpublished PhD dissertation, Cornell University, Ithaca, NY.

O'Donnell, Guillermo, and Philippe Schmitter. 1986. Tentative Conclusions about Uncertain Democracies, pt. 4 of G. O'Donnell, P. Schmitter, and Lawrence Whitehead, eds., *Transitions from Authoritarian Rule: Prospects for Democracy*. Baltimore: Johns Hopkins University Press.

Organization for Economic Cooperation and Development. 1999. OECD Economic Surveys 1998-99: Korea. Paris: OECD.

Overholt, William H. 1999. Thailand's Financial and Political Systems: Crisis and Rejuvenation. *Asian Survey* 39, 6 (November-December): 1009-35.

Pakorn Vichyanond. 1994. *Thailand's Financial System: Structure and Liberalization*. Research Monograph 11. Bangkok: Thailand Development Research Institute.

Pangestu, Mari, and Farid Harianto. 1999. Corporate Governance in Indonesia: Prognosis and Way Ahead. Paper presented at International Conference on Democracy, Market Economy, and Development, Seoul (26-27 February).

Park, Sang Yong. 1998. Financial Reform and Its Impact on Corporate Organization in Korea. Unpublished manuscript. Yonsei University, Seoul.

Park, Se-Il. 1999. Labor Market Policy and the Social Safety Net in Korea: After the 1997 Crisis. Unpublished manuscript. Washington: Brookings Institution.

Park, Yung Chul. 1996. East Asian Liberalization, Bubbles, and the Challenge from China. *Brookings Papers on Economic Activity 2: 357-71*.

Pasuk Phongpaichit and Chris Baker. 1998. *Thailand's Boom and Bust*. Bangkok: Silkworm Books.

Pasuk Phongpaichit and Chris Baker. 1999. The Political Economy of the Thai Crisis. *Journal of the Asia-Pacific Economy* 4, no. 1 (February): 193-208.

Pasuk Phongpaichit and Sungsidh Piriyarangsan. 1994. *Corruption and Democracy in Thailand*. Bangkok: Silkworm Books.

Pempel, T.J. 1999a. Introduction. In *The Politics of the Asian Financial Crisis*, ed. T. J. Pempel. Ithaca, NY: Cornell University Press.

Pempel, T.J, ed. 1999b. *The Politics of the Asian Financial Crisis*. Ithaca, NY: Cornell University Press.

Perkins, Dwight, and Wing Thye Woo. Forthcoming. Malaysia: Adjusting to Deep Integration with the World Economy. In *The Asian Financial Crisis: Lessons for a Resilient Asia*, eds. Jeffrey D. Sachs, Klaus Schwab, and Wing Thye Woo. Cambridge, MA: MIT Press.

Pettinato, Stefani. 1999. A Cross-Country and Cross-Quintile Analysis of Income and Education Distribution in Pre-Crisis East Asia. Unpublished manuscript. Washington: Carnegie Endowment for International Peace.

Pomerleano, Michael. 1998. *The East Asia Crisis and Corporate Finance: the Untold Micro Story*. Washington: World Bank.

Poppele, Jessica, Sudarno Sumarto, and Lant Pritchett. 1999. Social Impacts of the Indonesia Crisis: New Data and Policy Implications. Unpublished manuscript (March). Jakarta: Social Monitoring and Early Response Unit.

Przeworski, Adam. 1991. *Democracy and the Market: Political and Economic Reforms in Eastern Europe and Latin America*. New York: Cambridge University Press.

Przeworski, Adam, and Fernando Limongi. 1993. Political Regimes and Economic Growth. *Journal of Economic Perspectives* 7, no. 3 (Summer): 51-69.

Radelet, Steven. 1998. Indonesia's Implosion. *Harvard Asia Pacific Review* 2, no. 2 (Summer): 87-88.

Radelet, Steven, and Jeffrey Sachs. 1998a. The East Asian Financial Crisis: Diagnosis, Remedies, Prospects. *Brookings Papers on Economic Activity* 1: 1-90.

Radelet, Steven, and Jeffrey Sachs. 1998b. *The Onset of the East Asian Financial Crisis*. NBER Working Paper 6680. Cambridge, MA: National Bureau of Economic Research.

Robison, Richard. 1986. *Indonesia: the Rise of Capital*. Sydney: Allen & Unwin.

Rock, Michael T. 1995. Thai Industrial Policy: How Irrelevant Was It to Export Success. *Journal of International Development* 7, no. 5 (September-October): 745-59.

Rodrik, Dani. 1994. *Getting Interventions Right: How South Korea and Taiwan Grew Rich.* NBER Working Papers 4964. Cambridge, MA: National Bureau of Economic Research.

Rodrik, Dani. 1997. *Has Liberalization Gone Too Far?* Washington, DC: Institute for International Economics.

Sachs, Jeffrey, Aaron Tornell, and Andrew Velasco. 1996. Financial Crises in Emerging Markets: the Lessons of 1995. *Brookings Papers on Economic Activity* 1: 147-217.

Satyanath, Shanker. 1999. Doomed to Fail? Capital Mobility and Crony Capitalism in the South-East Asian Banking Crisis. Unpublished manuscript. Columbia University: New York.

Sauwalak, Kittiprapas, and Chedtha Intaravitak. 1998. Impacts of the Asian Economic Crisis: Case of Thailand. Paper presented at conference on Impacts of the Asian Economic Crisis, Thailand Development Research Institute, Bangkok (23-24 November).

Schedler, Andreas. 1999. Conceptualizing Accountability. In *The Self-Restraining State: Power and Accountability in New Democracies.* Boulder, CO: Lynne Rienner.

Schopf, James C. 2000. The End of Political Bank Robbery in the Republic of Korea. Unpublished manuscript. University of California, San Diego.

Schwarz, Adam. 1994. *A Nation in Waiting: Indonesia in the 1990s.* Sydney: Allen & Unwin.

Schwarz, Adam. 1999. *A Nation in Waiting: Indonesia's Search for Stability,* 2nd edition. St. Leonards, Australia: Allen & Unwin.

Searle, Peter. 1999. *The Riddle of Malaysian Capitalism: Rent-Seekers or Real Capitalists?* Sydney and Honolulu: Allen & Unwin and University of Hawaii Press.

Sen, Amartya. 1999. *Development as Freedom.* New York: Alfred A. Knopf.

Sheng, Andrew. 1992. Bank Restructuring in Malaysia, 1985-88. In *Financial Regulation: Changing the Rules of the Game,* ed. Dmitri Vittas. Washington: World Bank.

Shin, Doh Chull, and Richard Rose. 1998. *Responding to Economic Crisis: The 1998 New Korea Barometer Survey.* Studies in Public Policy 311. Glasgow: Centre for the Study of Public Policy, University of Strathclyde.

Sicat, Gerardo. 1999. The Philippine Economy in the Asian Crisis. In *Southeast Asia's Economic Crisis: Origins, Lessons, and the Way Forward,* eds. H.W. Arndt and Hal Hill. New York: St. Martin's Press.

Soesastro, Hadi, and M. Chatib Basri. 1998. Survey of Recent Developments. *Bulletin of Indonesian Economic Studies* 34, no. 1 (April): 3-54.

Song, Ho Keun. 1999. Politics of Crisis Management and Social Policy. Paper prepared for the conference on Globalization and the Future of the Welfare State: Interregional Comparisons, Brown University, Providence (22-23 October).

Stiglitz, Joseph. 1999. Reflections on Mobility and Social Justice, Economic Efficiency, and Individual Responsibility. In *New Markets, New Opportunities? Economic and Social Mobility in a Changing World,* ed. Nancy Birdsall and Carol Graham. Washington: Brookings Institution Press and Carnegie Endowment for International Peace.

Suchit Bunbongkarn. 1999. Thailand's Successful Reforms. *Journal of Democracy* 10, no. 4 (October): 54-68.

Suryahadi, Asep, Sudarno Sumarto, Yusuf Suharso, Menno Pradhan, and Lant Pritchett. 1999. *Poverty Measurements in Indonesia: Comparisons over Time (1996-99) and Across Regions* (November). Jakarta: Social Monitoring and Early Response Unit.

Thillainathan, R. 1998. The Current Malaysian Banking & Debt Crisis and the Way Forward. Paper delivered at ADB/World Bank Senior Policy Seminar on Managing Global Financial Integration in Asia: Emerging Lessons and Respective Challenges, Manila (revised, 6 May).

Thillainathan, R. 2000. Malaysian Financial and Corporate Sector under Duress: A Midterm Assessment at Restructuring Efforts. Paper presented at World Bank Conference on Corporate Restructuring. Tokyo, Japan (January).

Thomas, Duncan, Elizabeth Frankenberg, and Kathleen Beegle. 1999. Household Budgets, Household Composition and the Crisis in Indonesia: Evidence from Longitudinal Household Survey Data. Paper prepared for the 1999 Population Association of America meetings, New York (25-27 March).

Thompson, Eric C. 1999. Indonesia in Transition: The 1999 Presidential Elections. National Bureau of Asian Research Briefing. http://www.nbr.org.

Thorn, Bret. 1994. The Silent Foreign Policy Coup. *Manager* (Bangkok)(May): 34-40.

Tsebelis, George. 1995. Decision Making in Political Systems: Veto Players in Presidentialism, Parliamentarism, Multicameralism and Multipartyism. *British Journal of Political Science,* 25, no. 3: 289-325.

Tyabji, Amina. 1993. Social Security in the Asian-Pacific Region. *Asian Pacific Economic Literature* 7, no. 1 (May): 53-72.

United Nations. 1999. *World Population Prospects: The 1998 Revision. Volume 1: Comprehensive Tables.* New York: United Nations.

US Social Security Administration. 1999. *Social Security Programs Throughout the World.* http://www.ssa.gov/statistics/ssptw99.html.

Wade, Robert, and Frank Veneroso. 1998. The Asian Crisis: the High Debt Model vs. the Wall Street-Treasury-IMF Complex. *New Left Review* 228 (March-April): 3-22.

Warr, P. 1998. Thailand. In *East Asia in Crisis: From Being a Miracle to Needing One?,* eds. R. McLeod and R. Garnaut. London: Routledge.

Wei, Shang-jin. 1997. *How Taxing Is Corruption on International Investors?* NBER Working Paper W6030. Cambridge, MA: National Bureau of Economic Research.

West, James. 1997. Martial Lawlessness: The Legal Aftermath of Kwangju. *Pacific Rim Law and Policy Journal* 6, no. 1 (January): 85-168.

Winters, Jeffrey. 1996. *Power in Motion: Capital Mobility and the Indonesian State.* Ithaca, NY: Cornell University Press.

Wolf, Charles, Jr. 1998. Too Much Government Control. *Wall Street Journal,* 4 February: A22.

Woo, Jung-en. 1991. *Race to the Swift: State and Finance in Korean Industrialization.* New York: Columbia University Press.

Woo-Cumings, Meredith. 1999. The State, Democracy and Reform of the Corporate Sector in Korea. In *The Politics of the Asian Economic Crisis,* ed. T.J. Pempel. Ithaca, NY: Cornell University Press.

World Bank. 1993. *The East Asian Miracle.* New York: Oxford University Press.

World Bank. 1998a. *East Asia: Road to Recovery.* Washington: World Bank.

World Bank. 1998b. *Indonesia in Crisis: A Macroeconomic Update.* Washington: World Bank.

World Bank. 1998c. *Korea: Second Structural Adjustment Loan.* World Bank document R98-253 (2 October). Washington: World Bank.

World Bank. 1999a. *Indonesia: Social Safety Net Adjustment Loan.* Report P7307-IND. Washington: World Bank.

World Bank. 1999b. *Indonesia from Crisis to Opportunity.* Washington: World Bank.

World Bank. 1999c. *Malaysia: Structural Policy Review: Path to Recovery.* Report 18647-MA. Washington: World Bank.

World Bank. 2000a. *Global Economic Prospects and the Developing Countries.* Washington: World Bank.

World Bank. 2000b. *East Asia: Recovery and Beyond.* Washington: World Bank.

World Bank Thailand Office. 1999a. *Thailand Social Monitor 1: Challenge for Social Reform,* (January). Bangkok.

World Bank Thailand Office. 1999b. *Thailand Social Monitor 2: Coping with the Crisis in Education and Health,* (July). Bangkok.

Yoo, Seong Min. 1999. Corporate Restructuring in Korea: Policy Issues Before and During the Crisis. Unpublished manuscript (February). Seoul: Korean Development Institute.

Yoong, Chung Kek. 1987. *Mahathir Administration: Leadership and Change in a Multiracial Society.* Petaling Jaya: Pelanduk Press.

Yos Vajragupta and Pakorn Vichyanond. 1999. Thailand's Financial Evolution and the 1997 Crisis. In *East Asia's Financial Systems: Evolution and Crisis*, eds. Seiichi Masuyama, Donna Vandenbrink, and Chia Siow Yve. Tokyo: Nomura Research Institute and Singapore Institute of Southeast Asian Studies.

Young, Alwin. 1995. The Tyranny of Numbers: Confronting the Statistical Realities of the East Asian Growth Experience. *Quarterly Journal of Economics* 110, no. 3 (August): 641-80.

Young, Ken. 1998. Post-Suharto: A Change of Regime? In *Reformasi: Crisis and Change in Indonesia*, eds. Arief Budiman, Barbara Hatley, and Damien Kingsbury. Clayton, Australia: Monash Asia Institute.

Zainuddin, Daim. 1994. *Daim Speaks His Mind*. Kuala Lumpur: Pelanduk Publications.

Zakaria, Fareed. 1994. Culture is Destiny: A Conversation with Lee Kuan Yew. *Foreign Affairs* 73, no 2: 109-26.

Index

Bapindo, 26
Barisan Alternatif (Alternative Front), 108, 110-114, 111*n*, 112*n*
Barisan Nasional (National Front), 62
BBC. *See* Bangkok Bank of Commerce (BBC)
BCA. *See* Bank Central Asia (BCA)
BCB. *See* Bumiputra Commerce Bank Bhd (BCB)
BDNI. *See* Bank Dangang Nasional Indonesia (BDNI)
BIBF. *See* Bangkok International Banking Facility (BIBF)
Big Deals, 151-153, 152*t*, 156
BNM. *See* Bank Nasional Malaysia (BNM); Bank Negara Malaysia (BNM)
BNN. *See* Bank Kusa Nasional (BNN)
Board of Audit and Inspection (BAI), 37
BOK. *See* Bank of Korea (BOK)
boutique scandal, 106*n*
Brady bond deal (Philippines), 128
Brazil, 4
build-operate-own (BOO) contract, 169
BULOG, 203-204
bumiputra, 22, 23*n*
　banking sector, 27
　corporate restructuring, 22, 23*n*, 168, 170
　ethnic redistribution, 62
　financial crises (1985-87), 27
　financial market liberalization, 36
　stock market, 28
Bumiputra Commerce Bank Bhd (BCB), 167*n*
Burma, 79
business-government relations, 9, 15-46, 219-220, 224-230
　benefits of, 20-21
　crisis management, 47, 48*t*, 50-51, 90, 91*t*, 217-218
　economic reform-political change link, 89-90, 125, 224-230
　financial/corporate restructuring, 140, 162, 181
　government credibility, 88-89, 229
　Indonesia, 43-45, 124, 140, 177, 181, 219, 220
　Malaysia, 43-44, 46, 62, 108, 111, 140, 162, 167-169, 181, 219
　Philippines, 126, 127*t*, 129, 132
　policy networks, 21
　politics of, 38-46

reform of, 12-14
risk in, 2, 15-16, 16*t*, 21, 45-46
social dimensions, 184-185
South Korea, 28, 42-43, 102-103, 140, 219
Taiwan, 126, 127*t*, 135-136, 138
Thailand, 39-42, 97, 98-99, 140, 162, 219
transparency of, 139, 227-228
business lobbying, effect on crisis management, 50-51
business nationalism, 89
"buy British last" policy, 79

CAHB. *See* Commerce Asset-Holding Bhd (CAHB)
Camdessus, 68
capital account, opening of, 16, 214
　Indonesia, 32
　Malaysia, 73
　Philippines, 128
　South Korea, 37-38
　Taiwan, 134-135
　Thailand, 34
capital adequacy ratio (CAR), 6*n*, 172*n*-174*n*
Capital Augmented Preferred Shares (CAPS), 159*n*
capital controls
　Malaysia, 3, 6*n*, 62, 64, 180
　　economic effects, 74-75, 75*t*
　　elements, 73-74
　　financial support, 83-85, 84*t*
　　foreign policy of, 79-85
　　political economy of, 73-85
　Philippines, 130, 130*n*
capital flows, 4
　effect of capital controls on, 74-78, 76*t*
　role in triggering crisis, 15
Capital Structure Improvement Plans (CSIP), 151, 153
CAPS. *See* Capital Augmented Preferred Shares (CAPS)
CAR. *See* capital adequacy ratio (CAR)
car projects
　Indonesia, 66, 68
　Malaysia (Proton), 31, 43, 166-167, 170
CDA. *See* Constitutional Drafting Assembly (CDA)
CDRAC. *See* Corporate Debt Restructuring Advisory Committee (CDRAC)
CDRC. *See* Corporate Debt Restructuring Committee (CDRC)

and authoritarianism, 44
Hong Kong, 39, 40t-41t
and income distribution, 188, 201
Indonesia, 25-27, 39, 40t-41t, 44, 66-67,
  69-70, 116, 120, 122, 124, 201, 204-
  205, 220
Malaysia, 39, 40t-41t, 63, 108, 111
OECD, 39, 40t-41t
Philippines, 39, 40t-41t, 128-129, 132
and political change, 89
Singapore, 39, 40t-41t
South Korea, 29-30, 39, 40t-41t, 101,
  106, 106n, 206, 206n
Taiwan, 39, 40t-41t, 135, 136
Thailand, 39, 40t-41t, 92n, 99, 99n, 207
court protection (hwa ui pob), 56, 56n
court receivership (pasan), 56, 56n
CP. See Chart Pattana (CP)
CP market. See commercial paper (CP)
  market
cronyism, 25-27, 38-39, 71, 89, 129. See
  also corruption; nepotism
  and financial/corporate restructuring,
  140
  and income distribution, 188
  Indonesia, 44, 66-67, 69-70, 116
  Malaysia, 63
  Philippines, 128, 133
CSIP. See Capital Structure Improvement
  Plans (CSIP)
currencies. See also specific type
  floating of, 3
currency board, Indonesia, 69
currency crises (1997-98), 3-4
current account deficits, 5, 133
  Indonesia, 5, 65
  South Korea, 5
  Thailand, 5, 51
current account surplus
  Malaysia, 78
Taiwan, 133-134

Daewoo, 23t, 151-155, 154-155
Daewoo Motors, 154
Dagang Nasional Indonesia, 173n
Daim Zainuddin, 64, 81, 114, 168, 169,
  171
Danaharta, 62, 162-164, 167, 167n, 168,
  171, 180n
Danamodal Nasional Bhd, 62, 164
D and C Bank, 27n
DAP. See Democratic Action Party (DAP)
debt, external
  maturity profile of, 5

Philippines, 128, 138
  short-term, 18, 18t
debt-equity ratios, 151, 153, 156
debt rescheduling, South Korea, 28
decentralization, 90, 234n, 234-235
deliberation councils, 21
democracy
  business-government relations, 39-43
  effect of crisis on, 9, 11-12, 14
  financial/corporate restructuring, 140,
  181
  political change-economic reform link,
  87, 107, 124-125
Democratic Action Party (DAP), 110-114
democratization
  and crisis management, 2-3, 10-11, 47,
  50-51, 71, 217-218, 221-224
  and financial/corporate restructuring,
  140
  and government credibility, 88
  Indonesia, 90, 116, 121, 122-124, 205-
  206
  Philippines, 126, 222-224
  social dimensions, 183, 186, 190, 205-
  206, 214-215, 233-234
  South Korea, 28, 42-43, 101, 107, 190,
  221-224
  Taiwan, 126, 134, 136, 221-224
  Thailand, 35, 42-43, 190, 221-224
Democrat Party (Thailand), 87, 90, 94, 97,
  99n, 100, 162, 207-208
demographic changes, 187
deposit-taking cooperatives (DTCs), 27
developmental state, 20
dictatorships. See authoritarianism
Diversified Resources Bhd, 166
Dow Jones Publishing, 170
dwifungsi (dual function), 121

East Asian Economic Caucus (EAEC), 79
Eastern Seaboard project, 30
East Timor, 117
ECC. See Emergency Economic
  Committee (ECC)
economic vulnerability, 3-7, 15-46, 218-
  222
  political factors indicating, 47-85, 48t,
  90, 91t
Edaran Otomobil Nasional Bhd (EON),
  166n
education, 184-185, 185n, 198, 234
  Indonesia, 194, 194n, 204-206
  Malaysia, 208

Heavy Industries Corporation of
Malaysia Holdings Bhd (HICOM),
31, 166, 167*n*
hedge funds, 85
Hong Kong, 3, 39, 40*t*-41*t*
Hong Leong Bhd, 165, 171*n*
Hottick Investment Ltd., 168
human rights, 221
hwa ui pob (court protection), 56, 56*n*
Hyundai, 23*t*, 151-155, 211-212

IBRA. *See* Indonesian Bank Restructuring
Authority (IBRA)
IFCs. *See* investment and finance
companies (IFCs)
IFIs. *See* international financial
institutions (IFIs)
IMF. *See* International Monetary Fund
(IMF)
implicit intervention, 35
income, per capita, 192, 193*f*
income inequality, 187-190, 188*t*, 189*f*
and corruption, 188, 201
Indonesia, 187-190, 188*t*, 189*f*
Malaysia, 187-190, 188*t*, 189*f*, 196, 196*n*
South Korea, 187-190, 188*t*, 189*f*, 197
Thailand, 187-190, 188*t*, 189*f*, 195-196
Indian business groups, in Malaysia, 113
Indonesia
Asset Management Unit, 173*n*
bank failures, 173, 173*n*
banking sector, 23, 25-27, 33-34, 65-67,
69-70, 74, 219, 224-225, 227, 229
bank recapitalization, 171-175
bankruptcy laws, 70, 147, 175-176
budget conflicts, 67-68
business-government relations, 43-45,
124, 140, 177, 181, 219, 220
concentration of private economic
power, 21-24, 22*t*
constitutional reform, 116
corporate debt restructuring, 174-178
corporate restructuring, 140, 143-147,
144*t*-145*t*, 148*t*, 171-178, 181
corruption, 25-27, 39, 40*t*-41*t*, 44, 66-67,
69-70, 116, 120, 122, 124, 201, 204-
205, 220
currency board, 69
current account deficit, 5, 65
democratization, 90, 116, 121, 122-124,
205-206
education, 194, 194*n*
elections (1999), 121-122, 123*t*

electoral constraints, 66-69, 90, 115,
117, 119, 121-122, 124
ethnic considerations, 43-45, 115-116,
120, 124
financial market liberalization, 32-33,
74, 219
financial restructuring, 140, 143-147,
144*t*-145*t*, 148*t*, 171-178, 181
financial sector, government
involvement in, 24-30
fiscal policy, 191*n*
foreign direct investment, 180
IMF programs, 3, 65-70, 120, 177, 204
income inequality, 187-190, 188*t*, 189*f*
Islamic groups, 90, 115*n*, 115-117, 121-
122
labor relations, 115, 120*n*
lending growth, 17*t*, 17-18
macroeconomic policy, 64-65
military, 115-116, 119, 119*n*
Ministry of Cooperatives, 203, 205
monetary policy, 65
national car project, 66, 68
per capita expenditures, 194, 194*n*
per capita income, 192, 193*f*
political consequences of crisis, 11, 223
political constraints, 10-11, 48*t*, 50-51,
64-72, 220-221
and economic reform, 90, 114-125
political party composition, 121-122
poverty, 192-193, 194, 204
regionalism, 194-195
secessionist movements, 124
short-term obligations, 18, 18*t*
social policy, 192-195, 199*t*, 201*t*-202*t*,
203-206, 214-215
social unrest, 70, 116-119, 118*t*, 124,
203, 205
social welfare indicators, 190-191, 191*t*
subsidies, 70, 203
unemployment, 193-194, 201*t*
urbanization, 187, 194*n*, 204
Indonesia Association of Young
Businessman, 120*n*
Indonesian Association of Muslim
Intellectuals, 115
Indonesian Bank Restructuring Authority
(IBRA), 120, 171-174, 176-178, 181,
224-225, 229
Indonesian Chamber of Commerce and
Industry, 120*n*
Indonesian Debt Restructuring Agency
(INDRA), 175

Indonesian Democratic Party (PDI), 115, 115*n*, 121, 122
Indonesian Muslim Workers Brotherhood, 120*n*
Indonesian rupiah, 65
industrial organization, 21-22
industrial policy, 15, 20, 45, 219
  under authoritarianism, 186-187
  Malaysia, 30-32
  South Korea, 28, 30, 42, 55, 187
  Thailand, 30
institutional checks and balances, 49-50
interest groups
  disaffected, 87, 89-90
  social dimensions, 186, 214
interest rate policy, 61, 98, 129
interest rates, effect of capital controls on, 74-75, 75*t*
Internal Security Act (ISA), 109, 110, 223
international financial institutions (IFIs), 69, 207-208
internationalists, 4, 8
International Monetary Fund (IMF)
  Article VIII, 34
  letters of intent, 68-69, 98-99, 99*n*, 158-159, 172, 176, 206
  and Malaysian capital controls, 83-85
  policies of, effect on crisis, 4, 7, 125
  political analysis by, 8
International Monetary Fund (IMF) agreements
  Indonesia, 3, 65-70, 120, 177, 204
  Philippines, 3, 132
  social dimensions, 191-192
  South Korea, 4, 58-59, 100-101, 106, 179
  standby, 3, 132
  Thailand, 3, 54, 98-99
investment, growth of, 17*t*, 17-18
investment and finance companies (IFCs), 37
investment booms, bank-financed, 6
Investment Coordinating Board (Malaysia), 31
Irian Jaya, 124
ISA. *See* Internal Security Act (ISA)
Islamic groups
  Indonesia, 90, 115*n*, 115-117, 121-122
  Malaysia, 90, 110*n*, 110-111
  modernist vs traditionalist, 115, 115*n*
Islamic Party (PAS), 110, 110*n*, 208

Jakarta Commercial Court, 176
Jakarta Initiative, 175

Jakarta Initiative Task Force (JITF), 175, 175*n*
Japan
  business-government relations, 20
  lending to Malaysia, 79, 84-85, 192
  Overseas Economic Cooperation Fund, 84
Java, 194, 195*n*
Jinro, 55
Joint Public-Private Consultative Committee, 39
Justice Party (Malaysia), 110-114

KAMCO. *See* Korean Asset Management Corporation (KAMCO)
kamnan, 93
Kang Kyung Shik, 58
KCTU. *See* Korean Confederation of Trade Unions (KCTU)
KDIC. *See* Korean Deposit Insurance Company (KDIC)
Keadilan (National Justice Party), 109, 112
Kelantan, 208
Khalid Jafri, 64*n*
Khazanah Nasional, 81
Kia, 23*t*, 56, 57, 59
Kim Dae Jung, 11
  bankruptcy laws, 147
  crisis management, 100-104, 125
  election of, 100, 100*n*
  financial/corporate restructuring, 133, 143, 147, 150-156, 181, 228
  foreign direct investment, 179
  labor relations, 203
  political constraints, 43, 57-59, 87, 89, 90, 104-107
  social policy, 210-213, 215, 231
Kim Jong Pil, 100*n*, 105*n*
Kim Sun-Hong, 56
Kim Tae Joung, 106*n*
Kim Young Sam, 10
  financial/corporate restructuring, 28-30, 37*n*, 37-38, 101, 103, 143, 147, 149, 181
  foreign direct investment, 179
  political constraints, 43, 57, 57*n*, 132
  social policy, 212-213
KKN. *See korupsi, kolusi, nepotisme* (KKN)
KLCI. *See* Kuala Lumpur Composite Index (KLCI)
KLSE. *See* Kuala Lumpur Stock Exchange (KLSE)

KMT party. *See* Kuomintang (KMT) party

Konsortium Perkapalan, 170

Korea First Bank, 149, 150

Korean Asset Management Corporation (KAMCO), 56, 149n, 149-150

Korean Confederation of Trade Unions (KCTU), 104, 211-212

Korean Deposit Insurance Company (KDIC), 149

Korean Development Bank, 29

Korean Employers' Federation, 104n, 211

Korean Stock Exchange, 150

korupsi, kolusi, nepotisme (KKN), 116, 120, 122, 124

Krung Thai Bank, 158, 158n

Kuala Lumpur Composite Index (KLCI), 74, 75t

Kuala Lumpur light rail system, 109-110

Kuala Lumpur Stock Exchange (KLSE), 60n, 80n, 80-81, 82n

Kuomintang (KMT) party, 134-137

Kwik Gian Kie, 121

labor market
  Malaysia, 196, 208-209
  South Korea, 211, 214-215

labor relations, 58, 97, 233-234
  Indonesia, 115, 120n
  political role, 234
  social dimensions, 184, 186-187, 190n, 203, 213-215, 231-232
  South Korea, 103-104, 210-213, 231
  Thailand, 208

Labuan, 36

land ownership, 178

land reform, 185

Latin America, 124, 187, 188

Lee Hoi Chang, 57, 58, 100, 101, 107

Lee Hsien Loong, 82

Lee Kuan Yew, 221

lending growth, 17t, 17-18

letters of commitment, 175

letters of credit, 203

letters of intent (IMF), 68-69, 98-99, 99n, 158-159, 172, 176, 206

LG Group, 23t, 151-155

liberalization, 10, 16
  capture of, 32-38, 45, 219
  financial market (*See* financial market liberalization)
  foreign direct investment, 141t, 141-142, 178-181, 228, 230 (*See also* capital account, opening of)

and political change, 89

Lippo Bank, 173, 173n

loans
  bad, 29, 53
  nonperforming (*See* nonperforming loans (NPLs))

local business groups, 22-23

Lombok, 124

London Rules, 146, 147, 155, 158

"Look East" policy, 31, 79, 84-85

macroeconomic policy
  Indonesia, 64-65
  Malaysia, 78-79
  Taiwan, 134
  Thailand, 53, 97

Mahathir, Mirzan, 170

Mahathir, Mohamed, 10, 221
  business-government relations, 43, 63-64
  capital controls, 6n, 64, 73-74, 79, 82, 84-85
  conflict between Anwar and, 61-64, 63n-64n
  crisis management, 50-51, 60-61, 221-223
  financial/corporate restructuring, 165, 168, 168n, 169
  industrial policy, 31
  political constraints, 11, 63n, 63-64, 88-89, 107-114, 125
  pro-*bumiputra* policies, 63-64, 64n
  social policy, 210
  war on foreign investment, 60, 60n, 64, 79

Mahathir, Mokhzani, 170n

Malayan Banking, 167

Malaysia
  Anti-Corruption Agency, 108
  asset bubble, 59
  bank failures, 163
  banking sector, 27-28, 59, 61-62, 165, 165n, 219
  bank recapitalization, 162, 164, 171
  bankruptcy laws, 147
  bumiputra (*See* bumiputra)
  business-government relations, 43-44, 46, 62, 108, 111, 140, 162, 167-169, 181, 219
  capital controls (*See* capital controls, Malaysia)
  concentration of private economic power, 21-24, 22t

MIDA. *See* Malaysian Industrial
  Development Authority (MIDA)
Middle East, 188
military
  Indonesia, 115-116, 119, 119*n*
  Malaysia, 89
  and political change, 88
  Taiwan, 135
military intervention, 124, 190, 222
Millennium Democratic Party, 107
Ministry of Cooperatives (Indonesia),
  203, 205
Ministry of Finance and Economy
  (MOFE), South Korea, 57, 104, 104*n*,
  147, 147*n*, 211, 229
Ministry of Labor (South Korea), 104*n*
Miyazawa Institute, 84
Modern Bank, 173*n*
Mohamad Said Awang, 108*n*
monetary policy
  features of, 5
  Indonesia, 65
  Malaysia, 61-62, 64
  Philippines, 130
  Taiwan, 134, 138
  Thailand, 98
Moody's, 62
moral hazard, 7, 8-9, 15-16, 46, 219, 235
  financial/corporate restructuring, 139-
    140, 154, 161, 166
  government and financial sector, 24-30
  industrial policy, 30-32
  Philippines, 129
  South Korea, 101
  Thailand, 51
MOUs. *See* memoranda of understanding
  (MOUs)
MPR. *See* People's Consultative
  Assembly (MPR)
Muhammidiyah, 115, 122
Multi-Purpose Holdings, 170*n*
Musa Hitam, 63*n*
Muslim groups. *See* Islamic groups

Nahdlatul Ulama (NU), 115*n*, 122
NAP. *See* New Aspiration Party (NAP)
National Awakening party (PKB), 122
National Congress for New Politics
  (NCNP), 100*n*, 101, 104-105, 106*n*
National Counter Corruption
  Commission (Thailand), 93
National Economic Action Council
  (Malaysia), 208

National Economic Action Council
  (NEAC), 61, 62, 77, 162
National Economic and Social
  Development Board (NESDB), 35
National Equity Corporation. *See*
  Permodalan Nasional Berhad
  (National Equity Corporation)
nationalization, bank, 173, 224
National Justice Party (Keadilan), 109,
  112
National Mandate Party (PAN), 122
National Steel Corp of Philippines, 168,
  168*n*
NBFIs. *See* nonbank financial institutions
  (NBFIs)
NCNP. *See* National Congress for New
  Politics (NCNP)
NEAC. *See* National Economic Action
  Council (NEAC)
nepotism, 44, 63, 116, 170
NESDB. *See* National Economic and
  Social Development Board (NESDB)
New Aspiration Party (NAP), 52, 94*n*, 98,
  206
New Economic Policy (Malaysia), 28, 31,
  64, 114, 165
new fundamentalists, 4, 6-7, 8-9
New Order Indonesia, 115*n*, 223
New Taiwan dollar (NT dollar), 133, 135
nonbank financial institutions (NBFIs),
  141-142, 149*n*
nongovernmental organizations (NGOs),
  186, 201, 205, 207*n*
nonperforming loans (NPLs), disposition
  of, 141*t*, 141-142, 213, 224, 226-227
  Malaysia, 163-164, 167, 171
  South Korea, 149-150
  Thailand, 159
Northeast Asia, industrial policy, 30
North Korea, 223
NT dollar. *See* New Taiwan dollar (NT
  dollar)
NTS Steel, 160
NU. *See* Nahdlatul Ulama (NU)
Nukul Commission, 25, 35, 53

offshore trading, 73-74, 79
oil prices, 133, 180
Organization for Economic Cooperation
  and Development (OECD), 227-228
  corruption, 39, 40*t*-41*t*
  South Korean membership, 38, 179
Orient Bank, 129, 129*n*

Overseas Economic Cooperation Fund
(Japan), 84
over-the-counter (OTC) market,
Singapore, 80
overvaluation, 5, 5n
ownership concentration, 22t, 23

padat karya programs, 205, 233n
PAN. See National Mandate Party (PAN)
Park Chung Hee, 42, 187
Partai Persatuan Pembanguan (United
Development Party or PPP), 115n
PAS. See Islamic Party (PAS)
pasan (court receivership), 56, 56n
PCA. See Prompt Corrective Action
(PCA)
PDFCI Bank, 173n
PDI. See Indonesian Democratic Party
(PDI)
Pengurusan Danaharta Nasional Bhd. See
Danaharta
pension system, 207, 213, 231
People's Consultative Assembly (MPR),
69-70, 116-122
per capita expenditures, Indonesia, 194,
194n
per capita income, 192, 193f
Pergerakan Keadilan Social (Social
Justice Movement or ADIL), 109
Permodalan Nasional Berhad (National
Equity Corporation), 28
Perusahan Otomobil Nasional Bhd. See
Proton
Petronas, 27, 166-167, 167n, 170
Phileo Allied Bhd, 165, 171n
Philippines, 90, 126, 128-133, 138
    banking sector, 128-130
    business-government relations, 126,
    127t, 129, 132
    capital controls, 130, 130n
    central bank, 129-130, 130n
    charter change ("cha-cha") movement,
    130-131
    corruption, 39, 40t-41t, 128-129, 132
    currency float, 3
    debt crisis (1983-84), 128
    democratization, 126, 222-224
    electoral challenges, 126, 127t, 130-131
    exchange rate policy, 129-131
    financial market liberalization, 128-129
    foreign direct investment, 129
    IMF programs, 3, 132
    interest rate policy, 129
    monetary policy, 130

    political constraints, 126, 127t, 130-131
    political party composition, 131-132
    privatization, 128, 130
    tax reform, 132, 133
    "Philippines 2000," 129
PKB. See National Awakening party
(PKB)
PLUS. See Projek Lebuhraya Utara-
Selatan (PLUS)
PNB. See Permodalan Nasional Berhad
(National Equity Corporation)
50-Point Memorandum of Economic and
Financial Policies, 68
policy networks, business-government,
21
policy risks, 15-16
political change, and economic reform,
87-138, 222-224
political consequences of crisis, 9, 11-12,
222-224. See also democratization
political party composition
    Indonesia, 121-122
    Malaysia, 110-114
    Philippines, 131-132
    South Korea, 100n, 105-107, 106t
    Thailand, 94-100, 95t-96t
political uncertainty, 2, 10, 46, 220-221.
    See also electoral constraints;
    government credibility
    crisis management, 47, 48t, 71
    financial/corporate restructuring, 140
    sources of, 49-51
politico-military elite, loyalty of, 88, 116
poverty, 192
    Indonesia, 192-193, 194, 204
    Malaysia, 196, 208
    and political representation, 184
    social protection, 185, 213, 215, 230,
    235-236
    South Korea, 197, 197n
    Thailand, 195
PPP. See United Development Party
    (Partai Persatuan Pembanguan or
    PPP)
Prabowo Subianto, 115, 117
Prem, 35, 39
pribumi, 22, 45, 115n
private economic power, concentration
    of, 21-24, 22t, 46
private-sector groups. See also business-
    government relations
    confidence in government, 88-89

poverty, 197, 197*n*
regionalism, 106, 106*n*
short-term obligations, 18, 18*t*
social policy, 103-104, 196-198, 200*t*-
202*t*, 210-213
social welfare indicators, 190-191, 191*t*
transparency, 103, 103*t*, 150, 150*n*
tripartite commission, 103-104, 103*n*-
104*n*, 211-212, 231
unemployment, 104, 197, 201*t*, 210-213,
231
urbanization, 187
South Korean won, 3
Soviet Union, 9
Special Bumiputra Share Allocation, 64*n*
speculative attack models, 8
Standard & Poor's, 54, 62
Stapled Limited Issuance Preferred
Stocks (SLIPs), 159*n*
state-owned banks, 19, 29-30, 98*n*, 128,
172, 174
state-owned enterprises (SOEs), 31-32,
166-167, 169-170, 180
Stock Exchange of Singapore (SES), 80*n*,
80-82, 82*n*
Stock Exchange of Singapore Dealing
and Automatic Quotation
(SESDAQ), 80*n*
Stock Exchange of Thailand (SET), 34*n*,
54
stock market
effect of capital controls on, 74-75, 75*t*
government intervention, 28
Hong Kong, 3
Malaysia, 28
Taiwan, 133, 137
strategic industries, 32
striving class, 183, 184, 192, 198, 231
student movement, Indonesia, 70, 116-
117
subsidies, Indonesia, 70, 203
Suharto, 10, 221
crisis management, 50-51, 65-70, 115,
124, 223
fall of, 11, 63, 89, 116, 203
financial/corporate restructuring, 171-
177
health concerns, 66-67, 67*n*, 69, 114
political constraints, 66-67, 70, 88-89
social policy, 203
Suharto connection, 25-26, 44, 46
Sulawesi, 124, 194
Sumatra, 194

Sunkyong, 23*t*
Supachai, 98, 162
swindle banks, 33
systemic distress, 12, 139, 224
government management of, 139-140

Taiwan, 3, 126, 133-138
banking sector, 134-137
business-government relations, 126,
127*t*, 135-136, 138
central bank, 134-135
corruption, 39, 40*t*-41*t*, 135, 136
current account surplus, 133-134
democratization, 126, 134, 136, 221-224
electoral constraints, 126, 127*t*, 134,
136, 136*n*
financial market liberalization, 134-135,
137
fiscal policy, 134
macroeconomic policy, 134
military, 135
monetary policy, 134, 138
political constraints, 126, 127*t*, 135-136
stock market, 133, 137
Tansil, Eddie, 26-27
Tarrin, 98, 162, 179
taxes, exit, on foreign capital, 78, 78*f*
tax reform, Philippines, 132, 133
Telekom Malaysia, 82*n*
Tempo, 115
Tenaga Nasional, 169*n*
Thai baht, 3
Thai Danu Bank, 157
Thai Farmers Bank, 157
Thailand
bank failures, 157-158, 161
banking sector, 23-25, 52-55, 157-162,
219, 224, 227
bank recapitalization, 157, 159, 161
bankruptcy laws, 147, 160-162
business-government relations, 39-42,
97, 98-99, 140, 162, 219
concentration of private economic
power, 21-24, 22*t*
constitutional reform, 92*n*, 92-94, 100,
125, 230
corporate debt restructuring, 158-161
corporate restructuring, 140, 143-147,
144*t*-145*t*, 148*t*, 156-162, 181
corruption, 39, 40*t*-41*t*, 92*n*, 99, 99*n*,
207
current account deficit, 5, 51
democratization in, 35, 42-43, 190, 221-
224

electoral constraints, 87, 90, 99*n*

electoral system, 93-94

exchange rate policy, 51, 53

financial crisis (1983-84), 24-25, 45

financial market liberalization, 34-35, 51, 219

financial restructuring, 140, 143-147, 144*t*-145*t*, 156-162, 181

Financial Restructuring Agency, 97

fiscal policy, 98, 191*n*

foreign direct investment, 76*n*-77*n*, 178-179

Foreign Investment Law, 178

IMF programs, 3, 54, 98-99

income inequality, 187-190, 188*t*, 189*f*, 195-196

industrial policy, 30

interest rate policy, 98

labor relations, 208

lending growth, 17*t*, 17-18

macroeconomic policy, 53, 97

monetary policy, 98

National Counter Corruption Commission, 93

National Economic and Social Development Board, 35

nonperforming loan disposition, 159

per capita income, 192, 193*f*

political constraints, 11, 48*t*, 50-55, 71-72, 220-221

and economic reform, 90, 92-100, 125

political party composition, 94-100, 95*t*-96*t*

poverty, 195

prices, 196

regionalism, 196

rural population, 195, 208

Securities and Exchange Commission, 35

short-term obligations, 18, 18*t*

social policy, 195-196, 199*t*, 201*t*-202*t*, 206-208, 214-215

social unrest, 97-98, 100

social welfare indicators, 190-191, 191*t*

unemployment, 195, 201*t*

urban population, 187, 195, 207-208

Thailand Inc., 30

Thai Petrochemical, 160

Thai Stock Exchange. *See* Stock Exchange of Thailand (SET)

Thanong Bidaya, 53, 54

Tiara Bank, 173*n*

Ting Pek Khiing, 169*n*, 169-170

Tongkah Medivest Sdn Bhd, 170*n*

trade shocks, 4

transparency

business-government relations, 139, 227-228

measure of, 19, 21

South Korea, 103, 103*t*, 150, 150*n*

Transparency International, 39

Trengganu, 208

tripartite commission (South Korea), 103*n*, 103-104, 104*n*, 211-212, 231

Triskati University, 70

Tutut, 69

unemployment, 187, 231-232

Indonesia, 193-194, 201*t*

Malaysia, 196, 201*t*, 210

South Korea, 104, 197, 201*t*, 210-213, 231

Thailand, 195, 201*t*

unionization, 210

United Asian Bank, 28

United Development Party (Partai Persatuan Pembanguan or PPP), 115*n*

United Engineers Malaysia Bhd (UEM), 82*n*, 168, 168*n*, 170

United Liberal Democrats (ULD), 100*n*, 101, 105, 106*n*

United Malayan Banking Corporation (UMBC), 27*n*

United Malay National Organization (UMNO), 60

business-government relations, 167-169, 170*n*

misuse of funds, 108

politics, 43-44, 61, 63-64, 63*n*-64*n*, 110, 110*n*, 112, 114-115

social policy, 208-209

United Nations World Investment Report, 76*n*-77*n*

Universities and University Colleges Act, 109*n*

unsecured-corporate bond market, 137

urbanization, 187, 192, 194*n*, 230

Indonesia, 187, 194*n*, 204

Malaysia, 187, 196, 209-210

South Korea, 187

Thailand, 187, 195, 207-208

urban-rural migration, 195

veto gates, 49, 49*n*, 181

wage inequality, Gini coefficients, 188, 188*t*, 189*f*

wages, 195-196, 196, 197
Wahid, Abdurrahman, 115n, 121, 122,
    124, 177
Wan Azizah, 109, 112
Western models
  corporate governance, 225-226
  financial regulation, 225-226
  welfare, 184, 201, 213, 230-231, 232n
West Kalimantan, 117
Widjoyo Nitisastro, 65
window guidance, 74
Wing Tiek Holdings, 168, 168n
Wiranto, General, 116, 117
won (South Korea), 3
workfare programs, 212
World Bank, 67, 68, 69, 84
  East Asian Miracle report, 15
  foreign direct investment data, 77n
  Indonesian poverty estimates, 192-193,
    201
  social sector loans, 191, 204-207, 209,
    212-213, 233n
World Trade Organization (WTO), 66

Yahya Ahmad, 166
yen, 4
You Jong Keun, 106n

zone of vulnerability, 2

Toward Renewed Economic Growth in Latin America*   Bela Balassa, Gerardo M. Bueno, Pedro-Pablo Kuczynski, and Mario Henrique Simonsen
1986   ISBN 0-88132-045-5
Capital Flight and Third World Debt*
Donald R. Lessard and John Williamson, editors
1987   ISBN 0-88132-053-6
The Canada-United States Free Trade Agreement: The Global Impact*
Jeffrey J. Schott and Murray G. Smith, editors
1988   ISBN 0-88132-073-0
World Agricultural Trade: Building a Consensus*
William M. Miner and Dale E. Hathaway, editors
1988   ISBN 0-88132-071-3
Japan in the World Economy*
Bela Balassa and Marcus Noland
1988   ISBN 0-88132-041-2
America in the World Economy: A Strategy for the 1990s   C. Fred Bergsten
1988   ISBN 0-88132-089-7
Managing the Dollar: From the Plaza to the Louvre*   Yoichi Funabashi
1988, 2d ed. 1989   ISBN 0-88132-097-8
United States External Adjustment and the World Economy*   William R. Cline
May 1989   ISBN 0-88132-048-X
Free Trade Areas and U.S. Trade Policy*
Jeffrey J. Schott, editor
May 1989   ISBN 0-88132-094-3
Dollar Politics: Exchange Rate Policymaking in the United States*
I.M. Destler and C. Randall Henning
September 1989   ISBN 0-88132-079-X
Latin American Adjustment: How Much Has Happened?*   John Williamson, editor
April 1990   ISBN 0-88132-125-7
The Future of World Trade in Textiles and Apparel*   William R. Cline
1987, 2d ed. June 1990   ISBN 0-88132-110-9
Completing the Uruguay Round: A Results-Oriented Approach to the GATT Trade Negotiations*   Jeffrey J. Schott, editor
September 1990   ISBN 0-88132-130-3
Economic Sanctions Reconsidered (2 volumes)
Economic Sanctions Reconsidered: Supplemental Case Histories
Gary Clyde Hufbauer, Jeffrey J. Schott, and Kimberly Ann Elliott
1985, 2d ed. Dec. 1990   ISBN cloth 0-88132-115-X
                           ISBN paper 0-88132-105-2
Economic Sanctions Reconsidered: History and Current Policy
Gary Clyde Hufbauer, Jeffrey J. Schott, and Kimberly Ann Elliott
December 1990   ISBN cloth 0-88132-140-0
                   ISBN paper 0-88132-136-2

Pacific Basin Developing Countries: Prospects for the Future*   Marcus Noland
January 1991   ISBN cloth 0-88132-141-9
                      ISBN 0-88132-081-1
Currency Convertibility in Eastern Europe*
John Williamson, editor
October 1991   ISBN 0-88132-128-1
International Adjustment and Financing: The Lessons of 1985-1991*   C. Fred Bergsten, editor
January 1992   ISBN 0-88132-112-5
North American Free Trade: Issues and Recommendations
Gary Clyde Hufbauer and Jeffrey J. Schott
April 1992   ISBN 0-88132-120-6
Narrowing the U.S. Current Account Deficit*
Allen J. Lenz
June 1992   ISBN 0-88132-103-6
The Economics of Global Warming
William R. Cline/June 1992   ISBN 0-88132-132-X
U.S. Taxation of International Income: Blueprint for Reform*   Gary Clyde Hufbauer, assisted by Joanna M. van Rooij
October 1992   ISBN 0-88132-134-6
Who's Bashing Whom? Trade Conflict in High-Technology Industries   Laura D'Andrea Tyson
November 1992   ISBN 0-88132-106-0
Korea in the World Economy   Il SaKong
January 1993   ISBN 0-88132-183-4
Pacific Dynamism and the International Economic System*
C. Fred Bergsten and Marcus Noland, editors
May 1993   ISBN 0-88132-196-6
Economic Consequences of Soviet Disintegration*
John Williamson, editor
May 1993   ISBN 0-88132-190-7
Reconcilable Differences? United States-Japan Economic Conflict
C. Fred Bergsten and Marcus Noland
June 1993   ISBN 0-88132-129-X
Does Foreign Exchange Intervention Work?
Kathryn M. Dominguez and Jeffrey A. Frankel
September 1993   ISBN 0-88132-104-4
Sizing Up U.S. Export Disincentives*
J. David Richardson
September 1993   ISBN 0-88132-107-9
NAFTA: An Assessment
Gary Clyde Hufbauer and Jeffrey J. Schott/rev. ed.
October 1993   ISBN 0-88132-199-0
Adjusting to Volatile Energy Prices
Philip K. Verleger, Jr.
November 1993   ISBN 0-88132-069-2
The Political Economy of Policy Reform
John Williamson, editor
January 1994   ISBN 0-88132-195-8

DISTRIBUTORS OUTSIDE THE UNITED STATES

Australia, New Zealand, and Papua New Guinea
D.A. INFORMATION SERVICES
648 Whitehorse Road
Mitcham, Victoria 3132, Australia
tel: 61-3-9210-7777
fax: 61-3-9210-7788
e-mail: service@dadirect.com.au
http://www.dadirect.com.au

Caribbean
SYSTEMATICS STUDIES LIMITED
St. Augustine Shopping Centre
Eastern Main Road, St. Augustine
Trinidad and Tobago, West Indies
tel: 868-645-8466
fax: 868-645-8467
e-mail: tobe@trinidad.net

United Kingdom and Europe (including Russia and Turkey)
The Eurospan Group
3 Henrietta Street, Covent Garden
London WC2E 8LU England
tel: 44-20-7240-0856
fax: 44-20-7379-0609
http://www.eurospan.co.uk

Northern Africa and the Middle East (Egypt, Algeria, Bahrain, Palestine, Jordan, Kuwait, Lebanon, Libya, Morocco, Oman, Qatar, Saudi Arabia, Syria, Tunisia, Yemen, and United Arab Emirates)
Middle East Readers Information Center (MERIC)
2 bahgat Aly Street
El-Masry Towers, Tower #D, Apt. #24, First Floor
Zamalek, Cairo EGYPT
tel: 202-341-3824/340 3818;
fax 202-341-9355
http://www.meric-co.com

Taiwan
Unifacmanu Trading Co., Ltd.
4F, No. 91, Ho-Ping East Rd, Sect. 1
Taipei 10609, Taiwan
tel: 886-2-23419646
fax: 886-2-23943103
e-mail: winjoin@ms12.hinet.net

Argentina
World Publications SA.
Av. Cordoba 1877
1120 Buenos Aires, Argentina
tel/fax: (54 11) 4815 8156
e-mail:
http://wpbooks@infovia.com.ar

People's Republic of China (including Hong Kong) **and Taiwan** (sales representatives):
Tom Cassidy
Cassidy & Associates
70 Battery Place, Ste 220
New York, NY 10280
tel: 212-706-2200   fax: 212-706-2254
e-mail: CHINACAS@Prodigy.net

India, Bangladesh, Nepal, and Sri Lanka
Viva Books Pvt.
Mr. Vinod Vasishtha
4325/3, Ansari Rd.
Daryaganj, New Delhi-110002
INDIA
tel: 91-11-327-9280
fax: 91-11-326-7224 ,
e-mail: vinod.viva@gndel.globalnet.
ems.vsnl.net.in

South Africa
Pat Bennink
Dryad Books
PO Box 11684
Vorna Valley 1686
South Africa
tel: +27 14 576 1332
fax: +27 82 899 9156
e-mail: dryad@hixnet.co.za

Thailand
Asia Books 5 Sukhumvit Rd. Soi 61
Bangkok 10110 Thailand
(phone 662-714-0740-2 Ext: 221, 222, 223
fax: (662) 391-2277)
e-mail: purchase@asiabooks.co.th
http://www.asiabooksonline.com

Canada
RENOUF BOOKSTORE
5369 Canotek Road, Unit 1,
Ottawa, Ontario K1J 9J3, Canada
tel: 613-745-2665
fax: 613-745-7660
http://www.renoufbooks.com

Colombia, Ecuador, and Peru
Infoenlace Ltda
Attn: Octavio Rojas
Calle 72 No. 13-23 Piso 3
Edificio Nueva Granada, Bogota, D.C.
Colombia
tel: (571) 255 8783 or 255 7969
fax: (571) 248 0808 or 217 6435

Japan and the Republic of Korea
United Publishers Services, Ltd.
Kenkyu-Sha Bldg.
9, Kanda Surugadai 2-Chome
Chiyoda-Ku, Tokyo 101
JAPAN
tel: 81-3-3291-4541;
fax: 81-3-3292-8610
e-mail: saito@ups.co.jp
**For trade accounts only.
Individuals will find IIE books in leading Tokyo bookstores.**

South America
Julio E. Emod
Publishers Marketing & Research
Associates, c/o HARBRA
Rua Joaquim Tavora, 629
04015-001 Sao Paulo, Brasil
tel: (55) 11-571-1122;
fax: (55) 11-575-6876
e-mail: emod@harbra.com.br

**Visit our Web site at:
http://www.iie.com
E-mail orders to:
orders@iie.com**